LAND AS A HUMAN RIGHT

A History of Land Law and Practice in Tanzania

LAND AS A HUMAN RIGHT

A History of Land Law and Practice in Tanzania

Abdon Rwegasira

LL.B [Hons] (Udsm), LL.M (Udsm),
Assistant Lecturer, School of Law (Formerly Faculty of Law),
University of Dar es Salaam, & Advocate of the High Court of Tanzania

MKUKI NA NYOTA
DAR-ES-SALAAM

PUBLISHED BY
Mkuki na Nyota Publishers Ltd
Nyerere Road, Quality Plaza Building
P. O. Box 4246
Dar es Salaam, Tanzania
www.mkukinanyota.com
publish@mkukinanyota.com

ISBN 978-9987-08-152-3

Contents

Foreword . . . x

Preface . . . xi

Abbreviations and Acronyms . . . xiii

Introduction . . . xvii

Human Rights Movement and the Right to Land in Tanzania . . . 1

A General Overview on Political Discourse over the Right to Land . . . 2

Land Question in Historical Perspective . . . 7

Land Conflicts Arising from Colonial Occupation in Africa . . . 11

The Concept of Human Rights: A General Overview . . . 17

Land as a Human Right: The Position in International Law . . . 18

Land as a Human Right: The Law and Practice in Tanzania . . . 30

Land Law Reforms and Tenure Systems in Tanzania . . . 43

Land, Land Tenure and Land Law Reforms . . . 44

The Pre-Colonial Land Tenure Systems in Tanzania . . . 49

Tenure Systems and Land Law Reforms under German Colonial Rule . . . 53

Tenure Systems and Land Law Reforms under British Rule . . . 55

The Post-Independence Land Question . . . 65

The Land Acts as the New Land Law of Tanzania . . . 91

Land Delivery Systems: The Acquisition of Land . . . 93

Land Allocation by the State . . . 94

Land Acquisition by Purchase . . . 111

Land Acquisition by Adverse Possession . . . 111

Land Acquisition by Inheritance . . . 116

Land Acquisition by Gift . . . 117

Co-occupancy and Partition . . . 118

Rights and Obligations of the Holder of a Right of Occupancy . . . 126

Easement and Analogous Rights . . . 128

Land Delivery Syetems: Disposition of Land or Interests in Land . . . 133

Land Transfer by Sale . . . 134

Transfer of Land Interests by Lease . . . 152

Transfer of Land Interests by Mortgage . . . 181

Compulsory Acquisition of Land by the State . . . 203

Succession and the Law of Inheritance in Tanzania . . . 209

Testacy, Intestacy and Freedom of Testation . . . 211

Laws of Inheritance and their Scope of Application . . . 221

Rules of Procedure in the Administration of Estate . . . 234

Powers and Duties of Administrators of Estates . . . 246

The Role of an Administrator-General in Administration of Estate . . . 251

Women and the Right to Land in Tanzania . . . 253

The International Law Jurisprudence on Women's Right to Land . . . 254

The Domestic Jurisprudence on Women's Right to Land before the Land Acts . . . 259

National Jurisprudence on Women's Right to Land under the Land Acts . . . 278

The Right to Land of the Indigenous Minorities in Tanzania 283

General Comments 284

International Concern on the Right to Land of Indigenous and Minority People 284

The Tanzanian Jurisprudence on the Right to Land of the Indigenous Minorities 299

The Right to Compensation 305

The Right to Compensation in International Law. 306

Compensation and the Law in Tanzania 308

Grey Areas in the Realization of the Right to Compensation 314

Land Disputes, Litigation and the Role of Courts in Tanzania 323

General Overview on Land Disputes and the Role of Courts in Tanzania 324

Establishment, Composition and Powers of Land Courts 326

Legal Technicalities Affecting a Person's Right to Land 341

Conclusion 363

Appendixes 371

List of Cases 387

Bibliography 403

To my wife **Adrophina,** for her concern and care

&

my daughter **Aline**

&

my son **Allen,**

for their love

Foreword

Professor G. Mgongo Fimbo, Ph.D.

An academic work does not always carry a Foreword. The reason being that the author would already have a considerable number of publications in professional journals to his credit before being published in book form. He would be fairly well known and would not, therefore, require a senior academic to introduce him and his work. In this case I have willingly provided this Foreword for two reasons: first because literature on land and Land Law in East Africa is scarce and secondly because of the high calibre of the work of this relatively young academic.

Every one of us, except the present author, was intimidated by Megarry who wrote that the law of real property (Land Law) is a subject of great difficulty for the beginner because of the complexity of the language, which involves the use of many technical terms. In this book the author roundly disapproves Megarry by adopting a reader-friendly language and style. The author has chosen his topics well and treated them competently, drawing from international law, jurisprudence, human rights law, consitutional law, law of succession, history, anthropology and feminism. I am certain that this work will be of immense value in the teaching of Land Law and to legal practitioners in their handling of land issues and cases.

Dar es Salaam
2nd September 2011.

Preface

Given the focus of the book, "Land as a Human Right: A History of Land Law and Practice in Tanzania," it is encouraging to state, at the outset, that the use of the language of human rights to address various land issues (particularly acquisition, occupancy, and transfer of land) is a developing jurisprudence not only in Tanzania, but also at the international level. This means that in all matters of property relations, the modern language of a "human right" to access or deal with land by all is replacing the traditional language of a "legal right" to own land by the few and to the exclusion of many. However, we all know that rights (human or legal) and duties co-exist. It means that wherever there is a person's right to deal with land, there is a corresponding duty imposed upon that person to respect the rights of others. Having this in mind, then, my task in writing this book is made simple: to follow and document Tanzanian land law along its line of historical development whereby the thorny issues about "rights" and "duties" of the landed, landless and the intermediaries are demonstratively captured. It is, therefore, my hope that the form and content of the book will encourage students of land law, the practitioners in the Bar and the Bench, and any other interested party along the path to the enjoyment of land law (and practice) in all its aspects.

The work is presented in simple language and systematic style, whereby episodes and events are not only interconnected but also interrelated. Moreover, I have not limited my attention only to events in Tanzania, but have also traversed the jurisprudence of Land Law of other countries in order to tap some interpretative devices of our own land law by way of analogies. In this respect, I have referred to cases (reported and unreported, local and foreign) knowing that case law provides tangible content to what would otherwise be pure theory! At times, I have made references to local newspapers as a way of tapping public responses about land related matters. The information therefrom should not be taken as being authoritative; it simply stands as an expression of the public's attitudes towards the subject. Any deficiency or insufficiency therein need not discourage you, but it should instead breed into you new zeal and vigour as you reflect on the subject and consider making your own contribution to the discussion. I will have succeeded if this book gives voice to the voiceless landless, catalyses awareness on various aspects concerning the land rights, and sets plain ground on which the right to land of the landed and landless may be debated more fruitfully.

In writing this book I have relied not only on my own knowledge of the law and practice about the subject (land), but also on the knowledge of many others in and outside the legal profession who have equally written in many areas into which this book has necessarily ventured. Since I cannot fully record my indebtedness to the satisfaction of them all, I should be forgiven as I mention only Professors Issa G. Shivji, Gamaliel Mgongo Fimbo and Chris Maina Peter of the University of Dar es Salaam School of Law. The writing of this book was directed to the many sources which the trio identified. My learned brothers in the Bar and Bench, Mr. Martin Rwehumbiza (Advocate) of Kesaria and Company Advocates, Sigsbert Ngemera of Ntonge and Company Advocates and Honourable Augustine Karichuba Rwizile (SRM) provided me with some relevant authorities in the nature of unreported cases. To them all, and to many other unnamed members of academia, who have contributed to this publication with proposals, corrections and comments, I owe a heavy debt of gratitude.

Special and many thanks, again, go to Maria Malingumu Kashonda (Advocate) of Law Care Chambers and current chairperson of TAWLA and Professor H.I Majamba of the University of Dar es Salaam School of Law whose substantial review of the manuscript and comments have significantly enriched its form and content. It cannot go without a mention of my beloved family: wife and children. My wife, in particular has been a responsible woman as she has tolerated all the inconveniences involved in the preparatory work of the book. My children have been a source of pleasure and comfort especially during break times that followed the busy hours of writing.

Abdon Rwegasira
Dar es Salaam
June, 2011

Abbreviations and Acronyms

AC	Appeal Cases (Law Reports)
BC	Before Christ
Bom	Bombay
BRELA	Business Licensing and Registration Agency
CA	Court of Appeal
Cap	Chapter of the Laws
CCM	Chama Cha Mapinduzi
Ch	Chancery (Law Reports)
CJ	Chief Justice
Co	Company
CSOs	Civil Societies Organisations
CT	Certificate of Title
Doc	Document
EA	East Africa Law Reports
EACA	Law Reports of the Court of Appeal for Eastern Africa
Ed.	Editor

Eds.	Editors
ER	English Reports
et al	*et alia* (and other persons)
GA	General Assembly
GN	Government Notice
HC	High Court
HCD	High Court Digests
HC-Z	High Court of Zanziber
i.e	*id est* (that is to say)
IBDR	International Bank for Rural Development
Ibid	*Ibidem* (in the same place, book or source)
ICJ	International Court of Justice
IIED	International Institute for Environment and Development
ILO	International Labour Organisation
IWGIA	International Work Group for Indigenous Affairs
J	Judge
JA	Judge of Appeal
JJA	Justices of Appeal
KB	Kings Bench Division
LARRIT	Land Rights Research Institute
LHRC	Legal and Human Rights Centre
LL.B	*Latin Legum Bacclareus* (Bachelor of Laws)
LL.M	*Latin Legum* Magister (Master of Laws)
L.R.C	Law Report of the Commonwealth
L.R.T	Law Reports of Tanzania
Ltd.	Limited

Misc.	Miscellaneous
NAFCO	National Agricultural and Food Corporation
NBC	National Bank of Commerce
NGO	Non-Governmental Organisation
NHC	National Housing Corporation
No.	*numero* (number)
op cit	*opere citato* (in the work already cited)
OSCE	Organisation on Security and Cooperation in Europe
p..	page
para..	paragraph
PC	Primary Court/Privy Council
PCIJ	Permanent Court of International Justice
pp.	pages
PSRC	Presidential Parastatal Sector Reform Commission
QB	Queens Bench
R.E	Revised Edition
Resn.	Resolution
S.M.Z	Serikali ya Mapinduzi Zanzibar
SUKITA	Shirika la Uchumi na Kilimo
supra	Above
TAMWA	Tanzania Media Women Association
TANU	Tanganyika African National Union
TAWLA	Tanzania Women Lawyers Association
TGNP	Tanzania Gender Networking Programme
TLR (R)	Tanganyika Law Reports Revised
TLR	Tanzania Law Reports

Tshs.	Tanzanian Shillings
UDSM	University of Dar es Salaam
UK	United Kingdom
UN	United Nations
UNWGIP	United Nations Working Group on Indigenous People
USD	United States Dollars
v.	*versus* (against)
Vol.	Volume
WLR	Weekly Law Reports

Introduction

> Human rights approach has not been immediately relevant to arguments for particular types of land tenure systems. Such an approach, however, is of value in determining the moral weight of competing land rights, when claims made by those who need land but do not own it, are pitted against claims of those who own land but do not necessarily need it.
>
> - Winnie Bikaako and John Ssenkumba[1] -

1 BIKAAKO, Winnie and SSENKUMBA, John, "Gender, Land and Rights: Contemporary Contestations in Law, Policy and Practice in Uganda", at p. 241.

No idea comes from nothing. The idea to write and the choice of the subject matter in this work: *Land as a Human Right: A History of Land Law and Practice in Tanzania*, was triggered by my own understanding and belief that Human Rights, as a discipline, pervades all aspects of life at all levels of human society. Understanding Human Rights is *sine qua non* for the better understanding of society and of the laws governing social relations, be it Land Law, Jurisprudence, Family law, Tax Law and so on. As in any other country in the world, the History of Land Law in Tanzania, especially, has been evolving along the axis of rights. The intellectual works of resource persons such as Issa G. Shivji[2] and Ringo W. Tenga[3] are premised on the obvious fact that the land question has always been a struggle for land rights between, on one hand, those who need land but do not have it (the poor peasants; pastoralists; women; the indigenous people and minorities, on a long list) and, on another hand, those who have plenty of land but who do not necessarily need it. Gamaliel Mgongo Fimbo sees this kind of struggle as a historical phenomenon in the jurisprudence of land law when he notes very correctly that:

> *Historically, land has always been an arena of struggles between contending forces. From the 16th to the 19th centuries in England fierce struggles between the emerging bourgeoisie on the one hand and the feudal lords on the other culminated in land becoming a commodity. In this way the bourgeoisie was able to access land through the market. In Africa land was an arena of struggles between the colonized and the colonizer with the colonizer seeking to wrest control over land from the colonized. A Kenya settler, Colonel Grogan, once remarked graphically, "We have stolen his (Kikuyu's) land. Now we must steal his limbs. Compulsory labour is the corollary of our occupation of the country." Likewise, in the post-independent period the petty bourgeoisie in control of state power has insisted on vesting the radical title in land in the President in order to maintain control over land as against the peasantry.*[4]

---

2 See, for example, SHIVJI, Issa G., (1998): *Not Yet Democracy: Reforming Land Tenure in Tanzania*, London, Dar es Salaam: IIED, Faculty of Law, University of Dar es Salaam, HAKIARDHI.

3 See, foe example, TENGA, Ringo W., "Legitimizing Dispossession: The Tanzanian High Court's Decision on the Eviction of Maasai Pastoralists from Mkomazi Game Reserve", *Cultural Survival Quarterly*, Issue 22.4, January 31, 1999.

4 See FIMBO, G.M, (2004): *Land Law Reforms in Tanzania*, Dar es Salaam University Press Ltd.

W.R.Tenga and Sist J. Mramba consider struggle over land rights as part and parcel of the human life when they state that:

> *Nobody can live without land, and most people have to share it, creating competing rights. Disputes about rights in land cannot be avoided. People's relationships to land depend on many factors and have a strong cultural element.*[5]

Chris Maina Peter is even much more to the point when he establishes the link between land and human rights as he observes that:

> *Land is an important resource in the world today. It is the main source of livelihood and survival. Therefore, whoever controls land logically controls the lives of others. This is because that person or persons control what guarantees survival of human beings. Due to the proximity of land to survival, it is frequently related to the right to life*[6].

What is important to note here, is the fact that it is in the context of human rights that we record many of what I may call the ground-breaking or landmark cases; that is to say, the cases in which courts have either expressly or implicitly invoked the human rights language to deliver seminal decisions in favour of the marginalised landless or against them for the sake of the status quo. A cursory survey of such decisions in and outside Tanzania leads us automatically to judgements touching, for example, on women's right to matrimonial property[7] and inheritance[8]; individual[9] and collective[10] rights to land; and the right

---

5 TENGA, Ringo W and MRAMBA S.J., (2008): *Manual on Land Law and Conveyancing in Tanzania*, Tumaini University, (Unpublished).

6 See PETER, Chris Maina, "Human Rights of the Indigenous Minorities in Tanzania and the Courts of Law", A Paper presented at the University of Bergen, Norway, February 2007, at p. 16.

7 *Bi. Hawa Mohamed v Alli Seif* [1983] TLR, No.32. The full case also appears in Peter, C.M., (1997): *Human Rights in Tanzania: Selected Cases and Materials*, at pp. 396-405.

8 *Bernado Ephrahim v Holaria Pastory and Another*, High Court of Tanzania at Mwanza, Civil Appeal No. 70 of 1989. Reported in [1990] LRC (Const.) 757, and reproduced in Peter, C.M., *ibid*, at pp. 385-396.

9 The Attorney General of Tanzania v Lohay Akonay and Another [1995] TLR No. 80. See also PETER, Chris Maina, *ibid*, at pp.236-247.

10 *Mulbadaw Village Council and 67 Others v NAFCO* [1984] TLR 15 (HC), See also Peter, C.M., *ibid*, at pp. 228-236. See also *Likengere Faru Parutu Kamunyu and 52 Others v Minister for Tourism, Natural Resources and Environment and 3 Others*, Court of Appeal of Tanzania at Arusha, Civil Appeal No. 53 of 1998 (Unreported).

to land of the indigenous peoples[11]. Not only that, but even the recent land law reforms are inclined towards recognising, promoting, and protecting the right to land of all people, the emphasis being on the elimination of discrimination based, for example, on sex and status. The rights to land of the marginalised such as women, the disabled, and the poor are now well recognised through the current land law reforms. A cross section examination of the Tanzanian *Land Act,* [12] *Village Land Act*[13], *Law of Marriage Act,*[14] and the *Land Dispute Courts Act*[15] points to this conclusion.

However, as we may all agree, the general principle of human rights is that there cannot be rights without duties. It means, therefore, that the current land policy and law reforms keep on changing not only to respond to new demands, but also to ensure that the rights and duties of the landholders and the landless are clearly defined and protected. All these explain the meaning and essence of the choice of the topic, "**Land as a Human Right.**"

Let me also say that my understanding and experience over the subject of land, as well as my awareness of the legal wrangles that are being encountered by the various stakeholders in the administration of land law, make me believe that land law has remained poorly documented. Indeed, there is plenty of literature on matters of great concern about Land Law of Tanzania which appear in various forms including books, seminar and research presentations, academic dissertations and theses, and case law reports, and which are home to the old as well as new principles on land law, yet these sources are not easily available or even accessible to every interested person. The reasons behind the malaise include, among many, the fact that most of the sources are not meant for publication, or if published only few copies appear in public. Equally, some of the available literature is so old that it may not always depict land law and/or practice as we tend to understand it today. In other words, the available literature does not capture the latest reforms and newest laws.

---

11 See *Mabo and Others v Queensland* (No. 2) [1993] 1 LRC 194, and; *Alexkor Limited and the Government of the Republic of South Africa v The Rechtersveld Community and Others*, Case No. CCT 19/03. (South Africa).

12 [Cap. 113 R.E 2002].

13 [Cap. 114 R.E 2002].

14 [Cap. 29 R.E 2002].

15 [Cap. 216 R.E 2002].

The inevitable consequence, then, is that teaching land law in our law schools has always been uneasy task, not only on the part of the lecturers who need to make research and prepare lectures for students, but also to students who need in-depth understanding of the subject before they undertake to sit for examinations or carry out research for the purpose of writing compulsory papers (dissertations and theses). The end result is either poor training or training poorly. A similar story may be told of the legal practitioners in the field. At the end of it all, it becomes a case of a vicious circle of poor practice in the field of land administration for the reason that the beacons of the law faculties are not shining a light bright enough to lead to the next generation of law makers. It is in the view of this observation that I attempt, in this book, to rewrite land law of Tanzania in the context of its past and present forms. This is the essence of the second part of the title, "**A History of Land Law and Practice in Tanzania**".

It is appropriate, at this point, to say what the book is, and what it is not. It is not a comprehensive analysis of all land law legislation and how it has been interpreted section by section in the courts of law. My limited task is to unfold the history of land law in Tanzania and also to show how the law has been applied in practice. I do this by tracing and discussing land law along its line of historical development before independence, at the time of independence, and in the post independence period. The main object of writing is to try to have a single but comprehensive text on land law in which all the necessary land law principles are highlight with great precision. I do this with a human rights approach, believing that it is through this approach that the right to land, whether individual or collective, can best be explained, especially in this era when conflict over land is unabatedly becoming central in the family, communal and societal relations. I mean this era in which cases of a son rising against the father, a wife against the husband, a brother against a brother, an individual against the neighbour, a family against the community, a community against the State or even a State against another, are becoming the lifestyle of the time, all for the sake of securing land rights. This is the case, even if it means bloody struggles and sacrifice of human life for the sake of seeking or securing the right to land![16] Many scholars have explained the reasons behind the question of land

16 In Tanzania, we still have fresh memories about the recent brutal killings of innocent people (about 7) as a result of the fight over land rights between the Mabwegere villagers (pastoralists) and Mambegwa villagers (farmers) in Kilosa District, Morogoro, which occurred on 27th October 2008.

struggles. It suffices to remember Chris Maina Peter who says that, "Due to the importance attached to land and its immediate resources, many of the wars fought in the history of mankind and still being fought today centre on or are related to control over land and its resources".[17] Ngone Diop Tine and Mohamadou Sy, when speaking about the land question in Senegal, also join issue when they note that:

> *Land provides its owners with an essential means of survival. Land is therefore one of the Senegal's most complex issue. If it is not the explicit cause of fratricidal conflicts which Senegal has experienced, it is its implicit cause.*[18]

Although the book is written primarily for the land law students in our universities, the language of human rights is for all of us to speak. It follows, therefore, that practitioners both of the Bar and the Bench will as well find it useful for quick reference, much as will do the policy makers, law reformers and the general public in and outside Tanzania. One basic thing to note is that a mention of the name Tanzania in this work is strictly in respect of Tanzania Mainland. The reason is obvious since Tanzania is a Union of Tanzania Mainland and the Isles, and the land issue is not a union matter. Each part has its own system of land administration, including its own land tenure system and land legislation.

Chapter 1 – *Human Rights Movement and the Right to Land in Tanzania-* records the historical evolution and development of the concept of human rights at the global level, with particular focus being on the right to land, for which the general standards on the right to land as established by the international law are depicted. The main purpose of the chapter is, therefore, to enable the audience to assess whether or not the administration of land law in Tanzania conforms to these universal standards, which have been developing at the international level.

Chapter 2 – *Land Law Reforms and the Tenure System in Tanzania-* explicates the historical evolution of land law reforms and tenure systems that were in place in the pre-colonial, the colonial, and post-colonial periods through to present-day Tanzania. The relevance of the chapter is to make the audience appreciate that land law in Tanzania, as in any other country, has not been static, but has been changing in form and content in order to accommodate the social, demographic, economic,

---

17 Peter C.M., *op cit.*

18 "Women and Land in Africa: A Case Study from Senegal" in WANYEKI, L. Muthoni (ed.) (2003): Women and Land in Africa: *Culture, Religion and Realizing Women's Rights,* Zed Books Ltd, London: New York, David Philip Publishers: Cape Town, pp. 207-231.

and political challenges which are the typical characteristic of modern Tanzania. We all agree that learning from history is the only option available for one to better understand the present and, therefore, plan for the future. This is what the Court of Appeal of Tanzania highlights in the case of *Attorney General v Lohay Akonay and another, [1995] TLR 80* (CA), when it says at p. 1 that, "This case clearly demonstrates how an understanding of our country's past is crucial to a better understanding of our present, and why it is important while understanding our past, to avoid living in that past".

Chapter 3 – *Land Delivery Systems: Acquisition of Interests in Land*-is one of the chapters which I wish could have been written in "red ink". The reason for saying so is to try to draw the attention of the audience to look at it through the lens of human rights. This is because it is in the process of acquiring land or interests thereto, competing rights are borne out whereby the weak and voiceless are denied the right of access to land in favour of the Darwinian strongest individuals, especially so in the modern times when the market forces incline toward, and give favour to the few rich at the expense of the many, the poor.

Chapter 4 – *Land Delivery Systems: Disposition of Land or Interests in Land*- is almost a twin to Chapter 3. It discusses various legal principles and procedures that need to be followed to the letter. History has witnessed that most litigation in courts of law are rooted in the very failure to observe the law on disposition by those who take part in this vital process of transferring interests in land. In addition, there are some people who have been prejudiced as a result of unlawful disposition. All these collectively tell the importance of this chapter in the overall framework of administration of land law.

Chapter 5 – *Succession and the Law of Inheritance in Tanzania*. Although succession is not part of land law *per se*[19] most bloody litigations and even breaches of peace amongst our people are founded on contests involving land, one of the subject matter of inheritance. There are good reasons to explain this situation. As we may all agree, inheritance has traditionally been and remains the most common way of acquiring land in Tanzania. The main reason is that most of the land, especially in rural communities, is still owned collectively as family or clan land and, therefore, tends to pass from one generation to another by way of inheritance. Another reason is that as land is becoming more and more lucrative, so the majority of the poor, especially in rural communities,

---

19 It will later be seen that even the land court system under section 167 of the *Land Act, 1999* [Cap. 113 R.E 2002] and the provisions of the *Land Disputes Courts Act*, 2002, do not apply in all matters of inheritance.

find it difficult to participate in the cut-throat competition to purchase land. In other words, the majority of the poor are unable to dance to the "willing seller, willing buyer" drum. Thus the only major means of acquiring land remains that of waiting to inherit it when their relatives die. However, with population pressure and land scarcity in place, inheritance (bloody as it sometimes tends to be) has been one of the controversial areas of our socio-economic relations. The rights to land of vulnerable groups such as women and minors are perilously put to jeopardy by the dubious characters (greedy, unfaithful and treacherous) of the family or clan. All the above, has made it inevitable to have a chapter on succession in which the law governing inheritance is defined in clear terms, not only to ensure that the interests of the weak are known and protected wherever there is need to do so, but also create an arena for further discussion about the domains of inheritance in Tanzania.

Chapter 6 – *Women and the Right to Land in Tanzania*-looks carefully at women and their right to land. We all know that the status and rights of women are a major human rights concern in all parts of the world following their (women's) consistent and age-old oppression, discrimination, and denial of equality of rights by men. In other words, women have, more often than not, stood as losers at all levels of the social ladder. It is in this area that the language of human rights has played a very significant role in the efforts to reverse the malady.

Chapter 7 – *The Right to Land of the Indigenous Minorities in Tanzania*-seeks to record the growing jurisprudence of the international law on the right to land of the indigenous people and minorities, and to show how Tanzania, in particular, has endeavoured to protect these rights. It is my considered view that, as the issue of the right to land of these groups of people is currently turning into a universal agenda of the human rights camp, the book cannot satisfy the thirst of my audience without a proper record of the land rights of the indigenous minority in Tanzania.

Chapter 8 – *The Right to Compensation*- defines and elaborates the place of the right to compensation in Tanzanian land law jurisprudence. This is an area that has not been going smoothly both in law and in practice. It has, consequently, been an area of many bloody conflicts including resistance and contested litigation in the courts of law. It is submitted that our understanding about the nature and essence of the right to compensation is inevitable, especially now, when the issue of land grabbing and unlawful evictions of people from their land without compensations or adequate compensation is becoming a serious problem of land administration in Tanzania.

Chapter 9 – *Land Disputes, Litigation and the Role of Courts in Tanzania*-highlights the nature of land disputes and how individuals, singly or collectively, have resorted to courts of law for judicial redress. The chapter also discusses the court hierarchy in land matters. However, the most important part of the chapter is on legal hurdles facing plaintiffs in their pursuit of legal remedies in court, and whose effect has been a direct curtailment of some persons' rights to land. The chapter is useful to individuals and practitioners because it discusses the basic principles with which one is apt to "win or lose in the chamber."[20]

The chapter is immediately followed by a conclusion and appendices providing sample forms and content of various basic documents involved in the transfer of interests in land. These include the sale contract[21], lease contract[22], mortgage contract,[23] and will.[24] The essence of the appendices is simply to expose beginners to the drafting craft. As such, they play a tripartite role. Firstly, they stand as a guide as to form and content of the basic documents on land transfer; secondly they enable beginners to make similar documents when they are requested to do so in the day to day activities of lawyering and; thirdly, they build the capacity to challenge similar documents executed with apparent discrepancies.

Finally, there is a list of cases and a bibliography covering the most important sources that were consulted, and whose monumental contents have highly contributed to the development of this work. It provides for a formidable body of references which the audience might find useful to consult in cases where the in-depth understanding of the subject is at issue.

---

20 The phrase is taken from Professor Mgongo Fimbo, who has countlessly spoken it to students during his lecture presentation on Court Practice. The Professor's point is that law is never free of technicalities, and that it is only through the mastery of the same that one is able to sail safely through the legal turbulence (win) or else to be caught on the rocks (lose).

21 Appendix 1.

22 Appendix 2.

23 Appendix 3.

24 Appendix 4.

Chapter One

Human Rights Movement and the Right to Land in Tanzania

> Human rights have roots deep in the mists of time and yet the term itself dates back barely sixty years to international discussions proceeding the founding of the United Nations. Since 1945, the scope of human rights has been elaborated and the concept now permeates the fabric of international society. The origins of international human rights lie in the philosophical discussions evolved through the centuries.
>
> - Rhona K. M. Smith[25]

25 SMITH, Rhona K.M., (2005): *Textbook On International Human Rights*, 2nd Edition, Oxford University Press, at p. 5.

A General Overview on Political Discourse over the Right to Land

It is my understanding that the word discourse is simply used to connote a certain way of thinking and explaining things, feelings or actions. Therefore, as I undertake to talk about the political discourse over the right to land, I dare to record not only how political thinkers have philosophically and historically linked the individual person to the right to own land, but also to show how this thinking has, over the years, influenced the law and practice of land ownership and control. We learn from Johansson Dahre that "Discourses have effects. They are not just the way that social issues get talked and thought about. They structure the possibility of what gets included and excluded and what gets done or remains undone. Discourses impose themselves upon social reality, indeed they produce what is possible to think, speak and do"[26]. The available record shows that political discourse and the debate on the question of land is as old as the political thought itself. History has shown that the key questions of who is entitled to own land, and under what tenure system should land be owned, have very deep roots stretching back into the ancient Greek philosophy. In the time of the ancient Greece, women, children, slaves and land were all considered to be property for use by the few individuals, that is to say, the "citizens" and members of the *polis.*

Many political thinkers of the time had something to say about property relations. Aristotle (384-322 BC) considered the ideal State as being one that is founded on private, as opposed to communal, property ownership. Aristotle advanced three reasons in support of his proposition. First he argued that, "The greater the number of owners, the less the respect for common property. People are much more careful of their personal possessions than of those owned communally; they exercise care over common property only so far as they are personally affected"[27]. He argued further that, "Clearly then it is better for property to remain in private hands but we should make the use of it communal. It is a particular duty of the law giver to see that citizens are disposed to do this"[28]. His last line of argument was that, "The abolition of private property will mean that no man will be seen to be liberal and no man will ever do any act of liberality; for it is in the use of articles of property

26 See DAHRE, Johansson, (2002): *The International Discourse on Indigenous People: A Compilation of Legal and Political Documents*, Lund: Sociologiska Institutionen, at p. 16.

27 ARISTOTLE, (1962): *The Politics*, Penguin Books, paragraph 1261b 32.

28 *Ibid*, paragraph 1263a 30. Note that to Aristotle only men who owned property qualified to be citizens.

that liberty is practiced"[29]. It should not surprise us to see Aristotle write in favour of private property ownership. We learn from history that in the ancient past property qualification was, indeed, a determining factor for a person to participate in the processes of the State. That is to say, property ownership did not only confer social status to a person, but also political power to participate in decision making.[30]

I find it important to record that, despite the fact that Aristotelian political thought is over two millennia old, the debate on communal *versus* private ownership of property remains characteristic of land law in contemporary society, including Tanzania.

Another political figure, whose ideas on property rights have significantly influenced debates on land matters until today, is John Locke (1632-1704). Writing his *Two Treaties of Government* (1690)[31], Locke devotes quite some time to address issues of property relations in both of the Treaties. A cursory survey in his first book shows how Locke is against the idea that some people have plenty of property while others have nothing even for subsistence. His line of argument stems from the idea that God has not left one man to the mercy of another that he may starve him if he pleases. In that regard, it is Locke's moral observation that;

> *...therefore, no man could ever have a just power over the life of another by right of property in land or possessions, since it would always be a sin in any man of estate to let his brother perish for want of affording him relief out of his plenty; for as justice gives every man a title to the product of his honest industry and the fair acquisitions of his ancestors descended to him, so "charity" gives every man a title to so much out of another's plenty as will keep him from extreme want, where he has no means to subsist otherwise.*[32]

In his second book, Locke goes on to advocate for private property by saying that, "God who hath given the world to men in common hath also given them the reason to make use of it to the best advantage of life

---

29 *Ibid*, paragraph 1263b 7.

30 In colonial Tanzania, property qualifications remained factors determining one's right to vote or be voted until this was officially abolished in 1962 when Rashid M. Kawawa, the then Prime Minister of Mainland Tanganyika strenuously argued against property qualification in voting when commenting on the Voters Registration (National Elections) Bill, 1962 by saying that only citizenship and age, (not property) should be the only qualifications. See Parliamentary Debates (Hansard), National Assembly 1st Session June-July 1962, at p. 1116.

31 See LOCKE John, (1978): *Two Treaties of Government*, (Trans. Cambridge Bibliographical Society 1952), J.M. Deut & Sons Ltd.

32 *Ibid*, Book I, at p. 30, paragraph 42.

and convenience"[33] and, therefore, "Man puts the labour of his body and the work of his hand to convert what is common to be his own", under the condition that, "at least there is enough and good left in common for others"[34]. Locke's appeal is dominated by his move against taking too much, since if this is allowed it may lead to conflicts. He is very clear and to the point when he says:

> *For as a man had a right to all he could employ his labour upon, so he had no temptation to labour for more he could make use of. This left no room for controversy about titles, nor for encroachment on the right of others. What portion a man curved to himself was easily seen; and it was useless, as well as dishonest, to curve himself too much, or take more than he needed.*

The last aspect in Locke's account of property relations, which has been viewed negatively by analysts of modern times, was how he tried to relate land with commerce.

> *For, supposing an island, separated from all possible commerce with the rest of the world, where in there were but a hundred families, but there were sheep, horses, and cows, with other useful animals, wholesome fruits, and land enough for corn for a hundred thousand times as many, but nothing in the island, either because of its commonness or perishableness, fit to supply the place of money. What reason could any one have there to enlarge his possessions beyond the use of his family, and a plentiful supply to its consumption, either in what their own industry produced, or they could barter for like perishable, useful commodities with others? Where there is not something both lasting and scarce, and so valuable to be hoarded up, there men will not be up to enlarge their possessions of land…For I ask, what would a man value ten thousand or a hundred thousand acres of excellent land, ready cultivated and well stocked too, with cattle, in the middle of the inland parts of America, where he had no hopes of commerce with other parts of the world, to draw money to him by the sale of the product? It would not be worth the enclosing, and we should see him give up again to the common of nature whatever was more than would supply the conveniences of life, to be had there for him and his family.*[35]

33 *Ibid*, book II, p. 129. See paragraph 26.

34 *Ibid*, p. 130, at paragraph 27.

35 See LOCKE, John, Book II, at p. 140, paragraph 48.

Locke has, here, been criticised as justifying the grabbing of land of the indigenous peoples at different historical times: during the age of "discoveries" in which the "discovered land" was branded as *terra nullius*; during colonization when the lands of the colonised were massively and mercilessly taken; and in the post-colonial period when the right to land of many a people, such as the pastoralists, has remained moot even in Tanzania.[36]

The works of great thinkers never die. What Locke refers to as "charity" is not less than the principle of equity which has had wide application in modern legal systems. In Tanzania, the principle has been invoked frequently by courts in the course of deciding about people's right to land. In the case of *Didas Rwakalila and 3 Others v Thomas Matondane*[37], for example, the clan council, when distributing the estate of Mr Karaba who died intestate, knew that the respondent was the person entitled, according to the Haya rules of inheritance, to inherit as the heir in the first degree, but distributed the estate to the appellants after learning that the respondent had plenty of the property while the appellants had almost none. When the case finally landed in the Court of Appeal of Tanzania, the Court stated the principle that, "In practice, distribution is affected by many different circumstances, for instance in the case of one of the lesser heirs having a large family, he may be granted a larger share than is really his just due". The Court then noted that, "The reasoning of the clan council in coming to the decision they did what was plain and simple. They felt that since the respondent already had the plots of the two brothers who had died childless, then this plot in dispute belonging to the third childless brother, should go to the sons of the other two dead brothers, though the respondent was not moved by that philanthropy". Finally the court concluded that, "We are of the firm opinion that the clan council was justified in arriving at the decision they did and did not contravene the Haya customary law and its *equity*. (Emphasis is mine). Also in *Simon Byanyuma v A.E Haliday*[38], a case whose background was on double allocation, the court invoked the principle of equity when it said at p. 7 that:

---

36 See TENGA, Ringo W., "Legislating for Pastoral Land Tenure in Tanzania: The Draft Bill" in HORN, F., (ed.) (1998) *Economic, Social, and Cultural Rights of the Maasai*, Rovaniemi: The Northern Institute for Environmental and Minority Law, University of Lapland, at p. 94. Also, TULLY, J., "Aboriginal Property and West Theory Recovering Middle Ground" in Paul *et al.*, (1994): *Property Rights*, CUP, London, at p. 153.

37 [1992] TLR 314 (CA).

38 High Court of Tanzania (Land Division) at Dar es Salaam, Land Case No. 27 of 2004 (Unreported).

> *Let me also observe that I consider that it would not be equitable that the plaintiff should be given two plots leaving the defendant who was the original occupier of the disputed land with nothing.*

What Locke says is that it is useless and dishonest for an individual to to take too much land while there is not enough left for others. Conflicts arise because people tend to "curve"to themselves more land than they need, as Locke states, and, therefore, Tanzania has it as one of its fundamental principles of the national land policy to "regulate the amount of land that any person or corporate body may occupy or use"[39]. We learn from the current media reports that Tanzania is on the move to ensure that the landless majority get land from the landed individuals with unused tracts of land[40], possibly after it came to light that majority landlessness is a potential breeding ground for social instability.

The third line of thinking is one deposed by Jean-Jacques Rousseau (1712-1778) who develops the concept of public property as we have it today. In his *Social Contract*, Rousseau argues that, "What a man loses by the social contract is his natural liberty and the absolute right to anything that tempts him and that he can take; what he gains by the social contract is civil liberty and the legal right of property in what he possesses"[41]. He sees *natural* liberty as having no limit but the physical power of the individual concerned, and *civil* liberty as limited by the general will[42]. Rousseau argues further that, "…as the resources of the nation are incomparably greater than those of an individual, public possession is in simple fact more secure and more irrevocable than private possession"[43]. He is against mere *possession* of a piece of land if that *possession* is based only on force or what he calls "the right of the first occupant." He instead favours *property* which, to him, must rest on a legal title.[44] To Rousseau, there can be justification for the right of possession or the right of the first occupant to any peace of land only when the following conditions, as a general rule, are met: first, that the

---

39 Section 3 (1) (d) of the *Land Act*, 1999, [Cap. 113 R.E 2002].

40 See for example, The Editor, "Kikwete's stance on Land Soothing", *The Guardian*, (Tanzania), March 26, 2007; IHUCHA, Adam, "J. K. Moves to Prevent big Land Conflict", *Sunday Observer*, (Tanzania), March 25, 2007, and; MWENDAPOLE, Joseph, "Wamwomba Kikwete Awamegee Shamba la Dr. Abdallah Kigoda", *Nipashe*, May 8, 2007.

41 See ROUSSEAU, Jean-Jacques, (1962): *The Social Contract*, Penguin Books, at pp. 20-21.

42 *Ibid*, at p. 21.

43 *Ibid*, at pp. 21-22.

44 *Ibid*, p. 21.

land shall not already be inhabited by any one else; secondly, that the claimant occupies no more than he needs for subsistence; thirdly, that he takes possession, not by an idle ceremony, but by actually working and cultivating the soil- the only sign of ownership which needs to be respected by other people in the absence of the legal title.[45]

Rousseau concludes his argument on property ownership by saying that, "In whatever manner this acquisition is made, the right of any individual over his own estate is always subordinate to the right of the community over everything; for without this there would be neither strength in the social bond nor effective force in the exercise of sovereignty.[46] At the end of it all, Rousseau contemplates an ideal society whose social state is only advantageous to people: "when all possess something and non has too much"[47]; and when it is a state with "a people who is neither rich nor poor but has something to keep itself"[48]; and in which "no citizen shall be reach enough to buy another, and none so poor as to be forced to sell himself"[49].

In a word, we easily learn two things from Rousseau's presentation on property ownership. First, Rousseau presents what is equated with the present day classification of land as "public land" vested in President who is the trustee for and on behalf of all citizens.[50] Second, Rousseau's presentation of the right of the first occupant is equated with today's doctrine of adverse possession and the rule against absenteeism.

Land Question in Historical Perspective

We can agree in principle that the land question, involving struggles to acquire land and disputes for or against land ownership, is an age-old enterprise not only in Tanzania, but the world over because it is shown to be linked to human survival. Whoever is acquainted with the history of development of the earliest form of European capitalism (i.e., primitive capitalism), for example, shall agree with me that the land question was a central agenda of the time. What is commonly referred to, in history, as the "Discovery of the New World" by the early explores, like Christopher Columbus, means nothing more than the historical

45 *Ibid*, at p. 22.

46 *Ibid*, p. 24.

47 *Ibid*, p. 25.

48 *Ibid*, p. 27.

49 *Ibid*, p. 59.

50 See Section 4 (1) of the *Land Act, 1999* [Cap. 113 R.E 2002].

process of, among others, identifying and grabbing lands of the native people in the Americas. Indeed, the era of "discovery" witnessed some grave acquisitions of the "discovered" lands by European nations including Britain, Belgium, Spain and France, among others. The fact that this was done forcefully and against the wishes of the native owners does not need much emphasis. What is of great interest is to learn how the whole process was sponsored, on one hand, by the Roman Catholic Church (the Pope), and the European States' authorities, on the other hand. Johansson Dahre[51] has elaborately accounted for this aspect. From him we learn, for example, that Europe started to expand beyond the Mediterranean once the idea had been legitimised *vide* a legal discursive foundation at the Constance debate of 1414 to 1418, when it was agreed (in 1418) that the conquest of the "infidel" people and their lands could proceed according to a rule of law that imposed a duty on non-Christian peoples either to accept Christianity or face subjugation through a just war.[52] Efforts which followed later were manifold. The letter, (the *Romanus Pontifex* of January 8, 1455) issued by Pope Nicholas V confirming the right to the possession of lands invaded by King Alfonso of Portugal is an evidence of these efforts.

> *We [therefore] weighing all and singular the premises with due meditation, and noting that since we had formally by other letters of ours granted among other things free and ample faculty to the aforesaid King Alfonso- to invade, search out, capture, vanquish, and subdue all Saracens and pagans whatever, and other enemies of Christ whosesoever placed, and the kingdoms, dukedoms, principalities, dominions, possessions, and all movable and immovable goods whatsoever held and possessed by them and to reduce their person to perpetual slavery, and to apply and appropriate to himself and his successors the kingdoms, dukedoms, countries, principalities, dominions, possessions on goods, and to convert them to his or their use and profit-by having secured the said faculty, the said King Alfonso, or by his authority, the aforesaid infante, justly and lawfully has acquired and possessed, and doth possess, these Islands, lands, harbours and seas…*[53]

---

51 See note 2 above.

52 This was during the reign of Pope Innocent IV.

53 See DAHRE, Johansson, *op cit*, at p. 33.

It is on record that in the 1490s, when both Portugal and Spain started the discovery process, disputes over land started to show up over the "discovered" lands, for example, in South America where each of the two States claimed right over land constituting what is Brazil today. In his efforts to settle such disputes between the two States, Pope Alexander VI issued a letter, (the *Inter Caetera*, of May 3, 1493) calling upon the parties, Portugal then under King John and Spain under King Ferdinand (Aragon) and Queen Istabela (Castile), to settle their land dispute, before they (Portugal and Spain) signed the Tordesillas Treaty of June 7, 1494 to set the overseas demarcations between them. In another letter of 1514, (the *Praecelsae Devonionis*, issued by Pope Leo X, Roma, on November 3, 1514), the Portuguese dominion was expanded beyond Bojador, Nao and the Indies, to other places of the world, known and unknown:

> *And for greater security and virtue of the authority and in terms mentioned above, we hereby grant everything, all and singular, contained in the aforesaid letters, and all other empires, kingdoms, principalities, duchies, provinces, lands, cities, towns, forts, lordships, islands, harbours, seas, coasts, and all property, real and personal, wherever existing, also all unfrequented places, recovered, discovered, found and acquired from the aforesaid infidels, by the said King Emmanuel and his predecessors, or in future to be recovered, acquired or discovered and found by the said King Emmanuel and his predecessors both from Cape Bojador and Nao to the Indies, and any place or region whatsoever, even though perchance unknown to us at present; and we also extend and amplify the aforesaid letters, and their contents, all and singular, to the aforesaid concessions, and in virtue of the holy obedience and under penalty of our wrath, by the authority and in terns aforesaid, we inhibit all faithful Christians, even though adorned with imperial, royal, or any other rank, from presuming to hinder in any way the said King Emmanuel and his successors in respect to the aforesaid concessions, and from furnishing aid, counsel or favour to the infidels.*[54]

In almost similar terms King Henry VII of England commissioned (by Letters of Patent to John Cabot of March 5, 1496) John Cabot to conquer, occupy, and possess the lands of the "heathens and infidels" and to acquire titles and jurisdiction over them. All these efforts, whether by the by the Catholic Church, or by the King of England, meant nothing

54 *Ibid*, at p. 62.

but grabbing of the native lands in the "discovered" territories, and a direct infringement of the rights of the indigenous peoples to the benefits of their ancestral lands.

It is in that sense, I think, that when Pope John Paul III took the throne he immediately issued a letter, (the *Sublimis Deus*, of June 1537) whose effect was to revoke the earlier letters that purported to give the Spanish monarchy title over the Indians' land. Dahre considers this letter as the first declaration of human rights (to land) because it formally and for the first time recognised the right of the Indians to own lands regardless of their race, religion, and degree of civilization or any other circumstance.[55] The excerpt from the letter reads:

> *Desiring to provide ample remedy for these evils, we define and declare by these our letters, or by any translation thereof signed by the notary public and sealed with the seal of any ecclesiastical dignity, to which the same credit shall be given as to the originals, that notwithstanding whatever may have been or may be said to the contrary, the said Indians and all other people who may later be discovered by Christians, are by no means to be deprived of their liberty or the possession of their property, even though they be outside of the faith of Jesus Christ; and that they may and should freely and legitimately, enjoy their liberty and the possession of their property, nor should they be in any way enslaved; should the contrary happen, it shall be null and of no effect...the said Indians and other people should be converted to the faith of Jesus Christ by preaching the word of God and by the example of good and holy living.*[56]

This approach was much later followed by the Royal Instructions of 1761 issued by King George III of London in December 9, 1761 which required the English settlers to remove themselves from all lands acquired without formal licence. As an effort to implement these instructions and giving them the necessary force, Governor Belcher issued the Belcher Declaration of Halifax, Canada, May 4, 1762, in the following words:

---

55 *Ibid*, at p. 67. We still recall the devoted efforts of the late Pope Paul II in the field of human rights. This makes us conclude he lived by the legacy of his predecessor, Pope John Paul III in fighting tooth and nail for the equal rights of man.

56 *Ibid*, p. 68.

> *WHEREFORE, in dutiful obedience to His Majesty's Royal Order I do accordingly publish this proclamation in His Majesty's Royal Name, strictly enjoining and requiring all persons whatever, who may either wilfully or inadvertently have seated themselves upon lands reserved to or claimed by the said Indians, without any lawful Authority for so doing to, forthwith, remove there from.*[57]

Despite all these later efforts by the Church and State authority in recognizing the right to land of the natives, what happened to the native lands both in the Americas, Africa and the world over during the era mercantilism is well documented. Cases of native Indians in the Americans being pushed out of their lands only to be confined in limited reservations are typical characteristics of the period. In Africa similar cases of land confiscations were not uncommon. The controversial issue in the international law jurisprudence over the legal status of Western Saharan today,[58] for example, traces its history in the Spanish occupation of that part of Africa.

Land Conflicts Arising from Colonial Occupation in Africa

As it has been noted earlier that land was central to the age of "discovery", it is similarly noted, here, that land remained central to the colonisation process in Africa as well. We are witnesses to various forms of land disputes which are a product of the colonial land policy. To the colonizers, land was essentially and inevitably important to serve two major purposes: It would enable the investment of capital and also support human settlement. History is replete with examples ot how various colonial powers used whatever means they had (such as false treaties, negotiations, violence) to grab and alienate native lands, thereby dispossessing the majority of the natives, only to make them trespassers of their own land! The gravity and intensity of the matter, of course, differed from one region to another in one country or from one country to another depending on: who was the colonising power; what was the colonial attitude over the colony; the mode of entry into the colonial territory; the value of the land in question; the duration of stay in the colony; and the nature of the resources available therein[59]. It is not,

---

57 *Ibid*, p. 71.

58 See the Western Saharan Case, Advisory Opinion, ICJ Reports 1975 and FRANK, Thomas M, "The Stealing of the Sahara", in American Journal of International Law, Vol. 70, No. 4 (October, 1976), pp. 694-721.

59 All these factors are quite relevant for the better understanding of the history of land law and its development in Tanzania. See a discussion of this development in Chapter Two below.

therefore, surprising to learn from history that in the Republic of South Africa, for example, natives who formed 80% of the total population were statutorily[60] dispossessed of their land and were left with only 13%[61] of all the land in the country. Frankly speaking, I cannot tell the story about the land problem in the colonial State of South Africa better than Shahra Razavi who ably remarks:

> *The South African agrarian scene is deeply marked by a brutal history of colonial forced dispossession in the eighteenth and nineteenth centuries, and ferocious racial inequalities of land dispensation put in place by successive minority white governments after the 1910s... This was accompanied by a programme of spatial control, which forcefully resettled more than 3.5 million black people out of what were deemed "white" areas into labour reserves, or "Bantustans".*[62]

Also, apart from the *Native Lands Act, 1913* other discriminatory laws were enacted in different times, which greatly curtailed the right to land of the black people. We have on record for example the *Prevention of Illegal Squatting Act* 52 of 1951 which made it illegal for the black people to occupy any land without permission from the colonial government. Whoever contravened this Act was immediately labelled an "unlawful occupier", and, as a consequence, summary eviction and criminal conviction followed without any fear or favour. Expressing out its discontentment on the colonial land question in South Africa, the Constitutional Court of South Africa stated:

> *For all black people and for Africans in particular, dispossession was nine-tenth of the law. Residential segregation was the cornerstone of the apartheid policy. The policy was aimed at creating separate "countries" for Africans within South Africa. Africans were precluded from owning and occupying land outside the areas reserved for them by these statutes.*[63]

---

60 Native dispossession was done under the authority of the law, the *Native Lands Act of 1913*.

61 See WALKER, Cherryl, "Piety in the Sky? Gender Policy and Land Reform in South Africa" in RAZAVI, Shahra, (ed.) (2003): *Agrarian Change, Gender and Land Rights*, Blackwell Publishing, pp. 113-148, at p.116.

62 .RAZAVI, Shahra, *ibid* at p. 7.

63 See Port Elizabeth Municipality v Various Occupiers, Case CCT 53/03, decision of 1st October, 2004, at paragraph 9. The full discussion of the case appears herein below.

The above account of South Africa's colonial land issue forms the basis for intensive land law reforms of the 1990s by the post-apartheid government of South Africa which were inevitable in counterattacking the colonial vice which led to chronic landlessness for the majority of native South Africans.

Not only that: we are all witnesses to the most recent land question in Zimbabwe under President Robert Mugabe's regime as reported in both, academic writings[64] and in local and international media. Land problem in Zimbabwe is rooted in colonial land policy and it is hectic and moot at the moment since it touches the competitive rights of the landed (white settlers) and the landless (the indigenous Zimbabweans). The available record shows a clear gap that has been at the centre of land ownership in Zimbabwe and whose roots dig deep into the era of colonial domination over the country[65]. We note the gap at the outset through the record that:

> *Over six million indigenous black people live in Zimbabwe's marginal rural lands, the communal areas. These areas have poor soils and unreliable rainfall: producers lack control of water rights and are excluded from the bulk of the nation's natural resources. The unequal distribution of resources means that 4,500 mainly white, large-scale farmers dominate Zimbabwe's predominantly agrarian economy.*[66]

In the move to narrow or even to eliminate this gap the post-colonial government of Zimbabwe has, at different times, adopted different land policies directed to better use, management and control over land. It is the land policy of acquisition and distribution of the late 1990s which dominates the international and national debate to date, and among

---

64 See for example, MOYO, Sam, "The Political Economy of Land Acquisition and Redistribution in Zimbabwe 1990-1999", *Journal of Southern African Studies*, Vol. 26, No. 1 (Mar., 2000), pp. 5-28.

65 See "Mugabe says war was about land", *Daily News* (Tanzania), Wednesday, August 17, 2005. The paper summarizes the speech given by President Mugabe during the 2005 Heroes Day. The gist of the speech was about the relationship between the liberation struggle and the land question. His Excellency is quoted, in part, as having said "Freedom and Independence having been won, the ultimate goal was now the creation of a socio-economic environment in which the people would in common reap maximum benefits; these would, in the main, derive from the land, and land as their principal natural resource. That is why the Third Chimulenga became necessary. Without doubt our heroes are happy that a crucial part of this new phase of our struggle has been completed. The land has been freed and today all our heroes lie on the soil that is emancipated. Their spirits are unbound, free to loam the land they left shackled, thanks to the third Chimulenga. But they want you and me to protect and use that unshackled land in feeding and prospering our nation. They want the same land that was shackled yesterday to flower and feed our children".

66 MOYO, Sam, *ibid* at p. 6.

members from both the human rights and non-human rights camps[67]. Through this policy the government had determined to acquire 1, 471 farms from the previous owners (white settlers) and redistribute the same to the landless (native) people. The lands listed for acquisition and redistribution were, *inter alia*, those lands deemed to be under-used, under multiple farm ownership and, under farmer absenteeism.[68] Unfortunately, the policy has turned out to be a controversial issue of the international concern. However, many people see something fruitful in it. "The policy aims to uphold the general principle of 'one man one farm' whereby the commercial land ownership or tenure rights of each Zimbabwean who already holds land (hopefully including women, despite the terminology) are protected if they only hold one reasonably-sized farm", observes Sam Moyo.[69] There are also people outside Zimbabwe who see Mugabe as a hero not only in Zimbabwe but in the entire continent of Africa. In this sense, Filbert Kakwezi, a Tanzanian and independent writer, says:

> *We must seriously consider the sensitiveness of land and, in consequence, stop giving land to foreigners. There isn't a better message than this in line with Peasants' Day celebrated every year on August 8. The settlers are going to displace the indigenous population, and thereafter we'll become serfs, slaves or chattels if you so wish. Then we'll find ourselves in a chaotic situation same as Zimbabwe; thank God, President Robert Gabriel Mugabe is still strong and reliable enough to be our African consultant on how to reclaim misappropriated land.*[70]

Like what has been said about South Africa and Zimbabwe, all colonial governments in Africa undertook to establish their domination by first fixing boundaries over their respective spheres of influence, possibly to avoid potential hostilities that were likely to occur among themselves. This was done, for example, through some treaties, bilateral

67 The move towards this policy began with the government adopting the *Land Acquisition Act of 1992* before it declared its intent to acquire about 1471 farms from the previous owners in 1997.

68 MOYO, Sam, *op cit*, at p. 7.

69 *Ibid*, at p. 25.

70 See "Large –Scale Farming can make Tanzanians Landless" in *The African*, Saturday August 11, 2007 p. 17.

or multilateral, depending on who had what interests and over which specific areas of land. These artificial boundaries were later to be sources of tensions and confrontations among the various independent countries in Africa, the root cause being land issue. In order to settle these tensions and confrontations, some countries resorted to war when the amicable solutions proved failure while others sought the intervention of judicial bodies such as the International Court of Justice (ICJ).

According to the available record, the Kagera War of 1978/9 between Tanzania and Uganda may be cited as an example of such wars whose root cause was hostilities between the two countries over the border (border dispute). We read, albeit, from the literature that the root cause of the war was Idi Amin's claim that the Kagera salient belonged to Uganda. He overtly ordered his forces to invade the area in early 1972, which act prompted the convening of a meeting in Somalia and the subsequent signing of the Mogadishu agreement in Somalia[71] to address the unfriendly relations which had developed between Tanzania and Uganda over the border culminating in military invasion of Tanzania by Ugandan forces. The agreement called for, among others, cessation of military operations against each other's territory and a withdrawal of all military forces to a distance of at least ten miles from the common border.[72] Amin dishonoured the terms of the agreement by re-sending the troops to the border in the middle of October 1978, and by 27th October 1978 Amin's troops had invaded all area in the Northern part of the Kagera River, flying thereon a Ugandan flag while declaring the occupied part, part of Uganda.[73] Tanzania, then under the presidency of Nyerere, had no option but to declare war against Amin. Speaking through the media as he declared war, Nyerere said:

---

71 The agreement was signed in Somalia on 7th October, 1972 by Foreign Ministers from the three countries of Uganda, Tanzania and Somalia.

72 See a detailed account of the event in AVIRGAN, T. and HONEY, M., (1983): *War in Uganda: The Legacy of Idi Amini*, Tanzania Publishing House: Dar es Salaam.

73 By this act Amin had not only betrayed the terms of Mogadishu Agreement, but also disobeyed the general principle of international law, i.e, the principle of intangibility of frontiers inherited from the colonization process which is captured by the maxim, *uti possidetis juris*. This principle was domesticated in Africa in the famous Cairo Declaration of July 1964 (AGH/Res 16 (1) adopted at the first summit conference following the creation of the Organization of African Unity (OAU) whereby all member States solemnly…pledge themselves to respect the frontiers existing on their achievement of national independence.

> *Now what is to be done? We have only one task. It is to hit him. We have the ability to hit him. We have the reason to hit him. And we have the determination to do so. We want the world to understand this clearly that we have no other task; we ask our friends who are offering to meditate to stop these efforts.* ***To occupy other people's territory not that the forces have gone astray, but to announce the occupation of other people's territory is a declaration of war with that country.*** *We are not the ones who have done so.*[74] *(Emphasis is mine).*

As regards the peaceful means, there are States which decided to look for judicial remedies through the ICJ. The record provides us with several cases including, among many others: The Frontier Dispute between Burkina Faso and the Republic of Mali;[75] the Territorial Dispute between Libyan Arab Jamahiriya and Chad;[76] the case between Namibia and Botswana concerning the riparian boundary around the Kasikili/Sedudu Island and the legal status of the Island,[77]and; case concerning the Maritime Boundary between Cameroon and Nigeria[78], whose dispute was over the Bakassi Peninsula. We cannot keep our ears away from the current potential dispute between Uganda and Kenya about Migingo Island in which, each State claims ownership over this tiny Island, which is found on the east of Kenya-Uganda border within Lake Victoria.

In the determination of these disputes, especially the rights and duties of States, the International Court of Justice sought guidance in the various treaties which were concluded before, by the respective colonial governments in fixing the boundaries between one State and another.[79] In addition, the Court invoked the celebrated principle of international law, the *uti possidetis*[80], to require States to respect the international boundaries which were already fixed at the time of their independence.

---

74 This declaration was made on November 2, 1978 at Diamond Jubilee Hall in Dar es Salaam and communicated to the Tanzanians through the mass media: Radio Tanzania Dar es Salaam, and Daily News paper. See an article, "Mwalimu's broadcast to the nation" in *Daily News*, Friday November 3, 1978 at p. 1.

75 Judgment, ICJ Reports, 1986 p. 582. Judgment delivered on December 22, 1986.

76 Judgment, ICJ Reports, 1994 p. 6, Judgment delivered on February 3, 1994.

77 Kasikili/Sedudu Island (Botswana v Namibia) ICJ Reports, 1997, p. 1045.

78 Judgment, ICJ Reports, 2002 p. 303, Judgment of October 10, 2002.

79 For example the Court went back to the Treaty of Friendship and Good Neighbourliness of August 10, 1955 between French Republic and the United Kingdom of Libya when deciding the dispute between Libya and Chad and the Anglo-German Treaty of 1st July 1890, when deciding the dispute between Botswana and Namibia.

80 This is an important principle recognized by African States as part of the African legal order according to which African States' boundaries should follow those inherited at independence.

The narration above tells very clearly that land stands as a key factor of international peace, security and good relations of States. We can say much more about this hypothesis but in a different work dedicated only to that end. However, having a limited scope of this book, our preoccupation is directed to the current national and global debate over the right to land of individuals or groups.

The Concept of Human Rights: A General Overview

The term "Human Rights" is known to lawyers (and the majority of non-lawyers) as comprising of all entitlements that a person has or must have by virtue of his being born a human being (individual rights) or, in addition, by virtue of his being living in the community of human beings (collective rights). I share this understanding of the concept of human rights with other scholars in the human rights camp such as Manfred Nowak, who admirably describes the concept of human rights by saying that:

> *The focus of human rights is on the life and dignity of human beings. A person's dignity is violated when they are subjected to torture, forced to live in slavery, i.e* ***without a minimum of food, clothing, and housing****. Other economic, social and cultural rights, such as access to a minimum education, medical care and social security, are as fundamentally important to a life in dignity as are respect of privacy and family life or personal freedom.*[81] *(Emphasis is mine).*

The language of human rights, in the modern sense, is a 1940s phenomenon. History traces the birth of modern human rights from the foundational purposes of the United Nations. According to the 1945 Charter, one of the functions of the United Nations is to ensure that State Parties undertake to promote and encourage human rights and fundamental freedoms without distinction as to race, sex, language, or religion[82]. The Charter was followed by other international instruments on human rights in the form of Declarations, Conventions, Covenants, and Regulations which were sequentially formulated and adopted by the International Community to provide for these rights. These instruments may be classified according to their areas of application. In the first place, we have the Universal Declaration of Human Rights, 1948; the International Covenant on Economic, Social and Cultural Rights, 1966, and; the International Covenant on Civil and Political Rights, 1966 and

81 See NOWAK, Manfred, (2003): *Introduction to the International Human Rights Regime*, Martinus Nijhoff Publishers, at p. 1.

82 See Article 1 (3).

its Option Protocols[83], all of which cater for human rights generally and apply globally. In the second place, we have regional instruments which provide for human rights, but whose application is limited to a specific region. The list in this category would include the European Convention for the Protection of Human Rights and Fundamental Freedoms, 1950 and its Option Protocols, which is applicable in Europe; the American Convention on Human Rights, 1969 and its Additional Protocols, which apply to the member States in the Organisation of American States; and the African Charter on Human and Peoples' Rights, 1981 and its Additional Protocols, which apply in Africa. In the third place, we have instruments that provide for the rights of specific vulnerable groups such as the Convention on the Elimination of All Forms of Racial Discrimination, 1965 providing for the rights of all races; the Convention on the Elimination of All Forms of Discrimination against Women, 1979 and its Optional Protocol providing for the rights of women; the Convention on the Rights of Children, 1989 and its Optional Protocols providing for the rights of children; and the Convention Concerning Indigenous and Tribal Peoples in Independent Countries, 1989 providing for the rights of indigenous people. All these instruments comprehensively highlight the basic standards of human rights, including the right to land.[84]

Land as a Human Right: The Position in International Law

It should be understood from the outset that the international law of Human Rights does not say that every person must have land. Issues of land acquisition and transfer as well as the processes involved are part and parcel of the internal affairs of every individual State, and it is the responsibility of each State to decide on the proper mode of land acquisition, ownership and transfer[85]. However, what International law provides is a set of standards which need to be adhered, at various levels, by every State in the administration of land.

---

83 Reference is made to the Optional Protocol to the International Covenant on Civil and Political Rights, 1966, and the Second Optional Protocol to the International Covenant on Civil and Political Rights, 1989.

84 A compilation of these instruments is available in MELANDER, Goran, *et al.*, (eds.), (2004): *The Roul Wellenberg Institute Compilation of Human Rights Instruments*, Second, revised edition, Leiden/Boston: Martinus Nijhoff Publishes.

85 See the Tanzanian position with respect to the acquisition of landed property in Chapter Three.

At the first level the international law simply gives protection to any person who already owns property (land) to own it freely and without any unlawful interference or deprivation. The first instrument, in point of time, to stipulate the right of protection over property was the Universal Declaration of Human Rights, 1948 which states that, "Everyone has the right to own property alone as well as in association with others", and that "No one shall be arbitrarily deprived of his property"[86]. This article has been positively commended in the literature such that anyone from the human rights camp must take cognisance of the comment wholeheartedly:

> *The language of article 17 is broad and comprehensive. It applies to both individual and collective forms of property ownership... The right is not an absolute one, however, as it is foreseen that persons can be deprived of their property under certain circumstances, but this cannot be done arbitrarily. The term "arbitrarily" would seem to prohibit unreasonable interferences by states and taking property without compensation...*[87]

Other instruments with similar or additional provisions are the Convention on the Elimination of All Forms of Racial Discrimination, 1965, which also provides for the right to own property alone as well as in association with others, and the right to inherit property;[88] the Protocol to the European Convention for the Protection of Human Rights and Fundamental Freedoms, 1952, which provide for the right of every natural or legal person to peaceful enjoyment of his possession, and further that no one shall be deprived of the same except in public interest and subject to conditions provided for by law and by the general principles of international law;[89] the American Convention on Human

86 See Article 17 (1) and (2) respectively. Note that the Universal Declaration of Human Rights, 1948 was issued as a mere recommendation and not as as such legally binding on states. However, many international treaties on human rights based on it followed soon. Not only that, but even the Vienna Declaration of the World Conference on Human Rights, 1993 which was endorsed by the General Assembly in its resolution 48/121 (1993) expressed the view that the Universal Declaration of Human Rights now constitute customary international law.

87 See ALFREDSSON, Gudmundur, "The Right to Property" in EIDE, Asbojorn *et al.*, (1992): *The Universal Declaration on Human Rights: A Commentary*, Scandinavia University Press, at p. 257.

88 Article 5 (d) (v) and (vi) respectively.

89 Article 1.

Rights, 1969, which recognises the right of everyone to the use and enjoyment of his property except where the same is subordinated by law to the interest of society, and further, the right to a just compensation if the property is deprived for reasons of public utility or social interest[90]; and the African Charter on Human and Peoples' Rights, 1981, which guarantees the right to property and states that property may be encroached upon only in the interest of public need or in the general interest of the community and in accordance with the provisions of appropriate law.[91]

At the second level, international law provides for the right to adequate housing. The available record in favour of the right to adequate housing reads:

> *To live in a place, and to have established one's own personal habit with peace, security and dignity, should be considered neither a luxury, a privilege nor purely the good fortune of those who can afford a decent home. Rather, the requisite imperative of housing for personal security, privacy, health, safety, protection from the elements and many other attributes of shared humanity, has led the international community to recognise adequate housing as a basic and fundamental human right.*[92]

Following this recognition, several international legal instruments on human rights point directly to the right of every person to adequate housing. A cursory study of these instruments has identified, at the minimum, the Universal Declaration of Human Rights, 1948, which provides for the right of everyone to a standard of living, adequate for the health and well being of himself and his family including housing;[93] the Convention on the Elimination of All Forms of Racial Discrimination, 1965, which also recognise the right to housing;[94] the Covenant on Economic, Social and Cultural Rights, 1966, which recognises this right in similar terms;[95] and the European Social Charter (Revised), 1996,

90 Article 21.

91 Article 14.

92 See the United Nations Housing Rights Programme Report No.1, "*Housing Rights Legislation: Review of International and National Legal Instruments*" (2002), at p. 1.

93 Article 25.

94 Article 5 (d) (iii).

95 Article 11 (1).

which not only provides for the right of housing but also obliges State Parties to take measures to promote access to housing of an adequate standard, to prevent and reduce homelessness with the view to its gradual elimination and to make the price of housing accessible to those without adequate resources.[96]

However, despite the above elaborate on the right to housing, history witnesses that the realisation of the right to housing remains a practical nightmare, especially so in developing countries of the third world. We learn this discrepancy through the General Comments of the Committee on Economic, Social and Cultural Rights:

> *Despite the fact that the international community has frequently reaffirmed the importance of full respect for the right to adequate housing, there remains a disturbingly large gap between the standard set in article 11 (1) of the Covenant and the situation prevailing in many parts of the world. While the problems are often particularly acute in some developing countries which confront major resource and other constraints, the Committee observes that significant problems of homelessness and inadequate housing also exist in some of the most economically developed societies.*[97]

In essence, the right to housing, which according to the Committee is yet to be fully realised, is not all about having a house to reside in, it is all about having adequate housing. The Committee explains this point much better as it comments:

> *In the Committee's view the right to housing should not be interpreted in a narrow or restricted sense which equates it with, for example, the shelter provided by merely having a roof over one's head or views shelter exclusively as a commodity. Rather it should be seen as the right to live somewhere in security, peace and dignity.*[98]

Following this line of reasoning, the Committee has interpreted the right to adequate housing as capable of being realised through the following yardsticks[99]: *Legal security of tenure,* which ensures that all persons possess a degree of security of tenure which guarantees them

96 Article 31 (1), (2) and (3) respectively.

97 See General Comment No. 4 in which the Committee interpreted Article 11 (1) of the International Covenant on Economic, Social and Cultural Rights, 1966 at its Sixth Session, 1991 in United Nations Document, E/1992/23, paragraph 4.

98 *Ibid*, paragraph 7.

99 *Ibid*, paragraph 8.

legal protection against forced evictions, harassment or any other threat; *availability of services, materials, facilities and infrastructure*, which are essential for good health, security, comfort and nutrition; *affordability,* which is about enabling the needy to afford housing, for example where States undertake to subsidize some houses for those who are unable to pay or to invoke legal measures to protect tenants from rent hikes; *habitability,* which ensures that houses are free from threats to health such as structural hazards and disease vectors; *accessibility* to ensure that houses are accessible especially by the people who constitute vulnerable groups such as the disabled; *location* that facilitates access to places of importance such as workplaces, heath care centres, and schools; and *cultural adequacy* to provide for the cultural orientations of the people.

With the above elements in place, it is important to record that the primary obligation to promote the right to adequate housing is the responsibility of each State. However, international bodies, such as the United Nations acting through the United Nations Centre for Human Settlement (UN-Habitat),[100] as well as local bodies such as NGOs, have taken great efforts to advocate for the right to housing and lobby for its realisation. The least that can be said about the United Nations in this venture is to spearheading of international conferences and encouragement of debates about the right to land[101], as well as the launching of the World Habitat Day, which is currently commemorated annually by States every first Monday of October for certain specific purpose:

> *The commemoration of the World Habitat Day rests on Resolution No. 40/202 of the United Nations General Assembly adapted on December 17, 1985. This resolution calls upon UN member states to evaluate the conditions of habitats in their respective countries, with an objective of making them livable, safe, adequate and sustainable.*[102]

---

100 Tanzania is especially privileged to have had Professor Anna Kajumulo Tibaijuka as the Executive Director, UN-Habitat. The learned Professor is currently leading the Ministry for Land, Housing and Human Settlement Devepment in Tanzania. She has won public support by her promise and commitment to fight against corruption in the land sector and to restore open spaces illegally allocated to the rich individuals.

101 See for example the "Delhi Declaration by the United Nations Conference on Human Settlement", *Report of the Global Conference on Access to Land and Security of Tenure as Conditions for Sustainable Shelter and Urban Development*, New Delhi, India, January 17th-19th 1996.

102 An extract from the Statement of the Director General of the Tanzanian National Housing Corporation, Mr. Martin Madekwe, to commemorate the October 2008 World Habitat Day, *Daily News* Monday, October 6, 2008.

Equally, there are sufficient records of local NGOs that have been at the forefront in advocating for the right to housing. Suffice it to mention, by way of example, the *Shelter Forum*, a coalition of NGOs and individuals based in Kenya, founded in 1990 to facilitate sustainable access to affordable and decent shelter for all, particularly for vulnerable groups[103]. In this spirit, it is equally important to record that wherever situations of gross violation of the right to housing have occured such NGOs have even dared to take legal actions against the responsible States. For example, in one incident, a legal action was taken against the Republic of Sudan for the violations that took place in Darfur, Sudan, in the case of *Centre on Housing Rights and Eviction v Republic of Sudan.*[104] In this action, the main complaint was that: by attacking the people of the region (for example, the Fur, Masaalit and Zaghawa tribes), killing them and forcefully evicting others, the Government of Sudan and the Janjaweed violated their right to freedom of residence which is a right under article 12 (1) of the African Charter on Human and Peoples' Rights, 1981; and also that the action of the Government of Sudan and the Janjaweed involving forced eviction and housing and property destruction violated their right to property enshrined in article 14 of the African Charter. A similar scenario formed the subject of a litigation in the case of *The Social and Economic Rights Action Centre and Social Rights v Nigeria*[105] where the two complainants (NGOs) proceeded against the Government of Nigeria, accusing it for abetting human rights violations against the Ogoni people of the Niger delta, in Nigeria. According to the facts of the case the Nigerian armed forces had sided with Shell Petroleum Development Corporation to force people off their land to make room for the oil industry. The operation was undertaken violently, by burning farms and reducing houses to ashes, a factor which angered the complainants and forced them to proceed against the Nigerian government for violating the provisions of the African Charter on Human and Peoples' Rights, specifically the rights of the victims to property, housing and food.

At the third level international law provides for the people's right to self –determination. The jurisprudence on the right to self determination in international law is traced from the United Nations General Assembly Declaration of 1960, which declared that all peoples have the right to

103 See the details in KANJI, Nazneen, *et al.*, (2002): *Promoting Land Rights in Africa: How do NGOs make a difference?* London: International Institute for Environment and Development (IIED).

104 African Commission on Human and Peoples Rights, Communication 295/05.

105 *Ibid*, Communication 155/96 (2001).

self determination.[106] Thereafter, the right to self determination took its firm position in the arena of human rights under the common Article 1 to the International Covenant on Economic, Social and Cultural Rights, 1966 and the International Covenant on Civil and Political Rights, 1966. Specifically, the full article reads:

Article 1

> *All peoples have the right of self-determination. By virtue of this right they freely determine their political status and freely pursue their economic, social and cultural development.*
>
> *All peoples may, for their own ends, freely dispose of their natural wealth and resources without prejudice to any obligation arising out of international economic c-operation, based upon the principle of mutual benefit, and international law. In no case may people be deprived of its own means of subsistence.*

The clear wording of the provision that people may not be deprived of their own means of subsistence has some legal implication that people should not be deprived of their right to land and housing. This is what we grasp from the literature, for example, when we learn from Issa G. Shivji that, "Land was the underlying basis of struggle for self determination and independence"[107]. Also a comment on this right by the Human Rights Committee of the United Nations reads:

> *The right to self determination is of particular importance because its realization is an essential condition for the effective guarantee and observance of individual human rights and for the promotion and strengthening of those rights.*[108]

In contemporary international law the right to self determination is classified in two categories: external and internal right to self determination. The former involves the collective rights of the people of a particular State, in its relation to other States, to have the right to determine their affairs in terms of managing their own resources. The latter involves only individual groups within the State, say the indigenous minorities, to have the right to determine their destiny in terms of their

---

106 See declaration 2 of the 1960 General Assembly Declaration on the Granting of Independence to Colonial Countries, (GA Resn. 1514 (XV) 1960).

107 See SHIVJI, I.G., "Land: The Terrain of Democratic Struggle" in *Change*, Vol. 5, First Quarter, 1997, at p. 4.

108 See the General Comment No. 12 of the Committee at its Twenty First Session, 1984.

available resources. The provision of Article 3 of the 1995 United Nations Draft Declaration on the Rights of Indigenous People which provides that, "Indigenous peoples have the right to self determination" should be interpreted in the context of the right to internal self-determination.

At the fourth and final level, international law provides for equality of rights, equal protection by the law to all people, and the principle of non discrimination. Apart from these principles, international law obliges member States to various international human rights instruments to adopt some positive measures (such as national legislation) to ensure the realisation of the specific human rights. In this respect, we have for example Article 2 (2) of the International Covenant on Economic, Social and Cultural Rights, 1966, which obliges the State Parties to undertake to guarantee that the rights enunciated in the Covenant will be exercised without discrimination of any kind as to race, colour, sex, language, political or other opinion, national or social origin, property, birth or other status. A similar provision appears in Article 26 of the International Covenant on Civil and Political Rights, 1966, which provides that, "All persons are equal before the law and are entitled without any discrimination to the equal protection of the law. In this respect, the law shall prohibit any discrimination and guarantee to all persons equal and effective protection against discrimination on any ground such as race, colour, sex, language, religion, political or other opinion, national or social origin, property, birth or other status." Finally we have the International Convention on the Elimination of All Forms of Discrimination against Women which specifically obliges the member States to accord to women equality with men before the law,[109] and to take all appropriate measures to eliminate discrimination against women in all matters relating to marriage and family relations and in particular to ensure, on the basis of equality of men and women, *the same rights for both spouses in respect of ownership, acquisition, management, administration, enjoyment and disposition of property, whether free of charge or for a valuable consideration*[110]. (Emphasis is mine).

At all the above levels international law provides the international standards affecting the right to land and to adequate housing, which need to be observed by States in the administration of their respective land laws. However, one of the legal minds in the human rights camp is convinced that the international human rights instruments have meaning but only when State Parties thereto are willing to let them work.

---

109 Article 15 (1).

110 Article 16 (1) (h).

> *International human rights instruments are living organs, enshrining non-static norms, evolving in response to global developments and political reality...The lawyers have played their role, drafting norms of rights, codifying a philosophy on the rights of the individual. It is now for the politicians, the Governments of the States, to transform the theory into reality, the rights and freedoms into tangible norms enforceable before national courts and subject to international supervision.*[111]

It is on the basis of the above standards, that some States have undertaken concerted efforts to ensure that the right to land of all persons is seriously safeguarded. A pointer is directed to the Republic of South Africa which has incorporated the right to land, including the right to adequate housing in its Constitution of 1996, as part of the Bill of Rights. This is, of course, explained by the dark history of pre-independence South Africa's land problem which we have already rehashed herein above.[112] The relevant provision of the Constitution include section 25 which provides, in part, that, " No one may be deprived of property except in terms of law of general application, and no law may permit arbitrary deprivation of property"[113];... "A person or community dispossessed of property after 19 June 1913 as a result of past racially discriminatory laws or practice is entitled, to the extent provided by an Act of Parliament, either to restitution of that property or to equitable redress"[114]; and section 26, which provides that, "Everyone has the right to have access to adequate housing"[115];... "No one may be evicted from the home, or have their home demolished without an order of the court made after considering all the relevant circumstances. No legislation may permit arbitrary evictions"[116]. Besides the Constitution, South Africa has also enacted a law to provide for the right against illegal evictions.[117] Following these triumphant land law reforms, and the constitutional recognition of the right to land and adequate housing, litigation has flooded the Constitutional Court of South Africa, with

111 SMITH Rhona, K.M., *op cit*, at p. 370.

112 See footnote 36-39 above.

113 Section 25 (1).

114 Section 25 (7).

115 Section 26 (1).

116 Section 26 (3).

117 This is the *Prevention of Illegal Eviction from an Unlawful Occupation of Land Act* 19 of 1998.

litigants challenging, *inter alia*: the order of repossession of communal land[118]; the order against eviction[119]; discrimination in inheritance[120]; and the order of forfeiture of an immovable property.[121] Of all these, the jurisprudence laid down in the case of *Port Elizabeth Municipality v Various Occupiers* has raised an alarm, not only for its place in the developing philosophy of the right to land in Africa, but also for its guiding principles in addressing matters of illegal evictions that have, over the years, taken place even in Tanzania, to include the most recent unlawful evictions in the Tabata Dampo area in Ilala, Dar es Salaam, which attracted wide coverage by the Tanzanian media in its blended name, the " Tabata Dampo Demolition Saga.[122]"

A simplified survey of the *Port Elizabeth Municipality* case of South Africa shows the facts of the case to be that the applicant, Port Elizabeth Municipality, applied for an eviction order against the respondents (i.e. some 68 people including 23 children) who had occupied a privately owned land of Lorrain, within the Municipality, after they had been evicted from another land. Granting the eviction and demolition orders, the High Court of South Africa ruled that the occupiers unlawfully took the occupation of land. They were, thus, ordered to vacate, to have their housed demolished, if necessary with the assistance of the police, and to pay the costs of the proceedings. These occupiers successfully appealed to the Supreme Court which reversed the decision and ordered, instead, that the occupiers be provided with sustainable alternative land with some measures of security of tenure. Aggrieved by this decision, the applicant applied for leave to appeal to the Constitutional Court in that the matter involved a constitutional issue of the right to land of the legal owners.

---

118 *Alexkor Limited and the Government of the Republic of South Africa v The Richtersveld Community and Others*, Case CCT 19/03, decision of 14th October, 2003.

119 *Port Elizabeth Municipality v Various Occupiers*, Case CCT 53/03, decision of 1st October, 2004.

120 *Daniels v Campbell No and Others*, a decision of 11th March, 2004.

121 *Kumarnath Mohunran and Another v The National Director of Public Prosecutions and Another*, Case CCT 19/06, decision of 26 March 2007. The case is a result of an application for leave to appeal against the judgment of the Supreme Court of Appeal ordering an immovable property to be forfeited to the State in terms of the Prevention of Organised Crimes Act, 121 of 1998. The applicants' main argument was that, "The forfeiture constituted an unlawful and arbitrary deprivation of property and thus an infringement of section 25 of the Constitution."

122 This refers to the historical move of 29th February, 2008 in which the Ilala Municipality in Dar es Salaam, Tanzania unlawfully for what of proper procedure, undertook to demolish over 80 households thereby rendering homeless a total number of about 300 occupiers of various calibre: the elderly, children, and men and women of every description.

Before it gave out the decision of the case, the Constitutional Court first established the following points of law which form, very persuasively, the ideal principles that courts in Tanzania should make note of and follow when called upon to determine a matter of similar facts and arguments: One, that the rights involved in section 26 (3)[123] of the Constitution are defensive rather than affirmative. The land- owner cannot simply say: this is my land, I can do with it what I want, and then send in the bulldozers or sledgehammers; Two, that under the provision of section 6 (3) of the *Prevention of Illegal Eviction from an Unlawful Occupation of Land Act*,[124] the court, in deciding whether it is just and equitable to grant an order of eviction, must have regard to: the circumstances under which the unlawful occupier occupied the land and erected the building or the structure; the period the unlawful occupier and his or her family have resided on the land in question; the availability to the unlawful occupier of suitable alternative accommodation or land; and that justice and equity require showing special concern when settled communities or individuals are faced with being uprooted for the longer the unlawful occupiers have been on the land, the more established they are on the sites and in the neighbourhood, the more settled their homes and the more integrated they are in terms of employment, schooling and enjoyment of social amenities, the great their claim to the protection of the courts. A court will be far more cautious in evicting well-settled families with strong local ties than persons who have recently moved on the land and erected shelter there.

Applying these principles to the case before it, the court arrived at the following observations: One, that at the time of the occupation, the land was a vacant land upon which some trees and bushes were glowing and it was not being used by the owners at the moment for any productive purpose; Two that the occupiers' claim is that they had moved in the land with a permission of a person whom they believed was the owner, and had been there for a long time, with eight children attending school and several adults working nearby; Three, that the occupiers were willing to move but objected the Municipality's proposal that they move to Walmer, which they claimed was overcrowded and unsafe or to Greenbushes, which they claimed was too far from their places of work,

123 Footnote 82 above.

124 Act No. 19 of 1998 of South Africa.

and from the children's schools; Four, that the Municipality now sought to evict them without any discussion with them, or consideration of their request that they be provided with security of tenure on a stable peace of land pending their accommodation in the housing programme launched by the applicant.

After considered the above points, Sachs, J. speaking for the Court, did not find any difficulty in dismissing the application by holding that:

> *To sum up: in the light of the lengthy period during which the occupiers have lived on the land in question, the fact that there is no evidence that either the Municipality or the owners of the land need to evict the occupiers in order to put the land to some other productive use, the absence of any attempt by the Municipality to listen to and consider the problems of the particular group of occupiers and the fact that this is a relatively small group of people who appear to be genuinely homeless and in need, I am not persuaded that it is just and equitable to order the eviction of the occupiers.*[125]

Together with this seminal holding, the Honourable Court gave a directive statement to the applicant that:

> *In a case like the present it is particularly important that the Municipality [sic] not appear to be aligned with one side or the other. It must show that it is equally accountable to the occupiers and to the land owners. Its function is to hold the ring and to use what resources it has in an even-handed way to find the best possible solution.*[126]

Apart from South Africa, other countries in Africa, which have commendably recognised the right to land as a constitutional category in their Constitutions include Uganda and Kenya. One of the unique features about the Constitutions of the Republics of Uganda[127] and Kenya[128]is that they both recognise and protect the right of every person to own property either individually or in association with others and, therefore, prohibit deprivation of the same without payment of prompt, fair and adequate compensation. Another important feature borne by the two Constitutions is that they all give unlimited rights to every

---

125 See paragraph 59 of his Lordship's judgment.

126 *Ibid*, paragraph 61.

127 The Constitution of the Republic of Uganda is a people's democratic constitution which was adopted by all Ugandans on 22nd September 1995.

128 Like the Constitution of Uganda, the Constitution of the Republic of Kenya is also a people's democratic constitution which was adopted on 27th August, 2010.

person who has interest in a property to access the court of law for legal redress.[129] Further more, the two Constitutions maintain an independent Chapter on Land and Environment[130] which defines, among other items, land holding (tenure) systems of the respective countries.

Land as a Human Right: The Law and Practice in Tanzania

Throughout the pre-colonial, colonial and post-colonial eras (whether before or after the incorporation of a Bill of Rights into the Constitution of the United Republic of Tanzania, 1977[131]), land has never been recognised as a human right *per se* because it was never accorded the necessary status of being a constitutional category. It means that, until today a person's right to land, in any of its forms, is not specifically recognised and protected by the Constitution. However, this does not mean that the right to land is totally and constitutionally unknown. The jurisprudence on the Tanzanian land law tends to suggest that the right to land has been in place although alongside the policies or attitudes of discrimination in all its manifestations, including the superiority of some rights (granted rights of occupancy) against others (customary or deemed rights of occupancy) and the denial of some groups of people (say women) of the right to access land. It is in these kinds of situations, that the human rights approach has been a forward step in the fight against the above vices and the State (specifically through the courts of law) is now devoted to recognising, promoting, protecting and enforcing the right to land of all citizens, not only of the few.

A study of the pre-colonial land law and practice shows very clearly that one could not talk of a right to land as a private property in this period. This is for the simple reasons that the language of human rights of the individual was completely unknown. It was the period during which land tenure was purely communal, meaning that land belonged to a community and that an individual member would access it for use

---

129 Article 26 of the Ugandan Constitution and Article 40 of the new Kenyan Constituion.

130 Chapter XV of the Ugandan Constitution and Chapter V of the Kenyan Constitution.

131 The most profound account of the history of the Bill of Right in Tanzania is by PETER Chris Maina, "Blocking Fundamental Rights and Freedoms in Tanzania: The History of the Bill of Rights", *The Justice Review*, Vol. 7, No.1, 2008, pp. 1-35. The article was initially prepared to mark the 20th Anniversary of the justiciability of the Bill of Rights in the Constitution of the United Republic of Tanzania (1977) on 16th March, 2008 in Dar es Salaam, Tanzania. In summary, the Bill of Rights which covers Articles 12 to 29 of the Constitution of the United Republic of Tanzania (1977) was incorporated in the Constitution via the Constitution (Fifth) (Amendment) Act, 1984 (Act No. 15 of 1984, which became operational in 1985 and justiciable three years later as per the Constitution (Consequential, Transitional and Temporary Provisions) Act, 1984 (Act No. 16 of 1984).

purpose only. Furthermore, it was a period when commoditization of land was almost a sacrilege, because there was no selling or buying of land. Available literature records this very clearly:

> *To us in Africa land was always recognized as belonging to the community. Each individual within our society had the right to the use of the land, because otherwise he could not earn a living and one cannot have the right to life without also having the right to some means of maintaining life. But the African's right to it was simply the right to use it; he had no other right to it, nor did it occur to him to try and claim one.*[132]

The right to land during the colonial period was very limited. There are two reasons to account for the limitation. In the first place, the colonial administration made land confiscation a top item on the agenda of the colonial process. In grabbing land, the colonial government completely ignored the rights of the native people who occupied their traditional lands under their respective native laws and customs prior to colonial intrusion. In the second place land titles were deliberately accorded different status of superiority (granted titles) and of inferiority[133] (customary or deemed titles) by the colonial government. In such circumstances, it is only those who owned granted right of occupancy who could talk of "a right to land". The rest of the people were said to have only "a right to the use" of land, nothing more.

As regards the post colonial period, it is well on record that, "During the negotiations for independence the nationalists led by the Tanganyika African National Union (TANU) had taken a strong position against private ownership of property, especially land. They objected to the inclusion of a Bill of Rights in the Constitution which could, among other things, guarantee the right to ownership of private property".[134] However, from the early days of the post independence period until the date of incorporation of the Bill of Rights some limited steps were put in place to recognise and protect some kind of individual's right to land, but through non-legally binding documents such as the TANU Creed,

---

132 NYERERE, Julius Kambarage, (1968): *Ujamaa: Essays on Socialism*, Dar es Salaam, Oxford University Press.

133 See the cases of *Muhena Bin Said v Registrar of Titles* (1948) Vol. 16 E.A.C.A 71 *and Mtoro Bin Mwamba v Attorney General* (1953) 2 TLR 327 in Chapter Two below.

134 See PETER, Chris Maina, (1989): *Foreign Private Investiment in Tanzania*, Konstanz: Hartung-Gorre Verlag, at p. 11.

whose paragraph (e) of the Preamble provided that "Every individual has the right to receive from society protection of his life and *property* held according to law." Similarly, the right to land was expressed in a non-enforceable part of the law such as the Preamble to the Interim Constitution of 1965[135], whose first paragraph stated, "Whereas freedom, justice, fraternity and concord are founded upon the recognition of the equality of all men and of their inherent dignity, and upon the recognition of the rights of all men to protection of life, liberty and *property*, to freedom of conscience, freedom of expression and freedom of association, to participate in their own government and to receive a just return of their labours..." Notwithstanding this protection, the greatest weakness in this period is that land was occupied at the pleasure of the party and the executive branch of the government without the necessary legal protection. There were formulated various administrative policies above legislative measures, which greatly affected the people's rights to land. In this period, some of the most serious issues in land administration included: cases of unlawful evictions and dispossessions which were almost the order of the day, especially so at the hand of the government which was determined to formulate and implement various policies to meet the demands of socialism and self reliance; the legal gap in terms of recognition and protection between holders of granted titles over land and those who occupied lands under the native laws and customs[136]; and the prevailing negative attitude against women in land ownership which featured almost in all customary communities.

Turning to the period from the incorporation of a Bill of Rights in the state constitution until today, quite significant changes have been occasioned in Tanzanian land law, meaning that one can now undertake to consider the land issue in the context of human rights. As we have already noted above, the Bill of Rights was incorporated into the Constitution of the United Republic of Tanzania in 1984, providing for the basic rights and duties of every Tanzanian citizen, including the right to property (land). Specifically, the Constitution states in unambiguous terms that every person has the right to own property and the right to the protection of his property lawfully acquired,[137] and that a person shall

135 See Act No. 43 of 1965.

136 See the cases of *Methuselah Paul Nyagaswa v Christopher Mbote Nyirabu* [1985] TLR 103, and *Mulbadaw Village Council & 67 Others v National Agricultural and Food Corporation* [1984] TLR 15 in Chapter Two below.

137 See Article 24 (1).

not be arbitrarily deprived of his property for the purpose of acquisition or any other purpose without the authority of the law which shall set out conditions for fair and adequate compensation[138]. The basic law in this regard is the *Land Act, 1999*[139] and the *Village Land Act, 1999*[140], together with some other legislations including but not limited to the *Land Acquisition Act, 1967*[141].

As already noted above, the right to land appears in different forms including the right to the land itself, the right to housing (shelter), the right to compensation for a person's labour in the improvement of land and the right to participate in decisions affecting one's land. Of all these, only two rights, that is, the right to land and the right to compensation are taken to be the rights expressly protected by the constitution. However, it should be noted that the Bill of Rights was incorporated at the time when Tanzania had ratified various international instruments of human rights, such that these instrument are complementary to the Constitution. It is for this reason that history has witnessed some people going to court to seek protection of their land by invoking the provisions of Article 24 of the Constitution.[142] Equally, at times the courts have invoked the provisions of various international human rights instruments as aids in arriving at just decisions in support of the people's right to land.[143]

When looked at through the prism of human rights, three observations can easily be made in respect of the right to land in Tanzania. First, the constitutional protection of the right to land in Tanzania is still inadequate. A study of the land question in the three republics of South Africa, Uganda and Kenya, for example, shows clearly that Tanzania is still some steps behind when it comes to the constitutional recognition, promotion and protection of the right to land. Secondly, although article

---

138 See Article 24 (2).

139 [Cap.113 R.E 2002].

140 [Cap. 114 R.E 2002].

141 [Cap. 118 R.E 2002].

142 See for example *Lohay Akonaay and Another v Attorney General*, High Court of Tanzania at Arusha, Miscellaneous Civil Case No. 1 of 1993 (Unreported), and also *Attorney General v Lohay Akonnay and Another* [1995] TLR 80 (CA). The full discussion of the case is discussed in Chapter Two herein below.

143 See for example the case of *Ephrahim v Pastory and Another*, High Court of Tanzania at Mwanza (PC) Civil Appeal No. 70 of 1989. Reported in [1990] LRC (Const.) 757. See a full discussion about the case in Chapter Five herein below.

24 of the Tanzanian Constitution provides for a partial protection of the right to property (including landed property), the provision does not apply retrospectively to cover the pre-Bill of Rights land confiscations. This is what we can learn at once from the case of *Ami v Safari and Others*[144], which records the following facts: The appellant's father was the owner of a 25-acre parcel of land at Mamire village in Babati District. In 1974 his twenty acres were taken away during the villagilization exercise[145] and allocated to the families of the four respondents, each family being assigned five acres. The appellant did not react until his father's death in 1987. In 1991 the appellant commenced proceedings against the respondents to recover the twenty acres. He partly won in the Primary Court which awarded him only ten acres, that is, two and half acres from each respondent. He appealed in the District Court to recover the remaining ten acres. The District Court held that the ten acres awarded by the Primary Court was sufficient and constituted compensation under article 24 (2) of the Constitution. He was aggrieved further and appealed unsuccessfully to the High Court of Tanzania in Arusha where Munuo, J.- as she then was) dismissed the claim on point of law of limitation by saying that the claim was time barred. The appellant was, again, dissatisfied and appealed to the Court of Appeal of Tanzania. He cited, in favour of his argument, article 24 (2) of the Constitution and the Court's decision in *Attorney General V Akonnay [1995] TLR 80*. The Court, speaking through Lugakingira JA (as he then was) dismissed the appeal on the strength of the following statement:

> *It is not necessary to say much about the appellant's harping on his constitutional rights. As conceded by him at the hearing, the basic rights were enacted into the Constitution and became justiciable many years after his father's land was taken away. It was held in Akonnay upon which he purported to rely that "the provisions of the Basic Human Rights section are not retrospective" (page 95H). And so it is in this case. Article 24 (2) cannot be relied upon to determine the validity of confiscation of the property that took place in 1974. This is not to say that the confiscation of the property in question had any basis in law; what is at issue is that it could and should have been challenged at the appropriate time even though no Bill of Rights existed at the time.*

---

144 [2001]1 E.A 3. The judgment of the case is also available in East Africa Law Society, (2007): *Digest on Human Rights and Access to Justice*, LawAfrica Publishing Ltd, pp. 1-5.

145 For the full account of the villagilization program, see our discussion in Chapter Two below.

Thirdly, despite the fact that protection to land is now recognised by the Constitution, the practice tends to show that not all the citizens of the country can raise their voices high and claim to enjoy the right to land (individual) or the right to their land (collective). This is, at best, evidenced by, among many incidences, the rampant cases of illegal evictions of Tanzanians by their fellow Tanzanians who are, in most cases, assisted by the coercive apparatus of the government.[146] Of all the recorded cases of illegal evictions, the Nyamuma human rights violation case, the recent Tabata Dampo demolition saga and the ruthless eviction of Maasai pastoralists from Loliondo shocked Tanzanians the most.

According to the available record, the background of the Nyamuma eviction case is related to the intended extension of the border of the Ikorogo Game Reserve made by the Serengeti District Council vide a resolution in 1994. By this resolution a great part of the Nyamuma village was declared part of the Game Reserve and villagers were, accordingly, requested to leave the locality. It seems some of the villagers left in compliance of the request, but those involved in the case remained behind until October 8th, 2001 when they too were ordered to vacate by the government officials at the district level. Four days later, that is, on October 12th 2001, they were forcefully evicted from the area where their houses were mercilessly burned, other acts of violence apart. The villagers, assisted by the Legal and Human Rights Centre (LHRC) complained before the Commission of Human Rights and Good Governance[147] accusing the then District Commission and the Officer Commanding the District of Serengeti, Mara region, for setting fire to over 100 houses and the cereal storage facilities belonging to the villagers. They also accused the two government officials of forcefully evicting them from their fertile land of Nyamuma, an act that rendered them homeless.[148] The Commission made a thorough investigation of the matter and in December 2004 came to the conclusion which, indeed, touches the heart of human rights:

---

146 For some detailed account of the illegal evictions see LEGAL AND HUMAN RIGHTS CENTRE, "Tanzania Human Rights Report, 2005" pp. 43-47.

147 The Commission is established by Article 129 (1) of the *Constitution of the United Republic of Tanzania, 1977*, [Cap. 2 R.E 2002] and performs its duties under the guidance of the provisions of the *Commission for Human Rights and Good Governance Act, 2001*, [Cap. 391 R.E 2002].

148 See *Ibrahim Korosso and 134 Others & Legal and Human Rights Centre v Thomas Ole Sabaya and District Commissioner for Serengeti District*, Commission for Human Rights and Good Governance, Case No. HBUB/S/1032/2001/2002/MARA.

> *According to the evidence available to the Commission, the Commission is satisfied that the respondents...did evict the complainants from the area of disputed land and that eviction was carried out brutally and with excessive force. Some of the complainants had lived in the area for a long time and had enough properties to satisfy their needs but they were evicted without being given opportunity to take with them their belongings. They left while destitute. They were evicted without being told where to go. They found themselves refugees in their own country.*[149]

The Commission, therefore, decided in favour of the complainants, and ordered the government to pay them fair and adequate compensation for their property. The government strongly objected against the order, and at the end of the day, refused to comply with the Commission's recommendation. The complainants did not have any other alternative but to approach the High Court of Tanzania (Land Division) and lodge an application to execute the Commission's order through the service of the LHRC.[150] The application was, unfortunately, dismissed on legal technicalities.[151] However, LHRC has successfully appealed to the Court of Appeal of Tanzania[152], which, according to the recent media reports[153], has ordered that the matter should revert back to the High Court for its decision on merits. It is now about eight years from the date of the incident and the right to land of the innocent and homeless villagers is yet to be determined by a court of law! Whether they have any hope from the court, is, again a matter of time.

The history behind the Tabata Dampo Demolition Saga, again, is founded on competing rights between a registered owner, Allied Cargo Freighters on one hand, and the residents (non-registered owners) on the other. In 2002, the former required the latter to vacate from the disputed land on grounds that he was the registered owner of the land since 1996, but the residents ignored this claim and continued to reside on the land on grounds that they had lived there since the 1950s. Due

---

149 *Ibid.*

150 See *Legal and Human Rights Centre v Ole Sabaya and 4 Others*, High Court of Tanzania at Dar es Salaam (Land Division), Misc. Land Application no. 22 of 2005 (Unreported).

151 Court said it has no jurisdiction under section 28 (3) of the Act to entertain execution proceedings arising out of the Commission's recommendations, the same not constituting an award.

152 See *Legal and Human Rights Centre v Ole Sabaya and 4 Others*, Court of Appeal of Tanzania at Dar es Salaam, Civil Appeal no. 88 of 2006 (Unreported).

153 See, for example, PANCRAS, Primtiva, "Mahakama Yaafiki Maombi ya Wanakijiji," *Mtanzania*, January 5, 2009 at p. 4.

to this collision, Allied Cargo Freighters reported the matter, and the government preferred a criminal case[154] against one Mohamed Suleiman and 16 others. In this case the accused were charged with erecting buildings in the area without permits contrary to rules 4 (c) and 12 (2) and 64 of the then Township Rules, Cap 109. It was the prosecution's case that the area was surveyed and registered as Plot No 52 in which no one would build a house without holding a building permit. The accused denied the charge whereby one of them testified before the trial court that he had been in the area since 1954 as a farmer and that he never knew that the area was surveyed. The Trial magistrate held against the accused by ordering them to vacate from the area. Dissatisfied by the decision, the accused appealed in the High Court of Tanzania[155], raising four grounds of appeal, whereby the first three grounds related to the trial court's failure to assess and evaluate the evidence on record, while the fourth ground faulted the trial magistrate for ordering the appellants to vacate. Essentially, it was incisively argued for the appellants that they were in the area before the same was surveyed and named accordingly as Plot No.52 Mandela Road, and that they constructed their houses at a time when there was no requirement to have building permits. It was further argued that the responsible Authority did survey the area without first giving any notice to the appellants, the move being deliberately staged to avoid paying them compensation. Finally, it was the argument for the appellants that the magistrate had greatly erred in determining the issue of ownership when he ordered them to vacate. The Counsel for the appellants put it very correctly:

> *My Lord, there is no punishment of vacating the area for a person who constructs without a building permit because, in the areas which are surveyed, a person can be a lawful owner of the Plot but without Building permit, or he/she can not be the owner of the Plot, but the question of ownership is totally different to the other of having permit. Hence in our case there was a criminal charge on Building permit, which doesn't touch the ownership, which in our opinion is totally civil. Therefore, it was improper for the Court to touch the issue of ownership while the charge was of construction without Building permit.*[156]

---

154 See *Republic v Mohamed Suleiman and 16 Others*, Resident Magistrates' Court of Dar es Salaam at Sokoine Drive, Criminal Case No. 2552 of 2002. (Unreported).

155 See *Mohamed Suleiman and Sixteen Others v Republic*, Criminal Appeal No. 97 of 2003. (Unreported), judgement of 31st March 2004.

156 An extract from the Appellant's written submission filled in the Court on 12th February, 2004.

After directing its mind on the grounds of appeal and submission of the parties, the High Court of Tanzania (Massati, J. as he then was) found the conviction, sentence and order of the trial court to be bad in law and, therefore, allowed the appellant's appeal without fear or favour. "In the result, this appeal is allowed. The conviction is quashed the sentence and order of evacuation are set aside. This judgment, however does not decide on the issue of ownership of the said plot which may be the subject of civil litigation between the parties and does not bar the operation of Rule 12 of the Township (Building) Rules."

It can be said that the court's decision was the beginning of the cloudy days of the Tabata dampo residents. It seems that, apart from a criminal case that the residents won on appeal, Allied Cargo Freighters had also instituted in court and won a case against the Dar es Salaam Municipal Council for allowing the residents to remain on the land, which was legally allocated to it. In the move to satisfy the claims of a registered owner, the City Council ordered eviction of the residents at a very short notice or at no notice at all. It was on the afternoon of 29th February, 2008 when the situation deteriorated for the residents. The Ilala Municipality undertook to, and did, demolish over 80 households, rendering homeless over 300 residents of the said Tabata Dampo. The victims, like any other internally displaced persons, remained under the care of some good Samaritans who provided temporary shelter (tents) and food until a few months later when the government, moved by the public outcry, intervened by compensating them to the tune of Tshs. 20 million for each demolished household and allocating them new areas of residence in Mbuyuni. The government intervention, which was the inevitable rescue in the circumstance, is a clear indication that Ilala Municipality had moved illegally in evicting the residents, and was in clear denial of their right to land.

The last incident in the series is the ruthless eviction of the Maasai from Loliondo, in Ngorongoro District, Arusha region, which a known political figure from one of the opposition parties has had the courage to refer to as "*unyama dhidi ya wananchi wa Loliondo*" [i.e., inhuman acts done to the residents of Loliondo] when addressing a press conference recently in Dar es Salaam. According to records,[157] the Loliondo Controlled Area had, historically, been a traditional land of the Masaai,

---

157 See, for example, the LEGAL AND HUMAN RIGHTS CENTRE, "*Tanzania Human Rights Report,* 2009", at pp. 102, 125-128.

before it was declared a controlled area in 1959. This means that even after this declaration, people continued to claim and exercise residential and grazing rights over "their traditional land" until 4th July 2009 when they suffered shocking human rights abuses inflicted by government representatives. Before the fateful day, the then District Commissioner of Ngorongoro had formed the opinion that some people (who happened to be local residents of the villages of Ololosokwami, Saitsambu, Olerien, Magaiduru and Arash, in Loliondo), were trespassing in the hunting block which was licensed to a foreign company, the Ortello Business Corporation, for hunting activities. However, instead of dealing with the said "trespassers" according to law, the Commissioner, who is an executive arm of the government, issued an order dated 18/ 5/2009 that they should be evicted. The order was carried expetitiously by the Field Force Unit (FFU) of the police, who forcefully undertook to evict the Masaai families from the area by burning down their houses, destroying properties and sexually harassing their women! This predicament attracted various sympathizers both in and outside the human rights camp, including members of the parliament of the United Republic of Tanzania, the NGOs, CSOs, press, and the European Union delegation, some of which took the trouble to visit the *locus in quo*, to witness the result of the vicrous eviction.

Three things can be deduced from the three above cases, and similar cases on record. First, the government has turned out to be the greatest human rights violator by not respecting and protecting the right to land of the traditional land holders. Second, the government representatives have become promoters of lawlessness and anarchy by taking the law into their hands in total disregard of the rule of law and good governance. Evictions of people from their traditional land through imperious means, including the employment of fire against their properties, torture, rape and all kinds of sexual harassment, without paying them adequate and prompt compensation is, to say the least, an unfortunate chapter in the jurisprudence of the Tanzanian land law. Third, similar acts of lawlessness and violation of the people's right to land by arms of the government stand to cause negative reactions if it maintains its recalcitrant attitude toward the rights to land of the voiceless, and if it doesn't learn from past atrocities against its people or heed the public outcry.

Over and above the numerous cases of land confiscations and illegal evictions of the land holders, the shelter (housing) problem also has its unique place in the history of land administration in Tanzania. A personal comment about the housing problem in Tanzania reads:

> *The United Nations through its various organizations and programs has been pushing for actions which ensure that governments take appropriate steps in order to promote, protect and ensure the full and progressive realization of the right to adequate housing... My feeling is that Tanzania is far behind many countries, as far as advocating for a right to housing is concerned.*[158]

It means that the state of housing facilities is still a great challenge in Tanzania, especially in urban areas because of the urbanization process that is currently in place due to massive rural urban migrations. Inadequacy of house supplies, and poor housing facilities, the prevalence of slums, overcrowding, and serious deficiencies in basic urban infrastructure such as water, roads, electricity and drainage facilities, are among the key indicators of the problem. The immediate impact of the lack of habitable houses in towns, it has been noted, has been the prevalence of crime, especially in most slums of the unplanned areas. It is noted by an observer that:

> *Densely-populated residential areas or the 'uswahilini', as they are commonly known in Tanzania, are both a target and source for criminal groups. These groups generally involve themselves in a multiplicity of activities, for example, drugs, theft and child and women sexual abuse. A survey conducted in 2000, which covered the years 1995-2000, when the country was going through a transition period following a series of economic crises over three decades, indicated high levels of crime in Dar es Salaam's seething unplanned settlements.*[159]

158 See KIRONDE, Lussunga, "Human Rights to Adequate Housing", *Sunday News*, August 2, 2009. See also KIRONDE Lussunga, "Rent Control Legislation and the National Housing Corporation in Tanzania 1985-1990", *Canadian Journal of African Studies*, Vol. 26, No. 2, 1992, pp. 306-327.

159 KALOKOLA, Sharifa, "Crime Forces Parents to Keep their Kids Indoors", *Sunday Citizen*, October 4, 2009.

Two factors have been cited to account for the housing problem in towns. The first factor relates to the incapacity of the government to provide houses adequately, or at all, to the satisfaction of the urban dwellers, thus, leaving the citizens to go it alone through the self-help housing schemes. This is what we learn from Martin Madeke who states that:

> *On the other hand, housing demand by far outstrips house supply. Furthermore, the Government lacks the capacity to deliver housing; land; infrastructure and social services to match the urban population growth. Consequently, problems of poor and inadequate housing; deepening poverty; diminishing holding capacity of the existing infrastructure, and disintegration of the social fabric are interrelated and are life in our urban areas.* [160]

The second factor is the financial incapacity of the majority urban population to access surveyed and serviced plots of land[161], or to construct good and adequate houses, or to rent decent houses constructed by those who can afford. The National Housing Corporation (NHC)[162] is a parastatal organization that strives to provide adequate housing to the urban population. However, the available record shows that the Corporation is underperforming for reasons related to, among others, low financial position of consumers.

> *NHC's efforts to provide decent housing are, however, hampered by two factors. First, there is a widespread low affordability for housing consequent to low levels of income among the majority of Tanzanians. A study undertaken in 2001, indicated that the affordability indices are between 15 and 64 for welloff households and poor households respectively. This means that in Tanzania, it take 15 and 64 years household income to construct a decent house. These indices are low compared to three (3) years income equivalent in the developed world.*[163]

---

160 An extract from the Statement of the Director General of the Tanzanian National Housing Corporation, Mr. Martin Madekwe, to commemorate the October 2008 World Habitat Day, *Daily News* Monday, October 6, 2008.

161 The detailed historical account of the problem is recorded in MGULLU, Francis Peter, (1978): "Housing: A study of Tanzania's National Sites and Services Schemes," LL.M Dissertation, University of Dar es Salaam; STREN, Richard E., "Underdevelopment, Urban Squatting and the State Bureaucracy: A Case Study of Tanzania," *Canadian Journal of African Studies*, Vol. 10, No. 1 , 1982, pp. 67-91; KIRONDE, Lussunga, "Forms of Government Intervention to Encourage Rental Housing", *Sunday News* July 5, 2009, and; KIRONDE, Lussunga, "Affordability Consideration in Rental Housing", *Sunday News*, August 16, 2009.

162 See KIRONDE, Lussunga, *op cit*, for details about the establishment and the role of the Corporation in the housing sector.

163 Martin Madekwe, *op cit.*

All the above, tell one important story, that the right to adequate housing is still a serious problem for many Tanzanians. The right to adequate housing is part and parcel of a human right to land. It follows, therefore, that the government and citizens in their group or individual capacities are encouraged to find new solutions to the age-old problem of adequate and habitable houses. The government, especially, has been trying its best to resolve the problem of housing. It has, for example, developed the National Human Settlements Developing Policy whose vision is "to have well-organised, efficient, healthy, safe and secure settlements... where everyone has adequate and affordable shelter which is durable, accessible and which matches with the culture and living habits of the occupants"[164]. It is submitted that this and other government's efforts, including the 20,000 Plots Project which is currently taking place in Dar es Salaam and and in a few other regions, as well as the new legislation, including the the *Unit Titles Act, 2008*[165] and the *Mortgage Financing (Special Provisions) Act, 2008*[166] need to be commended and encouraged. The two acts are intended to improve, significantly, the prospect for mass houses production, and to satisfy increasing demands for financial mortgages.

164 See UNITED REPLIC OF TANZANIA, (2002): National Human Settlements Development Policy, Dar es Salaam, Government Printers.

165 [Act, No. 16. of 2008].

166 [Act No. 17 of 2008].

Chapter Two

Land Law Reforms and Tenure Systems in Tanzania

> The first thing to note about land law is that no subject can own land.
>
> - Judith-Anne Mackenzie.[167]
>
> Land is the basis of human life and all Tanzanians should use it as a valuable investment for future development. Because the land belongs to the nation, the Government has to see to it that it is used for the benefit of the whole nation and not for the benefit of one individual or just a few people.
>
> -Julius Kambarage Nyerere.[168]

167 MACKENZIE, Judith Anne, (1993): *A Practical Approach to Land Law*, 4th Edition, Blackstone Press Ltd, at p. 1.

168 NYERERE, Julius Kambarage, (1968): *Ujamaa: Essays on Socialism*, Dar es Salaam, Oxford University Press.

Land, Land Tenure and Land Law Reforms

Before going into a long discussion on the historical developments that gave rise to various tenure systems and land law reforms in Tanzania, it may be worthwhile to bring the readers' attention to the basic concepts, that is: land, land tenure and land law reform.

The Concept of Land

The old maxim regarding land, *quicquid plantatur solo solo cedit*, means that whatever is attached to the soil becomes part of it. However, the term "land" is, more often than not, known differently to different people depending on one's approach to the subject. What the term means to a lawyer is far more than what it does to a layman. But also the term may mean different things even among the lawyers themselves. The variation arises out of what I refer to as a broad (traditional) definition of land on one hand, and a narrow (non-traditional) definition on the other. Traditionally, therefore, the term land has a wide meaning and application. It includes the surface of the land (soil) and all other things on the soil which are considered to be part of the land by nature, such as rivers, streams, lakes, lagoons, creeks, mines and minerals, trees like palm trees, or by being artificially fixed to it like houses, buildings and any other structures whatsoever. It also includes any estate, interest or right in, to, or over the land or even any other things which the land denotes, for example, the right to collect herbs or to hunt. By this definition, a person may claim interest (s) in a piece of land without physically owning it!

We explore the non-traditional definition of land by way of a reference the statutory definition of land as provided by the Tanzanian *Land Act, 1999*[169]. In this Act:

> *..."land" includes the surface of the earth and the earth below the surface and all substances other than minerals or petroleum forming part of or below the surface, things naturally growing on the land, buildings and other structures permanently affixed to or under land and land covered by water.*[170]

---

169 [Cap. 113, R.E 2002].

170 See Section 2. It is also important to note that even within legal systems; there are significant variations in the definition of the term land. For example, while the term "mines and minerals" do not fall under the definition of land in Tanzania, the same is included in the definition of "land" under the English *Law of Property Act*, 1925. See section 25 (1) (ix) of this Act which defines "land" to include, among other things, "mines and minerals whether or not held apart from the surface..."

It means that under the statutory definition a person who owns land does not own any minerals or petroleum existing there. Once a discovery of minerals or petroleum is made into one's land, the holder thereof shall be compulsorily required to transfer the same to the government to give room for the mining industry if need be. It is important to note, here, that all land in Tanzania is public land and falls into three categories: general land, village land and reserved land.[171] As the names suggest, general land is public land, which is neither reserved nor village land, and includes any unoccupied land[172], while reserved land is land which is reserved for specific public uses including, for example, all land under the forestry and tourist industries.[173] Understanding the classification of land is important to a lawyer, because each of the three categories presents its unique features when it comes to land use and control, including the body of laws that govern them as well as the nature of the interests which go with them.

Land Tenure

The term tenure is derived from a Latin word, *tenere*, which means to "hold". Therefore, land tenure means a kind of a system of land ownership or control patterns. According to the available records, the idea of tenure in relation to land is foreign and is traced as far back as the Norman Conquest of the eleventh century[174]. Precisely, the idea of land tenure is historically linked with King William of Normandy under whose reign all land was declared *terra regis*, that is, belonging to the king who was not only the supreme, but also the largest land owner of the country and, therefore, the one who permitted the subjects to occupy and use land under given conditions and for a specified duration. Later developments in the English land law accommodated a similar scenario when the word King, as a superior landlord, was replaced by the word Crown[175]. Likewise under Tanzanian land law today, all land belongs to the public but it is vested in the President as trustee for and on

171 See section 4 (4) of the *Land Act, 1999* [Cap. 113 R.E 2002].

172 Section 2, *ibid.*

173 Section 6 (1), *ibid.*

174 See DIGBY Kenelm Edward, (1892): *An Introduction to the History of the Law of Real Property*, 4th Edition, Oxford, Clarendon Press. The learned author states at p. 37 that, "... the result of the Norman Conquest upon the customary law of land seems to have been the development of the idea of tenure, the more precise definition of the mutual rights and duties of lord and tenant.

175 This is the birth of the principle that the sovereign is the universal occupant of land.

behalf of all the citizens of Tanzania.[176] While the term tenure answers the question, "How is land held", there is a twin term, *estate*[177], which answers the question, "For how long is land held?". Tenure and estate are now recognised in the literature as constituting the basic doctrines in land law: the doctrine of tenure, which harbours the notion that all land is held of the Crown either directly or indirectly; and the doctrine of estate, which is home to the notion that a subject cannot own land, but can merely own an estate in it, authorizing him to hold it for some period of time.[178] Historically and especially under the English common law[179] system, estates in land were that of the freehold and the leasehold. The freehold estate was classified into three categories, namely, the fee simple, fee tail and the life estate. Of all the three, the fee simple has been described as the basic unit of ownership of land under English law and, therefore, the greatest interest holders of land can possess.[180] The estate in land was fee simple as soon as a piece of land was conveyed, *inter vivos*, to "A and his or her heirs", so that the estate would last as long as there were heirs to inherit that land. Until today, the English land law recognises fee simple as an estate which endures indefinitely as long as there are persons entitled to take the property under the provisions of the will of the previous owner, or under the statutory rules relating to intestacy. It means that if there is no heir the land will revert to the Crown at the death of the previous owner.[181] As regards the fee tail, this was created once a grant was made to "A and the heirs of A's body", meaning that the estate could continue as long as the original owner or any of his descendants survived. Under the fee tail estate, land passed from the ancestor to the ancestor's children, grandchildren, great grandchildren,

---

176 Per Section 4 (1) of the Land Act, Cap 113 (Revised Laws of Tanzania, 2002).

177 According to HAYTON, David J., (1982): *Megarry's Manual of The Law of Real Property*, Sixth Edition, London: Stevens & Sons Ltd, at p. 28, the term estate is defined to mean an interest in land of defined duration.

178 See an account of these doctrines in HAYTON, David J., *ibid*, at p. 24.

179 In the English legal system, reference to common law excluded local customs, statutory law and equity.

180 See BURKE, Barlow, *et al.*, (2004): *Fundamentals of Property Law*, Second Edition, LexisNexis, at p. 187.

181 See MACKENZIE, Judith Anne, *op cit* at p. 3.

etc., who were the heirs of his body, and not collateral heirs such as brothers or cousins. Finally, is the life estate, which was created when a grant was given to "A for life" and whose duration was measured by the duration of the life of the tenant. A life estate was not fee in that it was not an estate of inheritance, and could not continue forever. However, we are told that what was common to all the three estates of the freehold was that the duration of the estate was fixed but uncertain as nobody could say when the death would occur of a man and his heirs, or a man and all his descendants, or a man alone.[182]Freehold estate differs from a leasehold estate in that the leasehold is always an estate of limited duration, which is fixed and certain. Freehold tenures, reminiscent of the English fee simple, were introduced in the colonies and, to date, remain one of the tenurial systems in some countries such as Uganda till today[183]. In Tanzania, freehold estates were in place during both German and British colonial rules, but were abolished after independence[184]. According to the literature, we now identify three (3) land tenure systems in Tanzania which are: one, formal/official (statutory) land tenure where land is held under a Granted Right of Occupancy; two, Customary (indigenous) land tenure where land is held under a Customary (deemed) right of occupancy, and; three, informal (neither statutory nor customary) land tenure.[185]

Land Law Reforms

The term "land law reforms" has been used interchangeably with some other terms such as "land tenure reforms" or simply "land reforms." However in the context of land law and practice in Tanzania, preference is made for the term land law reform, for the reasons stated by the learned Professor of land law:

---

182 HAYTON, David J., *op cit* at p.29.

183 See BIKAAKO, Winnie, and SSENKUMBA, John, *op cit.* The learned authors give a detailed analysis on the freehold tenures in Uganda, relating it to the English fee simple, but distinguishing it in that the Ugandan freehold tenure is subject to statutory restrictions on development condition a freeholder has to abide by and the right to own the soil and the surface of the land, which excludes minerals and water rights. Another limitation is imposed by the public interests in that absolute ownership is never available to a freeholder of land, since what the landowners have to do with their lands has to take into account the public interest.

184 Freehold titles in Tanzania were abolished by the Freehold (Conversion) and Government Leases Act, 1963.

185 See an account of the three types of tenure systems in MUNDEME S., "Formalizing Informal Land Markets in Tanzania: The Role of the Private and Public Sectors", Paper Presented at the International Conference on the Interaction Between Formal and Informal Urban Land Management in Africa, Dar es Salaam, 25-26 November 1999.

> *In this study the process of change in land law reforms is referred to as "land law reforms." Two important expressions, "land tenure reforms" and "land reform" are not appropriate here because there has been no change in tenure forms. The main tenures which were introduced during the colonial period have been confirmed: thus the granted right of occupancy, customary tenure and leasehold estates have been confirmed by the 1999 Land Acts. Further, in Tanzania there has not been any land reform as is commonly understood. In South Africa land reform had three aspects; land restitution, land redistribution and land tenure reform.*[186]

The question that may rise is: What is land law reform? In the words of Muthoni Wanyeki, "Land [sic] reforms can be defined as legal and policy led changes with respect to rights affecting access to and control over land, with the aim of ultimately transforming land ownership patterns"[187]. We learn from the same author that land [law] reform is usually understood as being either conservative, liberal or revolutionary in terms of the rights being promoted and protected, as well as in terms of the process through which these rights are granted.[188] We quite agree with the learned author. History is replete of cases in which some individuals or groups of individuals have relied on revolutionary judicial processes to fight for their rights in land where the same were previously hindered by some conservative legislative measures. Some significant land law reforms in Tanzania are traced from the colonial invasion and the subsequent domination of German and British colonial governments. The reason is quite simple: the colonial occupation could not have been possible without land! The colonisers needed land for various purposes ranging from residential through agricultural to commercial goals. Acquisition of land from the native population in the colonies was a real necessity and could only be made possible through the introduction of the colonial land law whose actual impact was the suppression of the native law and customs governing land administration. Oppresive reforms were also in place at the demise of the colonial rule and were accelerated much later by the present-day demands, to wit: the increasing population in the midst of land scarcity; liberalisation and privatization at a time of stiff competition over land and resources;

---

186 FIMBO, G.M., (2004): *Land Law Reforms in Tanzania*, Dar es Salaam University Press, Ltd.

187 See WANYEKI, L. Muthoni, (ed.) (2005): *Women and Land in Africa: Culture, Religion and Realizing Women's Right*, at p. 25.

188 *Ibid.*

marital instabilities, and; new roles and responsibilities especially so at a time when the language of gender equality and human rights was taking off. All these have necessitated land law reforms at different times, until today when we are all witnesses to gender responsive land law reforms,[189] among many others[190].

The Pre-Colonial Land Tenure Systems in Tanzania

We cannot better address the pre-colonial land tenure system in Tanzania if we do not, in the first place, highlight the relations of production which were in place in this historical period. The rationale behind this approach is supported by the simple fact that it is the relations of production in any human society which determine not only who owns what and who produces what but also who appropriates what. The "what" phraseology in the "who owns what" scenario covers both real and personal property in its proper construction.

Pre-Colonial Relations of Production

If the year 1884/1885[191] is taken to be the historical dating for the beginning of the colonization process in Africa, then it cannot be disputed to say that the pre-colonial relations of production were not uniform in all of the African societies at that time. The same may be said of the Tanzanian societies as well. In this particular time some societies, constituted by hunting and gathering communities like the Hadzabe, Sandawe, and Mang'ati of Tanzania, for example, were still classless societies, based on the communal mode of production,[192] while many others such as the agriculturalist societies in the intercustrine region, were class societies

---

189 By "gender responsive land reforms" we mean changes in land law reforms that aim at ensuring equal access to and control over land for both men and women; also, equal land ownership patterns between men and women.

190 MINDE, Elizabeth Maro, " Law Reform and Land Rights in Tanzania", A Paper Presented to the XVI International Aids Conference, Toronto, Canada 13th-18th August, 2006 at p. 2 also identifies the factors that necessitated land reforms in Tanzania as including (1)The increased population of people and animals resulting in shortage of land and the subsequent conflicts, (2) The increased demand for land use leading to environmental degradation, (3) The increased awareness about the value of land leading to conflicts in both urban and rural areas, and (4) Changes in the mode of land ownership from clan based system to individual system brought by the introduction of land markets.

191 Reference is being made to the Berlin Conference of 188/5 which was responsible for the partition of the African Continent among the European colonial powers. The Conference is taken to mark the beginning of the colonization process. See the General Act of Berlin African Conference adopted in Berlin, Germany on 26th February, 1885.

192 The term "communal mode of production" is used interchangeably with the "Primitive Communalism".

founded on some forms of feudal relations of production. However, in all these societies the type of economy was essentially a natural economy in which the whole community participated in material production and also communally consumed what was produced. At the top of the political hierarchy, in all class societies were the ruling classes of the chiefs and their subordinates, who consumed the surplus. Since production was communal and labour was collective, it means that ownership and distribution were also collective. At the end of it all, this had a direct influence on the type of land tenure system that evolved in such relations of production.

Pre-Colonial Land Tenure System

In the pre-colonial societies, in Tanzania and elsewhere in Africa, property relations were communal. Land, the basic means of production and the object of life, was communally owned[193] and every member[194] of the society had a right to use it. The available literature explains this better than I can do. For example, S. Mundeme speaks in clear terms that:

> *Land in Tanzania during the pre-colonial days was a communal property belonging to the whole community, clan or tribe whereby all members of the community had equal access and right of use. The rights were usufractuary, i.e they were valid as long as the land held was utilized. The powers to allocate community land were vested into the Chiefs, Heads of the tribe or head of the clan.*[195]

The usufractuary right to land on the part of Africans as opposed to the right of individual ownership over the communal land is best analyzed by, and forms the legal precedent of, the case of *Amodu Tijani v The Secretary, Southern Nigeria*[196]. The appellant was one of the local chiefs heading the Oluwa family in Lagos, Nigeria. Sometime in 1913 certain lands under his jurisdiction were acquired by the British

193 We, therefore, talk of the communal land tenure system as characterizing the whole era of the pre-colonial period.

194 Membership was identified through kinship and consanguinity.

195 MUNDEME, S., *op cit,* at p.9. The learned author also appreciates and therefore cites, for our benefits, Mwalimu Julius Kambarage Nyerere who, writing in 1962, observed that, "In Africa land has always been recognized as belonging to the community and that each individual within our society had a right to the use of the land because otherwise he could not earn his living. But, the African's right to land was simply the right to use it, he had no other right to it nor did it occur to him to try and claim one".

196 (1921) AC 399.

Government under the *Public Lands Ordinance*[197] for public purposes. The appellant, a chief, claimed for some compensation, basing his claim on the ownership of lands. In other words, he claimed compensation for the whole value of the land in question. The trial court (Speed, C.J.- as he then was) found that the appellant was entitled to compensation on the basis of his having merely a right of control and management of the land, and not on the basis of absolute ownership. This decision was affirmed by the Supreme Court of Nigeria. Dissatisfied by the decisions of the two courts, the Appellant preferred an appeal against the judgment of the Supreme Court, which was granted and then determined by the Privy Council of the House of Lords. The question for determination by their Lordships was on what was the basis for calculation of the compensation payable to the appellant[198]. Writing the judgment of their Lordships, Viscount Haldane observed, *inter alia*, that according to the native custom, even in Lagos, land is held by the family. His Lordship went on to say that a very usual form of native title is that of a usufructuary right, which is a mere qualification of or burden on the radical or final title of the Sovereign. His Lordship found support in the 1898 Report of Land Tenure in West Africa by Rayner, C.J., and went on to state:

> *In the instance of Lagos the character of the tenure of the land among native communities is described by Rayner C.J in the Report on Land Tenure in West Africa, which that learned judge made in 1898, in language which their Lordships think is substantially borne out by the preponderance of authority: "The next fact which it is important to bear in mind in order to understand the native land law is that the notion of individual ownership is quite foreign to native ideas. Land belongs to the community, the village or the family, never to the individual. All members of the community, village or family have an equal right to the land, but in every case the Chief or Headman of the community or village, or head of the family, has charge of the land, and in loose mode of speech is sometimes called the owner. He is to some extent in the position of a trustee, and as such he holds the land for the use of the community or family. He has control of it, and any member who wants a piece of it to cultivate or build a house upon, goes to him for it. But the land so given still remains the property of the community or family. He cannot*

197 No. 5 of 1903.

198 See Judgment, p. 400.

> *make any important disposition of the land without consulting the elders of the community or family and their consent must in all cases be given before a grant can be made to a stranger. This is a pure native custom along the whole length of the coast, and wherever we find, as in Lagos, individual owners, this is again due to the introduction of English ideas. But the native idea still has a firm hold on the people, and in most cases, even in Lagos, land is held by the family. This is so even in land purporting to be held under Crown grants and English conveyances. The original grantee may have held them as an individual owner, but on his death all his family claim an interest which is always recognised, and thus the land becomes again family land. My experience in Lagos leads me to the conclusion that except where land has been bought by the present owner there are very few natives who are individual owners of land.*[199]

At the end of the matter their Lordships established the following principles as basis for calculation of compensation payable to the appellant. In the first place, their Lordship noted that the Crown was under no obligation to pay anyone for unoccupied lands as defined[200]. In the second place, it was noted that the Crown would pay the appellant (chief) for family lands to which he was individually entitled when taken. Also in all cases of other portions of the land under the appellant's control which he allotted to the strangers or even to individual members of his own clan community and from which he derived tribute or rent, he was to be compensated for the loss of it.[201] Under the circumstances, even the allottees, who had valid titles conferred on them would be compensated.[202] Finally, their Lordship noted that in all cases where land belonged to the community, but as to which no rent or tribute was payable to the chief, then the chief would not be entitled to compensation for the loss of such lands.[203]

What may be said to constitute the native ownership of land in the context of the above case also characterised most societies in the whole of Africa. In mainland Tanzania, for example, feudal (private)

---

199 Judgment, pp. 404-405.

200 Judgment, p. 410.

201 *Ibid.*

202 *Ibid.*

203 *Ibid.*

land ownership developed in areas with population density and agricultural economy in the form of *Nyarubanja* in Bukoba, *Kihamba*[204] in Kilimanjaro and *Obusi* in Ukerewe. This form of land tenure[205] was in place until it was formally abolished in 1968 under the *Customary Leasehold (Enfranchisement) Act*, 1968. Customary land tenure turned into a future potential victim of the colonial and post colonial land law reforms. The thorny area on the agenda in Tanganyika and Tanzania since colonial times to date has been the elimination of customary land tenure in favour of the granted rights of occupancy.

Tenure Systems and Land Law Reforms under German Colonial Rule

The history of German colonial rule in Tanzania is well documented.[206] My task in this book is to address the land tenure reforms that evolved under this rule. I share views with Nasani Batungi who observes that the first land tenure reform in Tanganyika (Tanzania mainland) occurred during German rule, which lasted from 1885 to 1914.[207] In essence, the German government passed a Decree in 1895[208] in which it expressly declared all land, except the land already in private ownership or possessed by indigenous communities, to be un-owned Crown land vested in the German Empire. In the later circular there was put in place a condition that proof of title to land was to be made by producing authenticated documents. In this regard, the *Land Registration Ordinance*, which was passed in 1903, established a registry system under which title to land had to be registered and documents of title issued to the owner. It should be noted that, although German rule recognised all land titles that existed, that is to say individual or tribal, the implication was the confiscation of all land which was not occupied into Crown land. Also, the requirement that title be proved by documentary evidence was

204 According to records, "Kihamba" is defined to mean a permanent homestead capable of disposition by the owner and inheritable by his heirs. See *Petri bin Joseph v Joachim bin Ndapoi, Appeal to Governor*, No. 78/1944. The case is discussed in JAMES, R.W. and FIMBO, G.M., (1973): *Customary Land Law of Tanzania: A Source Book*, East African Literature Bureau, Dar es Salaam.

205 This is properly referred to as the Feudal Land Tenure.

206 See, for example, ILIFFE, J., (1969): *Tanganyika under German Rule 1905-1912*, Cambridge: Cambridge University Press.

207 See BATUNGI, Nasani, "Land Tenure Reform in East Africa: Some Reflections on the Formalization of Customary Tenure" at p. 40.

208 This is the Imperial Decree Regarding Creation, Acquisition and Conveyance of Crown Land and regarding the Acquisition and Conveyance of Lands in general in German East Africa, of 26th November, 1895.

meant to favour certain categories of people, such as the white settlers who could get grants either from the German administration or from local chiefs.[209] Batungi expounds this point when he empirically says that by the end of the German administration in Tanganyika about 1,300,000 acres of land (about 0.5% of total landmass) on the coast and in the northern highlands were in the hands of the settlers.[210]

The history of the German administration in Tanzania is unique compared with that of the British rule[211] because of the stiff local resistance the Germans had to confront in the process of installing their administration[212]. Resistances of varying degrees were staged for reasons relating to, *inter alia*, opposition against forced labour and compulsory production of certain cash crops to meet some external demands.[213] The German colonisation of Tanganyika was a brief episode where nothing much, apart from resistances, is recorded concerning their rule, much less on the land tenure system. In a nutshell, we note the following tenurial systems of land ownership as characterising the German rule in Tanzania. First, there were freehold titles which were created out of the conveyance of property through such processes as purchase or sale of lands whose grants were available only to Europeans and subject to reversion. Second, there were leaseholds which were granted by the Empire up to the period of 21 years[214]. Third, there was customary land tenure, which was considered to be inferior and thus non-registerable as the owners thereof were not allowed to access the registry. The notion of the usufructuary native rights to land remained in full swing.

209 See JAMES, R.W., (1971): *Land Tenure and Policy in Tanzania*, Toronto: University of Toronto Press.

210 See BATUNGI, Nasani, *op cit.* p. 40.

211 The British employed the use of the indirect rule system, which played the preventive role against local resistances. The success of the indirect rule technique in Sukuma land, for example, has been well discussed in LITTLE, Marilyn, "Colonial Policy and Subsistence in Tanganyika 1925-1945", *Geographical Review*, Vol. 81, No. 4, (Oct., 1991), pp. 375- 388.

212 We have on record resistances such as the one led by Mkwawa, the Hehe leader of Iringa who resisted until his death in 1898, and the Maji Maji rebellion of 1905-1907. See an account of the latter in MAPUNDA, O.B. and MPANGARA, G.P., (1969): *The Maji Maji War in Ungoni*, East African Publishing House.

213 The Maji Maji rebellion against German rule in Tanzania has been called one of the most important anti- colonial movements in Africa. See MONSON, Jamie, "Relocating Maji Maji: The Politics of Alliance and Authority in Southern Highlands of Tanzania, 1870-1918", *Journal of African History*, Vol. 39, No. 1 (998), pp. 95-120, at p. 97.

214 Remember, land was Crown land administered by the Land Commissions as designated by the Governor.

Tenure Systems and Land Law Reforms under British Rule

The British took over the administration of the territory after the First World War[215] when Germany was defeated and gave up its overseas possessions[216]. Students and lawyers of international law recall the Versailles Peace Treaty of 1919[217], which is known for its outcomes: the creation of the League of Nations[218] and the dispossession of Germany of her colonies. Britain needed the mandate of the League of Nations before she could extend her colonial administration to Tanganyika, and immediately after receiving the mandate, enacted the *Tanganyika Order in Council*, 1920[219], which provided for the reception of English laws in the Territory[220]. This legal document also established the office of the Governor and provided for the establishment of the "Executive Council" to advise the Governor in the government of the territory.[221] All the legislative powers were vested in the Governor alone until 1926 when the Legislative Council was established under the *Tanganyika (Legislative Council) Order in Council*, 1926.[222] As far as administration of land is concerned, the available records show that the Order in Council vested all land control rights in Her Majesty. The land rights

---

215 The war lasted from 1914 to 1918, and Germany experienced some kind of an unprecedented defeat.

216 For an account of British history in Tanzania see MWAIKUSA, J.T., "Tanzania's Constitutional History and Development" in Binchy, W and Finnegan, C., (eds.) (2006): *Human Rights, Constitutionalism and the Judiciary: Tanzanian and Irish Perspectives*, Dublin: Clarus Press, pp. 3-19.

217 Adopted on 21 April 1919.

218 Established on 10 January 1920. For detailed account on the birth of the League of Nations, see the literature on International law such as VERMA, S.K., (1998): *An Introduction to Public International Law*, New Delhi, Prentice-Hall of India, at pp. 428ff.

219 Made under the English *Foreign Jurisdiction Act*, 1890 and proclaimed on 25th September 1920. See the Laws of Tanganyika, 1929, Vol. 3, at p. 6.

220 Article 17 (1) of the *Tanganyika Order in Council* established Her Majesty's High Court of Tanganyika, while sub-article (2) of the Order declared for the application of the Indian Laws in Tanganyika, the English common law, doctrines of equity and statutes of general application, as well as other laws which were in force in the territory at the date of the commencement of the order. Until this time the German law was still the law of the land, subject to the various proclamations and orders made under martial law during the occupancy by British forces. It was also retained by section 10 of The Peace and Order Ordinance of December 1920. See also the case of *Land Officer v The Motor Mart and Exchange* (1953-1957) 2 TLR 295.

221 See MWAIKUSA, J.T., *op cit* at p. 4.

222 *Ibid.*

became exercisable by the Governor in trust for Her Majesty in the form of grants or leases of public lands. The British administration recognised all existing German land titles and also made a small number of freehold grants.[223] As an effort to fulfil the obligation of dealing with the Trust Territories, the British government passed specific land legislation in the name of *Land Ordinance, 1923*[224]. This legislation marked the beginning of a legal dilemma on the security of customary titles that were in place during the pre-colonial period. The British government must have been aware of Article 23 (b) of the Covenant of the League of Nations[225] under which the High Contracting Parties agreed "to undertake to secure just treatment of the native inhabitants of the territories under their control." To keep the spirit of that Article, the Preamble of the Land Ordinance, for example, provided that:

> *WHEREAS it is expedient that the existing customary rights of the natives of Tanganyika Territory to use and enjoy the land of the Territory and the natural fruits thereof in sufficient quantity to enable them to provide for the sustenance of themselves, their families and their prosperity should be assured and preserved;*
>
> *AND WHERE it is expedient that the existing native customs with regard to the use and occupation of land should as far as possible be preserved;*
>
> *AND WHEREAS it is expedient that the rights and obligations of the Government in regard to the whole of the lands within the Territory and also the rights and obligations of cultivators or other persons claiming to have an interest in such lands should be defined by law;*
>
> *BE IT THEREFORE ENACTED by the Governor and Commander in Chief of the Tanganyika Territory as follows...*

Reading the provisions above at face value, one notes that there was a clear intention of the British government to preserve the native titles in land. However, the question that follows is how far these provisions of the *Land Ordinance* safeguarded the interests both present and future of the native population? In the reality the Ordinance did not safeguard the rights of the indigenous people for there continued to be massive

223 See BATUNGI, Nasani, *op cit* at p. 41.

224 This was Ordinance No. 3 of 1923, Chapter 113 of the Laws. The Ordinance is repealed by Section 183 of the *Land Act, 1999* [Cap. 113 R.E 2002].

225 This Covenant was adopted in Geneva Switzerland on April 21, 1919.

alienation of their lands. Specifically Section 2 of this law declared all lands whether occupied or unoccupied to be public land, while Section 3 put all public land under the control of the Governor. The section was followed by a proviso which saved the validity of the title or interest to which had been acquired lawfully before the commencement of the Ordinance. In a word, the Ordinance intensified land debate in Tanzania. Issa G. Shivji, a critical lawyer from the customary tenure camp describes the Ordinance as follows:

> *The Land Ordinance, the masterpiece of legal British draftsmanship, expropriated all lands of Tanganyika in two sections. Section 2 declared all lands, occupied or un- occupied, 'public lands'. Section 3 vested all public lands and interests over them under the control and subject to the disposition of the Governor to be held for the use and common benefit, direct or indirect, of the 'natives'. In one fell swoop, the ultimate ownership and control of land was vested in the State and the State became what the Court of Appeal was to call some sixty years later, a 'superior landlord'. Colonial courts were more circumspect. They did not call the colonial state a superior landlord but acted, behaved and decided as if it were one.*[226]

The practice of alienating native lands without fear was later faced with a severe criticism in the meetings of the Permanent Mandate Commission of the League of the Nations. Eventually, the Ordinance was amended in 1928[227] to give customary titles statutory recognition. The definition of the right of occupancy was, for the first time, extended to cover even "the title of a native or a native community lawfully using or occupying land in accordance with native law and custom". Before this amendment, the definition of a right of occupancy was simply restricted to "the title to the use and occupation of land". The amendment marked the birth of the customary right of occupancy, or deemed right of occupancy as it is sometimes called. In other words, the amendments recognised the native title such that anyone holding land under the indigenous property right system (customary law) would be declared the legitimate holder of the land without any deed whatsoever. Regrettably it was the amended definition that was later invoked by the court of law to deny the right to land to those who failed to prove

---

226 See SHIVJI, Issa G., "Lawyers in Neoliberalism: Authority's Professional Supplicants or Society's Amateurish Conscience," Valedictory delivered on the occasion of formal retirement from the University of Dar es Salaam, delivered on 15th July, 2006, at p. 11.

227 See the *Land (Amendment) Ordinance* No. 7 of 1928.

that they were natives.[228] Again, the question that remained a point of litigation in the courts of law was whether an occupier of the land under customary right of occupancy enjoyed the same rights as one occupying land under granted right of occupancy under the Ordinance. According to case law the answer to this question was a simple no. Customary right of occupancy was, by any interpretation of the law, inferior to granted right of occupancy. Also a person possessing land under customary right of occupancy had limited rights to land as against others, that is his counterpart who possessed land under the granted right of occupancy. This is what we gather from the two seminal cases of *Muhena Bin Said v Registrar of Titles (1948) Vol. 16 EACA 79, and Mtoro Bin Mwamba v Attorney General [1953] 2 TLR 327.* What the two cases communicate to us is that although customary titles were recognised, they were not protected by law.

Let me briefly present the facts of each case and the decisions of the court. In *Muhena Bin Said v the Registrar of Titles* the appellant had derived his title to land near Mwanza through an Arab prior to the German Administration over Tanganyika. He now applied to be registered as the owner of the land in fee simple. In 1931 the Land Officer, acting as Registrar of Titles wrote to the appellant's advocate informing him that "the claim to freehold by your client is admitted". In 1947 the appellant applied for registration as was required by Section 5 of the *Land Registration Ordinance.*[229] The Registrar held that the application failed. The appellant, dissatisfied by this decision, brought the matter in court against the Registrar. After the hearing of the parties' hot arguments the court construed two main issues relevant for the determination of the matter: (1) Whether the appellant could claim adverse possession over the land and, (2) Whether Mohamedan law, which recognised individual ownership could apply as to confer right of occupancy to an Arab and which later passed to the appellant. The court concluded the matter by establishing in the first place that the Arab had entered the land peacefully and was given the land through an arrangement with the Chief or Chief's representative. As such he was granted a tenure recognised by customary law of the tribe which, like in

228 See for example the case of *NAFCO v Mulbadaw Village Council and Others [1985] TLR 88.* In this case the Court of Appeal hesitated to recognise the title of some customary holders when it found that they had not proved to be natives. See a full discussion of the case below.

229 Cap. 70 of the Laws.

other African tribes, had no concept of freehold tenure. In the second place the court found that the appellant had also failed to prove adverse possession of the land for a period of 30 years prior to 26th January 1923. In the third place the court held that the occupation by the appellant was not in any way special or different from that of any other inhabitant of the Territory or inconsistent with it being just the general permissive occupation enjoyed by all inhabitants. At the end of the day the appeal was dismissed. The court set the doctrine of permissive occupation, which simply meant that all the land remained the property of the public, administered by the Governor so that all natives were only and simply permitted to occupy it, not to possess or own it. Issa Shivji is quite discontented by the decision in this case as he says:

> *Indigenous producers and communities had customary titles, theoretically in perpetuity. They were not registered. The Ordinance was ambiguous on the legal status of customary titles. Courts filled in the ambiguity. In the case of Muhena Bin Said (1949) the High Court of Tanganyika under, Sir Graham Paul, the Chief Justice, decided that customary titles and interests were 'permissive'. 'Natives' and 'native communities' possessed, occupied, and used land with the implied permission of the Governor. When the colonial state wanted the peasant to grow cotton, coffee, cashewnuts for metropolitan markets or food for manamba, the Governor's permission would continue to subsist and the natives would continue to use and occupy land. When the governor wanted to alienate customary lands to settlers, immigrants or companies, he could do it without legal restraint. He would be deemed to have withdrawn his 'constructive' permission from the customary owner. In short, customary rights were recognised by law, thanks to the Mandate requirements, but not protected by it, thanks to courts in the service of the State.*[230]

The above quotation makes the main theme of this book very clear in that what the law provided is not what was sanctioned by the practice on the ground.

Mtoro Bin Mwamba v Attorney General is not distinct from the position above. In the case we meet the appellant, who applied for registration as a beneficial owner of land in fee simple, which he claimed under the Washomvi laws and customs. In the alternative he claimed to be registered as an owner by virtue of adverse possession.

230 See SHIVJI, Issa G., *op cit*, at p. 12.

The argument in favour of his case was that the Washomvi tribe, of which he was a member, recognised an individual ownership of land equivalent to freehold and by Islamic law as applied by the Sultan of Zanzibar individual ownership could be acquired by clearing vacant land and planting it with coconut palms. In the alternative he argued that he was a owner by virtue of adverse possession in himself and his predecessor in title, that is, his father from whom he inherited the land since or before 16th January 1895. He concluded the argument by praying that he was, in the circumstance, entitled to be registered under the provisions of Section 5 (1) (a) of the *Land Registry Ordinance.*

In deciding the case, the court recalled the principle developed by Viscount Haldane in *Amodu Tajan v Secretary of South Nigeria* [231] in that the usual form of native titles is that of usufructuary right. The court then turned to *Muhena Bin Said v the Registrar of Titles,* whose effect was that the customary titles entailed the permissive (not adverse) occupational right. In essence, the court found that the Arabs arrived about the year 1860 by peaceful means, with the consent of the local native inhabitants, and not by conquest. As a result they did not impose their laws on the indigenous people nor did they interfere with the laws and customs already in force even if the natives were converted to Islam. The appeal was ultimately dismissed.

In short, the court in the two cases above, observed that the occupation of 'public land' by Africans was merely permissive. It did not establish any right as against the government. Legally speaking, the effect of Section 2 of the *Land Ordinance* was to vest the radical title in the State so as to allow it to exercise unlimited control over land. This law allowed the British colonial government to have full powers to deal with land according to whatever administrative policy they subsequently adopted. Native people never had security of tenure over their land.

Apart from the *Land Ordinance,* as amended from time to time, the British passed some other legislation, rules and regulations whose impact was to add salt to the unhealing injuries of the natives' dispossessions. Among these were the *Land (Law of Property and Conveyancing) Ordinance,* 1923[232] which for instance prohibited the natives from disposing interests in land to non-natives without the consent of the

231 The case has already been discussed above.

232 Orinance No. 2 of 1923, Chapter 114 of the Laws.

Minister;[233] the *Town and Country Planning Ordinance*, 1923[234] which, *inter alia*, divided Dar es Salaam into three zones according to race[235], and; the *Land Registry Ordinance*, 1923[236].

The post Second World War period was marked by intensive colonial pressure over land such that much grabbing of the native lands took place during this period, not only in Tanganyika, but also in the whole of East Africa and beyond, leading to grave grievances between the British colonial government and the local natives. In Kenya for example, the grievances culminated in the famous bloody war of Mau Mau[237]. It is well on record that:

> *White immigration in the post war- years resulted in a serious land shortage affecting Kenya's African population in general and the Kikuyu in particular. This land squeeze was further exacerbated by the mechanization of settler agriculture, rapid African population growth and the imposition of specific agricultural policies by the Colonial Administration. These policies included the eviction of African-usually Kikuyu- squatters from Maasailand and settler districts, followed by their forced resettlement back into Kikuyu reserves. The effect of these various demographic and economic pressures was thoroughgoing disruption of the material and moral economy of Kikuyu life.*[238]

233 Section 11 (1)of the law provided that, "A disposition of land belonging to a native in favour of a non-native or conferring on a non-native any rights over the land of a native shall not operate unless it is in writing and unless and until it is approved by the Minister". Despite the fact that this law was discriminatory in nature, some scholars have regarded the restriction imposed by it over the disposition of land by natives to non-natives as a positive colonial measure of protecting the property of the natives from exploitation by unscrupulous foreigners. See for example SAWYERR, Akilagpa, "Discriminatory Restrictions on Private Disposition of Land in Tanganyika: A Second Look," in OCHOLA, James Obol (ed.), (1969): *Land Law Reform in East Africa*, Militon Obote Foundation.

234 Capter 103 of the Laws. This was repealed and replaced in 1956. Now we have in place the *Town and Country Planning Act*, [Cap. 355 R.E 2002].

235 Zone I was an area in which residential buildings of European type were to be built, zone II was an area in which residential and commercial buildings were to be erected, and zone III which was meant for native quarters only.

236 Ordinance No. 15 of 1923, Chapter 116 of the Laws. The law was later repealed and replaced in 1953. We now have in place the *Land Registration Act*, [Cap. 334 R.E 2002].

237 According to MCADAM, Doug, *et al.*, (2001): *Dynamics of Contention*, Cambridge University Press, at p. 92, Mau Mau is defined to mean the armed insurrection that took place in Kenya in the early to mid-1950s, which pitted an irregular predominantly Kikuyu force of "freedom fighters" against both British troops and loyalist units of the Kikuyu Guards.

238 .MCDAM, Doug, *et al.*, *ibid* at p. 94.

> *The accelerated pace of white settler in migration and resulting loss of formerly Kikuyu land after the Second World War aggravated class, generational and gender tensions among the Kikuyu.*[239]

In Tanzania Mainland the situation was not dissimilar to that of Kenya. Many policies of land confiscation and control were also put in place. Some of these were strongly objected to by the peasants, for example, in the famous *Meru Land case*[240]. According to the record, the case has a background in what is known as the Wilson Report of 1947.[241] The Report's major proposal was the displacement of the natives in the Engare-Nanyuki area. Also, another recommendation was that as to compensation the displaced would be allowed to settle in the largely unoccupied area, further south on the lower slopes of Mt. Kenya. The Meruland people objected to this plan, arguing that the proposed new areas comprised land which was inferior, infested by the tsetse fly and very poorly watered. When it came to the implementation of the scheme, the people refused to move and as a result:

> *Their cattle were driven away by government forces, their household goods and movable property removed or burnt, and their houses, cattle pens and storage sheds razed to ground.*[242]

The people then presented their complaints to the United Nations Visiting Mission in 1951, which on return reported the matter to the Trusteeship Council of the United Nations, after which some representatives of the Meru people were summoned to argue their case before the United Nations General Assembly.[243] The outcome of this

---

239 *Ibid*, at p. 95. See also a full account of the war in KANOGO, Tabitha, (1987): *Squatters and the Roots of Mau Mau 1905-63*, James Curvey London: Heinemann Kenya, Nairobi: Uhio University Press, Athens and KILSON Martin L., "Land and the Kikuyu: A Study of the Relationship between Land and Kikuyu Political Movements" *The Journal of Negro History*, Vol. 40, No. 2, 1955, pp. 103-153.

240 The case is discussed at length by those who presented it to the United Nations in JAPHETI, Kirilo and SEATON, Earle, (1967): *The Meru Land Case*, Nairobi: East African Publishing House.

241 Judge Mark Wilson of the High Court of Tanganyika was commissioned by the government to study the distribution of alienated and tribal land in the Kilimanjaro-Meru area and make recommendations for its redistribution. He did the job and made recommendation thereafter without consultation of the native people in the area.

242 See JAPHETI, Kirilo and SEATON, Earle, *op cit*, at p. 19.

243 Tanganyika became a trust territory of the United Nations on 18th April, 1946 following the formation of the United Nations Organisation in 1945. The trusteeship ended on 21st April 1961 by virtue of the General Assembly Resolution 1609 (XV1) of 1962.

struggle was the amendment of the *Land Ordinance*[244] to provide, *inter alia*, that no land under the jurisdiction of a Native Authority could be alienated without consulting the said native authority. We learn from the literature that the Trusteeship Council particularly affirmed in its resolution[245] the principle that, "No African communities settled on the land should be moved to other areas unless a clear expression of their collective consent has been obtained"[246]. In a similar spirit, the British government passed the *Land Regulations* of 1948[247] which were later amended in 1960[248] and *Government Circular No. 4 of 1953*[249]. The effect of the regulations was to lay down some statutory control, especially on disposition of interests in land.[250] The effect of the circular can be looked into at four main levels. In the first place, the circular anticipated what later on came to be the recommendations of the East African Royal Commission, for it endorsed the hope that it would be possible to gradually initiate among Africans a system of holding land on individual titles. In the second place it explicitly provided that in all cases of urban areas all land should be alienated from tribal tenure, and that all Africans should obey the same laws of the territory in respect of the occupation of land, the same as any members of any other race on the other hand. In the third place the circular discouraged customary titles in town areas as it provided that customary rights of the Africans who would find themselves within the boundaries of the towns would be dealt with administratively by the District Commissioner by way of compensation for the loss of rights of their lands. Finally, the Circular interpreted the 1950 amendments in the *Land Ordinance*[251] by making it crystal clear that consultation of Native Authority meant "consultation" and not "consent". The final document that has a direct bearing on land reforms under the British rule in Tanzania is the report of the East African

---

244 See the Land Ordinance (Amendment) Ordinance, 1950, Ordinance No. 5 of 1950.

245 Dated 22 July 1952.

246 See JAPHET, Kirilo and SEATON, Earle, at p. 58.

247 Published as G.N 233 of 1948.

248 See G.N 101 of 1960.

249 See Land Utilization and the Allocation of Individual Rights over Land, 1953 (Government Circular No. 4 of 1953).

250 See for example regulation 3 (1) which prohibited disposition the holders of granted rights of occupancy to dispose land without if the disposition was not in writing and approved by the governor .

251 *I.e, Land Ordinance (Amendment) Ordinance* of 1950, Ordinance No. 5 of 1950. The amendment provided, *inter alia*, that no land under the jurisdiction of a Native Authority could be alienated without consulting the said native authority.

Royal Commission.[252] In this report the Commission saw customary tenure as a threat to development and therefore recommended for the individualization of land ownership. To the eyes of the Commission, a freehold system would expose land as a marketable commodity and, therefore, would give security to the efficient land user and also would ensure that land easily passed to this user from the inefficient user. The Commission was in this aspect very clear when it recommended that:

> *A free market gives to the buyer access to land for those economic purposes which are consistent with the price which he has to pay for it and ensures to the seller the opportunity to dispose of the land which he is unable to utilize adequately in relation to the prices which it would fetch. Where the market is not free, either because of tribal restrictions which prevent purchase, sale or lease or because it is encumbered by restrictions on transfer which have no relation to economic circumstances, access to land may be rendered impossible for those members of the community who are best able to use it in accordance with its market value.*[253]

This position of the Commission necessitated the adoption of the Government Paper No. 6 of 1958.[254] Essentially, the colonial state proposed, in this paper, to introduce "a form of tenure which is individual, exhaustive, secure, unlimited in time and negotiable", meaning the individual ownership of land in the form of freehold.[255] This proposal was never translated into law. The available records show clearly that the same proposal was strongly objected by Mwalimu J.K Nyerere.[256] Writing his article,[257] Nyerere argued against the freehold tenure, his right reasoning being that:

---

252 The Commission was called in 1953 to look into the ideal land tenure in East Africa. It gave its report in 1955. The report initiated the move towards customary tenure conversion under which customary tenures would be converted into other tenures preferable in the circumstances.

253 See the Report, paragraph 6 at pp. 49-50.

254 The paper was known as Review of Land Tenure Policy.

255 See p. 3.

256 Mwalimu Nyerere, born in the then small village of Butiama, in Mara region remains the most esteemed figure in the political history of Tanzania. He is not only remembered as the First President of Tanzania (1961-1985), but also as an individual who stood for the rights of the poor, peasants and workers of the Tanzanian community. He voluntarily stepped down from power in 1985 and died on 14th October 1999 at St. Thomas's Hospital, London.

257 "*Mali ya Taifa*".

> *If people are given land to use as their property, then they have a right to sell it. It will not be difficult to predict who, in fifty years time, will be the landlords, and who the tenants. In a country such as this, where, generally speaking the Africans are poor and the foreigners are rich, it is quite possible that, within eighty or hundred years, if the poor African were allowed to sell his land, all the land in Tanganyika would belong to wealth immigrants and the local people would be tenants. But even if there were no rich foreigners in this country, there would emerge rich and cleaver Tanganyikans. If we allow land to be sold like a robe, within a short period there would be only a few Africans possessing land in Tanganyika and all others would be tenants...If the two groups emerge-a small group of landlords and a large group of tenants-we should be faced with a problem which has created antagonism among peoples and led to bloodshed in many countries of the world. Our forefathers saved themselves from this danger by refusing to distribute land on freehold basis.*[258]

In short it is this, Nyerere's attitude over land that explains the land law reforms and tenure system that followed after independence. Traversed very briefly, we note the following as the tenurial system over land in Tanzania under the British colonial rule. First, there were freehold titles which were granted to the individuals during the German colonial rule in the Territory.[259] Second, there were granted rights of occupancy whereby one could apply and get a grant to occupy land under certain conditions[260]. The longest term of the grant was 99 years.[261] Third, there were leasehold titles. Fourth, there was customary or deemed right of occupancy, which was applicable especially in the unplanned urban areas as well as in the rural areas.

The Post-Independence Land Question

Tanzania is a union of the former independent nation states of Tanganyika (Mainland Tanzania) and Zanzibar, the two states having united on 26th April 1964. Any reference on the term "Tanzania" in this discussion is, unless expressly stated, confined to Tanzania Mainland

---

258 See NYERERE, Julius Kambarage, (1965): *Freedom and Unity*, at pp. 55-56.

259 The case of the *Attorney General v Motor Mart and Exchange Limited* [1960] E.A 689 tells us very clearly about freehold titles. The Court, in this case, ordered that the respondent be registered as owners of the freehold estate subject to German conditions in favour of the Government.

260 Section 6 of the Land Ordinance empowered the Governor to grant rights of occupancy.

261 This is still the law in Tanzania. See section 32 of the *Land Act, 1999* [Cap. 113 R.E 2002].

(i.e. the former Tanganyika) which attained her flag independence on 9th December 1961.There is a long list of land law reforms that took place during the post-independence period, which culminates in the present time's land law. Until the middle of the 1980s the land law reforms that took place were highly politically-motivated for the reasons related to: one, the absence of a Bill of Rights in the Constitution of Tanzania of that time[262], meaning that the land or interests therein were never protected by the Constitution and people would hardly approach the court of law to claim their rights to property including the land itself[263]; two, it was a time of the party supremacy whereby land administration and management fell squarely under the dictates of the party; three, it was a time of the political influence of Mwalimu Nyerere, who was capable of influencing decisions related to land use and control; and four, it was a time when the role of courts in the administration of land matters was still at its infancy. All these were in addition to the lack of professional academic institutions which would serve as centres of competence and professional training in land related matters including land law and land administration. F.N Lugoe notes that:

> *The professional servicing the lands sector were not deeply rooted in Tanzania's tertiary education system at independence, although that scenario is now changing at fast pace. Indeed, many years after independence not only were there no indigenous professional land surveyors, physical planners, valuers, photogrammetrists or cartographers, but also there was no university that was easily accessible to Tanzanians at which courses specialized in these disciplines could be offered, in spite of provisions made in the various sub-sectoral laws.*[264]

---

262 Since Independence, Tanzania has had a good number of Constitutions, namely: The Independence Constitution of 1961; The Republican Constitution of 1962; The Interim Constitution of 1964; The Interim Constitution of 1965, and; The Constitution of the United Republic of Tanzania of 1977.

263 F.D.A.M. LUOGA, observes that the absence of safeguards in the form of a Bill of Rights to protect the individual had given the executive an ever expanding margin (discretionary) of violating personal rights and freedoms. Since independence the citizenry went through successive and arbitrary erosions of their rights. The executive passed legislation after legislation to circumscribe personal rights and freedoms. See LUOGA, F.D.A.M, "The Tanzanian Bill of Rights" in PETER, Chris Maina and JUMA, Ibrahim, (eds.), (1998): *Fundamental Rights and Freedoms in Tanzania*, Mkuki na Nyota Publishers, pp. 37-46, at p. 39.

264 See LUGOE F.N., "Policy derived challenges impact greatly on land administration" in *The Guardian*, Wednesday September 12, 2007.

Nyerere's Conception of Land

During his political carreer[265], especially from the late 1950s and early 1960s, Nyerere undertook to express his personal feelings about many issues of great significance in relation to land administration. He made various statements which greatly impacted the post-independence land law reforms. A cursory survey of these statements has recorded, for example, some statements on the ideal land tenure system and on a person's right to compensation when his land is taken by another. Writing against individual land ownership, and suggesting the appropriate approach to land ownership, Nyerere said:

> *And in rejecting the capitalist attitude of mind which colonialism brought in Africa, we must reject also the capitalist methods which go with it. One of these is the individual ownership of land. To us in Africa land was always recognised as belonging to the community. Each individual within our society had a right to the use of land, because otherwise he could not earn his living and one cannot have the right to life without also having the right to some means of maintaining life. But the African's right to land was simply the right to use it; he had no other right to it nor did it occur to him to try and claim one.*
>
> *The foreigner introduced a completely different concept- the concept of land as a marketable commodity. According to this system, a person could claim a piece of land as his own private property whether he intended to use it or not. I could take a few squares miles of land, call them 'mine', and then go off to the moon. All I had to do to gain a living from 'my' land was to charge a rent to the people who wanted to use it. If this piece of land was in an urban area I had no need to develop it at all; I could leave it to the fools who were prepared to develop all the other pieces of land surrounding 'my' piece, and in doing so automatically to raise the market value of mine. Then I could come down from the moon and demand that these fools pay me through their noses for the high value of 'my' land-a value which they themselves had created for me while I was enjoying myself on the moon! Such a system is not only foreign to us, it is completely wrong. Land lords, in a society which recognises individual ownership of land, can be, and usually are, in the same class as the loiterers I was talking about: the class of parasites.*

---

265 Mwalimu Nyerere was the founder and leader of the Tanganyika African National Union (TANU) (1957-1977), and also the first President of Tanzania (1961-1985).

> *We must not allow the growth of parasites here in Tanganyika. The TANU Government must go back to the traditional African custom of land-holding. That is to say a member of society will be entitled to a piece of land on condition that he uses it. Unconditional, or 'freehold', ownership of land (which leads to speculation and parasitism) must be abolished.*[266]

Above all, Nyerere believed in the philosophy that land *per se* is a gift from God, it was never owned by the occupier, and what the occupier owns are the improvements over the land. In the light of his belief Nyerere stated that:

> *When I use my energy and talent to clear a piece of ground for my use it is clear that I am trying to transform this basic gift from God so that it can satisfy a human need. It is true, however, that this land is not mine, but the efforts made by me in clearing that land enable me to lay a claim of ownership over the cleared piece of ground. But it is not really the land itself that belongs to me but only the cleared ground which will remain mine as long as I continue to work on it. By clearing the ground I have actually added to its value and have enabled it to be used to satisfy a human need. Whoever then takes this piece of ground must pay me for adding value to it through clearing it by my own labour.*[267]

The statement concerning the right to compensation, especially, was later baptized with the name of "Nyerere's doctrine of land value," and became a very important element in the subsequent land law reforms. Laws were later enacted to accommodate a person's right to compensation whenever his land was to be taken.[268] Again, the doctrine captured by Nyerere's statement influenced judicial minds in that courts of law invoked the doctrine envisaged by the statement to adjudicate some land disputes where there was no clear written law to refer in awarding compensation[269], where the practice contravened the

---

266 See NYERERE, Julius Kambarage, (1968): *Ujamaa: Essays on Socialism*, Dar es Salaam Oxford University Press, at pp. 7-8.

267 See NYERERE, Julius Kambarage, (1966): *Freedom and Unity: A Selection from Writings and Speeches 1952-1965, Dar es Salaam*: Oxford University Press, at p. 53.

268 See for example the Preamble, Interim Constitution of the United Republic of Tanzania, 1965 which recognized, *inter alia*, one's right to liberty, property, and just return for his labour.

269 Members of the bar and bench would call this judicial hunch. See the application of the doctrine in *Lalata Msangawale v Henry Mwamlima* [1979] LRT No. 3.

written law on the right to compensation[270], or where the written law contravened the letter and spirit of this statement[271].

Generally speaking, Nyerere's articulations as shown above were followed by a series of measures by the post-independence Government, which tried to implement them in law and in practice. One of such measures was to recognise the *Land Ordinance* as a principle legislation governing land administration in independent Tanganyika. The legislation, though colonial in origin, was adopted both in letter and spirit, root and bark, save for a few amendments such as replacing the words "Crown" with "Public" and "Governor" with "President." Another such measure was to issue Government Paper No. 2 of 1962[272] in which the government proposed, among others things, the conversion of freehold titles into the government leases and the application of development conditions to all holders of rights of occupancy. The result of these proposals was the immediate enactment of two legislations: the *Freehold Titles (Conversion) and Government Leases Act*, 1963[273], which abolished freehold titles in Tanzania mainland[274], and the *Rights of Occupancy (Development Conditions) Act*, 1963[275], which made development conditions applicable to all land. Yet another measure in this series was to implement the recommendation of the World Bank[276] Report of 1961. The Report was centred on the economic development of Tanganyika and had recommended two approaches as viable tools

270 See *Ntiyahela v Kijiji cha Ujamaa Mutala*, High Court of Tanzania at Tabora, Civil Appeal No. 21 of 1987 (Unreported).

271 See *Lohay Akonaay and Joseph Loahay v Attorney General* [1995] TLR No. 80 (CA).

272 The paper was titled "Proposals of the Tanganyika Government for Land Tenure Reforms".

273 Act No. 24 of 1963, Chapter 523 of the Laws. The Act was repealed under section 10 of the Government Leaseholds (Conversion to Rights of Occupancy) Act, 1969, Act No. 44 of 1969.

274 The main reason behind the abolition of freehold titles as a post-independence measure need not be examined beyond the characteristics of freehold tenure itself. The Tanzanian National Land Policy highlights these characteristics with the utmost succinctness in that: (1) A freehold entails exclusive possession of land rights in perpetuity; (2) Under a freehold title there is no term on holding of land imposed on the owner; (3) The owner has the right to subdivide or lease the land, etc, so long as these actions do not violate land use policies as stipulated by zoning regulations and local by-laws; (4) There are no development conditions imposed on the title of the owner; and (5) The government has no right to interfere with the legal occupation and use of the land. See, Tanzania United Republic of, 1995 *National Land Policy*, Ministry of Lands and Human Development, Dar es Salaam, Tanzania paragraph 3.

275 Chapter 518 of the Laws.

276 See these recommendation in IBRD Mission Report, *The Economic Development of Tanganyika (Baltimore, 1961), p. 6ff.*

for organising the people for agricultural development. These were the improvement and transformation approaches. The former aimed at ensuring progressive improvement in the methods of crop cultivation and animal husbandry in order for peasants to improve production, while the latter aimed at transforming agriculture, land use and land tenure in order to organise the peasants in governmentally supervised settlement schemes.[277] It means that people had to be moved to new settlements which were created under that scheme. With transformation approach, about five goals would be met: incorporating the scattered rural hamlets into compact villages; liberating farmers from traditional controls; concentrating capital investment and technical power of a group of farmers living together as opposed to those scattered over large areas; enabling the government to easily supply local services; and discouraging freehold tendencies[278]. R.M. Kawawa, the Vice President of Tanganyika (as he then was) outlined the aim of this new programme as being, "To replace the existing patterns of shifting cultivation and living in scattered villages by the introduction of improved farming techniques and the provision of the essential services. To achieve this, it was planned to regroup and resettle farmers from the uneconomic semi-dessert areas on more favourable soils, and to introduce supervised crop rotation and mixed farming. The policy aimed at the creation of villages which would become centres of social and commercial development"[279]. Notwithstanding, some writers have viewed the process with ridicule. An extract from one of such writers reads that:

> *The transformation approach can be understood as a desperate reaction to peasant resistance: if there was no other way of making the farmer grow more crops, then the last hope was to take him right away from his 'traditional' surroundings, to settlement schemes on which, in return for land, he could be made to follow the instructions of the agricultural staff.*[280]

---

277 BATUNGI, Nasani, *op cit* at p. 42. See also RWEYEMAMU, Anthony H., "Managing Planned Development: Tanzania's Experience", *Journal of Modern African Studies*, Vol. 4, No. 1 (May, 1966), pp. 1-16. According to the author (pp. 11-12) the improvement approach was home to the need to induce an increase in productivity without any radical changes in the traditional social and legal system, whereas in the transformation approach the essential part of it was the Village Settlement Programme.

278 *Ibid.*

279 Kawawa gave the statement during the seminar on Rural Development Planning dated 4th April 1966. It is reported in JACOBO, Abel, "Foreign Aid in Agriculture: Introducing Israel's Land Settlement Scheme in Tanzania", *African Affairs*, Vol. 71, No. 283 (April, 1972), pp. 186-194, at p. 188.

280 See COULSON, A., (1982): *Tanzania: A Political Economy*, Oxford University Press, at p. 162.

The fourth measure was to adopt the Five-Year Plan for Economic and Social Development[281], and as far as land matters were at issue, the Ministry of Lands, Settlements and Water Development was created in June 1964. All these measures went hand-in-hand with enabling legislationss, which the government passed. These included, but are not limited to: the *Rural Settlement Commission Act,* 1963[282]; the *Range Development and Management Act,* 1964[283]; the *Land Tenure (Village Settlements) Act,* 1965[284]; the *Nyarubanja Enfranchisement Act,* 1965[285]; the *Rural Farmlands (Acquisition Regrant) Act,* 1966[286]; the *Land Acquisition Act,* 1967[287]; the *Customary Leasehold (Enfranchisement) Act,* 1968[288]; and the *Government Leases (Conversion to Rights of Occupancy) Act,* 1969.[289] The first Act in this order[290] created [291]the Rural Settlement Commission (R.S.C)[292] to establish, maintain and develop rural settlements and to allocate priorities for the establishment of rural settlements. The day-to-day execution of village settlement was done by the Village Settlement Agency which was appointed by and answerable to the R.S.C. The second Act [293] set up associations to manage and administer the ranch lands. The third Act[294] did, *inter alia*, empower the Rural Settlement Commission to be granted the right of occupancy, called "settlement rights", so that the individuals (villagers) in the area would get derivative rights by way of

281 The Plan was adopted on May 12, 1964 and came into effect on July 1, 1964.

282 Act No. 62 of 1963.

283 Act No. 51 of 1964.

284 Act No. 27 of 1965.

285 Act No. 1 of 1965.

286 Act No. 8 of 1966.

287 Act No. 47 of 1967.

288 Act No. 47 of 1968

289 Act No. 44 of 1969.

290 *Rural Settlement Commission Act*, 1963.

291 The Commission was later dissolved by the *Rural Settlement Commission (Dissolution) Act*, 1967 (No. 17 of 1967).

292 RWEYEMAMU, Anthony H., *op cit* at p. 11.

293 *Range Development and Management Act*, 1964.

294 *Land Tenure (Village Settlement) Act*, 1965.

licences, leases or easements. The fourth Act[295] abolished the semi-feudal land tenure system called *nyarubanja* in some Districts of the West Lake Region. The fifth Act[296] aimed at acquiring land from those who had land but did not develop it themselves (absentee landlords) and re-granting it to those who occupied it under the principle of "land to the tiller". The sixth Act[297] was intended to empower the President to acquire any land for public interest. The seventh Act[298] intended to abolish all types of feudal tenure not only in the West Lake Region but also in other parts of Tanzania where such tenures existed; it means that the application of the Act was extended to cover other areas such as Pare, Moshi and Tukuyu in October, 1969.[299] The eighth and last Act on the list[300] abolished government leaseholds whereby all Government Leases were converted to Rights of Occupancy effectively on 1st April 1970, when the Act came into force.[301] From this date until today, there is only one land tenure in Tanzania, namely, the "Right of Occupancy", which is either granted or deemed (held under native laws and customs). According to Issa Shivji[302], all the above measures had some implications: the land tenure was removed from the domain of customary law and assimilated in the statutory system of right of occupancy; there was evolution of some form of individual tenure system under the supervision of the statutory body or government department; the land tenure and land use systems were to be administered and managed from the top through a series of detailed regulations, rules and by-laws, the breach of which would result in criminal sanctions as well as loss of land rights; and the participation of peasants and pastoralists in the use, planning, administration and management of land came to an end.

---

295 *Nyarubanja (Enfranchisement) Act*, 1965.

296 *Rural Farmlands (Acquisition and Regrant) Act*, 1966.

297 *Land Acquisition Act*, 1967.

298 *Customary Leasehold (Enfranchisement) Act*, 1968, Act No. 47 of 1968. See *Peter Nderia Mushi v The Minister for Land, Housing and Urban Development* [1984] TLR 64 (ca).

299 See Government Notice No. 263 9f 1969. We are made to know, for example, that this Act came into operation in Kilimanjaro Region on 10th October, 1969.

300 *Government Leases (Conversion to Rights of Occupancy) Act*, 1969.

301 Per Government Notice No. 85 of 1970.

302 See SHIVJI Issa G., (1998): *Not Yet Democracy: Reforming Land Tenure in Tanzania,* IIED/ HAKIARDHI/ Faculty of Law, University of Dar es Salaam, at p. 6.

Customary Tenure Extinction: The Role of the Arusha Declaration and other Subsequent Developments

The year 1967 has a special place in the history of Tanzania. It is the time when the policies of the so-called Arusha Declaration were launched[303]. The declaration developed two basic doctrines: socialism and self-reliance[304]. The Government's move in the creation of a socialist society was, of course, based on the desire to create an egalitarian society free from exploitation of one man by another. Nyerere stated this intention when he wrote:

> *We have said that we want to create a socialist society which is based on three principles: equality and respect for human dignity; sharing of the resources which are produced by our efforts; work by everyone and exploitation by none. We have set out these ideas clearly in the National Ethic; and in the Arusha Declaration and earlier documents we have outlined the principles and policies we intend to follow.*[305]

Nyerere believed that true development of the time would be achieved if great emphasis was placed on the availability of land (other necessities being people, the policies of socialism and self-reliance, and good governance). He was emphatic in stating that:

> *Land is the basis of human life and all Tanzanians should use it as a valuable investment for future development. Because the land belongs to the nation, the Government has to see to it that it is used for the benefit of the whole nation and not for the benefit of one individual or just a few people.*[306]

In order to implement the letter and spirit of the above doctrine over and above the doctrine of socialism and self-reliance, Nyerere's Government formulated some policies whose impact in land control and management cannot be overemphasized. These were essentially the policies of nationalization and villagization. By nationalization, it was meant that all major means of production would be placed under national control for the benefit of all the people. Through this policy,

---

303 The Arusha Declaration is the official statement by the National Executive Committee of TANU meeting in Arusha from 26th to 29th January, 1967 to set out the country's policy of socialism and self reliance.

304 The common reference in Swahili is "*Ujamaa na Kujitegemea*".

305 See NYERERE, Julius Kambarage, Ujamaa: Essays on Socialism, at p. 50.

306 *Ibid*, at p 33.

various governmental and parastatal bodies were created to carry out some agricultural and ranching activities in the rural areas[307]. These alienated lands were granted lands previously held under customary law titles. The alienation was done without recourse to legal procedure, the justification being that the lands were needed for public interests or that the various projects, established in the process, were of national significance or *mradi wa taifa* (national programme), as it was known. It means that native lands in various customary communities were taken administratively and by force, without the consent of the communities or individuals concerned.[308]

The bitter side of the matter was the villagization programme. In this programme the government had undertaken to create what were called *ujamaa* villages, a move which was followed by relocating the villagers from other ancestral land into the newly-established villages. According to literature, the villagization process passed through three phases. That is to say, from 1967 till the beginning of 1970, the movement into the *ujamaa* villages was done on voluntary basis, mostly in the southern regions of Lindi, Mtwara and Ruvuma while other areas such as Tanga, Kilimanjaro, Mwanza and West Lake remained untouched. The second phase covered the period from 1970 until 1974 and was the dividing line between voluntary and forced movements into *ujamaa* villages, with many more villages created in other parts such as Dodoma and Singida. The third phase, 1975 onwards, witnessed the use of more force in that movements were no longer voluntary[309]. The kind of force which was employed in the process is starkly illustrated by Zaki Ergas who points out that:

> *Elsewhere force was used to 'persuade' pastoralists to settle down in villages, including the Masai who turned out to be more deeply allergic to settlements than the Government had expected. For them the policy of creating ujamaa villages was nothing but a trick to get hold of the lands on which they had been grazing their heads for centuries.*[310]

---

307 We learn from Shivji that nationalization created over 400 parastatals, including a number of big agricultural and ranching corporations which were involved in what are called national projects. See SHIVJI, Issa G., "Land: The Terrain of Democratic Struggle" in *Change, The Magazine of Business Politics and Economics*, Vol.5, First Quarter, 1997 at p. 6.

308 See the case of *National Agricultural and Food Corporation (NAFCO) v Mulbadaw Village Council and Others* [1985] TLR 88. (CA).

309 See BRIGGS, John, "Villagization and the 1974-6 Economic Crisis in Tanzania" *Journal of Modern African Studies,* Vol. 17, No. 4 (Dec., 1979), pp. 695-702.

310 See ERGAS, Zaki, "Why Did the Ujamaa Village Policy Fail? Towards a Global Analysis", *Journal of Modern African Studies, Vol.18, No.3, (Sep. 1980),* pp. 387-410, at pp. 399/40.

A very important point to highlight is that relocating villagers into the villages was done without any sound legal framework and in the absence of clear terms as regards to compensation for the land that was to be taken for the *ujamaa* village. The only legislation that followed the event included the *Rural Land (Planning and Utilization) Act*, 1973[311] and the *Villages and Ujamaa Villages (Registration, Designation and Administration) Act*, 1975[312]. The former Act, according to Shivji, had little to do with planning and utilization. It was a thinly-veiled attempt to confer open-ended powers on the President and appropriate Ministers in order to extinguish customary rights without due process or any legal redress.[313] Specifically, the Act gave the President the power to declare any part of Tanzania a specified area. Once a specified area had been declared as such, the Minister responsible for Local Government would make regulations for the effective control of that area. Such regulations would be for the extinction, cancellation or modification of the rights, titles and interests in or over the parcels of land falling wholly or partly within the specified area, or over any building within the specified area.[314] On record, there is an incident when the Act was invoked in declaring the Rufiji area a specified area under Government Notice No. 125 of 1974. The latter Act created the District Development Council at the District level, and the Village Assembly and Village Councils at the village level to control and manage land respectively. The Act empowered the responsible Minister to issue regulations for the effective operation of the Act. One such regulation was issued vide Government Notice No. 168 of 1975, which provided for the allocation of the villages by the District Development Council. The Village Council would, in turn, allocate land to the individual households for farming and dwelling houses. Again, under the provisions of this regulation an allocatee of the land was not allowed to dispose it without the approval of the Village Council. The disposition in contravention of this regulation was later declared by the Court of Appeal of Tanzania to be void and of no legal effect[315]. In brief, the villagization policy turned out to be a serious threat to the security of tenure of the customary holders, and the same is said on the part of the two Acts cited above. The general criticism in the literature is that:

---

311 Act No. 14 of 1973.

312 Act No. 21 of 1975.

313 See SHIVJI, Issa G., (1998): *Not Yet Democracy: Reforming Land Tenure in Tanzania*, at p. 13.

314 *Ibid.*

315 See the Case of *Metthuselah Paul Nyagaswa v Christopher Mbote Nyirabu* [1985] TLR 103 (CA).

Villagization in effect meant the expropriation of customary rights and the compulsory acquisition of land under customary regimes. No recognisable legal procedures were followed in carrying out the process. Even the colonial policy of prior consultation was ignored. In general, post-independence government practice had little regard for law.[316]

Simon Coldham's comment is:

The cost of implementing the policy was, however, considerable. The displacement of a large segment of the population, often by force and with inadequate planning, caused much social and economic disruption, and left in its wake a legacy of bitterness and distrust, not to mention a substantial number of land disputes.[317]

Ben Lobulu is also to the point as he says:

The Villagization Program was, in conception and implementation, high-handed, illegal, and criminal. As force was employed to group people together, the socialist dream changed into a socialist nightmare. There was no legislative basis for the program or its implementation; it was ill-conceived and ill-prepared; and it led many Tanzanians to become very bitter towards the State.[318]

Also commenting on this programme, the Court of Appeal of Tanzania had the following to say:

We all know that Operation Vijiji was implemented with high-handedness. Objections were not allowed. The role of those affected by Operation Vijiji 1974 was not to reason why. Theirs was but to comply, the irrationality of the operation notwithstanding.[319]

Other process, apart from nationalization and villagization, which have had a direct impact on the customary tenures, were the urbanisation and the ongoing liberalization processes. Under the urbanisation process, which is rooted in the colonial era but was inherited by the

316 SHIVJI, Issa G., *op cit* at p. 13.

317 See COLDHAM, Simon, "Land Tenure Reform in Tanzania: Legal Problems and Perspectives", *Journal of Modern African Studies*, Vol.33, No. 2 (June, 1995), pp. 227-242, at p. 228.

318 See LOBULU, Ben, "Dispossession and Land Tenure in Tanzania: What Hope from the Courts?, *Cultural Survival Quarterly*, Issue No. 22.4 of January 31, 1991.

319 See *Mohamed Hassan Hole v Keya Jumanne Ramadhani*, Court of Appeal of Tanzania at Dodoma, Civil Appeal No. 19 of 1992 (Unreported), at p. 3.

post-independence government, the lands previously under customary occupation were being engulfed within what were later called planning areas. Once this was done, then the administrative belief and practice was that on declaring the area a planning area, the existing customary rights were automatically extinguished with effect from the date of the declaration, even if there were no other legal procedure to observe. This practice was later challenged in the court of law and either affirmed accordingly, although it was not stated anywhere in a written law[320], or rejected. As regards liberalization, this meant a package of economic policies and measures adopted especially by the government in the middle of the 1980s to privatize economic resources and encourage foreign investors. The process saw alienations and reallocations of the rural village lands to outsiders.

> *Many of these allocations have become a veritable source of complaints and land disputes in that, either the customary land rights have been disregarded, or the present and the future land requirements of village communities have not been considered, or both.*[321]

The Eye of the Courts towards Customary Tenure Up to the Mid-1990s

Going by the discussion above, it is quite easy to note that the customary titles to land were put in jeopardy by the merciless hands of the colonial and post- colonial governments in Tanzania. It is the judiciary, which later came to their (customary titles) rescue. We learn from the literature that the higher judiciary, particularly in the late 1980s, began to take some steps towards providing greater security of tenure to customary landowners.[322] It means that customary tenures were, in away, protected by the higher judiciary if not by the lower. A cursory survey of the judicial pronouncements on the status of customary tenures at this time appears herein below. First in a long list is the case of *National Agricultural and Food Corporation (NAFCO) v Mulbadaw Village Council and Others*[323]. The background of the case is that in 1969

320 See *Kasubi v Kakubukubu*, High Court of Tanzania at Mwanza, Civil Appeal No. 23 of 1987 (Unreported); *Omari v Bilali*, High Court of Tanzania at Dar es Salaam, Civil Appeal No. 22 of 1987 (Unreported).

321 United Republic of Tanzania, (1994), *Report of the Presidential Commission of Inquiry into Land Matters*, Volume I,Chapter I, paragraph 50.

322 See SHIVJI, Issa G, (1998): *Not Yet Democracy: Reforming Land Tenure in Tanzania*, at p. 15.

323 [1985] TLR 88 (CA).

NAFCO was statutorily established[324] as one of the largest parastatals organizations to run a wheat project in the country. The project required substantial tracts of land to operate. This necessitated and, therefore, involved acres and acres of the best grazing land belonging to the Barabaig people in Arusha region, such that the most important sources of water, ancestral places of worship and some of the best agricultural lands were alienated by NAFCO without any consultation of the native people, the customary owners.[325] The people staged severe resistance against the encroachment of their lands but were often assaulted by the NAFCO employees and sometimes the police, forcefully evicted, and their houses and property reduced to ashes. Finally, the Village Council and the villages decided to approach the Court to seek the judicial protection of the right to their land, hence, *Mulbadaw Village Council and 67 Others v National Agricultural and Food Corporation.*[326] In this case the Plaintiffs sued the defendant corporation and claimed the return of their large tracts of land in Hanang District, damages for trespass and other connected reliefs. Two central and paramount issues were: whether NAFCO had a lawful right of occupancy over the disputed land, and whether the proper procedure to acquire land under the *Land Acquisition Act*[327] was necessary and followed. As regards the first issue it was argued for the plaintiffs that they were in occupation of the disputed land prior to its encroachment by NAFCO in 1978, and that their village was a registered village under the *Villages and Ujamaa Villages Act*[328], a fact that demonstrated their occupation of the land. The defendant's argument was that NAFCO entered the land lawfully and with the blessing of the government and party leaders and had obtained a granted right of occupancy. The court (D'Souza, Ag. J.- as he then was) was of the view that the right of the natives to occupy land was recognizable under the provisions of the *Land Ordinance*,[329] that the Village was registered and that, therefore, the Village Council was in lawful possession and control of the land in question. The court went on to say that the rights of the peasants and the Village Council could not be extinguished or superseded except by due operation of law. As far as

324 See Act No 17 of 1969.

325 See more details in SHIVJI, Issa G., *ibid*, at pp. 9-11.

326 [1984] TLR 15 (HC).

327 Act No. 47 of 1967. It is now [Cap. 118 R.E 2002].

328 1975.

329 Then Cap.113.

the second issue was in question, it was argued for the defendant that the provisions of the *Land Acquisition Act* were not applicable to land held under customary land tenure but were applicable only to formal rights of occupancy. The court was of the view that the Act was applicable to such land and stated that where someone is in lawful occupation of land, no valid right of occupancy can be offered to any one else over the same land unless the provisions of the *Land Acquisition Act* have been complied with. The court's conclusion was that the right of occupancy offered to NAFCO was not valid, that NAFCO's entry into the land was illegal and that the defendants were entitled to all their prayers.

NAFCO was aggrieved by this decision and successfully appealed against it in the Court of Appeal of Tanzania.[330] Allowing the appeal, the Court of Appeal of Tanzania considered first the issue of the competing titles between the Village Council and the appellant on one hand, and between the villagers and the appellant on the other. In the first place the court found that the Village Council did not own land since there was no evidence to show that the land was allocated to it by the District Development Council under directive 5 of the Directions under the Village and Ujamaa Villages Act.[331] In the second place the court observed that among the 67 villagers only five had appeared before the court to testify for their claim while the rest pretended to have authorized the five to stand for them. As regards those who did not show up in court, the court dismissed their claims after stating as follows:

> *Each claim is different from the other in terms of date of possession, of acreage, of the method of acquisition, and so on. They were individual claims. A person may act and represent another person, but we know of no law or legal enactment which can permit a person to testify in place of another.*

As regards those who appeared before the court, it was held that the *Land Ordinance* recognizes only natives as capable of occupying land customarily. The court found that none of the villagers who testified could be said to have held land on customary tenure as none had established, or even averred that he was a native. That they were not occupiers in terms of the *Land Ordinance*, but were in land as licensees. By way of an *obiter*, the court said:

---

330 See *National Agricultural and Food Corporation v Mulbadaw Village Council and Others* [1985] TLR 88 (CA).

331 See Government Notice number 168 of 22.8.75. Directive 5 herein provided that "5 (1) Land for the use of a village shall comprise such areas of land as may be reserved for the purpose and allocated to the village by the District Development Council.

> *If the villagers who had testified could have established that as natives they had right of occupancy by virtue of customary tenancies, then the view of the Judge that such villagers in this case could only be evicted or disposed under the provisions of the Land Acquisition Act, No 47 of 1967 is sound.*

The observation of the two courts is commended for having recognized customary titles and accorded it equal status to titles under the granted right of occupancy. The positive comment in relation to the judgments of the two courts comes from Issa Shivji who says that:

> *In the Mulbadaw case, for instance, the High Court held and the Court of Appeal agreed (obiter) that the customary rights stood on the same footing as granted rights in so far as the procedures for compulsory acquisition were concerned. The due process procedures of Land Acquisition Act, 1967 were applicable to both types of rights. In effect, the Courts were saying that the grant of a right of occupancy made by the President under Land Ordinance on a piece of land previously held under a deemed right of occupancy would be invalid unless the deemed right was first lawfully acquired in terms of the provisions of the Land Acquisition Act. This was undoubtedly a big step forward in land law jurisprudence, with far reaching consequences.*[332]

Another case almost similar in nature to *Mulbadaw's* case was the case of *Yoke Gwaku and 5 Others v NAFCO and Another.*[333] The case shares the same background as the Mulbadaw's case. The plaintiffs were members of the Barabaig Tribe, their claims were that NAFCO and Gawal Wheat Farms Ltd had unlawfully and forcefully evicted them out of their land. In court four issues were considered and determined: whether the plaintiffs had title over the disputed land; whether the plaintiffs were natives in terms of section 2 of the *Land Ordinance*[334]; whether the defendants lawfully acquired the disputed land; and whether the right of occupancy can be granted over land for which there is a subsisting customary title. As regards the first issue, the Court (Mroso, J.- as he then was) was of the view that in order for one to claim title over a piece of land he must prove ownership having been allocated the same by a competent authority or having inherited it from the past parent or

332 See SHIVJI, Issa G., (1998): *Not Yet Democracy: Reforming Land Tenure in Tanzania*, at p. 15.

333 High Court of Tanzania at Arusha, Civil Case No. 52 of 1988 (Unreported).

334 Cap. 113 as amended by Act No. 28 of 1970.

having cleared it and developed it without rival claims. The Court found that the first plaintiff proved to have acquired the land by inheritance while the second and third plaintiffs had acquired it by clearing their respective pieces of land and remaining in occupation without any challenge from anybody. In determining the second issue, the Court was of the view that the plaintiffs were natives since they were members of the Barabaig tribe.

A third case in the series but which stands on a different scenario[335] is the case of *Methuselah Paul Nyagaswa v Christopher Mbote Nyirabu.*[336] It is the first case in which the Court of Appeal was called upon to rule on the status of customary titles in urban areas. The facts were that the respondent sued the appellant in the High Court of Tanzania at Dar es Salaam[337]for trespass. His argument was that he was the registered owner of the right of occupancy over plot No. 130 in Mbezi Beach area after he had applied for, and been granted the same by the City Council of Dar es Salaam in 1978. His further claim was that the appellant had trespassed on his land and had commenced building thereon. He therefore prayed for an order of injunction to restrain the appellant from entering or remaining on the said plot. The appellant's argument, on the other hand, was that he [appellant] had purchased the disputed land from one Vincent Patrick three months before as an unsurveyed land in the then Mbezi Beach Village. The trial Court (Bahati, J.- as he then was) made an observation that Mbezi Beach had been declared a planning area within the provisions of section 13 of the then *Town and Country Planning Ordinance*[338] and under Government Notice No. 171 of 1966, and that once an area is so declared, customary law concerning land holding ceases to apply and a person who has a right of occupancy over a piece of land by virtue of native law and custom loses that right to a party who obtains a right of a occupancy under section 6 of the *Land Ordinance* over the same peace of land. The Court finally determined the matter in favour of the respondent by holding that the respondent's right of occupancy extinguished all prior rights and interests of the appellant in that plot. The appellant was aggrieved by the trial Court's decision and sought to challenge it in the Court of Appeal of Tanzania.

---

335 That is to say, the status of customary title over a piece of land in the area that is declared as planning area under the provisions of the Town and Country Planning legislation.

336 [1985] TLR 103.

337 See Civil Case No. 61 of 1980, Judgment of 17th January 1985.

338 Cap. 378. It is now *Town and Country Planning Act*, Cap. 355.

Arguing for the appellant, the learned Professor Mgongo Fimbo said that section 2 of the then *Land Ordinance* recognized ownership and granted right of occupancy under native law and custom. He further stated that since there was no evidence of revocation of the appellant's right, the subsequent grant was ineffectual. It was argued for the respondent on the other hand that a right of occupancy granted under section 6 of the *Land Ordinance* conferred a superior and overriding title. Reading the majority decision of the Court of Appeal[339] Mustafa, J.J.A. had the following to say:

> *In my view the law in Tanzania on Land and Tenure is still developing and certain areas are unclear and would have to await the necessary legislation. At any rate I am not prepared, on the rather inconclusive and tenuous arguments advanced in this appeal, to hold that the right of a holder of a right of occupancy by virtue of native law and custom is extinguished and he thereby becomes a "squatter" on an area being declared a planning area.*

The Court was saying that the mere declaration of an area as planning area does not automatically extinguish customary titles over the land in that area, that is to say, such titles would be extinguished if certain legal procedures had been followed, including clearing the previous third party's claims[340]. Notwithstanding this sound observation of the Court, the appellant lost the appeal on the ground that he had bought the land from a third party,[341]under improper procedure[342] such that the sale was declared null and void. Mustafa, J.J.A.- as he then was had the following to say:

> *I am of the view that the sale by Vincent Patrick Mmole to the appellant (Nyagaswa) of the land in Mbezi was void and ineffective as it took place without the approval of the village council. The appellant had not acquired any right or title in the land which could defeat the title in the land acquired by the respondent (Nyirabu) by virtue of the certificate of occupancy issued to him. There was no extinguishing of the appellant's anterior title to the land; he never had acquired a title to or interest in the land in dispute...*

339 Mustafa and Omary J.J.A., Makame, J.A. dissenting.

340 It should be noted that Mbezi Beach Village, though within the jurisdiction of the City of Dar es Salaam, was a registered village under the Villages and Ujamaa Villages Act, 1975. It was therefore classified as a rural area within the City of Dar es Salaam.

341 Christopher Mbote Nyirabu.

342 The sale of land to Nyagaswa was done without approval of the village council. The omission was considered by the Court of Appeal of Tanzania as fatal and therefore incapable of passing title to the appellant.

It is important to note that while the Court found that the sale of the land to the appellant was done in contravention of the provisions of directive 5 (6) of the Directives issued vide Government Notice No 168 of 1975, which made it a condition to obtain the consent of the village council before effecting any transfer of land, which process was not fulfilled thereby nullifying the sale of land to the appellant, the legality of acquiring land on the part of the appellant was not considered by, and did not form part of the majority's judgment. In the circumstances, Makame, J.A. decided to depart from the majority's decision by dissenting. His lordship's point on the case was that:

> *When the respondent was made an offer of the parcel of land in dispute on 18th July, 1978 the area had already been designated and registered as Mbezi Village, under the Villages and Ujamaa Villages Act, 1975. The spirit and effect of the Act, and the various regulations made under it, is among other things, to place the land within the jurisdiction of the Village at the disposal of the village and its kayas, under the administration of the village, for the economic and social transformation and development of the village and its inhabitants. The State decided that it should be so, and it would defeat the objective of the law if grants over the same land were made, even by superior authorities without consultation, or at the very least knowledge, of the village authorities. This, I am satisfied, is what happened in the instant case, as is clearly brought out by the testimony of D.W.3 Ally Kibwana, the C.C.M. Branch Chairman of the area and one of the persons who witnessed the transactions between the appellant and Mmole. There is no evidence that at the time of the said transaction the area had already been surveyed; in fact the Defence evidence is that it had not been. Once the appellant got the plot, in April, 1978, he contacted the Kinondoni District Land Office for a survey and title, and the same District Land Office turned round and made an offer to the respondent in July, 1978, behind the appellant's back as it were, when it knew that the appellant was in possession and wanted a title.*

The learned justice of appeal was finally of the view that the respondent's Right of Occupancy was issued in improper circumstances and did nothing to disturb or extinguish the appellant's right. He would therefore allow the appeal. The failure to agree on the part of the judges suggests that there was, until this time, much confusion on the legal status of customary titles. Shivji observes very correctly that, "These inconsistent and contradictory opinions of the judges demonstrate, at least, utter confusion in the legal framework of the village land tenure"[343].

Another case similar to but distinguishable from *Nyagaswa*'s case is the case of *Mwalimu Omari & Ahmed Baguo v Omari A Bilali.*[344] In this case, the respondent had commenced an action against the appellants in the Resident Magistrate's Court of Kisutu, Dar es Salaam whereby he claimed to have been the owner of land in plot No. 60, Block E in Magomeni area since 1 June, 1978. He prayed for the appellants to demolish all the improvements they had carried out, perpetual injunction and damages. The appellants' on their side, argued that they had acquired title over the land by adverse possession in that they had been in uninterrupted possession and control over the land since 1965, and that the respondent's title could not operate to extinguish their claim in adverse possession. The appellants lost the case in the trial court on two grounds. The first ground was the trial Court's observation that, since the appellants were merely holders of a deemed right of occupancy (as their tenure was under customary law) their rights were those of licensees and that, therefore, they could not hold land in adverse to anyone:

> *The owner of the land in customary land tenure does not have title on the land. He has only the right to use or in other words he has usufructuary right over the land.*

The second ground was the trial Court's view that because customary law could not apply in an urban area, then the appellants were therefore squatters and they could not defeat the respondent's claim over the plot, the claim of which was supported by statutory grant of right of occupancy.[345] The appellants lost their appeal in the High Court of Tanzania[346] when the Court (Masanche, J.- as he then was) upheld the decision of the trial court by stating that the customary title cannot override the grant under the *Land Ordinance*. The appellants, aggrieved for the second time, appealed to the Court of Appeal of Tanzania.[347] In

343 SHIVJI, Issa G., (1998): *Not Yet Democracy: Reforming Land Tenure in Tanzania,* at p. 16.

344 [1999] TLR 432. See a brief discussion of the case, FIMBO, G.M, "Customary Tenure and the Court of Appeal of Tanzania" in BISIMBA, H.J. and PETER, C.M. (eds.), (2007):*Law and Justice in Tanzania: Quarter of A Century of the Court of Appea*l, Dar es Salaam: Mkuki na Nyota Publishers, pp. 139-159.

345 See the judgment at p.3.

346 Civil Appeal No. 22 of 1987, Judgment delivered on 15th May 1990 reported in [1990] TLR 9 (HC).

347 Civil Appeal No. 19 of 1996.

the Court of Appeal, as was the case in the lower courts, the contentious issue for determination was whether holders of land under customary law in planned areas have inferior title to those who are subsequently allocated. The argument for the appellants was that the *Land ordinance* provided for the possibility of holding land under another system other than the land ordinance, and that the occupier under deemed right of occupancy must be informed of the impending plan so that he can apply for a granted right of ocupancy, if he fails to get the grant then he is entitled to compensation. On the part of the respondent, it was argued that the respondent's offer had priority over the appellants' because it was issued first in point of time.[348] In deciding the matter, the Court of Appeal of Tanzania first determined the status of customary titles by saying that the title of a holder of a right of occupancy under customary law is recognised by the law of the land, the *Land Ordinance,* such that the holder thereof cannot be said to be a squatter, his title being protected by statute[349]. The Court went on to say that such a title can only be taken away from the holder by an act authorised by a relevant law, i.e, the *Land Acquisition Act,* but certainly not by a single act of declaring an area as planning area.[350] The Court, however, distinguished the case before it from the *Nyagaswa*'s case in that in the former case the land claimed by both Nyagaswa and Nyirabu was in a village registered under the *Villages and Ujamaa Villages Act*, 1975 while in the latter the plot in dispute was situated in the Magomeni suburb of the City of Dar es Salaam, where customary law on land tenure did not apply. The Court observed, therefore, that the appellants had occupied the land without any authority, and were therefore squatters. At the end of the day, the Court stated the following seminal principles, that:

> *The question of application of customary law in urban areas or the right of the holders of land under customary law in planned or urban areas was not directly answered in Nyagaswa. But we want to say now that customary law cannot apply in urban areas for the very good reason that a deemed right of occupancy is not compulsorily registerable whereas in urban areas all titles to land must be registered. This is necessary for smooth urban planning.*[351]

---

348 *Ibid*, p.5.

349 *Ibid*, p.10

350 It is in this point that the Court of Appeal expressly stated that it agreed with the minority judgment (Makame J.A) in the *Nyagaswa*'s case, also said the appeal in that case would have been allowed had it not been for the sticky problem of consent by the Village Council.

351 p.17.

As regards the status of the customary title after the area has been declared a planning area, the Court stated:

> *A deemed right of occupancy is equal to the granted right of occupancy under the Land Ordinance, hence none takes precedence over the other. Therefore all that the holders of deemed rights of occupancy need do is to convert these into granted rights of occupancy by having their holdings surveyed and title deeds issued to them.*[352]

The appellants lost the appeal in that they failed to prove of whom they possessed land in adverse.

In parallel to all the above decisions, the Court of Appeal of Tanzania had another opportunity to address the question whether land is a property capable of protection under the provisions of Article 24 (1) of the Constitution of the United Republic of Tanzania, 1977. This was done in the case of *Attorney General v Lohay Akonaay and Joseph Lohay.*[353] The facts of this case are crystal clear. The respondents, a father and son, had held land under customary law during the colonial days[354]. In 1970s they were moved into another land in the same village of Kambi ya Simba in Mbulu District, Arusha Region, during the Operation Vijiji programme[355]. In 1987[356], they successfully

---

352 *Ibid.*

353 [1995]T.L.R.80. (CA). This case has unique position in the development of the Tanzanian legal system. It touches the doctrinal and constitutional principle of separation of powers and independence of the judiciary. It is quite familiar not only land law students, but also to constitutional and administrative law.

354 Way back to 1943.

355 We read from this case that during Operation Vijiji, a significant number of people were deprived of their of land, which they held under customary law, and were given in exchange other pieces of land in the villages established pursuant to Operation Vijiji. This exercise was undertaken, not in accordance with any law, but purely as a matter of government policy. It is not apparent why the government chose to act outside the law, when there was legislation which could have allowed the government to act according to law, as it was bound to.

356 Note that in 1987, the government issued the Customary Land Rights Order, 1987, Government Notice No. 83 of 13th February 1987, which extinguished customary rights in 92 villages named under the schedule, including the Kambi ya Simba village in which the respondents resided, and vested the same to the respective District Council. However, we read from LOBULU, Ben, *op cit*, that, "The validity of the Government Notices were considered in High Court Civil Case No. 27 of 1985, Tito Saturo and Seven Others versus Matiya Seneya and Others. This case emanated from Mareu Ujamaa village. The peasants sought to recover their ancestral land from the current occupants who were also the village leaders. The High Court accepted the contention that the Government Notices were ultra vires or beyond their control; only the minister responsible for regional administration could make the regulations and only after consulting the minister responsible for lands. The Government Notice did not, in any case, indicate that such consultation had ever taken place. The court further upheld the unconstitutionality of the principal legislation and resulting notices for failure to provide those affected with an opportunity to be heard - not to mention the unfair, slow, and inadequate compensation and for overriding the general principles of law."

instituted a case against the judgment debtor in the Resident Magistrates' Court for Arusha Region[357]. The trial Court's decision was appealed against in the High Court.[358] While the appeal was pending, the government passed a new law[359] which did, *inter alia*: declare extinction of customary rights in the disputed land; prohibit payment of compensation for such distinction; oust the jurisdiction of the courts;[360] terminate proceedings pending in the courts, and; prohibit the enforcement of any court decision or decree concerning matters in respect of which jurisdiction was ousted. The new law was, to state the obvious, detrimental to the interests of the respondents. They were very aggrieved and, therefore, petitioned against the Attorney General in the High Court[361] under the provisions of the Constitution of the United Republic of Tanzania, 1977.[362] The Court granted the petition by striking out the new law in its entirety. The attorney general was dissatisfied, hence the appeal in the Court of Appeal. The first ground of appeal, and probably the most serious of all the grounds[363], was that the Honourable Trial Judge erred in fact and law in holding that a deemed Right of Occupancy as defined in s 2 of the *Land Ordinance* Cap. 113 is 'property' for the purposes of Article 24(1) of the Constitution of the United Republic of Tanzania 1977 and as such its deprivation is unconstitutional. It was argued for the appellant that customary rights in land is not property within the meaning of Article 24(1) and is not, therefore, protected under the Constitution.[364] This was strongly opposed on the part of the respondent, the argument being that whatever nature of the customary right in land, this was property and was protected. The Court of Appeal of Tanzania approached this issue by way of an *obiter*:

---

357 See *Lohay Akonaay and Joseph Lohay*, Resident Magistrates' Court for Arusha, Civil Case No. 4 of 1987.

358 See Civil Case No. 6 of 1991.

359 *Regulation of Land Tenure (Established Villages) Act* No. 22 of 1992.

360 The Act established a special tribunal with exclusive jurisdiction to deal with matters taken out of the jurisdiction of the courts.

361 See *Lohay Akonaay and Joseph Lohay,* High Court (Arusha Registry), Civil Case No.1 of 1993.

362 That is to say Articles 26(2) and 30(3). The former confers the right to any person who, being aware that the provisions of the Constitution of the United Republic of Tanzania are being abrogated, to undertake a legal action to ensure that the Constitution is preserved, while the latter empowers any person whose constitutional right has been infringed to institute a case in the High Court of Tanzania.

363 The Court of Appeal of Tanzania noted, in this case, that, "Ground number one raises an issue which has far-reaching consequences to the majority of the people of this country, who depend on land for their livelihood".

364 The cases cited in support of this contention were: *Amodu Tijani v The Secreatary Southern Nigeria* [1921]2A.C 399 and *Mtoro bin Mwamba v The Attorney General* [1953] 20 E.A.C.A 108.

> *If the Deputy Attorney-General is correct, then most of the inhabitants of Tanzania mainland are no better than squatters in their own country. It is a serious proposition. Of course if that is the correct position in law, it is our duty to agree with the Deputy Attorney-General, without fear or favour, after closely examining the relevant law and the principles underlying it.*

After going through rigorous reasoning the Court came to the conclusion that customary or deemed rights in land, though by their nature are nothing but rights to occupy and use the land, are nevertheless real property protected by the provisions of Article 24 (1) of the Constitution and, therefore, that deprivation of a customary or deemed right of occupancy without fair compensation is prohibited by the Constitution.

Toward a New Hope: Shivji Commission and the Debate on Land Law in Tanzania

The study on land reforms and tenure systems in Tanzania shows that there are several shortcomings which surrounded the land question before the new land law. These included but were not limited to: lack of a clear national land policy to govern the over all management and administration of land; existence of conflicting land laws; lack of people's participation in decisions affecting their right to land; disrecognization of the existing system of land control of native occupiers; the problem of multiple land allocation authorities with overriding jurisdiction, leading to the age old issue of double allocation; people's discontentment as evidenced by violence and an increase in lawsuits; failure of the dispute settlement machinery; corrupt practices in land control and management; existence of discriminatory customary rules especially on succession by women; increased land demand by investors, local and foreign, and; higher court decisions affecting customary tenure rights, especially in areas affected by villagization. In the midst of all these was the external pressure for political and economic reforms from the World Bank, the International Monetary Fund[365], and other international donors. These were factors sufficient enough to compel the government to reconsider the land question, to find durable solutions to the above mentioned setbacks on one hand, and to work out measures necessary for economic liberalization on the other. The government began by appointing a Commission of Inquiry into land matters, which would move around the whole country and identify land-related problems and make recommendations. Simon Coldham ably described the Commission:

---

365 Refer to, for example, to the Structural Adjustment Programme (SAP) of the early to mid 1980s.

> *In January 1991 President Ali Hassan Mwinyi appointed a Commission of Inquiry into Land Matters, under the chairmanship of Professor Issa Shivji, with extremely broad terms of reference. It was mandated not only to review laws and policies concerning the allocation, tenure, use, and development of land, and to make recommendations for reforms, but also to examine the nature of disputes that had arisen, and to propose measures for their solution. More generally it was to hear complaints from the general public and look into any other matters connected with land that it deemed appropriate. The appointment of the Commission might be interpreted as tacit official acknowledgement that the land policies of the proceeding 25 years had, in many ways, been a failure, and that now was the time to formulate a new approach in keeping with the economic changes embraced in the mid-1980s.*[366]

The Commission was given terms of reference to include: reviewing laws and policies concerning land and to make appropriate recommendations in that regard; to study the nature of land disputes which had arisen as a result of these policies and suggest solutions, and; to look into other matters and issues connected with land which it deemed fit for investigation. We read from the literature that the Commission visited all but two districts of the country.[367] At the end of its mission in November 1992, the Commission prepared a report which remains a point of reference in the history of land law in Tanzania.[368] A cursory survey of the report reveals that the Commission addressed various areas of concern including the pervasiveness of insecurity of tenure; radical title[369] to land vested in the presidency; overlapping institutional structures of land allocation and administration and

---

366 See COLDHAM, Simon, *op cit* at p. 227.

367 See the Preface, at p.vii in SHIVJI, Issa G., (1998*): Not Yet Democracy: Reforming Land Tenure in Tanzania.*

368 The Report was published in 1994. See TANZANIA, United Republic of, (1994): *Report of the Presidential Commission of Inquiry into Land Matters, Volumes I (Land Policy and Land Tenure Structure) and II (Selected Land Disputes and Recommendations),* Dar es Salaam: Ministry of Lands, Housing and Urban Development in Co-operation with the Scandinavian Institute of African Studies.

369 The concept of radical title may be difficult to grasp with ease. However, the term is defined by Okoth-Ogendo to mean the final or ultimate root from which all other land rights recognised by the judicial system of a given polity are derived. See OGENDO, Okoth "Legislative Approaches to Customary Tenure and Land Reform in East Africa" in TOULNINE, C. and QUAN, J. (2000): The Evolving Land Rights, Policy and Tenure in Africa, London: IIED.

dispute adjudication; lack of transparency and popular participation in the administration of land, and; poor institutional structure for adjudication of land rights and disputes. On the basis of these areas the Commission made recommendations including, *inter alia*, that matters of land and the right thereto be constitutionally recognised and protected; that the tenure system should allow for the classification of land into national land and village land in order for the radical title to be diversified and democratised into the Board of Land Commissioners and the Village Assemblies respectively, instead of the pre- existing system that created a monopoly of the radical title into the President; openness and transparency in land allocation procedures; peoples participation in land administration and a viable system of dispute adjudication.

"Those recommendations", notes Tsikata Dzodzi, "were to become the subject of vociferous national debate involving the Government, academics and NGOs. The debates were sparked off by the Government's drafted National Land Policy document, judged to have rejected some of the fundamental recommendations of the Land Commission"[370]. In addition and possibly without due regard to the Land Commission's recommendations, the Government hurriedly published the National Land Policy in 1995 and stated therein the Government's vision about various land matters in Tanzania[371], which is said to have been formulated on consideration of the recommendations of the Land Commission, the National Workshop on Land Policy,[372] and comments and suggestions from the public and the mass media[373]. Later on the Government hired an expert in the jurisprudence of land law, one Patrick McAuslan, Professor and consultant of the University of London who drafted the Land Bill[374] which was presented to the Parliament in 1998 before it was made into law in 1999. These documents, namely the Shivji Commission Report, the National Land Policy and the Draft Land Bill led to an acrimonious national debate immediately before the adoption of the new land law. Invariably people in their private or collective capacity were accorded

---

370 See DZODZI, Tsikata, "Securing Women's Interests within Land Tenure Reforms: Recent Debates in Tanzania," *Journal of Agrarian Change*, Vol. 3, Nos. 1 & 2, January 2003, pp. 149-183 at p. 161.

371 See United Republic of Tanzania, (1997): *National Land Policy*, Second Edition, Ministry of Lands and Human Settlement Development, Dar es Salaam.

372 This workshop was held in Arusha on January 16-18, 1995.

373 Paragraph 1, National Land Policy.

374 The literature shows that the drafting of the Land Bill was made under the sponsorship of the British Overseas Development Agency.

reasonable opportunity to debate for or against the content of the Land Bill without fear or favour. Some of these debates were documented and form part of the recorded literature.[375]

The Land Acts as the New Land Law of Tanzania

The *Land Act*[376] and *Village Land Act*[377] were subsequently passed into law in 1999, after rigorous debate for and against the Land Bill, and they, now, form the new land law of Tanzania.[378] These Acts have been well commented in that they have achieved, *inter alia*, security of tenure of the landholders and the opportunity of the people to participate in land administration. [379]

The *Land Act* essentially provides for the basic law in relation to land, other than the village land, that is to say: the management of land; and settlement of dispute and related matters. According to Robin Parmer[380], the *Land Act* deals with general land, including urban areas and private estates outside the customary sector. The Act is quite extensive, comprising 186 provisions, unlike its predecessor, the *Land Ordinance*, which appeared in 24 Sections only. The provisions of the Act are grouped into 14 main parts. These are: preliminary provisions[381], the fundamental principles of the National Land Policy,[382] classification

375 These include, but are not limited to SHIVJI, Issa G., "Land: The Terrain of Democratic Struggles", in *Change*, Vol. 5 First Quarter, 1997, pp. 4-8; SHIVJI, Issa G., "Grounding the Debate on Land: The National Land Policy and Its Implications" in *Change*, Vol. 5 First Quarter, 1997, pp. 37-47; SHIVJI, Issa G. and KAPINGA, Wilbert, B.L., "Implications of the Draft Bill for the Land Act" in *Change*, Vol. 5 First Quarter, 1997, pp. 48-63; SHIVJI, Issa G., "Reflections on the Women Question and Land: Some Debating Points" in *Change*, Vol. 5, First Quarter, 1997, pp. 64-71; KAPINGA, Wilbert B.L., "Some Reflections on the Presidential Commission Report and the National Land Policy" in *Change*, Vol. 5, First Quarter, 1997, pp. 9-17; JUMA, I., "Problems of the National Land Policy" in Change, Vol. 5, First Quarter, 1997, pp. 18-30; MWAIKUSA, J.T., "The Policy Paper and Its Implications on Pastoral Lands" in *Change*, Vol. 5, First Quarter, 1997, pp. 31-36; NATIONAL LAND FORUM, "Azimio La Uhai (Declaration of NGOs and Interested Persons on Land" in *Change*, Vol. 5, First Quarter, 1997, pp. 72-76; MANJI, Ambreena, "Gender and the Politics of the Land Reform Process in Tanzania" Journal of Modern African Studies, Vol. 36, No. 1 (Dec., 1998), pp. 645-667.

376 [Cap. 113 R.E 2002].

377 [Cap. 114 R.E 2002].

378 The Acts came into force on 1st May 2001 by virtue of G.N number 485 of 2001.

379 See FIMBO, G. Mgongo, "Participation of Local Communities in Land Administration and Management", *Nyerere Law Journal*, Vol. 1 (2003), pp. 1-12.

380 See PARMER, Robin, "The Tanzanian Land Acts, 1999: An Analysis of the Analysis," March 1999. The author identifies himself as Land Policy Advisor, Africa, Oxfam GB.

381 Part I, Sections 1&2.

382 Part II, Section 3.

and tenure of land,[383] administration,[384] rights and incidents of land occupation,[385] granted rights of occupancy,[386] conversion of interests in land[387], dispositions affecting land,[388] leases,[389] mortgages,[390] easement and analogous rights,[391] co-occupancy and partition,[392] dispute settlement,[393] and miscellaneous matters.[394] Also at the end of the Act there is a schedule which repeals some laws which were previously in force in Tanzania.

The *Village Land Act*, on the other hand, provides for the management and administration of land in villages, or, put otherwise, the village land, and for related matters.[395] The Act appears in 6 main parts, that is: preliminary provisions;[396] transfers and hazard lands;[397] allocation of fundamental principles of the national land policy;[398] management and administration;[399] dispute settlement,[400] and miscellaneous provisions.[401]

---

383 Sections 4-7.

384 Sections 8-18.

385 Sections 19-23. Note that sections 19 and 20 have been amended by the Land (Amendment), Act, 2004.[Act No. 2 of 2004]. There is a further amendment of section 19 through the *Written Laws (Miscellaneous Amendment) Act*, 2004 [Act No. 12 of 2004].

386 Sections 24-52. Note that section 37 has been amended by the *Land (Amendment) Act, 2004. [Act* No. 2 of 2004], and section 50 has been amended by the *Written Laws (Miscellaneous Amendment*) (No.2) Act, 2005 [Act No. 11 of 2005].

387 Sections 53-60.

388 Sections 61-76.

389 Sections 77-100. Note that sections 77, 78, 102, 103, 104, 105, 106 and 108 have been amended by the *Written Laws (Miscellaneous Amendment) (No. 2) Act*, 2005 [Act No. 11 of 2005].

390 Sections 112-143. Note that the entire part has been repealed and substituted by the provisions of the *Land (Amendment) Act*, 2004. [Act No. 2 of 2004].

391 Sections 143-158.

392 Sections 159-166.

393 Section 167. See also the *Land Dispute Courts Act*, [Cap.116, R.E 2002] which provides for land dispute settlement machinery by creating courts and conferring them jurisdiction to deal with land matters.

394 Sections 168-186.

395 See the Long Title to the *Village Land Act*, [Cap. 114 R.E 2002].

396 Sections 1-2.

397 Sections 4-6.

398 Section 3.

399 Section 7-59.

400 Section 60-62.

401 Sections 63-66.

Chapter Three

Land Delivery Systems: The Acquisition of Land

Land has intrinsic value which cannot be likened to a bag of beans or maize which can easily be purchased from the market.

- Judge H.R. Nsekela[402] -

402 *Mazaher Limited v Murray K. Chume and Another*, High Court of Tanzania (Commercial Division) at Dar es Salaam, Commercial Case No. 89 of 2002 (Unreported).

The discussion on land delivery system, in this chapter centres on the processes involved in accessing land in Tanzania. The topic covers one main area, namely the acquisition of land, and answers the basic question: How does a person, who is in need of land get it? Traditionally, there have been in place several systems through which land can be accessed or acquired. Some of these systems in Tanzania recognised and, therefore, protected by the *Land Acts*. These include, for example, the system of land allocation by the State, and land purchase in the market. However, the Acts are silent with regard to other systems such as acquisition of land by adverse possession, inheritance, allocation by the head of the family or clan, and gift *inter vivos*. My pre-occupation in this chapter is to discuss these systems and show how they operate in law and in practice.

Land Allocation by the State

Application, Grant and Revocation of Title

We learn from the *Land Acts*[403] that a person who acquires title to the use and occupation of the land in Tanzania, including title of a Tanzanian citizen of African descent or a community of Tanzanian citizens of African descent using or occupying land in accordance with customary law, has a right of occupancy over that land. It follows that when such title is obtained through a process of application and the subsequent allocation or grant by the established authority such as the state or village government, then we say it is granted right of occupancy. When the title is granted to a person by virtue of customary law, or when a person occupies and uses land under native laws and customs, this is known in the land law jurisprudence, as customary right of occupancy. The history of granted right of occupancy in Tanzania dates back to 1923 when it was introduced as one form of land tenure system by the *Land Ordinance*[404]. However, what was not in place until the coming in of the *Land Acts* was the framework on the legal procedures to be involved in the acquisition of a granted right of occupancy. In 1978, there was even an administrative attempt to address this *lacuna*. Precisely, the Ministry of Lands issued an important circular[405]. The circular introduced, in the

403 See section 2 of both the *Land Act* and the *Village Land Act*.

404 Section 6 of the Ordinance provided for granted right of occupancy, while section 10 provided for its revocation by the Governor if such revocation was necessary for public interests.

405 This is Circular No. MLHUD-C-1133/11/23 of 13 November, 1978. See *Colonel Kashimiri v Naginder* [1988] TLR 163.

first place, the procedure of issuing a letter of offer as a necessary step before a person was given a certificate of occupancy. In the second place, the circular established what was known as Plot Allocation Committees, such as the Urban Planning Committee, which were mandated to receive applications, make considerations and issue letters of offer to the successful applicants. However, we read from the literature[406] that since the institution of Plot Allocation Committees was created, two problems remained intact. In the first place, plot allocations were sometimes made without the meeting of the committees. In the second place, there were serious double allocations which were mainly caused out of the existence of several institutions with concurrent jurisdiction to allocate land, such as the Plot Allocation Committees on one hand, and the District Land Officers on the other hand. It is also on record that corruption[407] was another problem that adversely affected the process of land allocation.

As can be seen from the foregoing discussion, one of the greatest achievements of the *Land Acts* is that the Acts now provide for a clearly detailed and succinct procedure for the application and grant of rights of occupancy. According to the *Land Act*, for example, the procedure begins by a formal application of a right of occupancy in a prescribed form[408] which is delivered to the Commission for Lands.[409] The Commission has a legal duty to maintain a register of applications which is available for inspection by members of the public at a reasonable time, during the office hours.[410] It is submitted that this duty is inevitable in the prevailing situations which call for transparency in all matters affecting the well being of the citizens.

The second step is a determination of the application by the Commissioner.[411] It means that the Commissioner has a legal duty, upon an application being made, to make a determination as to whether or not

---

406 See for example, FIMBO, G.M., "Land Delivery Systems in the Land Acts: The Land Act, 1999 and the Village Land Act 1999" (Undated) at p. 7.

407 The problem of corruption in the land allocation processes, especially so before the coming in of the Land Acts, is well conversed in KANIKI, Abdulrahman O.J., "Prevention of Corruption in Land Administration and Delivery in Tanzania: A Brief Glance at the 'New' Land Law Regime", *The Justice Review*, Vol. 7, No. 1, 2008, pp. 117-137.

408 See Form No. 19 of the Land (Forms) Regulations, 2001, in Government Notice No. 71 of 2001.

409 The Application is made under the provisions of section 25 (1) of the Land Act, save that the office of the Commission for Lands is established under section 8 of the same Act.

410 See section 25 (6).

411 Section 26 (1).

to grant the application and also as to whether to grant the application with or without further conditions. When the application is refused, the aggrieved party (applicant) has the right to appeal against the decision to the Minister.[412] The law is silent as to whether or not there is a right to appeal against the Minister's decision. This silence suggests that the decision of the Minister is final and conclusive. It is submitted that since the Minister decides matters in his official capacity, his decisions need to be made judiciously and in accordance with the rules of natural justice lest they become a subject of judicial review by the competent court of law.

Untill 2008, the third and fourth steps were respectively the issuing of a letter of offer to, and the acceptance of it by, the successful applicant.[413] The letter of offer used to be made in a prescribed form[414] and contained all necessary conditions that go with a granted right of occupancy.[415] Let it be on trecord that before the coming of the *Land Act*, the question that troubled the minds of most of practitioners at the bar and the bench was about the legal status of a letter of offer. Courts of law were, more often than not, being asked to decide whether or not an offeree of the letter of offer had legally acquired the land before he or she was issued with a certificate of occupancy. The case of *Sarjit Singh v Sebastian Christom*[416] is one of the cases in which this question was at the core of litigation between the parties. The facts of the case are very simple: the appellant had applied for a granted right of occupancy over Plot No. 978, Msasani Peninsula, and was granted the same by the Kinondoni District Land Office through a letter of offer which he accepted, and then paid the necessary fees for a certificate of occupancy. Before the certificate was issued, the District Land Development Officer wrote to the appellant revoking the appellant's offer. The same plot was subsequently offered to the respondent who finally got the certificate of occupancy. The appellant sued and lost the claim in the Resident Magistrates Court at Kisutu, but he successfully appealed to the High Court of Tanzania. In both Courts, there were raised two issues of great significance. The first was whether the offer of a right of occupancy and its acceptance conferred title to land to the appellant, and; the second was whether

412 Section 26 (5).

413 Section 27 (1).

414 Form No. 20 of the Land (Forms) Regulations, 2001.

415 See the contents in section 27 (2).

416 [1988] TLR 24 (HC).

revocation of a right of occupancy by persons other than the President constituted revocation in law. It was argued for the appellant on both issues that the offer and its acceptance conferred title, and that the certificate of occupancy was only an evidence of that title. It was further argued that the appellant had acquired the right in land, which right was revocable only by the President. On the other hand, it was the argued for the respondent that the offer was not a certificate of occupancy; and that it did not confer any title to the appellant, it being a mere expression of commitment on the part of government to issue a certificate of occupancy. It was further argued that what the appellant had was not a right of occupancy which required revocation by the President. The High Court of Tanzania (Kyondo, J.- as he then was) held that land becomes legally owned or a right of occupancy is established once an offer is made and the offeree pays the fees. In other words the Court was saying that a certificate of occupancy is not a conditional precedent before the right of occupancy is created. The Court went further and held that the District Development Officer had no power to revoke title but the President or his delegate did.

The Land Act set the position very clearly on the legal status of the letter of offer. It conferred legal powers to the Commission to withdraw a letter of offer even if an affirmative reply was made by the applicant, save that the applicant was entitled to compensation for any loss suffered in the process.[417] The Act also provided that no liability could lie on the part of the State until a certificate of occupancy was issued and signed by the applicant.[418] All these provisions suggested one thing; that the legal title to land was conclusively created after the issuing of a certificate of occupancy and when the said certificate was signed by the applicant and not before. However, the point of emphasis is that the case of Sarjit Singh above, and many others[419], was of the proposition that if the same plot was allocated to two persons in what we know as double allocation, the original offeree took precedent over the subsequent offeree even if the latter managed to manipulate the process and obtain a certificate of title first. Yet another important feature of the Land Act was that the Act gave a right to an offeree who accepted the offer but was not issued with a certificate of title within one hundred and eighty days, to register

---

417 See section 27 (3).

418 See section 29 (4).

419 See a discussion on double allocation below.

his letter of offer under the Registration of Documents Act[420] for the purpose of creating a notice of impending ownership.[421] Once this was done, the letter of offer conferred to the offeree all the rights over the land as if it was a certificate of occupancy and to the extent of creating liability even on the part of the State.

However, with the enactment of the *Mortgage Financing (Special Provisions) Act, 2008*[422], which repeals sections 27, 28 and 30, and modifies section 29 of the *Land Act, 1999*, the procedure calling for the giving and acceptance of the letter of offer is no longer part of the law. To date, applicants for granted rights of occupancy have the right to be considered and granted rights of occupancy outlight, without going into the lengthy procedure and legal uncertainities involving letters of offer. The law only saves the validity and legal force of offers issued before the 1st December 2008.[423]

The third and last procedure is the issuing of the certificate of occupancy[424] in a prescribed form.[425] The Certificate is issued in the name of the President and signed by the Commissioner.[426] It bears an official seal[427] and creates liability on the part of the state when it is signed by the applicant.[428] It is important to note here that the certificate of occupancy is compulsorily registrable under the provision of the *Land Registration Act*[429], and failure to do so may lead to some adverse consequences on the part of the applicant. Applicants are strongly advised to register their titles in order to avoid the consequences that go with non-registration of a certificate of occupancy.

Once land is granted, the grant may be classified according to the duration of the grant[430], such as long term right of occupancy of 99 years; short term right of occupancy from 5-99 years, and; periodic

---

420 See [Cap. 117 R.E 2002].

421 Section 30 (1).

422 Act No. 17 of 2008.

423 See the Written Laws (Miscellaneous Ammentments) Act, 2009 (Act No. 3 of 2009).

424 Section 29 (1).

425 Form No. 22 of the Land (Forms) Regulations, 2001.

426 Section 29 (2).

427 Section 29 (3).

428 Section 29 (4).

429 Cap. 334, section 27.

430 Section 32.

right of occupancy of year-to-year. Alternatively, the classification may be based on the functions or use or purpose of the grant, that is: whether the land granted is for the purpose of agricultural, pastoral, residential, commercial or mixed purposes.[431] Land delivery always goes with land control systems for economic development. For example, a granted right of occupancy goes with certain conditions, which requires strict compliance by the holder of the right of occupancy, meaning that the security of tenure of the holder of a granted right of occupancy is dependent on fulfilment of these development conditions which may include: payment of premium as may be required by the Minister;[432] occupying land for a specific term which comes to an end by the affliction of time but which may be subject to renewal;[433] payment of annual rent;[434] and other general or specific conditions that are imposed or may be imposed by the Commissioner under the law;[435] and the need to apply to the Commissioner for change of the land use or variation of the conditions of the right of occupancy when the same is proposed by the holder.[436] Failure to comply with the above conditions is a breach of the contract of grant of the right of occupancy and may lead to revocation of the same by the President.[437] The common condition attached to a right of occupancy has always been the "use-condition", which tends to restrict the use of the property, the subject matter of a grant. It is quite common, for example, to read from certificates of titles a restrictive clause such as this:

> *"Only one main building together with the usual and necessary outstanding buildings shall be built on the land and the same shall be used for residential purposes only".*

---

431 See regulation 6 (2) of the Land (Conditions of Right of Occupancy) Regulations, 2001, Government Notice No. 77 of 2001.

432 Section 31 (1).

433 Section 32 (1) (2) and (3).

434 Section 33 (1).

435 Section 34 (1).

436 Section 35 (1).

437 See section 45 (1) (v). Other instances where revocation can be preferred by the President include where there is good cause to revoke the right under section 45 (2) and where, in the opinion of the President, revocation is necessary for public interest under section 45 (3).

It is important to note, here, that it is a fundamental principle of the National Land Policy that land be used by Tanzanian citizens[438]. It follows that non-citizens (foreigners) are not allowed to apply for and be granted right of occupancy, derivative right or interest in land except for the purpose of investment approved under the *Tanzania Investment Act*[439]. It means that any application for a granted right of occupancy made by a non–citizen or foreign company must be accompanied by, among others things, a Certificate of Approval granted by the Tanzania Investment Centre which is established by, and carries out its duties under the provisions of the *Tanzania Investment Act.*[440] That is why even an attempt by a holder of a right of occupancy to dispose a right of occupancy to a non-citizen contrary to the provisions of the Act amounts to good cause that may lead to revocation of the right of occupancy of the holder by the President.[441]

Looking at it through the prism of Human Rights, the *Land Act*[442] is commended for two reasons. In the first place, the Act now provides a detailed but also transparent procedure in applying for and being allocated a right of occupancy. In the second place, the Act enhances and protects security of tenure of the holders of granted rights of occupancy. It can be learned from the Act, for example, that when it comes to revoking titles, the law requires revocation not only to be for good cause, but also it is a gradual process involving a sequence of procedures. We note, for example, that if revocation is for breach of conditions attached to the grant, the Commissioner has to make a finding as to the nature and gravity of the breach, and also the likelihood of the occupier to remedy the breach. Next the Commissioner must to issue a letter warning the occupier that he is in breach of the conditions of the right of occupancy.[443] If the Commissioner finds that the title is to be revoked, he has to issue a notice to the occupier requiring the latter to show cause as to why fine should not be imposed upon him in respect of

---

438 See Section 3 (1) (a) of the *Land Act*, 1999 [Cap. 113 R.E 2002].

439 See section 19 (2) of the *Land Act*, 1999, as amended by the *Land (Amendment) Act* No. 2 of 2004.

440 See Section 25 (1) (e).

441 See section 45 (2) (i).

442 [Cap. 113 R.E 2002].

443 Section 45 (4).

the breach,[444] requiring him to pay a fine,[445] or to remedy the breach.[446] Other procedures that follow include: the Commissioner to serve a notice of revocation,[447] and to recommend to the President to revoke the right of occupancy.[448] When the President approves the revocation,[449] then follows the publication of the revocation in the Gazette and in a newspaper or newspapers circulating in the area where the land which is the subject of the revocation is situated;[450] and payment of compensation to the former occupier for unexhausted improvements[451] made on the land, the subject of the revocation order. It is not difficult to note that the above procedures embrace, in root and trunk, the basic rules of natural justice, that is to say, the right to be heard on the intended revocation, and the right to know the reasons for the revocation. The eyes of the judiciary, long before the coming in of the *Land Acts*, were pointing to these rules of natural justice as we learn from the case of *Director of Lands and Mines v Sohan Singh.*[452] In this case the plaintiff, acting on behalf of the Governor, granted a right of occupancy to the defendant in 1937 for a period of 33 years on conditions including payment of annual rent and erecting a building of value not less than 3000/= on approval by the competent authority in the township of Moshi. The building was supposed to be erected and completed by 21 January 1939. The defendant was unable to finish the building due to a shortage of materials following the outbreak of the war in 1939. The matter was rested without any further action by either party until 1948, when a notice was issued to the defendant requiring him to show cause as to why the right should not be revoked for the breach of the building covenant. He replied and time was extended in that he was now required to finish the building in 1949 at value of not less than 10,000/=. It seems that the defendant had also

444 Section 46 (1).

445 Section 46 (3).

446 Section 47 (1).

447 Section 48 (1). See the content vide Form No. 11 which is the notice of revocation of a right of occupancy. The Notice is effective 90 days from the date of issue.

448 Section 48 (3).

449 Section 49 (1).

450 *Ibid.*

451 Section 49 (3).

452 (1952) 1 TLR 63.

acknowledged that failure to observe the conditions would constitute a good cause for revocation of his right of occupancy without further notice. The defendant breached the conditions so that the competent authority wrote to the plaintiff recommending that, as there was no prospect of the building being completed within the time specified in the covenant, then the defendant's right of occupancy be revoked. The Governor was moved by this recommendation to revoke title. When the matter landed in court, the court invoked equity and the principles of natural justice in deciding the case. Precisely, the court was of the opinion that:

> *It is entirely contrary to justice that a certificate of occupancy should have been revoked on the mere opinion of someone that a building cannot be erected by a specified date.*

As already stated, revocation of the right of occupancy can be done if, apart from breach of conditions, there is good cause to do so[453], or if it is for the purpose of public interest[454] as observed from the following two cases, respectively. In *Patman Garments Industries Ltd v Tanzania Manufacturers Ltd*[455], both parties to the case claimed to be lawful occupiers of the disputed land. The facts indicate that the appellant had applied for the right of occupancy, received a letter of offer over the same on 24th January 1978 and accepted it a day after. On 5th February the offer was revoked. On the other hand, the respondent applied for the right of occupancy over the same Plot, received the letter of offer on 29th May 1978 and accepted it on the same day. The Appellant was not satisfied the way things were going; he referred the matter to a court of law. In the court two main issues were framed for determination by the court, i.e, whether the right of occupancy held by the appellant was lawful, and whether the President's powers of revocation could be challenged in the court of law. The court held, *inter alia*, that the law[456] empowered the President to revoke the right of occupancy for good cause but held further that the President could not do so unless the conditions prescribed by law for its exercise were fulfilled. It was also observed that revocation in this case was unlawful because it was made for no

453 Section 45 (1) lists some situations amounting to "good cause" for the purpose of revocation of a right of occupancy.

454 See section 45 (3).

455 [1981] TLR 303 (CA).

456 Section 10 of the Land *Ordinance*, Cap.113 of the Laws of Tanganyika.

good cause, but was an unlawful exercise of powers conferred by law. Finally the court ruled that since the revocation was unlawful, then the appellants continued to be the right owners of the right of occupancy.

Another case is that of *Agro Industries v Attorney General*[457]. The facts of this case were that a person X mortgaged his two farms to a Bank. He failed to repay back the debt so that the Bank exercised the right of sale by selling the farms to the appellant after obtaining the consent of the Regional Development Director of Morogoro Region. Later on another firm applied through the Msovero Village Government, was allocated the same farms and took possession thereafter. The dispute arose between the appellant and the firm. The matter reached the Minister who, on failure to reconcile the litigants, recommended to the President to revoke the right of occupancy of the appellant in favour of the other party, a public parastatal. The President endorsed the Minister's recommendation by writing on the recommendations the word, "*Nakubali*" meaning "I agree", and the Minister issued a revocation letter in the name of the President. The appellant was aggrieved and filed a case but lost the claim in the trial court, which he successfully regained in the Court of Appeal of Tanzania. Essentially, the Court of Appeal addressed, among other things, the issue on the need to serve a notice of revocation to the occupier of land by holding in unambiguous terms that, "the purpose of notice is to afford a party an opportunity to put up a case". It is submitted that the Court's holding on the aspect of the need to issue a notice of revocation is the corollary of the right to be heard, which is a rule of natural justice. The court found that in this case, the appellant had notice of revocation but the said revocation was had been tampered with and not for the purpose of public interests as defined in various decisions of the court to include *Bp Bhatt and another v Habib Versi Rajan*[458] in which the court cited with approval, and the Indian case of *Hawabai Franjee Petit v Secretary of State of India*[459], which defined the term public interest in these words:

> *...the phrase, whatever it may mean, must include a purpose, that is to say an aim or object, in which the general interest of the country, as opposed to the particular interest of individuals, is directly or vitally concerned.*

---

457 [1994] TLR 43 (CA).

458 (1958) E.A 536.

459 (1915) 39 Bom 279.

It should not be forgotten that the right to apply for and be grated a right of occupancy over the village land is also available under, and is regulated by, the *Village Land Act*[460]. The procedure of applying for a right of occupancy over a village land under the *Village Land Act* is not dissimilar from the procedure obtaining under the *Land Act*. This begins by a formal application for the right of occupancy to the Village Council[461]. The Village Council determines the application within ninety days after the application[462] and issues a letter of offer.[463] A reply to the offer either accepting or not accepting the offer is made within ninety days of receipt of the offer.[464] The issuing of a certificate of a customary right of occupancy[465] closes the procedure. As is the case with conditions accompanying the grant of a right of occupancy under the *Land Act*, the *Village Land Act,* too, has conditions that go with the granted right which may include: occupying the land indefinitely or within a prescribed length of time;[466] payment of rent,[467] and; other conditions that are or may be described from time to time.[468] In case the conditions are breached[469] the right can as well be revoked but on fulfilling certain procedures. The procedure covers the Village Council issuing a warning to the occupier advising the occupier that he or she is in the breach of condition,[470] the occupier making a representation about the matter within fourteen days of receipt of the notice,[471] determination of the representation by the Village Council in order to decide whether or not to proceed with exercising the customary law remedy against the occupier,[472] depriving the land if the customary law permits, [473] and

460 Cap. 114. Read the Act together with the Village Land Regulations, 2001 (GN No. 86 of 2001).

461 Section 22 (1), (3).

462 Section 23 (1)

463 Section 24 (1).

464 Section 24 (2).

465 Section 25 (1).

466 Section 27 (1).

467 Section 28 (1).

468 Section 29 (1).

469 Section 37.

470 Section 38 (6).

471 Section 39 (1) (b).

472 Section 39 (1) (c).

473 Section 39 (2).

when the consent of the Commissioner for lands has been obtained.[474] The question how and when can the village authorities allocate land or re-allocate land to applicants was admirably answered by the court in the case of *Village Chairman KCU Mateka v Anthony Hyera*[475] . It is submitted that the case stated a very important legal principle which must guide village authorities in the exercise of their powers of land allocation.

Double Allocation in Law and Practice

No one can be faulted who holds that before the adoption of the *Land Acts*, one of the most serious and common problems in land administration in Tanzania which created unwelcome discontentment of the citizens against land allocation authorities was the issue of double allocation. Double allocation had been a long term problem, not only over the land held under granted rights of occupancy, but also over the village lands.[476] We say there is double allocation where two persons are each allocated the right of occupancy over the same plot of land, that is, one person is allocated a plot of land first on point of time, and the other is subsequently allocated the same plot. In all cases of double allocation it appears that all of the allocatees are legally allocated a piece of land and may have procured all the necessary documents of title over the same plot of land. Historically, double allocation happened as a result of a number of factors including, but not limited to: lack of a clear procedure in land allocation process; multiplicity of land allocating authorities, lack of or failure to keep proper records of allocates; and corruption on the part of the land allocating officials.

The questions that come straight are: do we still face the problem of double allocation after the arrival of the *Land Acts*? What are the current causes of double allocation, if any? The answer is that double allocation is still a problem, even though it is less serious compared to the time before the *Land Acts*. Double allocation is now attributed mostly to the negligent or even fraudulent undertakings as is promoted by the personnel in the Ministry of Land and Housing Development. The cases of *Simon Byanyuma v A.E Halday*[477] and *Mohamed Dossaji v Frederick Lwezaula*[478]are cited in support of this fact.

474 *Ibid.*

475 [1988] TLR 188 (HC).

476 See the old case of *Lukasi Masinori Kateti v Oloo Sebege* [1969] HCD no. 11.

477 High Court of Tanzania (Land Division) at Dar es Salaam, Land Case No. 27 of 2004 (Unreported).

478 High Court of Tanzania (Land Division) at Dar es Salaam, Land Case No. 25 of 2004 (Unreported).

In the *Simon Byanyuma* case, for example, the plaintiff claimed to be the rightful owner over Plot No. 46 Mandela Expressway Buguruni Industrial area by virtue of title no. 43260 dated 12th April 1994, which was in his name and which comprised of two plots, No. 45 and no. 46. The defendants on the other hand claimed to be the rightful owner of plot no 46 by virtue of a letter of offer dated 19th February 1990. The evidence in court showed that the plaintiff applied for the offer of the disputed plot on 12 April 1994 and was issued a Certificate of Title on 19th April 1994. The court held that the certificate of title no. 43260 was improperly obtained, because the rush manner in which the plaintiff obtained the title raised many questions, especially as the plot was not free for allocation. The court made severe attack against the officers in the Ministry of Lands as either being irresponsible in the performance of their duties or being dishonest and, at the end, decided the case in favour of the defendant.

> *Indeed if the Officials in the Ministry had been prudent they would have carried on diligent investigation and would have discovered that the plot was not free for allocation...*
>
> *Both assessors were of the opinion that the extraordinary speed with which the plaintiff obtained the title raises many question. I entirely agree. I cannot help but think that the circumstances of this case strongly suggest that there was some dishonesty somewhere, which led to the plaintiff being offered plot no. 46 while the same plot had previously been obtained.*

In the end the court invoked the principle of equity by holding that, "It would not be equitable that the plaintiff should be given two plots, leaving the defendant who was the original occupier of the disputed land with nothing."

In *Mohamed Dossaji case*, again, the court did not hesitate to blame the Ministry of Lands, whose irresponsibility was said to have caused double allocation of the land to the parties in dispute. The facts of the case are that the plaintiff, holder of a certificate of occupancy with title no 25715 for plot no 168 Msasani Village sued the defendant for trespass and harassment and, therefore, prayed for the following orders: a declaration that the defendant was not entitled to enter and use the land; an injunction restraining the defendant from entering the land; and the eviction of the defendant and his servants, agents and/or his employees. The defendant counterclaimed that he was the lawful owner of the said plot by virtue of a letter of offer issued to him on 2/8/1979. In other words, the defendant's case averred that he was the first one to be offered the disputed plot and that he should be declared the rightful owner as there was no evidence to show that his right to that land had been revoked. Going through the evidence the court discovered that the defendant purported to have obtained the letter of offer at a time when the land in question was not even surveyed, and the letter of offer issued to the defendant and which was contained in the file was a photocopy and had been tempered with. It was the court's opinion that the defendant might have been tricked by the land officials into giving him an offer of a plot that had no yet been surveyed. For that reason, the court had the following to say at p. 8:

> *This is one of those cases, which display the kind of problems that exist in the Ministry of Lands. Apparently, there are two files for the same plot. According to Dw2, Erick Makundi, an official from the Ministry of Lands, the position of the Ministry in this case is that there was a double allocation.*

At the end of the matter the court decided in favour of the plaintiff saying the plaintiff had successfully established his case to the standard required in civil procedure. From the foregoing, we note that double allocation has always been a recipe for land disputes, especially so in the post-independent period. However, in the course of deciding disputes of double allocation, courts have built a body of principles which control this practice, and which are worth highlighting in this discussion.

The case of *Village Chairman KCU Mateka v Anthony Hyera* [479] is based on the following set of facts and principles. The respondent had a piece of land in Mateka village, Mbinga District which he had possessed since 1953 and developed by building a house. There were also some permanent trees (coffee trees), among other things. In 1973, DW 3, a teacher, was transferred to Mbinga and applied to the Mateka village government for land. The appellant granted him the land of the respondent. The respondent was aggrieved. He applied to the court for relief against the appellant and won in the lower courts. On the appellant's appeal in the High Court at Songea, one of the main issues was: whether a village government can lawfully allocate land within its jurisdiction which is under the possession of another villager who is developing it. It was the court's wise holding that:

479 [1988] TLR 188 (HC).

> *I do not hesitate to answer that question with a big emphatic no. Common sense will not allow it. Equity will forbid it. While saying so I should not be taken to question the power of a village government to allocate land within its jurisdiction which has not been allocated to any person. Nor do I question the powers of a village government to allocate land which is already allocated to another person if the person in possession of such land is consulted prior to the re-allocation and he had consented to the proposed re-allocation. A village government which allocated land, as in the present case, which is already under development and in the possession of another person would not only bring lawlessness and anarchy to the villages but would also retard the development of the villages.*

In *Colonel Cashimir v Naginder Singh Matharu*[480] the facts of the case were that the respondent applied for and was allocated land by the Urban Planning Committee. Two months later the appellant was allocated the same plot, and the dispute between the parties arose as a necessary consequence. When the matter went to court, the appellant lost his claim and appeal in the High court and later in the Court of Appeal of Tanzania. In dismissing the appellant's appeal, the Court of Appeal of Tanzania observed that the respondent had followed the procedure to make his application as laid down in the circular No. NLUUD-C-1133/11/23 of 13.11.78 issued by the Ministry of Lands, Housing and Urban Development. According to the Court, the circular not only laid down the procedures to be followed in plot allocation, but also warned that any infringement of it would call for cancellation of the certificate of title so obtained. The Court went on to state that the circular was geared to avoid the confusion and embarrassment emanating from the practice of multiple allocations. It was the Court's conclusion that the evidence showed that the plot was properly allocated to the respondent, not the appellant.

The case of *Paul Michael Simbaine v Asina Hassan Ramadhani*[481] is seminal when it comes to double allocation. The facts of the case were that the respondent's farther, one Hassan Ramadhani Sefu had applied for and been granted title over plot No.435/43 in Kijitonyama area with Certificate of Title No. 21201 of 26th March 1977. However, earlier on, this plot plus many others were collectively allocated to Mwenge Co-

480 [1988] TLR 163 (CA).

481 High Court of Tanzania, at Dar es Salaam, Civil Appeal No. 150 of 1999 (Unreported). Judgment delivered on 14th September 2000.

operative Society, to which the appellant was a member under Certificate of Title No. 18859 of 21st June 1973. This type of property ownership by the Hassan and Paul was a clear case of double allocation which eventually led to a land dispute between the parties. Asina Hassan appeared as an administrator of the estate of her deceased father, Hassan Ramadhani Sefu. The appellant lost the claim in the Resident Magistrate's Court of Kisutu and regained it in the High Court of Tanzania. Adjudicating the matter, the High Court (Katiti,J.- as he then was) had the following to say, which we consider to be the correct jurisprudence in the determination of the rights of the parties to a land dispute in all cases of double allocation:

> *What, then is the legal position? It appears trite learning, and it is trite law, that where a party has been granted a Right of Occupancy over a piece of land, or plot, a subsequent grant, or allocation of the same land, or plot to another person, before the first grant is revoked, the subsequent grant is not only irregular, but also, it allocates, or grants what in law is not there to be granted...It is equally worth observing in this case, that both Certificates of Occupancy, were registered as Nos. 18859 and 21201, respectively, under the Land Registration Ordinance Cap.334. It seems to me that, though both were on different dates registered under the mentioned Ordinance, Section 32, it still seems to be the position of the law, that the first Certificate of Occupancy Title to be registered legally takes precedence and prevails over any subsequent ones, even if subsequently registered. If anything, for even practical reasons, in law there is no longer anything to offer, and I would venture to say that the respondent's father got nothing in law. Without, shilly-shallying therefore, I have confidence to conclude that, when the respondent's father came in the Plot, which was undivided, it already belonged to Mwenge Cooperative Society Ltd, the whole of it had already belonged to Mwenge Cooperative Society Ltd. I would therefore say, that Hassan Seif irregularly got, what already belonged to Mwenge Cooperative Society, and therefore in law got nothing...*

In summary, the court developed a principle that in the determination of a land dispute founded on double allocation, a party who was first allocated in point of time takes priority over a party who is later allocated when there is no evidence to show that the first title has been revoked.

Another area of importance when it comes to cases of double allocation has been the issue of compensation on the part of the person who loses the claim, but who has, fortunately, made substantial improvements on the disputed land. The principles governing the awarding of compensation in such a case were clearly stated in the case of *Anna Benedict v Mrisho*[482] and followed in *Salum Juma Mzeru v Omari Ubaya.*[483]

The facts in Anna's case were that a committee allocated a plot of land to the respondent when the same was already allocated to the appellant (Anna Benedict). The appellant filed a suit in the Resident Magistrates' court, claiming ownership of the land. The court held that the land belonged to her and ordered the respondent to vacate. However, the court upon declaring the appellant as a rightful owner of the land, ordered her to pay compensation to the respondent for the improvements he had put on the land. The appellant was aggrieved by the order of the court directing her to pay compensation to the responded and appealed against that order to the High Court of Tanzania, and later to the East African Court of Appeal. The argument in favour of the appeal was that the responded went on to build on the land even after he had notice that the land was in dispute. Both higher courts submitted to the general principle that a party should not reap the benefits of the improvements to the land affected by the opposite party without paying for such benefit and compensating the opposite party for this expenditure in so improving the value of the land. However, in this case, the East African Court of Appeal did not find it reasonable to force the appellant to take up a building which she might not have wanted to build in such a fashion since she might want to build a less expensive building altogether. The court was of the opinion that the most reasonable thing to do was to order the respondent to demolish his building and take away all his building materials within a certain, specifies period. With this jurisprudence on record, when Salum's case landed in the High Court of Tanzania based on similar facts, the Court did not hesitate in holding that:

> *Our present case is on all fours with Anna Benedict's case. Like the Court of Appeal in Anna Benedict's case, I do not see any reason for compensation. The respondent should demolish his building. I therefore allow this appeal. I order that the respondent demolish his building and carry away his building materials within two months from the date of this judgment. If by that date the respondent has not done so, then the materials on the plot will become the property of the appellant.*

482 East African Court of Appeal, Civil Appeal No. 41 of 1976 (Unreported).

483 [1984] TLR 31 (HC).

The two cases suggest that compensation being a human right[484], a party will be entitled to compensation who is allocated land and develops it unaware of any encumbrances thereto. Likewise, a party will not be entitled to compensation who is allocated land and undertakes to develop it having notice of the encumbrances thereof.

Land Acquisition by Purchase

This is the method of acquiring land by buying it in the market. It is the preferable, safe means of acquiring land, but it is available only to the people with deep pockets, meaning those who are able to compete with others in the free market.[485] Acquisition by purchase presupposes the presence of a willing seller and willing buyer and it enables one to have land according to the money he has. Tanzania passed the *Land Acts* having intended to regulate the amount of land that any one person or corporate body may occupy or use.[486] It is submitted that this intention, however good it may be, may not become a reality under this era of the free market economy. When it comes to acquiring land by purchase, the amount of land a person may occupy is determined by two factors: the amount of many one has in his pocket, and the presence of a willing seller.

Land Acquisition by Adverse Possession

In law, one may acquire the right to occupy a piece of land by way of the common law doctrine of adverse possession. This doctrine operates within the four walls of the law of limitation. We can better understand the doctrine of adverse possession only if we are acquainted with the basic tenets of the law of limitation[487]. As far as land law is concerned, the law of limitation imposes a duty to any person who claims to have been interfered with in the occupation or use of land to bring an action to recover the land within 12 years[488]. If the action is not brought within this (statutory) period, the law of limitation then permits a wrongful possessor of land to have a good title to it as against the true owner and

---

484 See a detailed discussion about the right to compensation in Chapter 8 below.

485 A detailed discussion of the legal position in relation to disposition of land by sale or purchase appears in Chapter 4 below.

486 See section 3 (1) (d) common to the *Land Act* and the *Village Land Act* which state the fundamental principles of the National Land Policy.

487 See the *Law of Limitation Act*, [Cap. 89, and R.E 2002] and Magistrates Courts (Limitation of Proceedings under Customary Law) Rules of 1963 (GN. No. 311 of 1964) discussion at length in Chapter 9 below.

488 See item 22 of the First Schedule to the *Law of Limitation Act* and item No. 6 of the Schedule to the Customary Law (Limitation of Actions) Rules.

the public at large[489]. When a person acquires the right to occupy land in this way, then we say that he has acquired it by operation of the doctrine of adverse possession and he may proceed to register it according to law.[490] It is observed that the Kenyan case of *Benjamine Kamau Murima and Others v Glady's Njeri*[491] remains the landmark case in which adverse possession was clearly pleaded and established. The facts of this case were as follows: Sometimes in1953 the respondent's husband died. She moved into, and took possession of the suit land believing the land to belong to her father. Unfortunately, the same land was registered in the name of Kamau Murima in 1959, i.e, during land consolidation and demarcation, while the adjacent land was registered in the name of the respondent's father. However, Kamau Murima never took possession nor occupied the land and the respondent continued to occupy it, carrying out on it various developments. By 1972, she had been in possession of the land as against its registered owner for a period exceeding 12 years. In 1980 the first appellant instituted succession proceedings over the land when Murima, his father, had allegedly died. He succeeded and a certificate in title in respect of the suit land was issued in his name. He later sold the land to the second appellant who sub divided it in portions to the rest of the appellants. The appellants' efforts to evict the respondent met with spirited resistance by the respondent, until the dispute landed in the court of law. The respondent claimed that her possession of land was adverse to the title of the original registered proprietor of the said land. The trial court held in her favour in that she had established her entitlement to the suit land by way of adverse possession. The appellants were aggrieved and appealed to the Court of Appeal of Kenya. In dismissing the appellants' appeal, the Court set the following admired principles of law: first, it was the Court's reasoning that the combined effect of the relevant provisions of section 7, 13 and 17 of the *Limitation of Actions Act*, Cap. 22 of the laws of Kenya is to extinguish the title of the proprietor of land in favour of the adverse possessor of the same at the expiry of 12 years of adverse possession in that land. Second, the Court

---

489 According to the literature, the fundamental principle of the law of limitation is that unless claims are enforced within a limited time, they become barred. See Megarry at p. 520.

490 Section 16 of the *Land Registration Act*, [Cap. 334 R.E 2002] declares that an application for first registration may be made by a person claiming to have acquired a title to a registrable estate by adverse possession or by reason of any law of prescription.

491 Kenya Court of Appeal Reports, Vol. 8, pp. 64-70. Judgment of 30th June 1997.

said in determining whether or not the nature of actual possession of the land in question is adverse, one needs only to look at the position of the occupier and if it is found that his occupation is derived from the proprietor of the said land in the form of permission or agreement or grant, then such occupation is not adverse, but if it is not so derived, then it is adverse. Third, the Court said that even if the respondent's possession of the suit land was taken to run from the date of its first registration in Murima's name, that is to say April 1960, such possession was inconsistent with and in denial of Murima's title to the said land because her occupation of land was not derived from him in form of permission or agreement or otherwise whatsoever. After April 1972, the respondent's continuous actual possession of the suit land in the manner aforesaid would not be interrupted and any subsequent dealings with the land including succession proceedings were subject to the respondent's interests in the land.

The Tanzanian case of *Jumanne s/o Mazebele v Bukombe s/o Kihongwe*[492] is also a record of the appellant who claimed title to a piece of land by way of adverse possession but lost the claim in court. The facts of the case tell that sometime in the past the respondent had permitted one Bugeke Magushi to erect a hut on his parcel of land and settle there during her lifetime. Bukene Magushi died and her daughter, Holo Kwande, sold the said hut to the appellant without the respondent's knowledge. When the appellant attempted to collect building material on the land, the respondent was brought to notice and instituted a suit against the appellant, which he lost in the Primary Court, but won in the District Court. The appellant appealed to the High Court but lost the appeal. Before dismissing the appeal, the court (Mwita, J.- as he then was) held at p. 3 that:

> *If Bugeke Magushi had taken Bukombe's parcel of land and retained possession of it for twelve years, then Bukombe's title would be barred and Bugeke would have acquired a good title to that parcel of land. If Bukombe's title is to be barred after twelve years, Bugeke's occupation must have been without Bukombe's authority, her possession must have been "adverse possession", that is adverse to Bukombe's title...*

---

492 High Court of Tanzania at Dodoma, (PC) Civil Application No. 76 of 2002 (Unreported).

> *As Bugeke Magushi was in occupation of the disputed parcel of land with the permission of Bukombe Kihongwe, she could not have acquired title to the disputed parcel of land by adverse possession. Hence, she had no title to which her daughter could have inherited after her death. In such circumstances, Holo Kwande had no title to the disputed parcel of land which she could sell to Jumanne Mazebele, the appellant.*

We learn from the two cases above that to be able to prove adverse possession of land, the following elements need be established: first, possession must be actual, meaning that the adverse possessor must physically occupy the land in dispute. Actual occupancy means the ordinary use of the land including any actual visible means, which gives notice of exclusion from the property to the true owner or to the public. In other words, any act that suggests control over the land by a person other than the true owner may prove actual possession for the purpose of adverse possession, for example, cultivating the land, planting permanent trees or erecting a building on the land. In the absence of any of such acts the defence of adverse possession on the part of the defendant cannot arise. Second, possession must be continuous for the statutory period of 12 years, that is to say, the adverse possessor of the land must remain himself in possession and control of the land for the entire statutory period of limitation. This is necessary for the easy accounting of the limitation time. Third, possession must be exclusive meaning that the adverse possessor of the land must do so by first claiming right over the land in question, and secondly must have the intention to exclude others, including the true owner and the public over that specific piece of land. Intention is a mental element and is captured by the maxim *animus possidendi*, meaning the intent to exclude the world at large. Fourth, possession must be hostile, that is, the occupation of the land must be without permission or agreement on the part of the original occupier and the defendant. The Court of Appeal of Tanzania,[493] once stated that, "In adverse possession there must be an act, or conduct on or in relation to the property which is inconsistent with the rights of the owner and which is not authorised by the owner". The effect of permission or agreement is to entitle the original owner to claim the right to land despite the fact that 12 years may have passed, and the defendant shall be taken to have been on the land as a tenant at

493 See *Jackson Reuben Maro v Hubert Sebastian*, Court of Appeal of Tanzania at Arusha, Civil Appeal No. 84 of 2004 (Unreported), at p. 11.

will.[494] Finally, possession must have an object, meaning, a person against whom the claimant claims to possess land in adverse to. This element was well discussed in the case of *Mwalimu Omari and Ahmed Baguo v Omari A. Bilali.*[495] The case involved a dispute between the appellants and the respondent over a piece of land. The respondent claimed to be the lawful holder of Plot No. 60 Block E, Magomeni area in the City of Dar es Salaam, having been granted the right of occupancy over that Plot by the land allocation authority. The appellants, on the other hand, stated that they had a title over the plot in dispute by adverse possession, after having been in uninterrupted possession and control of the said plot since March 1965. They therefore submitted that the respondent's alleged right of occupancy for a term of thirty-three years effective from 1st July 1978 cannot legally operate to extinguish their claim in adverse possession. Addressing the matter on adverse possession the Court of Appeal of Tanzania held that:

> *As we indicated at the beginning of this judgment, the appellant's claim to this plot was grounded on adverse possession. The pleadings are silent as to whom the appellants held this plot in adverse because adverse possession must always have an object.*[496]

Reading the quote above it is simple to note that when the court says adverse possession must have an object, it means that there must be the original occupier of the land to whom the subsequent occupier holds possession in adverse. It is important to state, that in Tanzania, no person can claim adverse possession in relation to the government's land.[497] The two case of *Jayantilal P. Rajan v City Council of Dar es Salaam*[498] and *Pravinnchandra Mohanlal Mevada and Two Others v Muhimbili Medical Centre and Another*[499] support this observation. The background of the latter case, for example, was that the applicants sued the respondents in

494 See *Mkakofia Meriananga v Asha Ndisia* (1969) HCD no. 204. In this case, a person was allowed to claim back the land in 30 years later after the same was, by permission, given to the other person to use.

495 Court of Appeal of Tanzania, at Dar es Salaam, Civil Appeal No. 19 of 1996 (Unreported). The case is substantially discussed in Chapter Two above.

496 *Ibid*, p. 6.

497 See section 38 (a) of the *Law of Limitation Act* [Cap. 89 R.E 2002].

498 [1983] TLR 385 (HC).

499 Court of Appeal of Tanzania at Dar es Salaam, Civil Appeal No. 106 of 2001 (Unreported). See also *Abdallah Chapila v Mwinyigoha & Others* (1965) L.C.C.A.D/30/65.

the High Court[500] seeking, *inter alia*, a declaration that the applicants were the owners of the suit premises by reason of adverse possession. The second respondent's averment was to the effect that he was the owner of the premises. The applicants raised a preliminary objection that the second respondent was time barred for the reason that it was more than 30 years when the respondent raised a claim, and that he should not be heard as the matter involved land, which is time barred under the *Law of Limitation Act*. The applicants lost the case both in the High Court and the Court of Appeal of Tanzania. It was stated by the Court of Appeal of Tanzania that:

> *From the record, what the applicants were seeking in the suit was a declaration that they were the owners of the premises by reason of adverse possession. On the other hand, the second respondent claimed that he was the owner of the suit premises because it was allocated to him by the government. On such facts I do not think that limitation comes into play. In such circumstances where one of the parties claims ownership over the premises by virtue of adverse possession, and the other, also claims ownership because it was allocated to him by the Government, I do not think that limitation arises.*[501]

Land Acquisition by Inheritance

Historically and traditionally, inheritance has been the commonest means of acquiring land for the obvious reasons: the process of application and grant by the state has not only been a foreign concept to the majority of citizens but also it has always involved procedures and costs unfriendly to the common man. Again, purchasing land in the highly competitive market is only open to the well-to-do, leaving the majority poor as onlookers. For the two main reasons above, the majority of people appear to have no option other than to keep their hands folded, waiting to inherit land after the death of their beloved family members. However, inheritance is not an easy venture. Scarcity of the family or clan lands due to population growth, and the nature of extended families may be marked as factors that have created a rough road to inheritance. Although the law is in place to regulate and control inheritance, the practice thereof is not so smooth in the field[502].

---

500 Civil Case No. 334 of 1990.

501 See the ruling of the case at p. 5.

502 See a detailed discussion about inheritance in Chapter 5 below.

Land Acquisition by Gift

A person's land is his own property. He can dispose of it in any manner he likes, including offering it *inter vivos* to another person of his choice subject to conditions and limitations as may be prescribed by law. Where a person acquires land by way of an unconditional gift, the land becomes his as if he was allocated the same or purchased it from the market. In other words, his title cannot be inferior only for the reason that the land is a gift. Unconditional gift *inter vivos* confers good, absolute and irrevocable title. The position at common law in respect of gifts, which the Tanzania land law subscribes to, is that:

> *It is on legal and equitable principles clear that a person sui juris acting freely, and with sufficient knowledge, ought to have and has power to make, in binding and effectual manner, a voluntary gift of any part of his property, whether capable or incapable of manual delivery, whether in possession or reversion, and howsoever circumstances.*[503]

Whenever a dispute arises between persons over land where one person claims to have obtained it by way of a gift, the court of law will consider the following issues in order to decide who of the litigants has got a better title over the disputed land: whether the donor of the gift was *sui juris* and competent to give the disputed land; whether there is sufficient evidence of the donation of the disputed land; whether the act of giving was not induced by fraud, undue influence, mistake or misrepresentation, or was not tainted with illegality; whether the gift was unconditional, and; whether the donee of the gift has registered or transferred, in his own name, the interest in land in accordance with the provisions of the *Land Registration Act* where such interests are compulsorily registrable. History is full of cases through which persons have approached the court of law for remedies arising out of disputes involving land obtained by way of gift. A traverse through the cases of *Salum Mateyo v Mohamed Mateyo*[504] and *Mkamangi Elifuraha v Mwinyishehe Mwinyishehe*[505] bears the best testimony. The former case was decided in favour of the donee who had registered the land in his own name after it was donated to him by the adverse party. Likewise, the latter case was decided in favour of the donee after it was proved by means of a document (a deed of gift) that the land was donated to her

---

503 See *Halsbury's Laws of England*, 3rd Edition, Volume 18, at p. 366.

504 [1987] TLR 111 (HC).

505 [1991] TLR 191 (CA).

by the donor. Of many such other cases founded on land acquisition by gift, the case of *Leyla Nassoro Kiruka v Muakwe Mohamed Maukwe & Another*[506] may not be left out of the record. The parties disputed over the ownership of house No. 35 on Plot No. 99, Block "D" in Turiani Street, Magomeni area, Dar es Salaam. The recorded facts indicated that the house belonged to X, (deceased at the time of litigation) who, being the stepmother of, and having lived very amicably with, the defendants for about thirty years, donated the house to the defendants through a deed of gift. The plaintiff, being then the administrator of the estate of X, strongly disputed the deed of gift by challenging its genuineness. She alleged that the same was a forgery. Furthermore, the plaintiff stated that if X ever donated the house to the defendants, she had revoked the donation during her lifetime. On the other hands, the defendants insisted that the document was genuine and that X had donated the house to them of her free will, and the she never revoked the said donation.

The court resolved the matter in favour of the defendants after believing their story, which was supported by the evidence from other sources, including an advocate to whom X had told that she was giving the house to the defendants. We submit that good practice would encourage parties to have deeds of gift executed properly and witnessed in order to avoid unnecessary litigation of this nature.

Co-occupancy and Partition

Co-occupancy Defined

The concept of co-occupancy is used in relation to two or more persons who own property jointly or in common. According to the *Land Act*, the term co-occupancy is defined to mean, "The occupation of land held for a right of occupancy or a lease by two or more undivided shares and may be either joint occupancy or occupancy in common"[507]. Co-occupancy, therefore, appears in two forms: joint occupancy and; occupancy in common. In the jurisprudence of English land law, the words joint tenancy and tenancy in common are employed to connote the two forms of co-occupancy as well.

The principles governing co-occupancy are of great importance in the administration of land law, especially so in the following situations: when a co-occupier dies, and; when one co-occupier intends to dispose

506 High Court of Tanzania (Land Division) at Dar es Salaam, Land Case No. 10 of 2003 (Unreported).

507 Cap. 113, Section 159 (1).

or purports to have disposed his interest in the property under co-occupancy. In the event of the occurrence of any of these situations, there is a great chance for the eruption of disputes between the co-occupiers, or between a co-occupier and a third party. For example, if one co-occupier dies, the question that may arise for determination by the court is whether a remaining co-occupier is entitled to hold the land in severalty, meaning to hold it alone without any interference from a third party. Likewise, when a co-occupier intends to dispose, or when he actually disposes his interest in the property, the question that may arise is whether he is holding the property concurrently with others, and; whether, under the circumstance, he is free to dispose the same without involving a co-occupier or other co-occupiers. In order to resolve such issues finally and conclusively, there is always a need to distinguish, at the outset, the two forms of co-occupancy, namely, joint occupancy and occupancy in common. This is because of the fact that different principles apply differently to each of these two forms of co-occupancy. It is on record that:

> *There are important distinctions between these two forms of ownership. In the first place, a joint tenancy arises where land is conveyed to two or more persons and no words of severance, such as 'in equal shares' are used in the grant. Thus a grant: 'To A and B', or 'To A and B jointly' creates a joint tenancy, while a conveyance 'To A and B equally', or 'To A and B in common' creates a tenancy in common. Whether land is granted in such a way as to suggest that the grantor intends the tenants to have distinct shares, even though the land remains physically undivided, a tenancy in common arises. Words which show this intention of distinct shares are known as words of severance.*[508]

Joint occupancy is pegged on two main doctrines: the doctrine of the right of survivorship, or *jus accrescendi* as it is sometimes known to lawyers, and the doctrine of four unities. The doctrine of the right of survivorship, on one hand, seeks to explain the legal position of the rights of a surviving joint occupier at the death of another joint occupier. The doctrine provides that when a joint occupier dies, all the interests in the property pass to the surviving joint occupier. If there are more than one surviving occupier, the right of survivorship continues until there is but one survivor who then holds the property as a sole owner. The *jus accrescendi* takes precedence over any disposition including

508 See BARKER, David & PADFIELD, Colin, (1996): *Law*, 9th Edition, Madesimple Books, at p. 250.

a disposition made by a joint occupier through a will. This principle applies even if a joint occupier dies intestate. It is from this that we come to a general conclusion that a joint occupier holds nothing and yet he holds the whole. The law in Tanzania states very clearly that, "If one or two or more joint owners of an estate or interest dies, his name shall be deleted from the land register on the application of any interested person, accompanied by proof of death."[509] The *Land Act,* in particular, provides that, where the land is occupied jointly under the right of occupancy or lease no occupier is entitled to any separate share in the land, and that on death of a joint occupier, his interest shall vest in the surviving occupier or occupiers jointly.[510] The law, therefore, allows a joint occupier to transfer his interest *inter vivos* to all other occupiers, but prohibits him from doing so to a third party. Any attempt to do so shall be declared to be invalid.[511] It is important to note that, unlike in England where the law allows corporations to acquire and hold land jointly as if they were individuals,[512] the law in Tanzania restricts the right to own land jointly only to spouses, and that persons other than spouses can hold the same with the leave of the court.[513] The doctrine of the four unities, on the other hand, seeks to explain the elements that constitute and define a joint occupancy. It means that the court shall look at certain elements (the four unities) in order to establish whether or not a joint occupancy subsists between the litigants. These are: the unity of possession; the unity of interests; the unity of title, and; the unity of time. Explained very briefly, the unity of possession shall be said to exist when each occupier is entitled to the possession of the land as are his co-occupiers. It means further that no one among them can raise his finger and point to any part of the property as his own to the exclusion of others, and also no one can dispose any interest thereof. The *Land Act* supports this position as it provides that, "disposition may be made only by all the joint occupiers".[514] The unity of interests is established when each joint occupier has the same interests in terms of extent, nature and duration. For example, in cases where the occupiers are entitled to

509 Section 69 (1), [Cap. 334 R.E 2002].

510 Section 159 (4) (b).

511 Section 159 (4) (c).

512 See the English *Bodies Corporation (Joint Tenancy) Act, 1899.*

513 Section 159 (8).

514 Section 159 (4) (a).

rentapayment, the same is divided equally between or among them. The unity of title, again, is established when each joint occupier is entitled to the claim of title under the same act (e.g., conveyance) or document (e.g., through a legal will). Lastly, the unity of time is established when the interests of each occupier shall have vested to that occupier at the same time with others, the exceptions being for example where land is conveyed to the use of "A for his life with the remainder to the use of B's children". In such a case, then, each child of B born in A's life acquires the vested interest at birth.

Occupancy in Common differs greatly from joint occupancy on the following grounds: first, the co-occupiers in common hold undivided shares in the property, meaning that each occupier in common has a distinct and fixed share in the property which has not yet been divided. Secondly, there is no *jus accrescendi*. It means that when a co-occupier in common dies his interests pass under the will or under the rules of intestacy to his survivors since such occupier has the freedom to dispose his shares according to his wishes. The *Land Act* requires that an instrument, which is made in favour of two or more persons, must show the share of each occupier if they are occupiers in common.[515] It also states that on the death of an occupier, his share shall be treated as part of his estate.[516] Thirdly, only the unity of possession is required to show that each of the occupiers is as much entitled to the *physical possession of every part of the property as every other occupier. As to w*hether an occupier in common has the right to dispose of his undivided share during his life time, the case of *Mutual Benefits Limited v Patel and Another*[517] as well as section 159 (6) of the *Land Act* state the legal position. In this case the appellants lodged a *caveat*[518] claiming for interest as a lessee over a certain land belonging to the respondents, and praying for an order to prohibit absolutely any dealing with that land. The respondents successfully applied to the High Court for an order to remove the *caveat* from the Register. On further appeal by the appellants to the East African Court of Appeal, the issue for determination was

515 Section 159 (3) (b).

516 Section 159 (5).

517 (1972) EA 496.

518 Section 2 of the *Land Act* defines a "caveat" to mean "a notice in the form of an entry on a register that no action of a specified nature in relation to the right of occupancy in respect of which the notice has been entered may be taken without first informing the person who gave the notice". A caveat is normally lodged to the Registrar of Titles under the provision of section 78 of the *Land Registration Act*.

whether the documents on which the appellant company relied proved a right in the appellant's company to call on the respondents to grant a lease to it. The Court held that it is of the essence of tenancy in common that owners can deal with the titles to their shares, but that possession is common to them and cannot be by one alone. From this the Court dismissed the appeal by holding that Patel as a co-owner had no ostensible authority to enter into agreements to lease the godowns which would be binding to the other tenants in common. The Court's position was later legislated into the *Land Act* to provide that:

> *No occupier in common shall deal with his undivided share in favour of any person other than another occupier in common, except with the consent in writing or in any other manner which signifies clearly that the consent is given freely and without undue pressure, of the remaining occupiers, but such consent shall not be unreasonably withheld.*[519]

The two authorities above suggest two things in respect to occupancy in common. Firstly, an occupier of land in common with others can dispose his undivided share in the property after he has sought the consent of other co-occupiers. Secondly, an occupier of land in common with others can dispose his share freely if the consent from others is unreasonably withheld. What is unreasonable shall depend on the facts and circumstances of each case.

Common Law, Equity, the Land Act, and Co-occupancy

During the development of the English common law (during the feudal era) land was not only a property but a sacred property. It means that in common law, when the estate was granted to two or more persons, other than a husband and wife, and without the language explicitly describing the type of ownership, the estate was said to be held in joint occupancy unless either one of the unities was missing or it was granted with the words of severance such as "to be divided amongst," or "in equal shares between." The common law preferred a joint occupancy for the obvious reasons, one being the operation of the doctrine of *jus accrescendi.* Since the doctrine made it more likely that the land could ultimately vest in a single occupier who would then enjoy the fruits thereof alone, it means, therefore, that occupiers bided their time waiting for such opportunity to come. Equally important, it was considered simple to investigate a single title of the occupiers than it was to investigate the titles of every occupant

519 Section 159 (6).

in common ownership. Occupancy in common was seen as capable of creating more problems where, for example, an occupant in common died leaving his share to a large number of persons. Their consents and signatures would be difficult to obtain in order to effect a conveyance.

Equity, on its part, was against the operation of the doctrine of *jus accrescendi,* and, therefore, favoured occupancy in common. Let it be stated, here, that "equity" of that time is equated with "human rights" of our times. The principle that prevailed in equity is that "equality is equity". This carries with it the notions of treating the equal equally and the unequal unequally. By applying this principle it would be expected, for instance, that if two persons purchased property by contributing unequal shares, the property would be divided proportionally to each according to his advances, and only this would be fair and just. In other words, equity considered occupancy in common as being ideal in business transactions including partnerships, trusts, and mortgage transactions.

The *Land Act*, for all purposes and intentions, favours occupancy in common. We learn this from the provision of section 159 (8) which makes the right to occupy land jointly only available to spouses. The section requires any other joint occupancy to be made only with the leave of the court.

Determination of Co-Occupancy

Co-occupancy, if joint, can be converted to occupancy in common, or brought to an end, as is the case of occupancy in common. This can be effected through one of the following ways: one, determination of joint occupancy by a deed of severance. This is where the joint occupiers execute an instrument in a prescribed form[520] signifying that they agree to sever the joint occupancy and register the same as occupancy in common in the register of joint occupiers and occupiers in common.[521] The effect of a deed of severance is to convert joint occupancy into occupancy in common. Two, determination of co-occupancy by transfer or disposition of the right of occupancy, or part of it. Disposition of the right of occupancy, if made by all joint occupiers to one sole joint occupier or to a third party,[522] has the effect of bringing the joint occupancy to an end. But if disposition is made only over part of the property[523] enabling

520 See Form No. 61 of the Land Forms Regulations, 2001.

521 Section 159 (7) of the *Land Act* [Cap. 113 R.E 2002].

522 Section 159 (4) (a) of the *Land Act* [Cap. 113 R.E 2002].

523 *Ibid*, section 159 (4) (c).

one occupier to have a bigger share of the interest, then joint occupancy is converted to occupancy in common. Three, determination of co-occupancy by partition of property occupied in common. Before the coming in of the *Land Act*, courts invoked the provision of the English *Partition Act* of 1868 and 1876 to administer partition.[524] Now, partition is governed by section 162 of the *Land Act*. In a situation, for example, where the occupiers in common are disunited, one or more of them may apply to the Registrar with or without the consent of others for the order of partition[525]. The law does not make the right to apply for partition available only to the co-occupiers, but also to any person in whose favour an order has been made for the sale of an undivided share in the property in the execution of a decree.[526] The Registrar has the duty, upon an application for partition being made, to hear the applicant and any other co-occupiers who may wish to appear and be heard, before he makes an order for partition.[527] Note that partition of land which is mortgaged cannot be effected without the consent of the lender.[528] A right of appeal against the order of the Registrar by an aggrieved party is available to the High Court under the provisions of the *Land Registration Act*.[529] Four, determination of co-occupancy by sale of the property held under co-occupancy and distribution of the proceeds of the sale. This may happen if the property, the subject matter of an application for partition, is incapable of partition or if partition would adversely affect the proper use of the land.[530] The application is made to the court and the order for sale shall, therefore, be granted by court on conditions that the court shall deem fit in the interest of justice.

The case of *Omari Mohamedi v Awadhi Abdallah*[531] is an illustration of the practice of sale of property held under co-occupancy. The facts of the case are that the parties, cousins as they were, jointly bought a piece of land and jointly constructed thereon a house. They divided the

---

524 See *Aggrawal v Dhillon* (1969) HCD No. 167.

525 Section 162 (2) (a) of the Land Act [Cap. 113 R.E 2002].

526 *Ibid*, section 162 (2) (b).

527 *Ibid*, section 162 (3).

528 *Ibid*, section 165 (1).

529 See section 102 of the Act.

530 See section 164 (1) of the *Land Act* [Cap. 113 R.E 2002].

531 [1992] TLR 35 (HC).

said house equally and each occupied some rooms with relatives. Later on they were in a serious wrangle over the house. The plaintiff went to court seeking for the order of sale by public auction so as to let the parties divide the proceeds of the sale. He prayed, in the alternative, for the order that any of the parties be allowed to purchase the share of the other party and that a party whose share is purchased should vacate the house. The court made its finding that the defendant was not a party to blame for the conflict that had risen between him and the plaintiff. For that reason, the court decided the case by giving orders and stating the grounds for such orders that:

> *I think it is then for this court to adopt the fairest method of dealing with the house as between the parties. Selling it at a public auction would certainly render the defendant homeless, for no fault, as held, of his. The plaintiff on the other hand has another house and does not live in the suit house. I am of the view then that selling the house by auctioning it will result in grave injustice to the defendant.*
>
> *There is a method which both the parties agree to... The method is the division of the house in terms of its value, and then giving the parties an option of purchasing the other's share and the one whose share has been purchased to move out of the house. The plaintiff says that if this is the option adopted, he should be the one to be given the opportunity to buy...*
>
> *I think this method is fair. As I have said the plaintiff pleads it in his plaint as an alternative relief. He is bound by his pleadings and he cannot now wriggle out of them as he now attempts to do. Also I do not see why he should be the one to be given the first option to buy. As I have said the defendant is not to blame for the conflict which has arisen in relation to the house. Also he is the one now in occupation of the house. I think it would be fair therefore to let him see if he can purchase the plaintiff's share first and if he fails then the plaintiff should be given the chance to purchase the defendant's share. In the result then, the house is to be divided in two shares in terms of value. Then the defendant is to be given the first chance to purchase the plaintiff's share. If he fails to do so within three months from the date of the delivery of this judgment, then the plaintiff is to purchase the defendant's share.*

> *I have made the above order because I am satisfied on the evidence that the parties cannot possibly continue to co-own the house. They are in serious conflict over it now, and it is best that one of them ceases to be associated with it altogether. This will disengage them from further contacts over the house, which contacts have been the reason for the present conflict between them.*

It is submitted that the principles developed in determining this case are ideal and should guide other courts faced with a similar situation. The case was decided on the principle of fairness, which accommodated the right to land of the defendant who would have been left landless if the court had reached a different conclusion.

Rights and Obligations of the Holder of a Right of Occupancy

Land is something so lucrative as long as it remains the basic means of survival, not only for human beings, but also for all fauna and flora. It is for this reason that a son is prepared to raise his hand against his father or against his brother, even at the cost of blood, in order to protect his interest in this most valuable asset. It has earlier been noted that history is full of protracted hostilities, some leading to bloody wars because of land. We also witness endless litigation in our courts of law because of land. All these happen because of the rights which are conferred to, and obligations which are imposed on, the holder of a right of occupancy. It should always be remembered that in Tanzania all land is public land vested in the President as trustee for and on behalf of all the citizens of Tanzania[532]. The citizens do not own land as if it was a chattel. What they hold is simply a right of occupancy which is limited only to the right to use and occupy the land.

A holder of a right of occupancy over a piece of land has the right to use and occupy that land for various socio-economic reasons. He can use the land for residential purposes through building a house or houses on the land, for use as a residence for himself and his family. To most holders residential areas are also used for ritual activities such as worshiping and burying of the dead. In the alternative, the holder of a right of occupancy can use the land for commercial purposes by establishing on the land commercial projects of all known categories, ranging from those in the nature of social services, such as schools, health, and religious centres, to those which are purely economic, such as shops and recreational centres. In another alternative, the holder of a right of occupancy can use the land for agricultural purposes

532 Section 4 (1) of the *Land Act*, [Cap. 113 R.E 2002].

through crop cultivation and animal husbandry whether on small or large scale depending on the size of the said land and capital involved. Furthermore, holder of land has the right to transfer his interest in the land, for example, by selling it in the market or leasing it or by creating a mortgage to secure loans from financial institutions. All these are regulated by law. Equally important, the holder of a right of occupancy has a right to adequate and prompt compensation when his land is taken for whatever reason, including compulsory acquisition by the state. Lastly, the holder of a right of occupancy has a right of action in tort against trespassers into his land, where he can sue for vacant possession, mesne profits, and damages.

In addition to all the rights that a holder of a right of occupancy may exercise over his land, the law recognises certain other rights which extend over the land of the neighbour. These are rights known in law as servitudes and may take the form of easements or *profits à prendre*.

However, as it has already been stated in the preface, rights and duties co-exist. This means that the holder of a right of occupancy has, over and above rights, legal obligations imposed upon him by virtue of the right of occupancy that he holds. One of the basic obligations is the obligation to occupy and use the land in accordance with the law on development conditions, including the obligation to pay property taxes[533]. We say this is basic because failure to observe development conditions which attach to the right of occupancy may lead to immediate revocation of the same by the President[534]. Another important obligation is the obligation to dispose his interest in land in accordance with the law on transfer the moment disposition is preferred. Again, failure to observe the law on transfer may lead, not only to the invalidation of the transfer, but also to revocation of a right of occupancy.[535] Equally important, the holder has the obligation to respect all contractual obligations that he may create with third parties, such as financial institutions in case of a mortgage involving land, the subject matter of a right of occupancy. The omission of this noble duty may lead the holder into being sued for damages on one hand, and his land being sold by the mortgagee on the other hand. Yet another obligation is the obligation to occupy and use the land in accordance with the law of the neighbour by respecting the rights of the neighbours to quite enjoyment of their lands. Failing to do this, the holder

533 Proprty tax is payable as per the provisions of, among other, the *Local Governments (Finance) Act, 1982* and the *Urban Authorities (Rating) Act, 1983*..

534 Section 45 (1) and (2) (v) of the *Land Act*, 1999 [Cap. 113 R.E 2002].

535 *Ibid*, Section 45 (2) (iv).

of a right of occupancy may be sued for damages in actions of trespass and nuisance, among others. Finally, the holder has the obligation to cooperate with the authorities in case his right of occupancy is acquired by the President for public interest, and when the government has fulfilled its obligation under the provisions of the *Land Acquisition Act, 1967* including payment of fair and prompt compensation. The same obligation shall arise when the Minister exercises his powers under the *Land Act* to create a public right of way in the form of a wayleave or communal right of way.[536] The call for observing this duty stems from the obvious fact that all land in Tanzania is public land entrusted to the President for the benefit of all citizens. For this reason, a holder of a right of occupancy may not raise his voice high and vehemently oppose a lawful presidential acquisition of land where the land is secured for the common benefit of the citizens.

Easement and Analogous Rights

Meaning and Classification of Easement

The law governing easement in Tanzania is the *Land Act*. Although the Act does dos not define the term "easement" clearly, easement is known in the land law jurisprudence to be "a nonpossessory interest in the land of another person or legal entity".[537] In other words, an easement is the right of a holder of a right of occupancy to use or to restrict the use of the land of another person in the same way. According to the *Land Act*[538] the rights that are capable of being created by an easement are: any right to do something over, under or upon the servient land; or any right that something should not be done; or any right to require the occupier of the servient land to do something over, under or upon the land; and any right to graze stock on the servient land. It follows that, when easements permit the use of the land of another person in certain specific ways we say they are affirmative easements, and when they restrict a person's use of his own land we say they are negative easements. The most important and, therefore, common easements include: the right of way including the right to walk across the land of another for ingress to or egress from the dominant land; the right of light or air which constitutes the rights to prohibit the owner of the servient land from blocking the light from reaching the adjoining land; the right of drainage, and; the right to the support of the building.

---

536 The Minister responsible for land matters has such powers under section 151 of the Act.

537 See BURKE, Barlow, *et al.* (2004): *Fundamentals of Property Law*, p. 619.

538 Section 144 (1) (a) to (d).

Pre-requisite for the creation of an easement

An easement may be created where the following features exist: firstly, there must be two parcels of land called the dominant land and the servient land; secondly there must be separate ownership of the dominant and servient lands, that is, both must not belong to the same owner, and; thirdly, the easement must be capable of forming the subject of matter of grant, for example, by way of a deed. This means that there must be a grantor of easement (owner of the servient land) and a grantee (owner of the dominant land). The *Land Act* defines "dominant land" to be "the land for the benefit of which any easement is created, and "servient land" to be "the land of the person by whom an easement is created".[539] To put it more graphically, if "**A**", the owner of land on Plot X, grants a right of way to "**B**", the owner of land on Plot Y, then "B" has an easement. Plot Y becomes a dominant land, while Plot X is a servient land. An easement in this sense is, in relation to the dominant land, referred to as "benefiting" that land and is, in relation to servient land, referred to as "burdening" that land.[540] Note also that when easements benefit the owners of adjacent lands (dominant lands) they are called appurtenant easements, and when they benefit persons who are not necessarily owners of the dominant lands they are called easements in gross. Ordinarily, appurtenant easements are treated as integral parts of the dominant land, meaning that when the land is transferred from one person to the other, the easement passes along with it, even without an express grant of "appurtenances". The important aspect in all relations created by easements is the general rule that if an easement is appurtenant to a particular parcel of the land, any extension thereof to another parcel (nondominant land) shall be construed to be a misuse of the easement. This is also the case when there is an attempt to convey the benefit of appurtenant easement to a person who has no interest in the dominant land. However, when an easement is created by grant or reservation and the instrument creating the easement does not limit the use to be made of it (e.g when it is not created for "*a single family only*" or for "*private roadway only*", then the easement may be used for any purpose to which the dominant land may be devoted. In other words an easement created by a general grant without words limiting it to any particular use of the dominant land shall not be affected by any reasonable change in the use of the dominant land, for example,

539 Section 145 (1).

540 Section 145 (2).

from domestic to commercial use of the land. However, no use of the easement may be made if it is completely different from that established at the time of its creation and whose effect is to impose an additional burden upon the servient land. Equally, the owner of the dominant land has the right to make reasonable improvement of the easement so long as such improvement does not unreasonably increase the burden upon the servient land.

Creation and Termination of Easements

Under the common law system, an easement may be created through various ways. The most common ways include: creation by express grant or reservation through a deed; creation by implication through the doctrine of implied grant, and creation by prescription through lapse of time. Creation of an easement by express grant or reservation takes place when the owner of servient land (the grantor) executes a deed agreeing to let his land to be used in a particular way for the benefit of the owner of the dominant land (grantee). Such an easement normally contains the conditions to be observed by the grantee including the duration of the easement. It terminates at the expiration of the term for which it was granted, unless there is a contrary intention of the parties thereof. The same can come to an end through other processes including: merger; release; abandonment; forfeiture for misuse; changed conditions, and; adverse possession.

Creation by implication comes in when it is shown that there has been a pre-existing use of an easement prior to the conveyance of the property (easement implied by past use) or that the use of the easement is essential to the beneficial enjoyment of the land conveyed (easement by necessity). Such implication is commonly available in relation to landlocked property with the overt problem of access. In such an eventuality, the court shall infer the intent of the parties to create an easement but only if the following set of facts may be established: that there was prior common ownership of the dominant and servient lands; that subsequently, there was transfer of one of the estates by the common grantor creating the lack of access to the other estate, and; that there is necessity of an easement for making beneficial use of the transferred estate. It is important to note, here, that what is looked at is the necessity for an easement, not mere inconvenience that may be created against the owner of the dominant land. The test to be applied in order to infer the existence of an easement is whether an easement is required in order to provide reasonable access to the property or whether without it the land cannot be effectively used. As it may be observed, the implication is very strict, the rationale being attached to public policy which encourages productive use of the land, and discourages buyers from purchasing land without paying sufficient attention to problems of ingress to or egress from the land. Termination of implied easement may come through either of the processes discussed above, but most important is when the necessity that brought about its implication is no longer in existence.

Easement by prescription (or prescriptive easement) may be created under the conditions applicable in all cases of adverse possession. A party claiming entitlement to prescriptive easement needs to demonstrate that he took the easement under a claim of right (without the permission or licence of his adverse), that the use of the easement has been open and continuous and uninterrupted for the period of prescription, and that the owner of the servient land had knowledge of the use of the easement and acquiesced to it.[541]

Creation of an easement under the *Land Act* may be effected only through express grant[542] or reservation[543] by an occupier of the land or a lessor in the right of occupancy. The Act requires the instrument creating an easement to clearly specify: the nature of the easement and any conditions, limitations, and restrictions subject to which it is granted; the period of time for which the easement is granted; the land or part of it which is burdened by the easement, and the land benefited by the easement.[544] Unlike the common law which recognises prescriptive easements, the *Land Act* does not recognise, at all, any easement or any right in the nature of an easement that may be capable of being acquired by any presumption of a grant from long and uninterrupted use.[545] The exception to this general rule is when the right of way for persons and for stock is acquired. This is deemed to be property, and, therefore, confers title to the users.[546]

---

541 See the facts and decision of the court in the cases of *Bridle v Ruby and Another* [1988] 3 WLR 191; 3 ALL ER 64, and; *Mills and Another v Silver and Another* [1991] WLR 324; 1 ALL ER 449.

542 Section 146 (1).

543 Section 146 (2).

544 Section 146 (3).

545 Section 146 (7).

546 Section 146 (8).

Analogous Rights

Unlike the common law, which recognises implied easement by necessity, the *Land Act* provides the occupier of a land with some "analogous rights" in the nature of an "access order".[547] To be entitled to the right of access order, a person must: be occupying a landlocked land; apply for the access order in a court of law; and serve a notice of such application upon all persons having interest in the land which may be affected by the granting of the order, including the local authority having jurisdiction in the area where the landlocked land is located. However, the court has discretionary powers to grant or not to grant the access order to the applicant regarding attention being paid to, *inter alia*: the hardship that may be caused to the applicant by the refusal of the access order[548] and subject to the conditions that the court may deem fit to fix.[549] Once an access order is granted, it has the force of law as if it were an easement.[550]

It is very important to note, that the benefit of an easement or analogous rights under the *Land Act* may be enjoyed, during the term of their existence, by the occupier of the land or his successors in title[551]. However, a person to whom a grant of an easement or analogous rights has been made has the right to cancel the same, else it will subsist until it is terminated in accordance with the provisions of the *Land Act, 1999*.[552]

547 See Section 143 (3) and 148.

548 Section 148 (4).

549 Section 148 (5).

550 Section 148 (6).

551 Section 149.

552 Section 150

Chapter Four

Land Delivery Syetems: Disposition of Land or Interests in Land

> … There is now no freehold tenure in Tanzania. All land is vested in the Republic. So land held under a right of occupancy is not a freely disposable or marketable commodity like a car. Its disposition is subject to the consent of the superior and paramount landlord as provided in the relevant Land Regulations.
>
> - Court of Appeal of Tanzania -[553]

553 *Nitin Coffee Estate Ltd and 4 Others v United Engineering Works Ltd and Another* [1988] TLR 203 (CA).

This chapter discusses the process involved in the disposition or transfer of interest in land. Although the definition of disposition is very broad under the *Land Act*,[554] the discussion in the chapter is confined to a few forms of disposition, namely, sale, lease and mortgage.

Land Transfer by Sale

Sale and the History of Sale of Land in Tanzania

The term "sale" as used in relation to a right of occupancy means a transfer of an interest in or over land subject to the conditions attached to a granted right of occupancy[555]. The term "sale" is often used interchangeably with other terms such as transfer or conveyance. As it is noted in Chapter Two above, the pre-colonial societies never knew the commercialization of land. Each member would access land and continue to occupy it as he needed it. The question of land being seen as a commodity in the market may, therefore, be traced along some historical developments. Before the new land law in the form of the two *Land Acts*, the holder's power to dispose land by sale was customarily and statutorily controlled and, therefore, somewhat restricted.

As regards control under customary law, the records show, for example, that there was clan control over the sale of the clan land[556] under the natives laws of many, if not all, customary communities in Tanzania. That is to say, under the customary law, clan land was supposed to be sold to a clan member, and not to a stranger (non clan member). The occupier of a clan land could only sell the land to a non clan member if none of his clan member was able to purchase the land, and after seeking the consent and approval of the other clan members. It means that if a clan land was sold to a stranger without the consent of the clan elders, it stood to be redeemed by the owner or by any other clan member if the owner could not redeem it. The case of *Nicolaus Komba v Kondrad Komba*[557] supports this fact.

This kind of restriction was intended to promote social harmony by discouraging intruders from occupying clan land. Until today,

554 See section 2 of the Act.

555 The definition of the term is provided for under section 2 of the *Land Act* as amended *by Land (Amendment) Act* No.2 of 2004.

556 The concept of clan land was defined by Mwalusanya J (as he then was) in the case of *Jibu Sakilu v Petro Miumbi* (1993) TLR 75 (HC) to mean a "land that has been inherited successfully without interruption from the great grandfathers or from a grandfather by members of the same clan."

557 [1988] TLR 172 (HC).

this remains the position of the customary law of the Haya because, according to Cory and Hartnoll[558], it is a rule that a man must inform his nearest paternal relatives before he undertakes any transaction over the land with an outsider[559], and that should the relatives concerned not be so informed then they have the right to invalidate the sale by bringing an action against the vendor, who must return the purchase price he received or allow his relatives to do so if he cannot get the money himself.[560] Originally, the customary law required a legal action to nullify the sale to be instituted within three months of the date on which the relatives first heard of the sale.[561] However this was later modified by the Customary Law (Limitation of Proceedings) Rules, 1963[562] which provides for the limitation period to be 12 years[563].

Statutory limitation, on the other hand, was at different levels depending on the nature of the land involved. To begin with, section 11 (1) of the *Land (Law of Property and Conveyances) Ordinance*[564] provided that a disposition of land belonging to a native in favour of a non-native or conferring on a non-native any right over the land of a native shall not be operative unless approved by the Governor. It is not disputed that at independence the term Governor was replaced by the term President, meaning that this legal restriction on disposition of the native land to a non-native was retained in letter and in spirit by the Independent Government of Tanzania. The President was empowered to delegate to any person the powers of approving dispositions made under this law, [565] so that in 1962 the powers and duties of the President were transferred to the Minister for Lands, Forests and Wild Life,[566] and later to the Commissioner for Lands, Assistant Commissioner for Lands and Land

---

558 See CORY, H. and HARTNOLL, M.M., (1945): *Customary Law of the Haya Tribe*, Tanganyika Territory, Frank Cass, London.

559 Paragraph 560 of the rules.

560 Paragraph 561 of the rule.

561 Paragraph 568 of the rules. See also the case of *Lutalaza Biteya v Haji Selemani* [1975] LRT No. 43; *Jeremiah Venant v Clementina Alexander* (1983) TLR 137 (HC).

562 GN No. 311 of 1964.

563 See the case of *Erizeus Rutakubwa v Jason Angero* [1983] TLR 365 (HC), which discusses the issue of limitation of actions to redeem a clan land.

564 Cap.114 of the Law of Tanzania. The Act now stands repealed by the Schedule to the *Land Act*.

565 *Ibid*, section 11(5).

566 See GN No. 478 of 1962.

Officer and other officers in the management of land issues.[567] The effects of this law appeared on two levels. On the first level, the Registrars of documents and titles were required not to register or give effect to any disposition made in contravention of the law on approvals.[568] On the second level, a disposition so made without approval was declared unenforceable in law. This is what happened, for example, in the case of *Mohamed Alladitta v El- Harthi.*[569] In this case, the respondent was a native and holder of a land in Ipuri, Tabora. He agreed to sell the land to the appellant, a non-native. However, the agreement was not approved by the Governor as required by law. The respondent handled the title deeds to the appellant's advocate but later sued for its return. The appellant counter-claimed for specific performance. The High Court allowed the respondent's claim and dismissed the counter claim. Aggrieved by the decision of the High Court, the appellant appealed to the East African Court of Appeal. It was the Court's holding that the whole agreement was caught by the provisions of section 11 and was therefore unenforceable, and that the decision of the High Court was perfectly correct.

This kind of restriction embedded in the above-named law was once positively commended by Akilagpa Sawyerr[570] who happened to say that it was necessary for the protection of the property of natives from exploitation by unscrupulous foreigners. According to Sawyerr, the approving authority was able to investigate, before giving an approval, matters related to: the nature and situation of the land in question, including whether it was developed or not; the condition of the alienee such as his social standing in the community and whether he is amassing too much property and what he is proposing to do with the land; the situation of the alienor, that is, what is he like and why is he disposing his interest in the land, and; whether he will be destitute as a result of the disposition. Besides the above, the author argues that restriction was necessary to safeguard the interests of the natives and also to discourage absentee landlordism.

However the question that may be posed from the human rights camp is: why was the law addressed only to the natives? It is submitted that the law was, to state the obvious, discriminatory in nature as it tended

567 See GN No. 124 of 1963.

568 Section 11 (7).

569 (1955) 22 EACA 84.

570 See SAWYERR, Akilagpa, *op cit.*

only to restrict the natives from enjoying their right to land through free disposition of their property.

The second level of control was that stated by regulation 3 (1) of the Land Regulations of 1948, as amended. The regulation stated that:

> *3-(1) A disposition of a right of occupancy shall not be operative unless it is in writing and unless and until it is approved by the Governor.*

The interpretation of this rule has, for a long time been a moot issue and has engaged the minds of the judiciary in a litany of cases before it was finally settled by the full Bench of the Court of Appeal of Tanzania in the case of *Abualy Alibhai Azizi v Bhatia Brothers Ltd*[571] and later by the *Land Act*. The bone of contention in this case may be traced from, among others, the decision of the Court of Appeal of Tanzania in the case of *Nitin Coffee Estate Ltd and 4 Others v United Engineering Works*[572], whose facts are as follows: the 4th and 5th appellants, shareholders and directors of the 1st and 2nd appellants' companies sold the assets to one Manik, the 2nd respondent in 1984. The assets included two farms held under the right of occupancy. The agreement was made orally, but the respondent was put in the occupation of the farms as the buyer. In 1986, the appellants sought to repudiate the agreement arguing that they did not sell the farm to Manik and that in the alternative if they did, the agreement was not enforceable for lack of writing and consent as required by regulation 3 (1) of the Land Regulations of 1948. The Court of Appeal of Tanzania pointed out that, land held under a right of occupancy is not a freely disposable or marketable commodity like a motor car. Its disposal is subject to the consent of the superior and paramount landlord, as provided for in the relevant Land Regulations. The Court also said that an oral agreement to sell land held under a right of occupancy is inoperative and of no effect in terms of Regulation (1) of the Land Regulations, 1948. The Court went on to say that the doctrine of part performance cannot help as in Tanzania the regulation requires both writing and consent. Finally, the Court held that the respondent must vacate from the two farms and hand over possession of them to the appellants or their nominees, and that the appellants must pay costs that the respondent incurred up to the date of filing the suit and also refund the initial payment made by Manik for the purchase.

---

571 [2000] TLR 288 (CA).

572 [1988] TLR 203 (CA).

At a later time, the Nitin's decision found itself in severe conflict with another decision of the same court in the case of *George Shambwe v National Printing Co. Ltd*[573]. The facts in *George Shambwe's* case were as follows: The appellant was the owner of the house on Plot No. 86 Mkulima Road in Kinondoni. He mortgaged the house to the National Bank of Commerce as a security for a loan. The respondent company, then a lessee of the appellant, entered into an agreement to buy the house, where he was to pay the initial amount to the Bank in order to redeem the mortgage, and the balance to the appellant. The respondent executed part of the agreement by advancing some amount of money to the Bank but which money was not enough to redeem the house. The appellant decided to pay the remaining amount to redeem the property and to treat the amount paid by the respondent as rent for the period that the respondent had occupied the house. This triggered a dispute between the parties. The appellant insisted that the respondent vacate from the house, while the respondent claimed the right to the house as founded on the sale agreement. The appellant sued unsuccessfully in the High Court of Tanzania[574], and later appealed to the Court of Appeal[575]. It was argued for the appellant that the sale agreement was void for it was not in writing and was not approved by the Commissioner for Lands and that there was no agreement in terms of Regulation 3 (1) such that the appellant could not be said to have breached any agreement, and that if there was an agreement, it was not legally enforceable. On the other hand, it was the respondent's argument that the maxim, "He who resorts to equity must come with clean hands" applied. It was further argued that the parties had entered into a sale agreement which was legally binding upon them. Finally, it was argued that on the basis of the agreement there was consideration from the respondent, which the appellant benefited from. The Court of Appeal of Tanzania held that the appellant had refused to sign the document to execute the sale agreement even before the consent of the Commissioner could be sought. He was therefore in breach of the sale agreement and could not validly resort to reg. 3 (1) of the Land Regulations 1948 in his defence.

The case of Abualy Alibhai Azizi came to clear the position between the two conflicting decisions of the Court of appeal. In this case, the parties had a dispute over the sale of land but in contravention of the

573 [1995] TLR 262 (CA).

574 See Civil Case No. 123 of 1990 (Mkude J.,- as he then was).

575 Civil Appeal No. 19 of 1995.

provisions of reg. 3 (1) of the Land Regulations of 1948. The appellant had lost the case in the High Court and appealed to the Court of Appeal of Tanzania.[576] In the Court of Appeal, a bench of three justices of the Court of Appeal, sitting as an ordinary court referred the case to the full Bench of the Court for its decision on point of law. The order referring the matter to the full Bench stated the case as follows:

> *After discussion between the Bench and the representatives of the parties, it is directed that the matter of the legal effect of lack of consent to a sale of registered land be referred for decision by the Full Bench, as there are conflicting decisions by the Court on the issue, and that pending such decision by the Full Bench, the case is stayed and will be fixed for continuation of hearing after such decision…*

The order was admitted and five justices of appeal[577] sat to resolve the conflict while Prof. G.M Fimbo of the Faculty of Law, University of Dar es Salaam was invited to be the friend of the Court (*Amicus Curiae*). The Court, after going through a long list of decided cases on the matter, made the following observation:

> *It is our considered opinion that a contract falling within the scope of regulation 3 has all the attributes of a valid contract, except those, of which performance before the requisite consent is sought and obtained, is prejudicial to the interests of the paramount landlord. Such are, for example, terms of which performance has the effect of replacing the holder of a right with another person without the consent of the paramount landlord. Such terms, though valid are unenforceable on the grounds of public policy which protects the interests of a paramount landlord. In our considered opinion, this unenforceability of valid contract is what is meant by the expression "shall be inoperative" under regulation 3.*
>
> *The corollary of what we have stated is that a contract for the disposition of land, which otherwise is proper but for the lack of required consent, is inoperative, that is, unenforceable to the extent that such enforcement is prejudicial to the interests of the paramount landlord. However, where such enforcement is not thus prejudicial, a party who has performed his or her part of the bargain may be assisted by the court to enforce the contract against the defaulting party. So a party who defaults to submit a*

576 Civil Appeal No. 42 of 1995.

577 Nyalali, C.J., Mfalila, J.A., Lubuva, J.A., Samatta, J.A. and Lugakingira, J.A.

> *written contract for consent or refusal by the specified authority may be compelled to do so if the other party has performed his or her part of the bargain. Of course where such consent is sought and is refused, the contract become wholly unenforceable, though valid, and any expenses incurred by the parties may be recovered by legal action, if necessary...This means NITIN's case is bad in law since it undermines the sanctity of the contract; and GEORGE SHAMBWE's case is only partly sound because it does not safeguard the interests of the paramount land lord.*

Stated very simply, the Court of Appeal held that the contract of sale entered into by the parties is valid and parties thereto may be assisted by the court especially where the consent of approving authority has not been sought deliberately.

Sale of Land under the Land Acts

In some other jurisdictions, there is specific law, such as the Indian *Transfer of Property Act, 1882*, which governs transfer of property, including sale of land. In Tanzania the sale of land may be made under the *Village Land Act* if the sale involves a village land, and under the *Land Act*, if the sale involves land other than village land. One thing must be noted that the *Land Acts* were passed as a reaction to two opposing sets of pressures: the internal pressure pointing towards strengthening the security of tenure of occupiers of land, and; the external pressure pointing towards the free market economy. This is what we learn from Professor Fimbo when he says:

> *The central issue in Land Law reform has been the tension between, on one hand, freedom to deal with the land in the market and, on the other, protection of occupiers and users of land.*[578]

In an attempt to reconcile these two tensions the *Land Acts* have removed the traditional restrictions on matters of consent over the disposition of land by sale. For example, the traditional requirement for consent of the Commissioner for Lands before disposition of land held under a granted right of occupancy has been dispensed with.[579] The only requirement is delivery of a notification in a prescribed form[580] to the Commissioner before or at the time of the disposition. The

578 FIMBO,G.M., "Privatization, Private Investment and the Land Law", A Paper Presented during Training of Land Law Reforms in Tanzania, Centre for Continuing Education, University of Dar es Salaam, May 7th-9th 2003, at p. 3.

579 See section 36 (2).

580 Form No. 29 of the Land Forms.

Commissioner then endorses the notification with his signature and official seal and sends a copy to the Registrar[581]. The only disposition which requires the consent of the Commissioner is a disposition in respect of land which is within three years of its grant to the transferor.[582] This requires the assignor to comply with certain procedures including: application for grant of approval of disposition[583] in a prescribed form;[584] determination of validity of the application by the Commissioner and issuance of a certificate of approval which is also copied to the Registrar.[585] Although the Act does not require consent of the Commission in all dispositions, the practice preferred mostly by practitioners has been to prepare and forward to the Commissioner, both the notification form and the approval form. When the seller is the legal representative of the deceased, and the property, the subject matter of the sale, is part of the deceased's estate, then the seller is also required to fill in a form of the assent to bequest a right of occupancy, made under section 68 of the *Land Act*.

The *Land Act* provides the criteria to be considered by the Commissioner when determining the application of approval. For example, the Commissioner may refuse to give approval if the intended disposition conflicts with the interest of high-risk groups such as displaced persons, children and any low income persons.[586]

A similar legal position over disposition is available in all cases of village lands governed by the *Village Land Act*. According to history, the requirement of consent prior to the disposition of land in the village was first imposed by the provisions of Directives contained in Government Notice No. 168 of 1975, which provided, *inter alia*, that: Except with the approval of the Village Council, no person shall: (a) transfer to any other person his right to the use of land in a village; or (b) dispose of his house, whether by sale or otherwise. This means that any disposition that was made in contravention of the requirement of consent of the village council was void and of no effect in law[587]. The *Village Land Act*

581 Section 36 (4).

582 Section 37 (2).

583 Section 39 (1).

584 Form No. 30 of the Land Forms.

585 Section 39 (6) and (7).

586 Section 41 (2) (e).

587 See the case of Nyagaswa in Chapter Two above.

allows the villager to transfer a right of occupancy to another villager[588] under the requirement that the parties notify the Village Council on a prescribed form of the proposed transfer in not less than sixty days.[589] The villager can transfer the right to a non-villager only when there is approval of the Village Council.[590] In all the above, a village Council is empowered to disallow an assignment for a number of reasons[591]. From the human rights perspective, some of these reasons are very sound and need to be always considered before a disposition is approved. These are: whether the transfer would or would not be likely to operate to defeat the right of any woman to occupy land under a customary right of occupancy, or a derivative right or as a successor in title of the assignor;[592] also, whether the transfer would result in the assignor occupying an amount of land insufficient to provide for his livelihood or, where he has a family or other dependants, for their livelihood.[593] It is submitted that the limitation imposed on the right to transfer a village land is necessary for the protection of vulnerable groups like women and children from disposition of land, especially so when land, the only means of survival, is under the sole control of some irresponsible men.

The traditional restriction of disposition by sale of a right of occupancy to foreigners has been retained by the *Land Acts,* which prevent foreigners from acquiring land in the form of a right of occupancy, except for the investment purposes, and in a form of derivative right of occupancy through the Tanzania Investment Centre. The jurisprudence laid down by the court in the case of *Saffique A.S Dhiyebi v Presidential Parastatal Sector Reform Commission*[594] is squarely in support of this fact. The facts of the case show that the plaintiff submitted a bid offering to purchase the house in response to the defendant's advertisement to the public inviting people to purchase various properties owned by the National Housing Corporation, including the suit property, a residential

588 Section 30 (1).

589 Section 30 (3).

590 Section 30 (2)

591 Section 30 (4) (a)-(e).

592 Section 30 (4) (b).

593 Section 30 (4) (c).

594 High Court of Tanzania (Land Division) at Dar es Salaam, Land Case No. 46 of 2004 (Unreported).

house at plot No. 186, Uganda Avenue. The defendant considered the bid, but asked the plaintiff to raise the purchase price, and further informed him that transfer of title would be affected on payment of the purchase price and production of acceptable evidence of the plaintiff's Tanzanian nationality. The plaintiff fulfilled all conditions except that he did not produce evidence of his Tanzanian nationality. On learning that the plaintiff was not a Tanzanian national, the defendant terminated the offer and wrote a cheque in his favour as a refund of monies that had already been paid. Following the non transfer of the property, the plaintiff went to court seeking, among others, an order for specific performance. The defendant's defence was that since there was no evidence that the plaintiff was a Tanzanian national then the whole transaction became illegal. The Court (Kileo, J.) dismissed the plaintiff's prayers without fear or favour but by insisting that there could be no contract between the plaintiff and the defendant because the plaintiff was unable to show evidence of his being a Tanzanian national, and that he only posed as a Tanzanian national to get the property, which he knew was available only to Tanzanian nationals. In other words, the court held that even if the plaintiff had fulfilled all the conditions of the offer, but to fulfil the fundamental condition, which was based on legal requirement, there was in law no acceptance and the agreement did not mature into a legally enforceable contract between the parties.[595] The court emphatically insisted on the need to observe the provisions of the law in a case like one before it:

> *If the land in Tanzania belongs to the citizens with the President holding it as trustee on behalf of all citizens, then it must be assumed that the citizens have a say in the way their land is administered. How can they have a say if courts allow themselves to be persuaded to ignore such significant provision as that contained in section 20 (2)[596] quoted above? I am not entitled to overlook these provisions as has been suggested by the plaintiff. I for one am enjoined and happily bound to ensure that provisions of the Land Acts are observed to the letter.*

---

595 The Court was making reference to sections 31 and 32 of the *Law of Contract,* [Cap. 345 R.E 2002]

596 The letter and spirit of section 20 of the *Land Act, 1999*, as a whole, is to deny non-citizens the direct right to acquire land in Tanzania unless the acquisition is through the Tanzania Investment Centre.

The Contract of Sale of Land

The contract of sale is just like any other contract and is, therefore, governed by the provisions of the *Law of Contract Act*.[597] The contract presupposes the presence of two parties to the contract, the vendor (seller) and vendee (purchaser or buyer) and, of course, consideration.[598] The case of *Mohamed Iddi Mjasir v Mrs Jayalaxmi Jayantilal Joshi* [599] points to this proposition. The facts of the case were that, the respondent's husband, one Mr. Jayantilal Joshi owned a house in Zanzibar in which he lived with his family up to 1972, when he left for Canada. Before he left, he entrusted his house, by way of power of attorney, to the appellant's father, Mr. Ahmed Iddi Mjasir who was to collect rent from tenants, to effect repairs where needed, to pay charges, and to sell the house when the price offered was reasonable. In 1987, Mr. Jayantial Joshi died. Ahmed Iddi Mjasir prepared a deed of conveyance purporting to be between himself and the owner, and indicating the purchase price of Ths. 150,000/=. He then prepared a deed of gift showing that, on consideration of natural love and affection for his son, he conveyed the house to him. The deed was promptly registered in the name of the son, now the appellant. The respondent brought an action against the appellant in the High Court of Zanzibar, in which she vehemently challenged the transfer of the house to Ahmed Mjasir, which she believed to be illegal. The issue for determination by the court was whether such transfer was in accordance with the law. In other words, the issue was, whether Ahmed Mjasir could transfer the house to himself alone. The court considered the matter and decided in favour of the respondent. Aggrieved by the decision, the appellant appealed to the Court of Appeal of Tanzania. Deciding the matter, the Court of Appeal of Tanzania held that the purported transfer by Ahmed Iddi Mjasir to himself contravened the clear provision of the *Transfer of Property Decree* of Zanzibar[600] which provided that:

> *Transfer of property means an act by which a living person conveys property, in present or in future, to one or more other living persons, or to himself and one or more other living persons; and `to transfer property' is to perform such act.*[601]

---

597 [Cap. 345 R.E 2002].

598 See appendix 1, a sample of sale contract at p. 284.

599 [1993] TLR 274 (CA).

600 Cap. 150 of the Laws of Zanzibar.

601 Section 5.

The Court observed that if a person decides to convey the property to himself, such a conveyance must include one or more other living persons, meaning that in the absence of other person or persons, there was no valid transfer to Ahmed, and consequently Ahmed had no property to transfer to his son.[602] It means that there was no contract of sale of land to Ahmed, the purported purchaser if there was no vendor. As another ground for its decision, the Court observed that there was no evidence to show that the purported consideration passed to the vendor and that the lack of consideration vitiated a contact of sale.

The above scenario is well covered by Section 65 (1) of the *Land Act,* which gives the right of a person to make a disposition to himself. The section provides that:

> *For avoidance of doubt it is hereby declared that any person may make a disposition to himself and any other person or together with any other person to himself alone.*

Transfer of land interests by sale has been one of the complex areas in the administratioin of land law in Tanzania and it is, for this reason, recorded to be one of the main sources of land disputes and litigation. The reason is obvious. The majority of people tend to rush thereby concluding land sale deals without satisfying themselves as to the legality of the sales and the procedural steps involved in the process.[603] It is emphasised that, in order to avoid unnecessary prejudices, purchasers of land ought to make thorough inquiries to discover the defects, if any, over the title of the vendor to the land, the subject matter of the transfer, immediadtely before entering into, or concluding, a deed of transfer of the land. This is very important in all cases especially where, for example, the land to be sold or purchased is or forms part of a matrimonial property, or is mortgaged, or is held under co-occupancy or in trust. In these circumstances, one needs to identify and establish the legal right (the right in *rem*) and/or the equitable right (right in *personam*) of the vendor over the land before he attempts to enter into a contract of sale. In other words, a purchaser needs to inquire into anything that appears to throw doubt over the land offered for sale by the vendor.

602 The transfer to the son was captured by the maxim: Nemo dat quod non habet, meaning that no one can give that which he does not have.

603 Experts in the law on transfer of a right of occupancy agree that from start to finish, a transfer consists of about eighteen (18) steps which need be known and strictly observed if the transfer is to be successful. For detailed account of these steps, see GONDWE, Zabron Steven, (2001): *Manual for Transfers of Rights of Occupancy* (Revised Edition 2010), Mkuki na Nyota Publishers Ltd, Dar es Salaam.

Things that may create doubt in the mind of the purchaser include: the presence of some occupants/tenants on the land; a right of way; doubtful boundaries with the neighbours; or, knowledge of suit pending in a court of law over the same land. Also the rights of a wife or wives, children, co-occupiers and creditors (both secured and unsecured) need be considered at this level in order to avoid prejudicial dispositions. Such inquiries may be done in various ways including making official search and requisition as to title in the office of the Registrar of Titles. This can assist the purchaser to ascertain the particulars of registration of vendor's registrable encumbrances, if any.[604] The *Land Act* envisages three kinds of knowledge that a purchaser is presumed to have at the time of executing the sale contract: actual knowledge; constructive knowledge, and; imputed knowledge[605]. The Act is silent as to what these may mean in practice. However, by actual knowledge it means knowledge based on one's own experience of the state of affairs as opposed to knowledge based on hearsay and vague rumours. On the other hand, by constructive knowledge it means the knowledge one has about the encumbrances in the title of the vendor, but, he has not taken the trouble to make inquiries to establish the facts of these encumbrances in order to establish actual knowledge. In other words, a purchaser has constructive knowledge of the fact if, (1) has actual knowledge of the encumbrances but makes no proper inquiries to establish what they are, and (2) has either deliberately or carelessly abstained from making those inquiries that a prudent purchaser would have made.[606] Lastly, if the purchaser employs an agent to act on his or her behalf, and if the agent obtains any knowledge, actual or constructive, then such knowledge is imputed to the purchaser and becomes imputed knowledge.

It may be said without any hesitation that there have been serious complaints, disputes and litigations arising out of the omission, whether deliberately or by mere negligence, of this duty on the part of the purchasers, or fraud vitiating the duty, on the part of the vendor. In either case, the purchasers have suffered the consequences. The cases

---

604 Section 3 (2) of the Land Registration Act [Cap. 334 R.E 2002] imposes a duty upon a Registrar of Titles to maintain in the land registry a land register for the registration of the title to land in Tanzania and the recording of dispositions, transmissions and encumbrance of land over registered land. Todate, there are five zonal land registries, namely Dar es Salaam, Dodoma, Mbeya, Moshi, Mtwara and Mwanza.

605 Section 71 (2).

606 See *Bailey v Barnes* (1894) 1 Ch. 25 at p. 35.

of *Mtumwa Rashid v Abdallah Iddi and Salum Omari*[607] and *Peter Mbararia and Another v Peter Tabu Massawe*[608] may be cited in support of this point.

In the *Mtumwa Rashid* case the facts show that the second respondent, a husband of the Appellant, one Salum Omari, agreed to sell a matrimonial house to the first respondent without involving the appellant, a wife and co-occupier to the matrimonial house. The appellant raised a spirited objection against the sale of the house and instituted a case to recover the house. The District Court held that the case fell under section 59 of the *Law of Marriage Act*[609], which expressly prohibits a spouse from selling a matrimonial home without the attention and, therefore, consent of the other spouse. The court decided in favour of the appellant but ordered her to pay the purchaser fair and adequate compensation. On appeal to the High Court, the judge gave a very strange, unreasonable and unpractical judgment that the purchaser should live with the appellant or re-sell the house to Salum Omari. On further appeal to the Court of Appeal of Tanzania, the issue for determination was whether or not the sale by Salum Omari was a nullity. The Court reacted to the issue by first establishing that section 59 of the *Law of Marriage Act* did not apply[610], but the applicable law in this case was the law regulating ordinary contracts. The Court observed that sale of property by Salum was made secretly and the purchaser knew that the matrimonial home was jointly owned. The secret sale, therefore, amounted to fraud[611]. Finally the Court observed that although the Commissioner consented to the sale as required by regulation 3 (1) of the Land Regulation, 1948

607 Court of Appeal of Tanzania, at Dar es Salaam, Civil Appeal No. 22 of 1993, Judgment of 23rd February 1996 (Unreported). See also: *Letisia Bugumba v Thadeo Magoma and Another*, High Court of Tanzania at Mwanza, Civil Appeal No. 8 of 1989 (Unreported); *Zakaria Barie Bura v Theresia Maria John Mubiru* (1995) TLR 211 (CA).

608 High Court of Tanzania at Moshi (PC) Civil Appeal No. 34 of 2003 (Unreported).

609 [Cap. 29 R.E 2002]. Section 59 (1) provides that, "Where any estate or interest in the matrimonial home is owned by the husband or the wife, he or she shall not, while the marriage subsists and without the consent of the other spouse alienate it by way of sale, gift, lease, mortgage or otherwise, and the other spouse shall be deemed to have an interest therein capable of being protected by caveat, caution or otherwise under any law for the time being in force relating to the registration of title to land or of deeds".

610 It was the Court's reasoning that the section is applicable only to protect a spouse who has no actual interest, but who is deemed to have the interest. Mtumwa Rashid was not such a spouse, but a co-occupier with actual interest.

611 See the constituents of fraud under section 17 of the *Law of Contact Act*, [Cap. 345 R.E 2002].

the consent was sought by misrepresentation and, therefore, it was non existent. As regards the rights of the purchaser, the Court directed that the purchaser would turn to Salum Omari for the refund of the purchase price which was paid to him under the abortive transaction. In simple terms, the court's decision meant that the purchaser must bear the consequences since he failed to exercise his duty to establish the title of the vendor before undertaking to purchase the land which was not free from encumbrances and/or that he was part of the fraud.

The facts in *Peter Mbararia's* case were that the first appellant sold a piece of land to the second appellant on 15th April 1999 and a sale agreement was dully executed. About three months later, the first appellant, for reasons best known to him and without notifying the second appellant, resold the same land to the respondent. The respondent, on discovering that the second appellant was encroaching on the land, brought an action against the appellants to recover the piece of land. He won the case in the lower courts but lost on appeal to the High Court of Tanzania. Allowing the appeal and declaring the second appellant as being entitled to the ownership of the land, the Court had the following to say at p.3-4:

> *This is indeed what the second appellant said in his defence. He clearly stated that he bought the suit land from the first appellant on 15/04/1999, about two and a half months before the transaction of 06/07/1999, the date on which the first appellant is regarded to have resold that same piece of land to the respondent. The story of the second appellant was corroborated by DW.4 Valentina Alphonce, DW.5 Bernard Ndengaso, DW.6 Andrew Laurent and DW.7 Cornell Majaliwa all of whom testified that they witnessed the transaction of 15/04/1999 between the first and second appellants in which the first appellant sold the suit land to the second appellant. I believe that such was the situation, therefore that the first appellant's act of reselling that same piece of land to the respondent constituted fraud.*
>
> *Since the first sale was effected on 15/04/1999, I agree with Mr. Urio that the second sale agreement of 06/07/1999 was ineffectual on the ground that the land handed over to the second appellant was no longer available for sale on 06/07/1999, for as properly submitted by Mr. Urio, the second appellant had, by virtue of the agreement signed on 15/04/1999, acquired a superior title over that land. I further agree with Mr. Urio that in the circumstances of this case, the respondent ought to have sought to recover from*

> *the first appellant Shs. 500,000/= he paid for the land already in the hands of another person. Reliance is on the case of Bi Amina Katume v Eustace Ndyakowa (1968) HDC 13 in which the High Court of Tanzania held that in fraudulent sale of land, vendee (purchaser) is entitled to purchase price and costs from the vendor. Indeed the respondent in the present case is entitled to just that.*

Rights and Obligations of the Parties to a Contract of Sale

In order for the parties to a contract of sale of land to enjoy the rights and obligations created by the contract, there are certain legal requirements which need be fulfilled in the first place. These include the requirement that the contract be in writing or that there is a written memorandum of its terms[612] and that the contract or the written memorandum is signed by the party against whom the contract is to be enforceable[613]. It is important to record, here, that there are other requirements which, although not mentioned in the *Land Act*, have been taken to be necessary to create rights and obligations. These include, for instance, the requirement to pay stamp duty in respect of the contract under the provisions of the *Stamp Duty Act*[614] in order to make the contract admissible in evidence in case there is a dispute between the vendor and vendee. We learn about this requirement from the case of *Zakaria Barie Bura v Theresia Maria John Mubiru.*[615] In this case, the respondent and her late husband had jointly acquired a plot of land and a matrimonial house thereon. The couple applied for and were jointly given a letter of offer of a right of occupancy, and jointly paid various fees in satisfaction of the conditions attached to the offer. Later on, the husband fraudulently obtained a title deed in his own sole name instead of joint names with the wife. He thereafter sold the house to the appellant. The sale was executed in two documents, one indicating a lower price of 500,000/=, which was intended to be presented to the revenue authority and the other indicating the price of 900,000/=, which was actually paid to the vendor. The respondent brought an action against the purchaser (the appellant in the case) arguing that the appellant was either a party to or knew of the fraud. It

612 Section 64 (1) (a). The memorandum may be any document containing (1) the names of the vendor and the purchaser, (2) the nature of the title to be conveyed, (3) the certificate number of the title, (4) the date of its execution, (5) statement of payment of interest in case there is default and (6) date of completion of the transaction.

613 Section 64 (1) (b).

614 [Cap. 189 R.E 2002].

615 [1995] TLR 211 (CA).

was the appellant's argument, on the other hand, that the respondent's husband had proceeded alone because of matrimonial problems, and that there was no fraud neither in acquiring title nor in the sale. The respondent won the case both in the High Court and the Court of Appeal of Tanzania. Two issues were the subject of the litigation: whether the title deed was fraudulently obtained, and whether the sale agreement of the suit premises was of any legal effect. In addressing the first issue, the Court of Appeal was of the view that the certificate of title bearing solely the name of the respondent's husband was obtained fraudulently-that is by deceit and for the purpose of depriving the respondent of her right on the suit premises. As regards the second issue, the Court held that the contract of sale of the suit premises in this case was executed in two documents aimed at depriving the Treasury as to the proper tax liable to be paid for the transaction. Clearly such a contract was void *ab initio*. Lastly the Court observed that even if the sale agreement had not been tainted with illegality, the document containing the agreement did not show any indication of payment of stamp duty and was accordingly inadmissible in evidence.

When the contract is executed in accordance to law, it remains the duty of the parties to ensure that each fulfils his obligations under the contract including: the obligation to pay the purchase price (purchaser); the obligation to surrender possession of the land and all relevant documents relating to the land (vendor); the obligation to process and complete the transfer in the office of the Registrar if sale involves a registered land (either of the parties) and the obligation to register the instruments of transfer[616] in the name of the purchaser. Failure to fulfil these obligations is fatal under the law and may lead any of the parties into adverse consequences. Usually in all cases of breach of the contract of sale, the innocent party has the right to seek the assistance of the court for orders such as specific performance, mesne profits, and damages, among others.[617] The *Land Act* provides for remedial measures to be undertaken by the innocent party when there is breach of the contract by another party. For example, the law empowers the

616 The documents of transfer (conveyancing documents) are compulsorily registrable under the *Registration of Documents Act*, [Cap. 117 R.E 2002]. See the cases of *Abdulkadri Mohamed v Registrar of Titles* [1992] TLR 21 (CA) and *Furaha Mohamed v Fatuma Abdallah* [1992] TLR 205 (HC). It follows that failure to register the documents shall make the title not to pass to the buyer. See *Mkubwa Said Omar v S.Z.M* [1992] TLR 365 (CA).

617 See the cases of *Jones v Gardiner* [1902] 1 Ch. 191; *Shah v Abdulla* [1964] E.A 742; and *Diamond v Campbell-Jones & Others* [1960] 1 ALL ER 583.

vendor to resume possession of the land in case a purchaser breaches the contract, for instance by not paying the purchase price. He can do this either peacefully or by the order of the court.[618] In addition, he can claim damages for the breach.[619] The law also empowers the purchaser to apply to court for relief against the rescission of the contract.[620] In this scenario the court, as custodian of justice, has the power to determine the applications and make orders in accordance with the law.[621] The case of *Riziki Habibu v Fatuma Juma*[622] supports the law. The parties to this case concluded a sale contract in respect of house No. 30 on the Plot No. 31 Block E along Moshi Street in Ilala District. The plaintiff, a buyer, performed her part by paying the purchasing price, Tshs. 9,000,000/=, leaving the balance of Tshs. 3,000,000/=. The defendant defaulted in his part, that is, did not surrender possession of the house. The plaintiff approached the court for the order of specific performance. The Court decided the case in favour of the plaintiff by saying that:

> *On the premises, prayers (a) (b) (c) and (e) are granted as prayed, that is, that the order for specific performance is allowed and therefore the plaintiff is declared legal owner of the suit premises; that all the relevant documents for the suit premises be surrendered to the plaintiff forthwith. Since the substantive purchase price was handed over, let the defendant be compelled to collect the reminder Tshs. 3,000,000/= from court.*

It is important to note that even before the adoption of the *Land Acts*, an innocent party to a contract of sale was protected in the event of breach of the contract of sale by the other party. The case of *Edwin Simon v Adam Mbala*[623] is authoritative in support of this fact. It should be pointed out that matters relating to dispositions of a customary right of occupancy are governed by customary law.[624]

---

618 See section 73 (1) (a) (b). Read this section together with section 74 which makes it mandatory for the vendor to serve notice to the purchaser stating the facts of the breach and the intention to resume possession by order of a court if the breach is not remedied.

619 Section 73 (2).

620 Section 75.

621 Section 76.

622 High Court of Tanzania (Land Division) at Dar es Salaam, Land Case No. 102 of 2004 (Unreported).

623 [1983] TLR 410 (HC).

624 Section 61 (3).

Transfer of Land Interests by Lease

Leases in Historical Perspective

The concept of lease is guided by the law on landlord and tenant. For this reason, the term lease is very often used interchangeably with other terms such as "tenancy" or "demise". A lease or tenancy, when taken by the tenant, creates interest in land for a fixed period of certain duration, usually in consideration of payment of rent. The contract of lease or tenancy presupposes the presence of two parties, that is, a lessee (a person to whom a lease is granted) and a lessor (a person by whom a lease is granted).[625] The granting of a lease by a lessor to the lessee is, in law, executed by way of a lease contract. Historically, there have been two remarkable features characterising the landlord-tenant relationship, not only in Tanzania, but also in other jurisdictions. First, there has been a tendency of the party with the stronger bargaining power (landlord) to impose harsher conditions in a lease or change them unilaterally, and forcing the week party (tenant) to dance to the tune. Secondly, many lease contracts have been observed more in breach than in compliance by the parties thereto. This trend is largely attributed to the competing rights between the landlords who look for super profits out of the rented premises and, the tenants who put forward the claim of right to housing and shelter against the interests of the lessors. In this scenario, then, cases of exorbitant increases in rent, unwarranted evictions from rental premises, harassment and annoyances against tenants on one hand, and the inability to pay rent whether deliberately or otherwise, and failure to maintain the demised premises by the tenants on the other hand, have not been uncommon.

The point of emphasis, here, is that if the above named vices were left unchecked by the State, and if the State were to remain indifferent in the matter or to act in vacuum without the necessary legislation, the result would be chaos, insecurity, and social disorder. This would be worse in urban areas where the increasing population due to urbanisation is not accommodated by the severely inadequate housing facilities. The seriousness of the problem is reflected not only by the history of legislation on leases but also by the litany of disputes and litigations in the courts of law which have been arising out of the landlord-tenant

625 For the full meaning of the terms "lessee" and "lessor" see section 2 of the *Land Act*, [Cap. 113 R.E 2002].

relationships[626]. It follows, therefore, that since serious issues on leases or tenancies have occupied a very significant part of the administration of land law in Tanzania, the state has always resorted to legislative measures to harmonise the landlord-tenant relationship. As it may be observed, legislative measure has a very important role to play, especially in the management of tenancies. James, E.M. Jesse is articulate and on point when he notes that:

> *'Housing deficit' in urban areas in Tanzania is great and consequently the Government has chosen, among other measures, legislative vehicles to ensure that the situation is not exploited for profiteering purposes at the expense of social justice and peace.*[627]

In this regard, Tanzania has always strived to balance the interests of parties to leases through legislative measures. Various statutory laws and common law principles have been in place to guide the landlord-tenant relationships despite the challenges posed on one hand by the market demands and on the other hand the protection of the consumers, the tenants. A study on the history of legislation on leases in Tanzania reveals the following statutes to have been in force on various dates: the *Rent and Mortgage Interest (Restriction) Ordinance*, 1941[628]; the *Rent Restriction Ordinance*, 1951[629]; the *Rent Restriction Act*, 1962[630]; the *Rent Restriction Act*, 1984[631], and; *the Land Act*[632]. The *Rent Restriction Act*, 1984 has been in force until it was officially repealed in 2005.[633] This means that to date all matters concerning leases of a right of occupancy are governed by the provisions of the *Land Act* except customary leases and sub-leases which are governed by customary law.[634]

---

626 See, for example, *Beno Chelele t/a General Intergrated Firm v National Housing Corporation and 2 Others*, High Court of Tanzania (Land Division) at Dar es Salaam, Land Case No. 96 of 2004 (Unreported); *Rashid Halfan v Pendael Singa and National Housing Tribunal* [sic], High Court of Tanzania (Land Division) at Dar es Salaam, Land Case No. 173 of 2004 (Unreported), and; *Shaidu Juma Kopwe v Seleman Mussa*, High Court of Tanzania (Land Division) at Dar es Salaam, Land Case No. 18 of 2006 (Unreported).

627 JESSE, James E.C.M., (2002): "Rent Control Legislation in Tanzania: A Critical Review of Security of Tenure in Residential Rental Housing", LL.M Dissertation, UDSM.

628 Act No. 26 of 1941.

629 Act No. 16 of 1951.

630 Act No. 42 of 1962.

631 Act No. 17 of 1984. It was latter named [Cap. 339 R.E 2002].

632 [Cap. 113, R.E 2002].

633 See the *Written Laws (Miscellaneous Amendment) (No.2) Act*, 2005. (Act No. 11 of 2005).

634 See section 19 of the *Village Land Act*, [Cap. 114 R.E 2002].

Salient Features of the Rent Restriction Act, 1984

The *Rent Restriction Act*, 1984, as amended from time to time, came into force on 1st June 1985 *vide* Government Notice No. 433 of 1985. The Act aimed, *inter alia*, at protecting tenants from unscrupulous landlords by trying to strike a balance between the interests of both. It was applicable to all dwelling and commercial houses, furnished or unfurnished situated, or in the course of erection, in a rent restriction area in mainland Tanzania.[635] The Act was not applicable to premises which were the property of the Government, parastatal organisations or local authority and used for their respective employees.[636] It was also not applicable to all cases where the Government was a landlord in government leases.[637] Moreover, the Act empowered the Minister responsible for land matters to exempt certain premises from the application of the Act.[638] The Minister exercised this power quite often but he was accordingly challenged in court by people who were aggrieved by the very exercise. The case of *Lausa Alfan Salum and 106 Others v Minister for Lands, Housing and Urban Development & National Housing Corporation*[639] is very clear.

One of the salient features of the *Rent Restriction Act* was about the institutional framework. The Act established the Regional Housing Tribunal,[640] which was composed of the Chairman, Deputy Chairman and not more than five members,[641] and stated the powers of the Tribunal as being, for example, to fix standard rent and to hear all civil matters arising out of the application of the Act.[642]. In addition, the Act established the Housing Appeals Tribunal with powers to admit, consider and determine appeals originating from Regional Housing Tribunals.[643] From the Housing Appeals Tribunal, a further appeal would go to the Court of Appeal of Tanzania but only if that appeal was on a point of law or a point of mixed law and facts.[644]

---

635 Section 2 (1) of the Act. The words, "Rent Restriction Area" mean areas falling in the jurisdiction of District Council, Municipal Council, Township Council and City Council.

636 Section 2 (1) (a).

637 Section 2 (3).

638 Section 2 (1) (b).

639 1994] TLR 237 (CA).

640 Section 9.

641 Section 10.

642 Section 12.

643 Section 6.

644 Section 45 (1).

Another salient feature of the Act was the machinery to assess standard rent. The Act imposed a duty to the landlord, whose premises were to be let for the first time, to apply to the tribunal for the determination of the payable rent (the standard rent),[645] meaning that the landlord would not, thereafter, impose rent above the rent determined by the tribunal. Also failure to apply for the assessment of standard rent amounted to commission of offence under the Act.[646] Equally, acceptance of rent in excess of the standard rent amounted to an offence under the Act.[647]

The third salient feature of the Act was the scheme of protection of tenants against eviction. The Act restricted or disallowed the common law landlord right of re-entry. It did that by imposing the duty to the landlord to apply to court for the order of re-entry. Essentially, the Act set out certain basic grounds that the court had to consider before granting an order of eviction or ejectment. These were for example: non payment of rent on the part of the tenant; the tenant becoming a nuisance or using the premises for immoral purposes; the tenant subletting the whole premises or part of it at higher rent than he himself paid; landlord requiring the premises for his own use; tenancy having been expired, and; premises being used for commercial or trade purposes without the consent of the landlord[648]. It means that if the tribunal was not satisfied that any one of the alleged ground existed, then it was bound to refuse to grant the order for vacant possession. The case of *Hamis Sakaya v Beda Joseph and Others*[649] is a case in point. The respondents were the tenants who entered the suit premises at different times when the premises were unfit for human habitation. They all agreed with their landlord to effect the necessary repair, and agreed further that the cost spent in the process would be set-off against the payable rent. Such an agreement induced them to renovate their respective rooms by installing the floor, fixing doors and mosquito gauze, and painting the walls. The premises looked beautiful and were now suitable for habitation. Having remained in the premises for not longer than six months, the landlord demanded his premises back by serving the notice to the respondents requiring them to vacate. His reason to demand back the premises was that his

645 Section 18 (1).

646 Section 18 (2).

647 Section 23.

648 Section 27.

649 Regional Housing Tribunal of Dar es Salaam, Application No. 134 of 2001 (Unreported).

son was about to marry and that he needed the house for that purpose. The respondent ignored the notice, so the landlord decided to apply to the Tribunal for the order of vacant possession. The evidence tendered in court indicated that there was no son who was planning to marry, but that the applicant had decided to demand the premises back as soon as it looked beautiful.The Tribunal was of the view that the applicant's claim had no merit, and the application was consequently dismissed.

Another feature of the protective aspect was the application of the doctrine of alternative accommodation. The doctrine was, to say the least, a thorn to landlords. In the application of this doctrine the court could only issue the order of vacant possession of the demised house against a tenant if it was established by the landlord that the tenant had or would get an alternative, reasonably equivalent accommodation. It means that even if the landlord needed the house for his own use and the use of the family, this alone could not entitle him to the order of vacant possession, if the tenant was not able to secure an alternative accommodation, meaning another house which was reasonably equivalent with the demised premises.[650]

Finally, the Act was being regarded to be more tenant than landlord-friendly. It is this aspect which led to its repeal in 2005. This is what we learn from the case of *Lausa Alfan Salum and 106 Others v Minister for Lands, Housing and Urban Development & National Housing Tribunal* (supra). In this case, the second respondent, the National Housing Corporation (NHC), then established under the *National Housing Corporation Act, 1990*, was required to charge rent subject to the provisions of the *Rent Restriction Act*. In 1994 the Minister exempted the premises of certain specified parastatals, including NHC, from being subjected to the provisions of *Rent Restriction Act*.[651] NHC took that opportunity to increase rent for all the premises including those occupied by the appellants. The appellants were aggrieved by this move and decided to go to the court to challenge, *inter alia*, the unilateral rent increase and the validity of the Minister's order which, they claimed, had deprived them their protection through the Act, rendering them defenceless as long as they were deprived the right to enjoy the services of the Housing Tribunals. However, the appellants lost the case in both the High Court and Court of Appeal of Tanzania. Essentially, both courts

650 See *PS Parmer and A.Adamjee v Paulo E. Maro* [1990] TLR 67 (CA) and *Issa Warsama v Salima Bhanji* [1984] TLR 122 (CA).

651 See the Rent Restriction (Exemption Specified Parastatals) Order, 1992 (GN 41 of 1992).

were of the view that the Minister did what he was legally empowered to do under the provisions of the Act, that is, to exempt certain premises from the application of the *Rent Restriction Act*. However, the Court of Appeal of Tanzania was of the opinion that the appellants would have questioned the reasonableness of the rent increase but not its validity. The point we emphasize, here, is that the tenants considered themselves more protected wherever the *Rent Restriction Act* applied than in any other eventuality. However, with the development of the power of the market, and the rise of the super profit-oriented generation, the Act lost its taste in the thinking of the government. The government's attitude towards the Act, before its repeal, is best expressed through its policy statement on Human Settlements Development when the government states:

> *People who invest in the rental housing do so with the intention of getting profit just as do other people who invest in other sectors. If they are subjected to rules that deter them from achieving their objectives, then they will be discouraged in investing in this sector. Certain sections of the Rent Restriction Act, 1984 are some of such deterrents, because they serve the intersests of the tenants more than those of landlords, thus discouraging investiment in rental housing.*[652]

The point of emphasis is that while the rent control scheme under the *Rent Restriction Act* was considered by some people as providing cheap and efficient means of assisting low income households to access affordable rental houses, yet others, including the government, treated it as a stumbling block whose effect was to discourage maintenance and investment in the housing sector. Such an antagonistic attitude was natural as long as there were two camps, one of tenants and another of landlords, which would hardly come to terms. Tanzania subscribed to the former view until 2005 by way of legislation in the nature of *Rent Restriction Acts*. However, for the reasons known best to the legislators, the *Rent Restriction Act* was wholly repealed in 2005[653] and the legal scheme of protection which the tenants enjoyed followed suit. This means that at the moment the tenants' safeguards, including the principle of standard rent and the doctrine of alternative accommodation are turning into matters of the past. In other words, today the rent payable is much more a question to be determined by the dictates of the market. The *Land Act* simply gives some guidelines in that in imposing rent, regard should be made to the size of the land, use of the land, value of the land as

---

652 See the National Human Settlements Development Policy, 2000, paragraph 4.2.7.1.

653 See the *Written Laws (Miscellaneous Amendment) Act* No. 11 of 2005.

evidenced by leases in the market in the area, location of the land and the condition of the land or building.[654] Five years now, following the repeal of the *Rent Restriction Act*, we are witnessing exorbitant increases in rent, a situation suggesting that the security of tenants is now placed under very serious jeopardy, meaning that those who have deep pockets and who can compete in the market are the most privileged to access quality rental premises than their counterparts who are economically handicapped. It is submitted that the human right to adequate housing and shelter by way of rented premises, especially in urban areas, is now very limited and only available for the economically advantaged few. The poor who form the majority of Tanzanians have no choice, their only refuge being slums and the geographically disadvantaged areas (*uswahilini*) in terms of infrastructure and other social services.[655]

Creation and Classification of Leases under the Land Act, 1999

Section 78 (1) of the *Land Act* empowers the holder of a granted right of occupancy to lease that right of occupancy to another person under certain specified conditions, while section 86 empowers the lessee to make a sub-lease. So, like sale, a lease is a disposition of interest over the land requiring, in the first place, a written contract[656] or memorandum, which is signed by the parties thereto before it can be enforceable in law[657]. A contract of lease may be completed on condition that there are parties to it;[658] there is land, the subject matter of the lease; there is reversion, that is, the right of the landlord to take back the demised property on termination of the lease; there is certainty of the term of the contract, and; there is a right of exclusive possession on the part of the lessee.[659] Again, we read from the *Land Registration Act*[660] that there are some leases which are compulsorily registrable under the Act, and there are some other leases which are not. Precisely, the law provides that:

---

654 See section 78 as amended by the *Written Laws (Miscellaneous Amendments) Act*, (No. 2), 2005 (Act No. 11 of 2005).

655 For details on the dangers that tenants are exposed to through the repeal of the Rent Restriction Act, see JESSE, James E.C.M., "The End of Protection from Forced Eviction through the Repeal of the Rent Restriction Act in Tanzania," *The Tanzania Lawyer*, Vol.2 No. 2 (2008), pp. 63-75.

656 See Land Form No.55 of the Land Forms Regulations, 2001.

657 Section 64 (1).

658 See this proposition also in *Rye v Rye* (1962) A.C 496.

659 See appendix 2, which is a specimen for a deed of lease, p. 286.

660 Cap. 344.

> *No lease shall be registered unless it is expressed to be for a term exceeding five years or contains an option whereby the tenant can require the landlord to grant him a further term or terms which, together with the original term, exceed five years.*[661]

The leases that are known in the jurisprudence of land law, some of which are expressly provided for under the *Land Act*, fall into the following classifications:

Lease for Fixed Period: a lease for a fixed period (or fixed term lease) means the lease that may be granted for a fixed duration, for instance, of 20 years. The condition in relation to this type of lease is that the term must be certain or must be capable of being made certain.[662] The maximum period under which a lease may be granted is ten days less than the period for which the right of occupancy has been granted for a definite term. It means, therefore, that the document creating the lease should specify when the lease commences and when it terminates. It is quite safe for example, if the lease agreement contains unambiguous clause providing, *inter alia*, that: "*IT IS HEREBY AGREED and DECLARED that this lease is for a fixed term of One year from the date of commencement*". If the period of commencement is not specified, the lease will be presumed to commence immediately unless it is a future lease[663]. As a general rule, a fixed term lease terminates at the affliction of time unless the lease provides for the option of unconditional renewal of the contract. The case of *Sands v Mutual Benefits Ltd*[664] is to the point. In the case the plaintiff sued the defendant for ejectment from a dwelling house which was demised to him for three years with an option to renew, "at such rent as may be mutually agreed". However, there was no arbitration clause in the lease. The lessee attempted to exercise the option but the parties could not agree on the future rent payable under the contract. The defendant contended that there was a binding option which had been exercised, and requested the court to determine a reasonable rent. In the court, the issue for determination was whether there was a binding option to renew the lease of the suit premises. The court, after making reference to a number of cases was of the view that

661 Section 54 (1).

662 See section 78 (1).

663 Section 83 (1) provides for the possibility to create a future lease, i.e a lease which may be made for the term commencing on a future date, but which is not later than twenty one years from the date on which the lease is executed.

664 (1971) EA 159.

the option to renew was not binding because of its uncertainty in terms of the rent payable. In essence, the court said that if an essential term, like the price of the commodity or service, or the rent of the house, is left uncertain and the agreement does not provide any means of ascertaining it, in the event of disagreement between the parties, that agreement is not a contract. In this case, the court awarded damages to the plaintiff at the rate he desired after the term of the lease had expired.

A point of emphasis, here, is that in order to avoid unnecessary litigations in the nature of the option to renew leases, parties are advised to insert in a lease contract a renewal clause which is unambiguous and certain, for example, that: "*The Landlord may in his absolute discretion renew (or decline to renew) the Lease for a further period of One year. No Court or Tribunal shall enquire in the matter of any decision made by the landlord*". However, sometimes avoiding litigations may not be guaranteed for at times parties to a lease prefer to go to court even where there are clear provisions about the option to renew in the lease contract. In *Juthalal Velji Ltd v The THB Estate Ltd*[665] the parties had created a fixed term lease through which the tenant had the option to renew the same by giving a three (3) months notice to the landlord before the term came to an end. Instead of abiding to this condition, the tenant gave a notice almost a month before and the landlord refused the renewal. The court decided in favour of the defendant in that the defendant had the right to refuse to renew the lease since the notice of renewal was not presented within the time stipulated in the contract.

Periodic Lease: periodic lease is a lease defined as per the provisions of section 79 (1) and (2) of the *Land Act*. According to this provision, leases shall fall under the category of periodic leases if they are made in the following alternative situations: Where the term of the lease is not specified and no provisions is made for the giving of notice to terminate the tenancy; where the term is from week to week, month to month, year to year or any other periodic basis, and; where the lessee remains in possession of the land with the consent of the lessor after a term of the lease has expired. The law provides for the manner of terminating a periodic tenancy, that is, by either party giving notice of intention to terminate to the other, the length of which shall not be less than the period of tenancy[666]. The period of tenancy, in this case, is presumed to be equal to the manner by which rent is reckoned. In *Adler*

665 [1983] TLR 391 (HC).

666 Section 79 (4).

v Blackman[667] the following were the facts and decision of the case: the premises were let by the landlord to the defendant on a weekly tenancy. An agreement was entered into between the parties, with one of the several clauses providing that, "To hold for the term of one year, at the inclusive weekly rent of £3 payable weekly in advance on Monday in each week during the whole of the tenancy." The tenant occupied the premises for the term provided on the agreement and thereafter he remained in possession, paying the rent reserved in the agreement. The plaintiff, having purchased the property, served a weekly notice on the defendant requiring him to quit. The defendant set a contention that the notice to quit was invalid, since he was holding over on a yearly tenancy. The Court held that where the rent is expressed to be per week, when the fixed period has come to an end one should not presume anything but a weekly tenancy, a tenancy for the period in respect of which the rent is expressed. In this case the notice was held to be valid. It is important to note that a periodic lease is leasehold whose term is indefinite, that is it automatically renews from year to year, month to month, or week to week until the landlord or tenant terminates it by notice to the other.

Short Term Lease: a short term lease is one that may be created under the provisions of section 80 of the *Land Act*. Examples of short term leases include: a lease that may be made for a term of one year or less, and; a periodic tenancy for periods of one year or less. Unlike other leases, a short term lease may be made orally or in writing[668] and does not create registrable interests in land[669].

Other Types of Tenancies: there are other categories of tenancies that are not expressly provided for under the *Land Act* but which have been recognised in the common law legal system. These include: Tenancy at will; tenancy at sufferance, and; service tenancy.

Tenancy at Will: This is created where the tenant, with the consent of the landlord, occupies the land qua tenant on the terms that either party may determine the tenancy at any time and that the tenant may occupy the premises at rent free. In other words, a person possessing the property of another without being required to make periodic rent payments is a tenant at will. However, if the tenancy at will is created and rent is subsequently paid and accepted upon some regular periodical basis (for example yearly, monthly, and weekly) then a periodic tenancy

---

667 (1953) 1 Q.B 146.

668 Section 80 (2).

669 Section 80 (3).

will be created. A tenancy at will normally comes to an end when either party does an act which is incompatible with the continuance of the tenancy such as assigning the interests in the land, or when there is notice of termination, or when either party dies.

Tenancy at Sufferance: this type of tenancy (also referred to as "statutory tenancy") arises where a tenant, having entered upon the land under a valid tenancy, holds over when the tenancy terminates, without the consent of the landlord. Such a tenant differs from a trespasser in that his original entry was lawful, and from a tenant at will in that his tenancy exists without the consent of the landlord. The rationale behind this classification is to avoid claims of adverse possession where the period of limitation has passed. Though no rent is payable, the tenant is liable to pay compensation (for example in the form of mesne profit). The tenancy may be terminated at any time or may be converted to periodic tenancy under the provisions of section 82 (2) of the *Land Act* which provides in part that:

> *...where the lessor continues for two months to accept rent from a tenant who remains in possession after the termination of the lease, a periodic lease from month to month shall be deemed to have come into force.*

Service Tenancy: this is a form of tenancy that is created when one occupies premises provided by his employer. In order to determine whether or not a service tenancy exists, one needs to establish whether the tenant pays rent directly or indirectly by having certain amount of rent being deducted from his salary. A service tenant is distinguished from a service occupant, that is, a person who occupiers the premises of his employer for the easy carrying out of his work. In Tanzania, people like the members of the defence forces who live in quarters form an immediate example of the service occupants. A service tenant does not enjoy the exclusive right of possession against the employer; he is regarded as a mere licencee and his tenancy over the premises ceases immediately when the tenant's employment ceases. It is submitted that this position of the law is sound and is well accommodated by public policy under which employers should enjoy the right of repossession of premises under the tenancy by their employees in order to be able to let such premises to other employees who come subsequently. The case of *Shell and BP Tanzania Ltd v Wilbard Fulgence Rwenyagira*[670] serves to illustrate a point on service tenancy, it being a case in which the appellant was granted an order of vacant possession on the termination of employment of the respondent (tenant).

---

670 1984] TLR 251 (CA).

Rights and Obligations of Parties to a Lease

It has been a common practice for the covenants creating rights and obligations of the parties to the lease/tenancy agreement to be adequately expressed in the lease deed. However, where, for some reasons, some important covenants are omitted in the deed, then such covenants will be implied under the common law as well as statutory law. These are what are termed as "usual covenants" under the provisions of the *Land Act*.[671] Usual Covenants are classified into two groups: implied covenants to bind the landlord[672] and implied covenants to bind the tenant[673]. The implied covenants falling in the former group confer rights on the part of the tenant, and impose a duty on the part of the landlord, and vice versa. These covenants are very diverse as discussed herein below.

Implied Covenants for Quiet Enjoyment: the law gives right to the lessee to peacefully and quietly possess and enjoy the land leased, provided that he pays rent, also observes and performs other obligations as may be imposed upon him by law or lease agreement.[674] The rationale behind the doctrine of quiet enjoyment relates much to protecting the tenants from unjustifiable interferences by the landlords. This is what we learn from the literature when we read that:

> *The phrase 'quiet enjoyment' connotes freedom from physical interference with the tenant's enjoyment of the land. "Quiet" here does not refer to freedom from noise but rather 'peaceable', though it is possible that noise might constitute a breach of the covenant. This right of quiet enjoyment is provided in order to guarantee security of tenure to a tenant. If this was not the case the landlord could decide to interrupt or harass the tenant from his quiet enjoyment of the premises as a measure to compel the tenant to vacate the demised premises.*[675]

This means that the landlord, or any other person claiming under him, has the obligation not to interfere with this right unless there are good reasons to do so. Breach of this obligation is condemnable and may even attract a penal sanction on the part of the landlord. In *R v Abdulrahman*

---

671 Section 91.

672 Section 88.

673 Section 89.

674 See Section 88 (1) (a). The section may be read together with section 56 (2) of the *Land Registration Act,* Cap. 334 in case of a registered lease.

675 JESSE, James E.M., *op cit.*

s/o Sima[676] the landlord was convicted for causing annoyance to the tenant. However, it is one thing to have the law being as good as this, but another thing to realise it in practice. Cases where the landlords opt for deliberate interference of the rights of tenants by deprivation are not minimal, including where a landlord decides to cut off the essential services such as water, electricity, telephone even toilet facilities for the purpose of compelling the tenant to vacate. This scenario is likely to aggravate in this time when the market tends to dictate the terms while the language of rights of the majority of tenants or potential tenants remains in its infancy. The case of *Shaidu Juma Kopwe v Seleman Mussa*[677] supports this observation. The parties in the case, a landlord and tenant, concluded a lease agreement for a fixed period of one year involving a room the respondent occupied as a haircutting salon and in respect of which he paid Tshs. 180,000/= as rent in lump sum. The respondent had also to pay Tshs. 5,000/= for electricity per month. Sometimes during the existence of the tenancy, the appellant raised the sum of the electricity contribution to Tshs. 10,000/=. The respondent declined to pay the same on grounds that it was not part of the agreement. The appellant decided to disconnect power (electricity) to the salon and the respondent filed a suit in court for, *inter alia*, an order of compensation for loss of business from the date of disconnection to the date of restoration. He won in the District Land and Housing Tribunal, and the appellant's appeal to the High Court was dismissed.

Implied Covenant for Non- Derogation from the Grant: it is the duty of the landlord not to permit any adjoining or neighbouring land to which he is the occupier or lessee, to be used in a manner that defeats the purpose for which the lease was granted[678]. In other words, the law prohibits the landlord from taking with his left hand whatever he has given with the right hand. However, in order to be able to hold the landlord liable for the breach, it needs be shown that his act has the effect of making the leased land or premises unfit or materially less fit for purpose of the lease and not otherwise[679]. We learn about this obligation from the case of *Aldin v Latimer Clark Muirhead and Co.*[680]

676 (1972) HCD 182.

677 High Court of Tanzania (Land Division) at Dar es Salaam, Land Case No. 18 of 2006 (Unreported).

678 Section 88 (1) (b).

679 See *Port v Griffith* (1938) 1 ALL ER 295.

680 (1894) 2 Ch. 437.

In this case, the land was leased to the appellant, a timber merchant. In order for timber to dry, there needed to be free flow of air to the sheds where the timber was stalled. The respondent retained the adjoining land. Thereafter, the lessor died and his interests passed to Latimer. Latimer proposed to build on the land such that, if the plan materialised, it would interrupt the free flow of air to the sheds. It was held, in court, that this constituted derogation from the grant and that the respondent was not, therefore, entitled to build so as to interrupt the free flow of air to the appellant's sheds.

Implied Covenant as to the Suitability/Fitness of the Premises: it is an implied term of a lease contract that "Where any dwelling house, flat, or room is leased, that house, flat or room is fit for human habitation at the commencement of the tenancy and will be kept fit for human habitation during the lease".[681] This provision gives the primary responsibility of ensuring that the premises are fit for habitation, at the commencement of the lease, to the landlord. Anything to the contrary needs to be expressly stated in the contract of lease. Following this obligation, the *Land Act* further provides that where the demised premises or part of them are destroyed by fire, flood, or explosion or other accident or natural disaster (e. g lightening, earthquake or volcanic activity) not attributed to the lessee's negligence or the negligence of his invitee or employees, so as to make that premises or part of it unfit for human habitation, the rent and any such other contribution payable by the lessee shall be suspended and cease to be payable until the premises are again rendered fit for occupation or use.[682] The law gives the lessee an option to terminate the lease by giving a one month's notice for that intention if the landlord does not remedy the damage within six months.[683]

Implied Covenant as to Repair and Maintenance: the law makes it an implied term that where only part of the building is leased, the landlord will have an obligation to keep the roof, all external and main walls and main drains and the common parts and installations in a proper state of repair.[684] It means that the landlord has no primary obligation to effect repairs where the lease is made to the whole of the building. It is submitted that since the law requires the landlord to ensure that

681 Section 88 (1) (d).

682 Section 88 (1) (e).

683 *Ibid.*

684 Section 88 (1) (c).

the premises are fit for human habitation, the duty to repair will arise depending on the nature of repair. In every case, the law makes it an implied term for the landlord's obligation, at all reasonable times to enter either personally or by an agent, the leased premises for the purpose of inspecting their condition and repair and for carrying out repairs and making good any defect.[685]

Implied Covenant as to Payment of Rates and Other Charges: the law makes an implied covenant that the landlord will be under the obligation to pay all rates, taxes, dues and other outgoings which are payable in respect of the leased land or building[686].

The second class of implied terms is comprised of terms that bind the tenant/lessee, meaning that they impose a duty to the tenant but create rights to the landlord.

Implied Obligation to Pay Rent: Section 89(1) (a) of the *Land Act* makes it an implied term of the lease that the lessee shall pay rent reserved in the lease at the time and in the manner specified in the lease. Failure to pay rent at the time specified in the lease or within the reasonable time thereafter is a breach of the contract of lease and it is, therefore, a good cause for eviction of the tenant from the demised premises. Judge P.A Rugazia of the High Court notes very correctly that, "Rent arrears and subletting are the two sins which normally bring landlords and tenants head on."[687] Before the repeal of the *Rent Restriction Act,* 1984 the rent payable under the lease was the standard rent as would have been assessed and fixed by the Regional Housing Tribunal[688]. However, with the repeal of the *Rent Restriction Act*, the question of rent payable under a lease is now determined by the market. It means that with the repeal of the *Rent Restriction Act*, the majority of tenants will hardly escape liability for non payment of rent, and cases of evictions will remain the common feature affecting the landlord-tenant relationships, especially so in many cases of residential premises.

---

685 Section 88 (2) (a).

686 Section 88 (1) (g).

687 See *Rashid Halfan v Pendael Singa and National Housing Corporation*, High Court of Tanzania (Land Division), at Dar es Salaam, Land Case No. 173 of 2004 (Unreported) at p. 1.

688 Section 16 of the *Rent Restriction Act*.

Implied Covenant not to Commit Waste: the covenant[689] imposes a duty to the lessee to keep the demised premises in a tenant-like manner, that is to say, to keep it in a reasonable state of repair[690]. Therefore, a lessee commits waste who undertakes to alter the premises by way of damage, destruction, addition, improvement or neglect. It is well stated in the literature that:

> *Any act of the tenant which, is not in accordance with the suitable use of the premises or in a manner inconsistent with the conditions in which it was leased may amount to commit waste and thereby becomes liable to an action for damages or eviction.*[691]

For that reason, we are strongly warned by Ihema, J.- as he then was in the case of *Fumo Co. Limited and National Housing Corporation v Jujent Import-Export Co. Ltd*[692] that, "Structural alterations in demised premises may not be carried out without express permission of the land lord". The case of *Hamid Mbaye v The Brigade Commander*[693] also supports this view. In this case the plaintiff had let his premises to the respondent. When he was later given vacant possession of the same, much damage had been done on the premises. The parties had not agreed on anything regarding maintenance of the suit premises. However the *Rent Restriction Decree*[694] of Zanzibar imposed a duty on the tenant to maintain the premises in the same state, fair wear and tear and damage arising from irresistible force excepted, as that in which the premises were at the commencement of the tenancy[695]. When this matter came to court, it was found that the defendant had made several alterations to the house where, for example, a toilet was sealed and turned into kitchen. The court held that most of the damages were not from irresistible force but a result of alterations. The defendant was, consequently, ordered to pay damages. The *Land Act* does not impose liability to the tenant if the waste results from: reasonable tear and wear; fire, flood or explosion, or other accident not attributable to the negligence of the lessee, his invitees, or employees; other natural disasters.[696]

---

689 See section 89 (1) (b) and (c).

690 Section 92 of the *Land Act* defines a "reasonable state of repair" to mean a state of repair which a prudent owner, might reasonably be expected to keep his own building, due allowance being made for the age, character and locality of the building.

691 JESSE, James E.M., *op cit.*

692 High Court of Tanzania at Dar es Salaam, Civil Appeal No. 135 of 1999 (Unreported).

693 [1984] TLR 294 (HC-Z).

694 Cap. 98 of the Laws of Zanzibar.

695 Section 28 (1) (b) (i).

696 Section 89 (1) (c).

Implied Covenant as to Restraint on Alienation: under the common law, a tenant was free to transfer, assign or sublet the demised premises unless this freedom was expressly restricted by the covenants. According to the literature, this is called the "lessee's common law right to freely assign or sublease"[697]. The possible exceptions would be: when the tenancy at will or sufferance was involved; where the lease required significant personal services from the lessee such that any transfer would substantially impair the lessor's chances of obtaining those services; or where the parties to the lease validly agreed otherwise.

In Tanzania, section 89 (1) (i) of the *Land Act* makes it an implied covenant restraining the tenant from transferring, mortgaging, charging, subleasing or otherwise parting with the possession of the land or building without the previous written consent of the lessor. However, the requirement of the law is that such consent must not be unreasonably withheld.[698] Consent will be said to have been unreasonably withheld, if for example, the landlord requires the lessee to pay money other than the reasonable expenses incurred in connection with the giving of consent or imposes on the lessee any unreasonable conditions.[699] Before the enactment of the *Land Act,* judicial authorities suggested that the effect of subleasing a premises without the consent of the landlord was to render the sublessee a trespasser. In *Onoratha Della Santa and Others v Peera,*[700] the landlord had leased the premises to Onoratha for a term of three years. The lease contained a term that the lessee was not to assign or underlet any part of the demised premises without first obtaining a written consent of the lessor. Onoratha, without obtaining the consent of the lessor assigned the demised premises to the "others". In the court the issue was whether the sublease was valid. The court held that the premises were unlawfully sublet and, therefore, the lessor maintained the right of re-entry. The court held the 2nd, 3rd and 4th appellants to be trespassers. This position of the court was followed in the cases of *Mrs Clara D'Souza v Charles Frank Kanyamala*[701] and *Gregory Mtafya v Zainabu Lyimo*[702] in which, again, the court held the sublease to be

697 See Burke B et al., *op cit*, at p. 378.

698 See section 89 (1) (i) and section 93 (1). Also the case of *International Drilling Fluids Ltd v Louisville Investment (Uxbridge) Ltd* [1986] 2 WLR 581 sets some propositions on reasonableness in the withholding of consent.

699 Section 93 (3).

700 (1970) HCD 22.

701 (1974) LRT 27.

702 (1976) LRT 3.

unlawful and that tenants were not protected by the *Rent Restriction Act* of that time, because the sublease was made without the consent of the lessor. The rationale behind this rule was probably to afford opportunity to the lessor to know who is coming into his premises and be able to object the subletting if, in his opinion, the intended sublessee could not be entrusted with the landlord's property, or would not perform the lease covenants, or be a good neighbour.

However, the *Land Act* tends to suggest that even if a lessee sublets the lease without the lessor's consent the sublease has effect, but the lessor is not precluded from seeking for remedy against the lessee.[703] This is the case even where there is an express prohibition against assignment or subleasing. This position of the *Land Act* is, to my opinion, commendable for two reasons: it takes into consideration the public policy which implies a covenant of good faith and fair dealing in every contract, and; it tends to protect the right of the innocent subtenants to the leasehold by recognising them as valid tenants rather than treating them as simply trespassers. It follows that a landlord whose premises have been sublet without his consent, has a cause of action, including the right to terminate the lease, not against the sublessee but against the lessee for breach of the lease contract. The case of *Rashid Halfan v Pendael Singa and National Housing Corporation* cited above points to this new position of the law. In this case the plaintiff was a tenant of the second defendant. He sublet the premises to the first defendant without the knowledge and consent of the second defendant at a monthly rent of 250,000/= while the lessee himself was paying the lessor a monthly rent of 27,000/= and later 35,000/=. When the matter came to light, the second defendant concluded a tenancy between him and the first defendant. The plaintiff was aggrieved and instituted this suit. Dismissing the suit as unfounded, the Court (Rugazia, J.) had the following to say at p. 3:

> *I find no difficulty in answering the first issue because there is no dispute that the plaintiff took it upon himself to sub-let the premises. Through that arrangement, which was done without the consent and knowledge of the landlord, the plaintiff reaped an illegal huge profit yet, he even failed to remit a mere shs. 35,000/- out of shs. 250,000/- he earned through unlawful means. This is the man who has the audacity to come forward seeking court protection! Which court does he expect to bless illegality?*

703 Section 98 (2).

> *I have to find which I now do, in respect of the first issue, that it was the plaintiff who breached the lease agreement.*
>
> *Having so found, I think it should follow, that having conducted himself the way he did; and having been served with a termination notice, the plaintiff was no longer a tenant so there was no reason for the second defendant not to re-allocate the premises to the 1st defendant.*

Implied Landlord's Right to View: The lessee has a statutory obligation to permit the landlord, his agent or employees to enter demised premises, to view and, where necessary, to effect some repair. However, the obligation arises where there is a prior reasonable notice by the landlord, his agent or employees and when entry is done at a convenient time. As to what is reasonable notice, this will depend on each particular case. The *Land Registration Act*[704] provides for three months notice to be reasonable. Any attempt by the lessor to exercise power of entry in contravention of the law is untenable, and the lessor may bear responsibility for interference which amounts to violating the lessee's right to exclusive possession of the rental property.

Implied Obligation for Repair and Maintenance: it has already been stated above that the *Land Act* imposes a legal duty of repair to both the tenant and the landlord. It means that, where only part of a building is leased, the landlord is obliged to keep the roof, all external and main walls and drains, the common parts and common installations, including common passage and walkways in a proper state of repair.[705] However, where the whole of the building is leased, then the tenant has the obligation to keep all buildings comprised in the lease in a reasonable state of repair.[706] Also where only part of a building is leased, a lessee has the obligation to keep the leased part of the building in a reasonable state of repair subject to the obligation of the landlord. [707]As to what is "reasonable state of repair", reference is made to a state of repair which a prudent owner might reasonably be expected to keep on his own building, due allowance being made for the age, character and locality of the building and the means of the person under the obligation to comply with such a covenant.[708] It means, therefore, that

---

704 Section 56 (1) (c).

705 Section 88 (1) (c).

706 Section 89 (1) (e).

707 Section 89 (1) (f).

708 Section 92.

a lessee has the duty to restore the building in the same condition as it was in when the lease began. There are two exceptions to the lessee's obligation to repair. First, is when damage or deterioration is caused by reasonable tear and wear; fire, flood or explosion or other accidents not attributable to the negligence of the lessee, his invitees or employees; civil commotion; lightening, storm, earthquake, volcanic activity or other natural disaster.[709] Second is when a person is a tenant of short term lease.[710] From the foregoing, it follows that whenever a tenant is relieved from the duty to repair, he has, nevertheless the reciprocal duty of maintenance.

Assignment, Subleasing and Enforceability of Covenants in a Lease

This area seeks to answer three basic questions about leases: who can enforce covenants in a lease, and against whom? What covenants are enforceable in a lease? What happens if the lease is assigned or sublet to a third party? In order to answer the above questions succinctly, reference is made to the literature and judicial precedents of great significance. It is said that:

> *...a lease is both a contract between landlord and tenant and a conveyance of an estate from the landlord to the tenant. The conveyance gives the tenant the right to possess land for a period of time without interference from the landlord and imposes on the tenant certain duties including the duties to pay rent, make repairs, and not commit waste. The rights and obligations of the landlord and tenant growing out of the conveyance are based on* ***privity of estate,*** *because both have an interest in the land; the tenant has possessory interest, and the landlord has a reversion. Leases also create a contract in which both parties make express covenants. The tenant, for example, may agree to make specific rental payments by the first day of each month, and the landlord may agree to maintain the premises. The landlord's and tenant's rights and obligations arising out of the express lease covenants are based on* ***privity of contract.***[711] *(Emphasis added).*

We note from the above extract that there two relationships that may be created under a lease. There is on one hand a relationship that arises out of *privity of estate* and on the other hand a relationship that

709 Section 89 (1) (c).

710 Section 89 (2).

711 See Burke B *et al., op cit* at p. 364.

is born out of *privity of contract*. Therefore, as regards enforceability of the covenants in the lease, there are three common law principles that may be invoked as guides: One, if there is *privity of contract,* then all covenants are enforceable by one party to the contract against the other. There is *privity of contract* when the parties have made a legally enforceable agreement creating therein terms and conditions to bind them. Their obligations in that agreement will bind them whether they have anything to do with land or not. Two, if there is mere *privity of estate*, only covenants which touch and concern the land are enforceable. There a privity of estate between two people who have interest over the land, one having possessory interest and another having reversionary interest over the same land. In such a case only covenants that "*affected the nature, quality, or value of the thing demised, independently of collateral circumstances; or if it affected the mode of enjoying it*"[712] shall be enforced. In other words, all covenants that are implied by law in a lease are covenants that touch and concern the land, and as such can be enforced by parties when their relation is either that of *privity of contract* or *privity of estate* or both. Three, if there is *privity* neither of estate nor of contract between the parties, then, the general rule is that the covenants are not enforceable at all against any party. The only exception would be where there are restrictive covenants touching and concerning land. These will be enforceable except against a *bonafide* purchaser for value without notice. Since a tenant can transfer part or all of his leasehold estate by means of subleasing or assignment, the above principle may apply in any of these cases.

There is subleasing (or subletting) when the original lessee contracts to lease part of his estate to a third party thereby becoming a sublessor and the third party becoming a sublessee. The parties to a sublease are in privity of contract as well as privity of estate. They can agree on anything provided that it is not inconsistent with the provisions of the original contract. Take the following to be a case scenario:

> ***B** who is a university student leases **A**'s apartment for twelve months commencing from January to December. In three month period (June-September) **B** subleases the apartment under a new contract to **C**, his friend for three months.*

In this case there is a twofold relationship, that is to say, B, a lessee, remains responsible to A, a lessor, on one hand, and as between them there is still both, privity of contract and privity of estate. For example,

712 As per Lord Ellenborough's words in *Congleton Corporation v Pattison* (1808), 10 East 130, 135.

A can sue B to recover the rent for the months of June-September, even if C did not pay B. On the other hand, C, a sublessee, is responsible to B, a sublessor, on the terms of the new contract, and as between them, there exists privity of contract and privity of estate. However, as between A and C there is only privity of estate but no privity of contract. As regards the assignment of the lease, the general common law rule may be stated that an assignee of a lease is bound by privity of estate to perform the covenants which run with the land and during such time as he holds the term.

There is an assignment of the lease when the original tenant, say B in the above case, transfers his entire leasehold to a third party, C. This happens, for example, if B decides to transfer the leasehold to C from June till December when the lease period comes to an end. In such a case, there is privity of contract between A and B, but there is no longer privity of estate since B has no more possessory interest in the estate. And as between A and C, there is no privity of contract but privity of estate, and C's primary responsibility is to A, not B. So, should it happen that C breaches any covenant, say non payment of rent, A can proceed against B, the assignor, on the basis that there is privity of contract between them, or against C, the assignee, on the basis that there is privity of estate between them. This is where the question of covenants that touch and form part of the land comes in because the assignee is liable only for the "usual covenants" in the lease unless he expressly assumes the tenant's lease obligation to the landlord. The express assumption may, for example, be in the following form: "*It is hereby understood that the assignee accepts, assumes, and agrees to perform all of the terms, conditions, and limitations in the lease*." Once this is made, then the privity of contract between the lessor and an assignee arises. However, even if the sublessee assumes the original tenant's obligation, the lessor retains the right of action against both the lessee and sublessee, unless he expressly releases the lessor from his obligation under the contract. If this happens, then we say there is *novation* that extinguishes the privity of contract between the lessor and the lessee.[713] It is, therefore, very important to ask whether the transfer that is created by the tenant to another is an assignment or a sublease. We read from the literature[714], that there are two tests to apply in order to make this determination: the traditional test and the modern test. According to the former, the

---

713 For the doctrine of *novation* in contract, see section 62 of the *Law of Contract Act,* [Cap. 345 R.E 2002].

714 See Barke B *et al.*, *op cit*, at p. 366.

question is whether the original tenant retains any interest in the leased estate. If the answer is in the affirmative, it is a sublease, and if it is in the negative, it is an assignment. According to the latter, the question is: what was the intention of the parties as evidenced by the totality of the factors and circumstances surrounding the transfer.

The above common law position has been substantially altered by the *Land Act* of Tanzania. Precisely, the Act has abolished the common law rule that a transferor or assignor of a lease remains liable on the personal covenant to the lessor for payment of rent and for all breaches of covenants even if he is no longer in possession or occupation of the leased land. The Act provides that the effect of a transfer or assignment of a lease is to discharge absolutely the transferor or assignor from any obligation to pay rent or to observe any covenants in respect of the land as from the date of the transfer or assignment.[715] The only exceptions in which the transferor or assignor will remain liable are: when he remains in occupation of the land, despite the transfer or assignment,[716] or; in respect of the obligation to pay rent or remedy the breaches that accrued during the term of the lease when such a transferor or assignor was still bound by all covenants in that lease, that is, those which accrued before the transfer or assignment.[717] The transferee or assignee undertakes obligations on the lease immediately after the transfer or assignment even if he does not acknowledge the lessor as such[718] or take possession of the land or building complied in the lease.[719] The person who becomes a lessee in this scenario has all the obligations under the lease even if the transfer or assignment is made with or without the consent of the lessor.[720] He will have all the rights and obligations to pay rent to the lessor,[721] observe and perform all covenants binding the lessee, expressed or implied in the lease[722], and enforce all covenants made by and binding on the lessor, expressed or implied in the lease.[723]

---

715 Section 97 (1).

716 Section 97 (2).

717 Section 97 (3).

718 Section 98 (1) (a).

719 Section 98 (1) (b).

720 Section 98 (2).

721 Section 98 (3) (a).

722 Section 98 (3) (b).

723 Section 98 (3) (c).

Termination of Leases

A lease may terminate following the occurrence of any of the factors discussed herein below and, of course, depending on the nature of the lease itself, or the applicable law, that is, whether it is common law or statutory law.

Termination by Expiry: as a general rule, a lease for a fixed term terminates automatically when that fixed term expires, the exception being in the case when the lease contract provides for an unconditional option to renew. A fixed-term lease need not be terminated by notice, except where it is expressly agreed upon in the contract of lease.

Termination by Notice: This applies to periodic leases, that is, leases in which the term of the lease is not specified, and no provision is made for the giving of notice to terminate the tenancy. The term of such leases may be from year to year, month to month, week to week or any other period. As it is stated above, the length of the notice must be equal to the length of the period of the tenancy. By period of tenancy, it means a period by reference to which rent is payable.[724] The essence of the notice of intention to terminate the lease by the lessor is, *inter alia*, to afford the lessee an opportunity to secure some alternative accommodation. When termination is by the lessee then the notice affords the lessor an opportunity to secure another tenant in order to avoid the possibility of losing profit if property is left unoccupied when the original tenant vacates.

Termination by Forfeiture: This is a common law method of termination of a lease. It occurs where the lease contains an express forfeiture clause which creates a legal right of re-entry. The clause makes the lease voidable at the option of the landlord when a covenant in the lease is breached, or in the case that there is no such express forfeiture clause, where the lease is granted "upon a condition" or "provided always that" certain things are done or not done, the lease may be forfeited on the breach of such a condition. In all these, a landlord can enforce forfeiture by issuing a writ of possession. This common law mode of termination of a lease by forfeiture has undergone some considerable statutory modifications. For example, forfeiture of a lease for non payment of rent requires prior formal demand by the landlord unless this is exempted by the express wording of the lease. Again, in all cases of forfeiture for breach of other covenants or conditions, the forfeiture is subject to the landlord's obligation to serve a notice to the tenant and allow reasonable time for

724 Section 79 (3).

the tenant to comply or seek relief.[725] In Tanzania, the lessor's power to terminate the lease by re-entry or forfeiture was initially abolished by the provisions of section 101 (1) of the *Land Act* for what might have been said to be the legislative measures to protect tenants. Under this provision the landlord's right of re-entry was not available even if it was expressly or impliedly provided for in the lease. However, following the amendment of the *Land Act*,[726] sub-section (1) of section 101 has been repealed in order to give much power to the market, meaning that the right of re-entry is now available to the landlord. Precisely, the law requires a lessor to exercise any right to terminate a lease for non payment of rent or for breach of any covenant or condition in the lease.[727] However, what the law requires is for the lessor to serve a notice of his intention to terminate the lease for non payment of rent (where rent has been in arrears for not less than thirty days)[728] or for breach of covenants other than non payment of rent.[729] The contents of the notice include[730]: the description of the breach; the action which the lessee may take to remedy the breach, and; the duration of the notice which is the period of not less than thirty days. This requirement of notice need not be overlooked since it strikes a balance between the fundamental right of a hearing, the *audi alteram partem*, by affording the lessee the opportunity to present his case[731] on why should the lease not terminate and to know the adverse act that may be taken against him on one hand, and the right of the lessor to the profit of renting on the other hand. The law obliges the lessor to serve a copy of the notice to sublessees, spouse of the lessee, mortgagee of the lessee or of sublessees, and, where the lessee

---

725 See section 146 (1) of the English *Law of Property Act, 1925*. Under this section, the enforceability of a right of re-entry or forfeiture is subjected to the requirement that the lessor first serves on the lessee a notice specifying the particular breach complained of, requiring that the breach be remedied where the remedy is available or requiring compensation in any other case.

726 See the *Written Laws (Miscellaneous Amendments) Act* No. 11 of 2005.

727 See section 103 (1) of the *Land Act* as introduced by the *Written Laws (Miscellaneous Amendments)* (No.2) Act No. 11 of 2005.

728 Section 104.

729 Section 105.

730 See sub section 2 of sections 104 and 105 respectively.

731 The case of *Assistant Registrar of Building v Fredrick Kibwana* [1987] TLR 84 is illustrative of this point. In this case the learned judge (Mwalusanya, J.- as he then was) held that since the tenant was not served with any demand notices for arrears of rent or letter of notices to quit the premises, the tenant was condemned unheard which was in breach of rules of natural justice.

is bankrupt, the trustee of the lessee[732] of whose names and addresses the lessor has notice.[733] The essence of notice to the persons, other than the lessee, is to enable them to know the adverse action that is likely to be taken against their interest in the demised property, if any, and to be able to take immediate action to rescue such interest, e.g., to apply for any relief in the court.[734] According to law and in the event that the breach is not remedied, the lease shall terminate at the expiry of thirty days from the date of service of the notice[735]. In case of an application for relief against termination by the lessee the court has the power to consider the matter and grant the relief after taking into consideration a number of factors[736] such as the age, means and circumstances of the lessor[737] and also the age, means and circumstances including the health and number of dependants of the lessee. The court, especially, needs to consider whether the lessee will be rendered homeless by grant of an order or whether the lessee will have any alternative means of providing for himself and his dependants or whether the spouse of the lessee will or is likely to suffer undue hardship if an order were made.[738] The law is, to this extent, commendable for it gives primacy to the lessee's right to housing, which tops the human rights agenda. Having made its mind, the court may or may not grant the order of termination, and when it does not, then it needs grant an alternative remedy that it thinks fit.[739] Other courses of action available to the parties, apart from an order of termination or relief against that order, include actions for damages, specific performance, injunction, and, in the case of an action by the lessor, recovery of debt as arrears of rent.[740]

Surrender, Abandonment and Transfer: Surrender of a lease happens when the tenant surrenders his lease to the landlord. When the landlord accepts the surrender, the lease merges in the landlord's reversion. A case scenario illustrating surrender would be where:

---

732 Section 106 (1) (a) - (d).

733 Section 106 (2).

734 Section 107.

735 Section 104 (2) (d) and section 105 (2) (c) of the *Land Act* as amended by Act No. 11 of 2005.

736 Section 108 (1).

737 See 108 (1). (g).

738 Section 108 (1) (h).

739 Section 108 (2).

740 Section 109.

> *In January 2007* **A**, *leased an apartment to* **B** *for affixed term of three years at monthly rent of Tshs. 200,000/= payable in advance on 1st January each year. The lease expires on 1st January 2009. In August, 2007* **B** *moved out of the apartment, he immediately notified* **A** *of his decision and further said that he would no longer be bound by the lease covenants, express or implied.*

In such a situation, the legal issue that need to be considered and, therefore, determined is whether the lease terminates automatically following B's decision. The second immediate issue is whether A, the lessor is entitled to any remedy. Reading the *Land Act* between the lines, we learn that under the common law the lessee remains liable to pay rent and observe all covenants of the lease until the expiry of the term of the lease in question. However, this position is different in Tanzania. The *Land Act*[741] provides that:

> *(4) As from the date of the commencement of this Act, the rule of the common law that a lessee remains liable to pay rent and comply with all the covenants, notwithstanding that he has, with the agreement of the lessor, vacated the leased land before the date for the termination of the lease, is abolished and the provision set out in subsection (5) shall forthwith apply.*
>
> *(5) A lessee who, with the agreement of the lessor, vacates land before the termination of a lease shall, unless the lease provides expressly for a shorter period, remain liable to pay rent and observe all the covenants in the lease for one year from the date on which he vacates the land or buildings except that where the lessor leases that land or any buildings to another person before the end of the period of one year, the provisions of subsection (1) shall apply from the date of the execution of that lease.*

Our understanding of the above provisions is that a lessee who vacates the leased premises on agreement with the landlord is protected. The law dictates the maximum period for the lessee to remain liable to the lease to be one year, that is, the lessee remain liable to pay rent and observe all the covenants for the period of one year. This period may be shortened by the landlord by the express terms or by leasing the land or building to another lessee. Public policy and logic would expect the landlord to lease the property to another lessee instead of leaving it unoccupied and, therefore, in immediate danger of damage. Again, from the above

741 See Section 97 (4) and (5).

provision we learn that the lessee, who vacates the demised premises without the consent of the lessor, will be said to have abandoned the premises, and this will constitute a breach of a contract for which the landlord will have an action for the breach and, thus, will be entitled to damages that would naturally follow from such a breach. In such a case, the landlord's obligation to mitigate the loss/damage by securing another lessee will arise under the doctrine of mitigation of losses in the law of contract or on public policy consideration which discourages economic waste and encourages productive use of the property.

Abandonment on the other hand, happens when a lessee leaves the demised property unattended with no intention of repossessing it again. Abandonment may be implied, for example, in a situation where a tenant stops occupying the property, ceases to pay rent for a considerable term and does not react to any adverse action against his interests in the property by the landlord or third party. The issue of abandonment, particularly, was central in the case of *Beno Chelele t/a General Integrated Firm v National Housing Corporation and 2 Others* cited above. The facts are that the 1st defendant (the National Housing Corporation) let the suit premises, that is the commercial premises known as apartment No. 004 situated on plot no 728 Block II along Makunganya Street in Dar es Salaam, to the 2nd defendant (Morogoro Stores (1976) Ltd) as early as 1976. Subsequently and with the permission of the landlord, the lessee sublet the premises to the 3rd defendant (Nevada Golden Coin Ltd). Later on the 1st defendant re-allocated the premises to the plaintiff saying that the original tenants had abandoned it. The plaintiff entered the premises through a District Court's order. The 2nd and 3rd defendants successfully applied for revision in the High Court whereby the District Court's order was nullified. The plaintiff was aggrieved and filed this action in court praying for, *inter alia*, that he be declared the lawful tenant of the premises. The arguments advanced against the defendants centred on the plaintiff's allegation that the two defendants had abandoned the suit premises. The defence argued that they had closed the premises in the process of changing their line of business. Evidence indicated that the defendants went to court to challenge the plaintiff's forceful entry into the premises about five days of the entry, and that they were not in rent arrears. To the court (Kileo, J.- as she then was) the two facts did not give an impression of someone who had abandoned, forsaken and deserted the premises, meaning that the fact of abandonment was not established, and the defendants remained the lawful tenants of the first defendants. The point we take, here, is that that mere allegation that the tenant has abandoned the demised premises is, alone, not enough to determine a lease. There must be sufficient evidence which establishes that there has been an abandonment of the demised premises, and that such an abandonment is for no good cause. In the above case it was emphasized that:

> *Premises may for some good cause be unoccupied for a time and someone may just spring up and force his entry on the ground that the premises are unoccupied. To allow this kind of thing to happen may result in anarchy and would certainly be against public policy. Even the court may allocate only those premises, which are left unoccupied without good cause.*[742]

The court had another ground to reject the plaintiff's claims. This is the question of notice. In brief, the court found that there was no proper notice of the intention of the 1st defendant to terminate the lease contract between him and the rest of the defendants. To the court this, again, was another defect in the procedures involved, and undermined the cherished principles of natural justice. The court was very clear to the point as it observed at p. 12 that:

> *In my considered opinion exhibit DI cannot be said to be proper notice. Termination of tenancy particularly where the tenancy agreement has been in existence for over twenty years without breach is a serious thing and any steps towards that end must be taken with strict observance not only of the law but also of principles of natural justice, including an opportunity for the tenant to be heard.*

Lastly, transfer occurs when, with the consent of the landlord, the original lessee transfers his interests in the demised property to a third party. Once this is complete a new tenancy is said to have been created as between the landlord and the said third party, while duties and obligations of the original parties cease.[743]

Termination by Frustration: A lease may be terminated due to the occurrence, during the tenancy, of a frustrating event such that no substantial use permitted by the lease and in the contemplation of the parties remains available to the tenant. For example, a three month lease of a hall would be frustrated if on the first day of the lease, the hall is burnt down, otherwise than through the fault of the tenant. Should this

---

742 Beno Chelele case, at p. 8.

743 See *Fatuma Ghahae v Mariam Ghahae and National Housing Corporation*, High Court of Tanzania (Land Division) at Dar es Salaam, Land Case No. 261 of 2004 (Unreported).

happen, then the normal rules of contract law will apply. The *Law of Contract Act* of Tanzania states very clear that a contract to do an act which, after the contract is made, becomes impossible of performance is void.[744] It follows that any person who has received any advantage under a frustrated contract is bound to restore it to the person from whom he received it.[745]

Transfer of Land Interests by Mortgage

Reading section 2 (1) of the repealed *Land (Law of Property and Conveyancing) Ordinance* , it is not difficult to discover that the law that governed, *inter alia*, matters of mortgage in Tanzania before the coming of the *Land Act*, was the English law that was in force in England on January 1st 1922. After the coming of the *Land Acts*, the main legal principles governing mortgages in Tanzania are derived from the content of Part X of the *Land Act*, especially under the provisions of sections 111-142. It is important to note, at the outset, that this part of the Principle Act was repealed and replaced by the *Land (Amendment) Act*, 2004[746] which has also been substamtially amended by the *Mortgage Financing (Special Provisions) Act, 2008*. It means, therefore, that any reference made of the *Land Act* in this part, takes into account these amendments. Essentially, this area of the law provides for all matters involved in the execution and enforcement of mortgages including, *inter alia*, creation of mortgages, classification of mortgages, as well as the rights and obligation of parties to a mortgage deed.

Definition, Creation, and Parties to, a Mortgage

The term mortgage may simply be understood to mean a conveyance of interest in property which is designed to secure payment of money or discharge some other obligations.[747] The law on mortgage empowers, in unambiguous terms, an occupier of land under the right of occupancy or a lessee to mortgage his interest in the land or part thereof to secure the payment of an existing or future or contingent debt or other money or money's worth or in the fulfilment of a condition.[748] It follows, therefore,

---

744 Section 56 (2).

745 Section 65.

746 Act No. 2 of 2004.

747 For the statutory definition of the term, see section 2, of the *Land Act* which defines mortgage as "an interest in the right of occupancy or lease securing the payment of money or money's worth or the fulfilment of a condition and includes a sub mortgage and the instrument creating a mortgage".

748 See section 113 (1).

that to talk of a mortgaged land is to talk of a mortgage over the land in the nature of right of occupancy, lease and sublease[749]. In order to create a mortgage which shall be recognised in law, there are certain basic requirements in terms of essential elements and procedures that need be observed.[750] First, the mortgage requires the presence of parties who agree to enter into a contract of mortgage. These are the mortgagor, meaning a person, occupier or lessee, who has mortgaged his right of occupancy or lease[751] (he is a borrower), and a mortgagee, meaning a person in whose favour the mortgage is created or subsists[752] (i.e., a lender, such as a bank). Second, the mortgage requires the presence of land (with or without structure erected on it) which is the subject matter of the mortgage, in the form of a right of occupancy or lease. Third, the mortgage must be created in a prescribed form, that is, in writing and signed by the parties thereto (formal mortgages)[753]. The exception to this requirement is in respect of the informal mortgages which might be created under the provisions of section 113 (5) of the *Land Act.* These may be created for example, when the borrower offers and the lender accepts a written and witnessed undertaking whose intention is to charge the borrower's land with the repayment of money obtained from the lender[754], or when the borrower deposits to the lender documents such as a certificate of a granted right of occupancy.[755] Fourth, the mortgage, once created, must be registered in a prescribed register, depending on the nature of land which is the subject matter of the mortgage. This means that for mortgages involving land which is compulsorily registrable under the *Land Registration Act,* a mortgage must be registered under the same Act,[756] and for mortgages involving any land, not compulsorily registrable under this Act, registration is through the *Registration of Document Act.*[757] Mortgages involving

749 Section 111 (3).

750 See appendix 4 which is a specimen of a deed of mortgage below at p. 290.

751 See section 112 (2).

752 *Ibid.*

753 Section 113 (1) makes it a requirement of a mortgage as to be executed by an instrument in a prescribed form, which may be varied or added to as the circumstances may require. To say the least, this is Land Form No. 40 of the Land (Forms) Regulations.

754 Section 113 (5) (a).

755 Section 113 (5) (b).

756 See section 57, [Cap. 334 R.E 2002].

757 [Cap. 117 R.E 2002].

customary land may be registrable under the Village Land Register. The obligation to apply for registration falls on the mortgagor, but should the mortgagee be so requested, such application can be done by the mortgagee at the mortgagor's cost. The effect of non registration of a mortgage which is compulsorily registrable renders the mortgage of no effect and, thus, incapable of enforcement in court. Section 57 of the *Land Registration Act* is very clear on the effect of non registration of mortgages registrable under that Act:

> *A mortgage shall,* ***when registered****, have effect as a security and shall not operate as a transfer of the estate thereby mortgaged, but the lender shall have all the powers and remedies in case of default and be subject to all the obligations that would be conferred or implied in a transfer of the estate subject to redemption. (Emphasis added).*

It is important to note, here, that the Registrar of Titles is compelled not to register a mortgage created by any company registered in Tanzania or incorporated outside Tanzania but which has established place of business in Tanzania and a mortgage created by a cooperative society, until he satisfies himself that such a company or society is registered in accordance with the provisions of the *Company Act*[758] and the *Co-operative Societies Act*[759] respectively[760]. Mortgages which are not registrable under the *Land Registration Act* are registrable under other relevant laws for the Land Act provides that:

> *In respect of a mortgage other than a mortgage of land registered under the Land Registration Ordinance [sic], it shall take effect only if it is registered in a prescribed register and a mortgagee shall not be entitled to exercise any of his remedies under that mortgage if it is not so registered.*[761]

Registration goes with another very important advantage on priority of mortgages, meaning that the mortgage first registered in point of time takes priority over the mortgages created over the same land and subsequently registered[762]. The exceptions to the above rules are in respect of all informal mortgages, which may not be registered and

758 Act No. 12 of 2002.

759 [Cap. 211 R.E 2002].

760 See section 59, [Cap. 334 R.E 2002].

761 Section 113 (4).

762 See 117 (1), [Cap. 113 R.E 2002], and section 60 (1), [Cap. 334 R.E 2002].

which takes priority according to the order in which they were made.[763] Fifth, if the mortgage is to be created in respect of a matrimonial home, then, the law requires prior consent of the spouse or spouses living in that matrimonial home.[764] Initially, the *Land Act* neither defined the term "matrimonial home" nor stated whether or not the right to consent was available to all spouses in a polygamous family. However, the amendment of the Act made in 2004 filled in the gap. Specifically, the *Land Act* now defines "matrimonial home" to mean, *inter alia*, the building or part of the building in which the husband and wife ordinarily reside together.[765] It equally makes it a legal requirement for all spouses living in a matrimonial home to give consent before the mortgage is concluded. This is, indeed, a progressive step in the jurisprudence of land law where the law does not only enhance the principle of equality of the spouses, but also it promotes the principle of legal protection where the spouse's right to land or housing (or shelter) is likely to be jeopardised by greedy and unscrupulous spouses who are, in most cases, men. It follows that the legal effect of creating a mortgage in respect of the matrimonial home but without the consent of the spouse(s) is to render the mortgage void and unenforceable in law. Equally, the mortgage may be set aside if the consent of a spouse is obtained through undue influence or misrepresentation. The law imposes a duty on the mortgagor to disclose whether he has a spouse or not and upon such disclosure, the mortgagee has the responsibility to take reasonable steps to verify whether the applicant (mortgagor) has or does not have a spouse.[766] The degree of the duty imposed on the part of the mortgagee has been a hot and contested issue in the courts of law and has lead to some commendable land law reforms. The cases of *Idda Mwakalindile v NBC Holding Corporation*[767] and *Samwel Olung'a Igogo and Two Others v The Social Action Trust Fund and 4 Others*[768] highlight the controversy graphically.

763 Section 117 (2).

764 Section 114 (1). See also section 59 (1) of the *Law of Marriage Act*, [Cap. 29, R.E 2002].

765 Section 112 (2).

766 Section 114 (2) of the *Land Act, 1999* as amended by section 8 of the *Mortgage Financing (Special Provisions) Act, 2008*.

767 Court of Appeal of Tanzania at Mbeya, Civil Appeal No. 59 of 2000, reported in [2001] 1 EA p. 148.

768 High Court of Tanzania (Commercial Division) at Dar es Salaam, Commercial Case No. 3 of 2004 (Unreported).

Mwakalindile's case records the following facts and court's decision. The appellant, a wife, filed a suit against the respondent and one Sam Saijen Mwakalindile, the husband, in the High Court of Tanzania at Mbeya, challenging the mortgage deed that had been concluded by and between the respondents in respect of house on Plot No. 22C Block 1 Usafwa Road in Mbeya without her knowledge and consent. The appellant told the court that she was not aware of the existence of the mortgage deed until a proclamation was made for the sale of the house via a local newspaper. Her main arguments in support of her case was that the house, the subject matter of the mortgage, was a matrimonial property in which she, the second respondent (husband) and their family lived, and that the mortgage deed was entered into in contravention of section 59 (1) of the *Law of Marriage Act*[769]. However, for the reasons known to the court, the High Court of Tanzania held that section 59 (1) did not apply and dismissed the appellant's claim. The Court of Appeal equally dismissed the appeal but on a different level of reasoning. The Court agreed that under the law the matrimonial house owned by a wife or husband ought not be alienated by way of sale, mortgage, lease, or gift without the consent of the other spouse. However, the Court decided in favour of the mortgagee on the reason that the mortgagee, the bank, was not aware that the house was a matrimonial property. It was the Court's view that the house was registered in the name of the husband and that although the appellant had registrable interest in the house, such interest was not protected by the caveat. The appellant did not register the caveat with the Registrar of Titles, which would have served as a warning to the husband that the house was a matrimonial property.

To any human rights activisit, the decision of the Court dismissing the appeal and, thus, affirming the sale of the house is quite unwelcome. It is not known as to what was the fate of the innocent wife and the family when the house was subsequently sold and in the absence of any other order by the Court! The Court's decision became its precedent to bind the lower courts in the judicial hierarchy before it was overtaken by the provisions of the *Land Act*. For example, in *CRDB Bank Ltd v Mazrui*

---

769 [Now Cap. 29 R.E 2002]. Section 59 (1) of the Act provides that , "Where any estate or interest in the matrimonial home is owned by the husband or the wife, he or she shall not, while the marriage subsists and without the consent of the other spouse, alienate it by way of sale, gift, lease, mortgage or otherwise, and the other spouse shall be deemed to have an interest therein capable of being protected by caveat, caution or otherwise under any law for the time being in force relating to the registration of title to land or of deeds".

Commission Agent Co Ltd and 4 Others,[770] the Commercial Division of the High Court at Dar es Salaam (Kimaro, J.- as she then was) relied, among other authorities, on the decision of the Court in Mwakalindile's case to dismiss the application against the execution of mortgage in respect of house on Plot No. 180, Regent Estate, Kinondoni, Dar es Salaam.

The case of Samwel Olung'a, having been decided much later and on the basis of the *Land Act*, records a different jurisprudence. The plaintiffs, Social Action Trust Fund (1st respondents in this case), executed a loan agreement with the defendants whereby the former extended millions as loan facility to the later, which was secured by a legal mortgage over the defendants' plots of land. The defendants failed to repay the loan and the plaintiffs sued for recovery of the amount, sale of the mortgage properties and interest at the court's rate. They were successful and applied for execution by attachment of the mortgaged properties. At this stage they met serious objections from, among other objectors, Rukia and Ruth who claimed to be wives of the defendants and, further, that since they had interests in the properties as matrimonial properties and as matrimonial homes, they had not given consent to their being mortgaged.

In their counter arguments the 1st respondents (decree holders) launched a challenge by making reference to Mwakalindile's case, insisting that there was no way the respondents could have known of the existence of the interests. The Court (Kalegeya, J.- as then was) dismissed the respondent's argument and allowed the objections. The learned judge had the following reasons in allowing the objections:

> *Under s. 59 (2)[sic] of the Law of Marriage Act, lenders could simply urge that there was no way they could have been aware of the existence of the spouse's interest as they did not see any encumbrance in the Land Register upon due search. I am satisfied that this was the line of reasoning adopted by the Court of Appeal in Mwakalindile case.*
>
> *The Court of Appeal did not deal with the provisions of the Land Act in question and I think primarily because it had not effectively been put into operation although legally, as per commencement date, it was.*
>
> *Now however, search in the Land Register alone is not enough. The lender has to go further and inquire about the existence of spouse and inquire whether due consent has been secured...*

---

770 High Court of Tanzania (Commercial Division) at Dar es Salaam, Commercial Case No. 97 of 2002.

> *What is obvious therefore is that the lenders (the decree-holders) did not conduct inquires regarding Rukia and Ruth's consent under s 161 (3)*[771] *and this takes us back to s, 112 (3)*[772] *of the Land Act and s. 59 (1) of the Law of Marriage Act (read together) which make a transaction without spouse's consent invalid.*

From the foregoing, it can be said that the degree of the mortgagee's duty to ascertain whether or not spousal consent has been obtained when a matrimonial home is in question has been widened. A mortgagee must not only confine himself into the Register of Titles to ascertain the existence of the registrable interests of a spouse, but must take further steps to verify whether the applicant has a spouse, whether that spouse has consented to the mortgage, and whether the spouse has signed or assented the documents creating a mortgage. To be able to ascertain this, the mortgagee will have to make a thorough search depending on the circumstance of each particular case. As to what should the mortgagees do, one of the legal luminaries proposes that:

> *Before accepting a house as a security, the lender should physically inspect the house, among other things, to know who lives there. They can even assess its value to know if it is sufficient to secure the loan. If it is difficult to do it alone they can contact ten cell leaders and ward officers, among others to get the necessary information. Admittedly, it is learned that ascertaining the existence and value of a matrimonial home has never been an easy task. That difficulty cannot, however, be said to be the impossible. ACD, for instance, hires a special company of consultants...for that purpose.*[773]

Not only that: the law states very clearly that, "A mortgagee shall be deemed to have discharged the responsibility for ascertaining the marital status of the applicant and any spouse identified by the applicant if, by

---

771 Section 161 (3) (a) of the *Land Act*, specifically imposes a duty to the lender to make inquiries of the borrower as to whether the spouse or spouses have consented to the mortgage in accordance with the provisions of section 59 of the *Law of Marriage Act*, [Cap. 29 R.E 2002]

772 Section 112 (3) before the 2004 amendments stated that the mortgage of a matrimonial home would be valid only if the document or form used in applying for a mortgage and any documents or form used to grant the mortgage over that property were signed or there were evidence that they have been assented to by the mortgagor and the spouse or spouses living in that matrimonial home. The 2004 amendments, section 114 (1) has retained this requirement, but added section 114 (2) that it shall be the responsibility of the mortgagee to take reasonable steps to verify whether the applicant for a mortgage has a spouse or spouses.

773 See PHILIP, Adam, (2006): "The Law on Consent of a Spouse in Securities: A Case Study of Commercial Banks in Dar es Salaam", LL.B Dissertation, UDSM.

an affidavit or written and witnessed document, the applicant declares that there was a spouse or any other third party holding interest in the mortgaged land".

The point of emphasis, here, is that the law does not protect the right of a spouse to give consent when a property, the subject matter of the mortgage, is a matrimonial property, other than the matrimonial home. Spouses who happen to have interests in such properties are advised to register them to avoid the inevitable consequences that might be occasioned by their irresponsible and greedy spouses.

Classification of Mortgages

Both, common law and the *Land Act* recognise and provide for two categories of mortgages, namely legal mortgage and equitable mortgage. A legal mortgage is essentially created by observing all formal procedures involving the making of a legal deed or document which is signed by the parties, sealed, and delivered for registration to the Registrar of Titles. This class of mortgage may be created under the provisions of section 113 (1) of the Act. This type of the mortgage is valid only when it registered under the provisions of the *Land Registration Act* and, of course if it involves a land registered under the said Act, or under any other law, when it is for unregistered lands. Equitable Mortgage on the other hand is the common law equitable mortgage which is created without due regard to legal technicalities or formalities. What matters in this type of a mortgage is the agreement between the parties, express or implied that an equitable interest in the property will pass to the mortgagee. In Tanzania, this class of mortgage is sub-classified into: "*informal mortgage*" which may be created when the borrower offers and the lender accepts a written and witnessed undertaking, the intention of which is to charge the borrower's land with the repayment of the money or money's worth obtained from the lender,[774] and; "*lien by deposit of document*" which may be created by a deposit of documents such as a certificate of a granted right of occupancy, a certificate of a customary right of occupancy, a document of a lease, or any other document which may be agreed as evidencing a right to an interest in land or any other document which may be agreed upon to secure any payment.[775]

The legal importance behind the classification of mortgages is in relation to the rights and obligations of the parties to each type of the mortgage created, and the enforceability of such mortgages in a court

774 Section 113 (5) (a).

775 Section 113 (5) (b).

of law. This is what can be learned, at best, from the jurisprudence of the case of *National Bank of Commerce Ltd v Manna Investment (Pty) Ltd and 2 Others*.[776] The facts of the case were that there was a litigation between Manna Investment (Pty) Ltd, the decree holder, and Mwananchi Engineering and Contracting Corporation (MECCO), the judgment debtor, which ended in favour of the former, and at issuing the order of execution by attachment and sale of the judgment debtor's property on Plot No. 2 Montovia Road, off Nyerere Road, Temeke Distrct in Dar es Salaam. Before the said execution, the applicant, a bank, filed objection proceedings to object the order of attachment and sale of the property which, it was argued was security for the money advanced by it to the judgment debtor. The application was opposed by the Counsel for the decree holder on grounds, among others, that the mortgage between the applicant and the judgment debtor was not registered in the Register of Titles by the time the order of attachment was issued, so that what the mortgagee had was an equitable mortgage and not a legal mortgage. It was further argued that the court could not be moved to release the property from attachment on the strength of an equitable mortgage. He further submitted that if the court allowed the property to be sold, the objector was not entitled to be considered first because it had only an equitable mortgage, which ranks second to a legal mortgage. In granting the application, the court (Kimaro, J.- as she then was) found, on evidence, that the judgment debtor, a limited liability company, had registered the mortgage with the Business Licensing and Registration Agency (BRELA) and obtained a Certificate of Registration of a charge.[777] Further, evidence indicated that the mortgage was registered with the Registrar of Titles some days after the court had issued the order of attachment. There was no evidence to show the date when the mortgage was submitted for registration with the Registrar of Titles. In that regard and noting that some matters at the Land Registry are not done instantly, the court opined that there was great probability to suggest that the mortgage was submitted for registration before the court's order of attachment, but registration was not done until the order of attachment was issued. When the court had considered the evidence and circumstances of the case, it arrived at the conclusion that, "I would not think that the court would do justice if the applicant/judgment

---

776 High Court of Tanzania (Commercial Division) at Dar es Salaam, Commercial Case No. 84 of 2002 (Unreported).

777 Section 59 (1) [Cap. 344 R.E 2002] requires all mortgages created by companies to be registered with BRELA first before they are registered with the Registrar of Titles.

debtor is blamed or penalized for a matter which it had no direct control over it." It is submitted that the court's conclusion would have been different if the mortgage was not registered as the counsel of the decree holder had wanted the court to believe. It is further submitted that a legal mortgage gives a better title to the mortgagee than an equitable mortgage. Lenders are accordingly advised to resort to legal mortgages unless there are special circumstances to the contrary.

Rights and Obligations of Parties to a Mortgage

Rights and Obligation of the Mortgagor

The basic right of the mortgagor to a mortgage contract is the right to redeem the mortgaged property. This right, to say the least, has a unique history in the development of land law jurisprudence. In the old days of the common law, say by or prior to the 15th Century, land was conveyed in fee simple to the mortgagee on condition that if the loan was repaid on the day which had been fixed by agreement, then the mortgagor was free to re-enter. However, if repayment was not made on the *exact date fixed by the agreement*, then the estate of the mortgagee became absolute and the mortgagor's interests in the land were extinguished. The mortgagor did not only lose the land to the mortgagee but also remained liable for the debt. This scenario was captured by the common law *legal right to redeem on the fixed day*. By the beginning of the 17th century, equity intervened by taking the view that the property mortgaged was merely a security for the money lent and that it was unjust that the mortgagor should lose his property merely because he was late in repaying the loan. Equity insisted that the mortgagor should be allowed to redeem his property on a later date, despite his failure to make repayment on the date fixed by the mortgage deed. So equity introduced the *equitable right to redeem after the fixed date*. The harshness born out of the common law position on the right of redemption is better explained in the literature:

> *In the early days the common law courts held parties to the agreement...strictly construed the contract, and enforced its terms. If the loan was not repaid on the date named in the mortgage deed the borrower would be deprived permanently of the land, the land then becoming "dead pledge". This caused some hardship; the lender obtained the land itself (more valuable than the loan advanced), and in addition could sue the mortgagor on the agreement to repay the sum advanced, plus interests thereof. Mortgagors could obtain no relief from*

> *this situation from the common law court and eventually approached the court of chancery. As a result, equity intervened in the mortgage transaction and gave borrowers certain rights, the most notable being the right to get back the lands (taken as security) if the loans were able to be repaid at some time later than the date of redemption named in the contract. This right became known as the "Equity of redemption". As was said by Lord Nittingham in 1675, "The principal right of the mortgagee is the money, and his right to the land is only as a security for the money.*[778]

From this historical development, two concepts emerged in respect of the law on mortgages, that is, the legal right to redeem, which is created the moment a mortgage is entered into by the parties, and the equitable right to redeem, which is born after the date fixed for repayment. These two concepts constitute what is known in law as the equity of redemption or simply the right of redemption. The case of *Samuel v Jarrah Timber & Wood Paving Corporation*[779] is referred to for the following facts and holdings: the defendant mortgaged a debenture stock to the plaintiff. The mortgage provided, *inter alia*, that Samuel should have the option to purchase the whole or any part of the stock at any time. When Samuel attempted to exercise that right, the Corporation claimed to be able to redeem it. When the matter came to court, the defendant asked for the declaration that the option clause was void and ineffectual as being a clog on the equity of redemption. The House of Lords held that the defendants were entitled to redeem on the basis of the principle that, "once a mortgage always a mortgage". The option clause was, in other words, fettering or clogging the equity of redemption for if the option was to be exercised, it would have made the property completely irredeemable. From judicial decisions similar to *Samuel's Case* it has been established that the right of redemption must not be unduly restricted, clogged or fettered. Statutorily, this is the gist of section 125 (1) of the *Land Act* which states that, "Any rule of law, written or unwritten, entitling a mortgagee to foreclose the equity of redemption in a mortgaged land is abolished". Under this law, a clause in the mortgage deed will be invalidated and hence unenforceable if it provides, for example, a condition that:

---

778 BARKER, David & PADFIELD, Colin, (1996): *Law*, at p. 259.

779 (1904) A.C 323.

> *AND the said mortgagor agrees with the said mortgagee that if the said mortgagor does not pay the amount of consideration on the tenth of March Two Thousands and Eight, the said mortgagee will be entitled to foreclose the said property and thereafter the said mortgagor, her heirs, executors and assigns shall be absolutely debarred of all rights to redeem the same.*

Such a clause shall be taken by courts to be a clog or fetter on the equity of redemption and shall render the mortgage void on the trite principle of "once a mortgage always a mortgage." It can be said without hesitation that the law in Tanzania is quite protective of the interest of the mortgagor as it speaks very loudly and in clear terms that a provision in the mortgage instrument which purports to deprive the mortgagor of this right, or seeks to fetter the exercise of this right, or stipulates for a collateral advantage which is unfair and unconscionable and inconsistent with the right to discharge shall be void[780]. It is, indeed, encouraging to learn that the right of redemption is available even in cases where customary law applies. There are detailed principles governing the right of redemption, for example, in cases of customary mortgages under the Haya customs as recorded by Cory and Hartnoll in paragraphs 572-574 which state that:

> *572. A plantation under family tenure may be pledged, but any relative may at any time, even in the absence of the owner, redeem it.*
>
> *573. If a relative does so, the payment of the money does not give him possession of the plantation. The redemption money is due to him as a common debt by the owner.*
>
> *574. If the plantation has been pledged on the condition that it will become the property of the creditor failing the repayment of the debt within an agreed time, a relative has the right to redeem it, even after the time has expired, as an invalid sale; in which case it follows that the plantation becomes the property of the man who redeems it.*

When interpreting the above paragraphs in the case of *Didas Rwakalila & 3 Others v Thomas Madondane*[781] the Court of Appeal of Tanzania said that when a mortgage is created under paragraphs 572 & 573 then the creditor can never become the owner of the plantation but is merely entitled to his debt, and that when a mortgage is created

780 See section 121 (1) (a) (b) (c).

781 [1992] TLR 314 (CA).

under paragraph 574 the creditor can become the owner of the shamba as can the relative who steps into the shoes of the creditor provided two conditions exist in the mortgage: first, there must be a time stipulated for the repayment of the loan, and; second, upon failure, it must be stipulated that the property becomes that of the creditor. It is submitted that this interpretation by the Court of Appeal does no longer state the legal position on redemption after the coming of the *Land Act,* which completely abolishes foreclosure of the right of redemption.

According to the legal position at the moment, a mortgagor may lose the right of redemption in any one of the following instances: first, by wilfully releasing the right to the mortgagee. This means that once the mortgage has been made, equity will not interfere if the mortgagor, by a separate and independent transaction, gives the mortgagee an option to purchase the mortgaged property. The legal effect of such an option shall cause the mortgagor to waive his right to the equity of redemption. What is important is that the option need not be contained in the mortgage itself,[782] but need be made later and in a separate transaction. This was the basis of the court's decision in the case of *Reeve v Lisle.*[783] Secondly, the right may be lost through lapse of time, meaning that when land has been in the possession of the mortgagee until the period of limitation lapses no action to redeem it shall be brought thereafter by the mortgagor or any other person claiming through him. The *Law of Limitation Act*[784] of Tanzania provides that, "Suit to redeem land in possession of a mortgagee is twelve years".[785] Thirdly, the right of the mortgagor to redeem shall be lost on sale of the land by the mortgagee when he exercises his statutory power of sale in accordance with the provisions of the *Land Act.*

Apart from the right to redeem the mortgaged property, a mortgagor has also obligations which he ought to fulfil. These are implied under any contract of mortgage.[786] They include the obligation to pay the principle money on the day appointed and agreed in the mortgage or the interest thereto as the principle sum remains unpaid; the obligation to pay all

---

782 See the Samuel's case above.

783 (1902) A.C 461.

784 [Cap. 89 R.E 2002].

785 See item No. 17 of the Schedule to the Act. See also the decisions of the court in the cases of *Malekela Maluta v Kibuwi* [1989] TLR 113, and *Elizeus Rutakubwa v Jason Angelo*, Court of Appeal of Tanzania at Mwanza, Civil Appeal No. 21 of 1987 (Unreported).

786 See section 124 (1).

rates, charges, rent and taxes; the obligation to repair or keep in repair all the buildings upon the mortgaged land; the obligation to insure either by insurance or any other appropriate means, and; the obligation not to dispose the interest in the mortgaged land without prior consent of the mortgagee, among others. The case of *NBC Holding Corporation v Shirika la Uchumi na Kilimo (SUKITA) and 63 Others*[787] underscores some of these obligations. In this case the plaintiff sued the defendants for breach of a covenant in a mortgage deed that was signed by the plaintiff and the first defendant where they agreed that the latter would not lease or agree to lease or sublet the mortgage properties without prior leave of the plaintiff. The first defendant leased the properties to the 64 other defendants without the leave of the mortgagee. Hence the mortgagee's action in court seeking for a declaration order that the lease agreements entered between the first defendants and his tenants is void and an order for vacant possession to all tenants.

Rights and Obligations of the Mortgagee

The basic right of the mortgagee is, in the first place, the right to be repaid his money secured by the mortgage. It is through efforts to ensure that this sacred right does not wither, that the majority of mortgagees have finally knocked at the door of the courts to seek judicial redress[788] against defaulting mortgagors. In *Emma Kichiku Kea v Anna Musa Mbaga*[789] the following facts and court's decision were recorded. The plaintiff sued the defendant on the basis of a loan agreement. The evidence showed that there was a mortgage contract entered into by the parties. The mortgagor defaulted in payment and the plaintiff sued to recover the amount. A consent agreement inter parties was concluded but, yet there was failure on the part of the defendant to fulfil his obligation created by the agreement. The plaintiff filed an application in court for the orders of attachment and sale of the property securing the mortgage (house on Plot Nos. 130 & 132 Mikocheni Area, Dar es Salaam). The defendant resisted the application, her argument being mainly that the property,

787 High Court of Tanzania (Commercial Division) at Dar es Salaam, Commercial Case No. 24 of 2001 (Unreported).

788 See, for example, *National Bank of Commerce Ltd v Manna Investments (Pty) Ltd and 2 Others*, High Court of Tanzania (Commercial Division) at Dar es Salaam, Commercial Case No. 84 of 2002 (Unreported), *Emma Kichiku Kea v Anna Musa Mbaga*, High Court of Tanzania (Commercial Division) at Dar es Salaam, Commercial Case No. 84 of 2000 (Unreported).

789 High Court of Tanzania (Commercial Division) at Dar es Salaam, Commercial Case No. 84 of 2000 (Unreported).

being a residential house of the applicant, was not liable to attachment and sale in execution under the provisions of section 48 (1) (e) of the *Civil Procedure Code, 1966*. The court's decision allowing the application and dismissing the defendant's arguments was supported by the terms of the loan agreements especially Article III which provided that:

3.1 ***As Collateral for the Loan Repayment***

> *The borrower shall offer the title deed in respect of a house on Plot No. 130 and 132 Mikocheni Area Dar es Salaam registered under CT No. 25573 with land office No. 64100 bought by Anna Musa Mbaga, the borrower (sic), but yet to be transferred from the name of the previous owner one Devotha John. This property may be dealt with in any manner by the lender to ensure full repayment of the obligation herein.*

Interpreting this provision of the loan agreement, the court (Kimaro, J,- as then she was) agreed that under the law, residential houses are protected from attachment and sale but said the reasoned opinion of the court is that such a protection cannot be given to a party who has voluntarily offered a residential house as a security for a loan and defaults to repay the loan. The Court cited with approval the case of *Simon Ngeleja v NBC*[790] in which Lugakingira, J.- as he then was, had rightly held that:

> *The true purpose of section 148 (1) (e) of the Civil Procedure Code is to protect from attachment and sale of a residential house occupied by a judgment debtor, his wife or wives and children... But here the judgment debtor has mortgaged the property, he has thereby waved the benefit of that protection and he is estopped from denying the right of the mortgagee to sell the property.*

The court concluded, at the end, that, "This Court will not be doing justice to the lender if such an application was to be granted by the court." The mortgagee's right of repayment goes together with other collateral advantages that may be created by the mortgage. By collateral advantage, reference is made with respect to something which is guaranteed to the mortgagee as condition to the return of his loan with interest. It is a collateral advantage, for example, when the mortgagor agrees that for a number of years he will purchase beer for sale on the premises only from the mortgagee. Strictly speaking, a collateral advantage is valid only if it

790 Civil Case No. 154 of 1999 (Unreported).

is not unfair or unconscionable, meaning that it needs not be oppressive, or unfairly restrictive of the right of redemption. The two old cases of *Biggs v Hoddinnott*[791]and *Noakes & Co Ltd v Rice*[792] are directed to this proposition. In the former, the facts were that Hoddinnott mortgaged his hotel to Biggs, the brewer in return for an advance of a sum of money. He also agreed that during the continuance of the mortgage, he would sell no beer, other than that supplied by the mortgagee. It was further agreed that the mortgage should not be redeemable nor should the loan be repayable for the period of five years. Two years later, the mortgagor made a claim that he was entitled to be released from the agreement and to procure beer elsewhere upon payment of the loan. In the court, his claim was rejected when the court held that the agreement remained a valid agreement, thus binding upon the parties. This was a clear case whereby the mortgagor had created a collateral advantage to the mortgagee. The latter case is distinguished. In this case, a tenant of a public house under a lease which had 26 years to run, mortgaged the premises as security for a loan and covenanted that for the duration of the lease, whether he had already paid the mortgaged money or not, he would not sell malt liquors except those provided by the mortgagee. Three years later, the mortgagor claimed a declaration that he should be released from the covenant upon payment of all moneys due under the mortgage. The House of Lords decided in his favour by holding that he was not bound by the clause after redemption.

In Tanzania, the law obliges the mortgagee to discharge the mortgage at any time, on payment of all monies and performance of all other conditions and obligations secured by the mortgage and at the request and cost of the mortgagor.[793]

Other rights, in the form of powers of the mortgagee, arise when the mortgagor defaults in repaying the mortgage debt. These powers, include; the power to appoint a receiver; the power to lease the mortgaged land or, where the land is under lease, to sublease; the power to enter into possession of the mortgaged land and the power to sell it[794]. However, before the mortgagee undertakes to exercise any of these powers, he is legally obliged to serve a sixty days notice on the mortgagor informing

---

791 (1898) 2 Ch. 307. See also *Kreglinger v New Patagonia Meat and Cold Storage Co.* (1914) A.C 25.

792 1902) A.C 24.

793 Section 121 (1).

794 Section 126.

him about the nature and extent of the default, and the nature of the action to be taken by the mortgagee, for example, that mortgagee may proceed to exercise his rights against the mortgaged land such as the right to sell that land.[795] The effect of not serving a notice on the Mortgagor by the Mortgagee renders any subsequent action by the Mortgagee a nullity. In *National Bank of Commerce v Walter*[796] the Court of Appeal of Tanzania held that because the appellant did not issue a demand notice to the mortgagor for payment of the outstanding debt before foreclosing and selling the mortgaged property in accordance with the provisions of the mortgage deed, therefore, the property sold prior to the fulfilment of this condition precedent was not legally sold and no title passed to the purchaser. The property remained to be that of the mortgagor. The powers available to the mortgagee need be highlighted with the greatest precision, because disputes arising out of the mortgagee's undertaking to exercise any of these powers are not minimal in the administration of land law.

The power to appoint a receiver of income of the mortgaged land: Section 128 (1) of the *Land Act* makes it an implied condition that the mortgagee shall have the power to appoint a receiver of the income of the mortgaged land. The mortgage instrument may provide that this power shall be available at any time after the mortgagee shall have demanded payment of any money or the discharge of any obligation or liability secured or if requested by the mortgagor to exercise such power. The important thing to note, here, is that the appointment of such a receiver needs to be in writing and signed by the mortgagee,[797] and that once appointed, the receiver has wide powers including the power of sale of the mortgaged property. He is, therefore, deemed to be the agent of the mortgagor such that the mortgagor is solely responsible for the receiver's acts or defaults.[798] The case of *Standard Charted Bank Ltd v Walker &Another*[799] is in support of this point. In this case, the company borrowed money from a bank on security, which gave the bank a floating charge on the company's assets and empowered it, on default of repayment and on demand, to appoint a receiver to take possession of the assets and sell them. On default, the receiver was accordingly

795 Section 127 as amended by the section 12 of the *Mortgage Finance (Special Provisions) Act, 2008*.

796 Court of Appeal of Tanzania, Civil Appeal No. 31 of 1995 (Unreported).

797 Section 128 (3).

798 Section 128 (5).

799 (1982) 3 ALL ER 938.

appointed and instructed to realize the company's assets as soon as possible. He immediately instructed an auctioneer to hold sale of the company's stock. The company's guarantors complained that the sale was conducted at a wrong time of the year that it was poorly advertised and, therefore, poorly attended and that the stock was sold under its value. The court held that the receiver is the agent of the company not the debenture holder, the bank. He owes a duty to use reasonable care to obtain the best possible price which the circumstances of the time permit. It was further held that the receiver also owes a duty to the guarantor because the guarantor is also liable to the same extent as is the company. Finally the court held that the debenture holder is not responsible for what the receiver does, except in so far as it gives directions or interferes with his conduct over the realisation of the sale.

It is important to note that once the mortgage instrument provides for the appointment of the receiver to exercise any of the statutory powers, in the absence of a contrary provision, the mortgagee will have no power to exercise his rights in the absence of the receiver. We learn this from the case of *Shinyanga Regional Trading Co. Ltd & Another v National Bank of Commerce.*[800] In this case the appellant had issued a debenture to the respondent to secure an overdraft facility of Tshs. 50,000,000/= granted to it by the respondent. The appellant failed to pay in time whereby the respondent sold the godown, one of the properties securing the debt, by public auction. The Court of Appeal of Tanzania invalidated the sale conducted by the respondent in the absence of the receiver. It was the court's finding that:

> *...under the debenture the respondent had no direct power of sale. All that the debenture provided was for the appointment of a receiver in the event of a default. The receiver would then act in the interests of both the lender and the borrower. The respondent could not act as receiver under the debenture.*[801]

When he has exercised his powers in accordance with the law, the receiver is obliged to spend the money in the order of priority as provided for under the provisions of section 128 (8) of the *Land Act.*

Power to Lease: section 129 (1) of the *Land Act* empowers the mortgagee to grant a lease in respect of the mortgaged land or any part thereof, or to accept surrender of a lease so granted on certain conditions, provided

800 [1997] TLR 78 (CA).

801 Note that in this case debentures are defined to mean species of documents issued by companies evidencing their indebtedness, and that in sum then debentures are a class of securities issued by companies.

that such power is not expressly restricted by the mortgage instrument or by the provisions of the *Land Act* or any other law applicable to leases. Other conditions in respect of the mortgagee's powers to lease include limitation of time during which this right can be exercised, that is fifteen years or the duration of the mortgage, whatever is shorter;[802] and the fact that the power is not available without the order of possession from the court if the mortgaged land is a dwelling house in which any person is in residence, or is a land in actual use for agricultural purposes, or is a land in actual use for pastoral purposes[803]. This last condition, which restricts the power of the mortgagee to lease unless there is a court order, is commendable for it protects the occupiers against the competing rights between the mortgagee and other persons who may have taken the occupation of the land, the subject matter of the mortgage.

Power to Take Possession of the Mortgaged Land: section 130(1) gives power to the mortgagee to take possession of the mortgaged land. This power may be exercised in three ways. On one hand, the mortgagee may enter into and take physical possession of the land or part of it peacefully, on the other, he may assert management or control over the land by serving a notice requiring the lessee or mortgagor or other occupier to pay rent or profit to him, which is ordinarily payable to the mortgagor, and yet he may do so by order of the court..[804] A mortgagee who takes possession of the land remains accountable to the mortgagor in that he is not allowed to commit waste or any other wanton destruction thereto[805]. The mortgagee will withdraw from the land when any of the conditions stipulated by law[806] is fulfilled, for example, when the mortgagor discharges his liabilities under the mortgage.

Power to Sell the Mortgaged Land: section 132 (1) empowers the mortgagee to sell the mortgaged land after the expiry of a sixty days notice served to the mortgagor[807]. The old rule is that, in these instances, and unless the mortgage instrument provides to the contrary, the mortgagee is free to sell the mortgaged land or part thereto without any interference from the court. This was the position in the case of *National Bank of*

---

802 See section 129 (3) (c).

803 Section 129 (5).

804 Section 130 (2).

805 Section 130 (6).

806 Section 131.

807 See the requirement to serve notice under section 127 of the *Land Act*.

Commerce v Dar es Salaam Education and Office Stationery.[808] The facts of this case are: the respondent borrowed money from the appellant bank. As a security, a house was mortgaged in favour of the appellant. Upon failure to repay the loan, the appellant exercised its right under the mortgage deed by selling the house. The respondent failed a suit praying for temporary injunction restraining the bank and the Registrar of Titles from transferring title of the house and evicting the tenants therefrom. The High Court of Tanzania granted the prayers, hence on dissatisfaction, the appellant appealed to the Court of Appeal. The Court held, inter alia, that, where a mortgagee is exercising its power of sale under a mortgage deed, the court cannot interfere unless there was corruption or collusion with the purchaser in the sale of the property. Today, the law has restricted the power of sale. For example, the power is only exercisable with the order of the court if the mortgaged land is a dwelling house in which any person is in resident, or in actual use for agricultural or pastoral purposes.[809] Also the law imposes upon the mortgagee intending to sell the property, a duty of care to the mortgagor or guarantor or any lender under a subsequent mortgage to obtain the best price reasonably obtainable at the time of sale[810], such that the breach of this noble duty gives a right of action for the mortgagor to apply to the court for a declaration that the sale is void[811]. Finally, the law limits the mortgagee to sell the mortgaged land to himself. However, he may do so, only by the leave of the court[812] or by bidding highly at the public auction.[813] It is important to note, here, that all applications to the court with respect to mortgages are made under the provisions of order XXXII of the *Civil Procedure Code Act.*[814] The case of *M/S Ilabila Industries Ltd and 2 Others v Tanzania Investment Bank and Another*[815] assists to explain the nature of the duty imposed on the mortgagee to ensure that he obtains the best price when exercising the right of sale of

808 [1995] TLR 272, (CA).

809 Section 132 (2).

810 Section 133 (1).

811 Section 133 (2).

812 Section 136 (1).

813 Section 136 (3).

814 [Cap. 33, R.E 2002].

815 High Court of Tanzania (Commercial Division) at Dar es Salaam, Commercial case No. 27 of 2002 (Unreported).

the property. The background of the case is in relation to the application made by the 1st Respondent to the court, whereby the applicant claimed the outstanding amount on a credit facility granted to the 1st Applicant and secured, *inter alia*, by a legal mortgage of the property in dispute. Following this application the parties concluded a consent agreement which the applicants, after all failed to honour. The respondent applied for and was granted an order for attachment and sale of a landed property on Plot No. 1472 Msasani Peninsular, composed in a certificate of title No. 32132, which was sold by public auction. The applicants filed this application to challenge the sale of the property, arguing that the sale price of the house at Tshs. 143 million was a throw away, as there was a Valuation Report from 2001, which reflected the value of the property at Tshs. 391 million and a real estate consultant who put its value at Tshs. 500 million. It was further argued by the applicants that selling property at less than 25% of its value was violation of section 132[816] of the *Land Act* which was introduced to protect borrowers. Dismissing the application[817], the Court (Kalegeya, J.) said at p. 14 that:

> *When it comes to value of a property, bare assertions by parties or their witnesses cannot determine the same but rather professionally arrived at analysis. And whoever wishes to invoke s. 132 of the Land Act, in my view, should start by equipping himself with such proof and not otherwise.*

The Court arrived at this remark after it had observed that there was no evidence to show how Tshs. 500 million was arrived at by the real estate consultant and that Tshs. 391 was not the current price for it was based on an evaluation made in 2001. The Court also observed that even if either of the prices (shs. 391 and 500 million) was correct, still the contested price of shs. 143million would have been above the 25% of each. Finally, it was the court's interpretation of the law that where the price is less than 25% of the value, there is a rebutable presumption that the lender did not exercise the duty of care imposed on him to obtain the best price reasonably obtainable at the time of sale, meaning that to rebut the presumption the court would look at various factors including the mode of sale used and the obtaining circumstances.

816 It is now section 133 of the Land Act as amended by the Land (Amendment) Act 2004.

817 The applicants intended to appeal against the decision of the High Court dismissing their application, *M/S Ilabila Industries Ltd & 2 Others v Tanzania Investment Bank & Another*, Court of Appeal of Tanzania at Dar es Salaam, Civil Application No. 159 of 2004 (Unreported), but the applicants' application for the leave to appeal was struck out for citation of wrong provision of the law to move the Court where section 5 (2) (i) was cited instead of section 5 (1) (c) of the *Appellate Jurisdiction Act, 1979* [Cap. 141 R.E 2002]

Priority of Mortgages and the Mortgagee's Right of Tacking

This area seeks to explain the mode of payment when the mortgagor has created more than one mortgage over the same property. Note that, it is an implied term of the mortgage[818] that the mortgagor may not transfer the right of occupancy without prior consent of the mortgagee, provided that such consent is not unreasonably withheld. Such transfer includes the subsequent mortgage. The legal question, here, is how do the mortgages rank in priority for the purpose of payment, especially in a case where the amount secured in various mortgages exceeds the value of the property. The old rule governing this area was stated in the case of *Manyara Estate Ltd and Others v National Development Credit Agency.*[819] In this case a right of occupancy was granted to one Mr. Coulter under the provision of the *Land Ordinance*. He later mortgaged it to secure a loan from the then Land Bank of Tanzania. The right was revoked, whereby Mr Coulter was paid compensation for unexhausted improvement. The respondent, then the successor in title of the mortgagee, claimed to be entitled to the benefit of the mortgage which Mr Coulter defaulted in payment. The respondent brought an action to recover the debt and judgment was entered in his favour for the amount of compensation payable for unexhausted improvements. The four appellants brought an action for the court to determine their rights as other creditors in respect of the amount of compensation. The court was also asked to determine whether the respondent had preferential rights by reason of its mortgage. The court held that the security in each case was the right of occupancy, such that when the right was revoked the security was destroyed and could not be substituted with payments for unexhausted improvement. The court, however, concluded that the money should be distributed rateably in favour of all the creditors.

The modern law, today, is that mortgages shall rank in accordance with the order in which they were registered[820]. As regards informal mortgage, the law states that they shall rank according to the order in which they were made, while registered mortgages shall take priority over unregistered mortgages.[821]

---

818 See section 124 (1) (g).

819 (1970) E.A 177.

820 Section 117 (1).

821 Section 117 (2).

As regards the mortgagee's right of tacking, this simply means a right of prior mortgagee to advance further monies, without being required to create a new mortgage instrument. However, according to the law this right is only available when the said right is stipulated in the mortgage deed.[822] Also to be able to rank in priority over subsequent mortgages, the mortgagee's right to tack must be noted in the register in which the mortgage is registered and the subsequent mortgagee must have consented in writing to the priority of the further advance.[823] In the absence of all of the above, the right of tacking is not available to the mortgagee.

Compulsory Acquisition of Land by the State

The discussion above has been directed to the processes involved in the voluntary transfer of interest in land, permanently or temporarily, by a person singly or jointly. This part seeks to explain the process involved when a holder of a right of occupancy is compulsorily required to transfer the same to the President for reallocation to another person, natural or legal, on grounds of public interests. There are three issues of great concern involved in the process. These concern the legal rights of the President to acquire land for public interests; the procedure involved in the process, and; the rights available on the part of the original holder of land from whom land is acquired. The *Land Acquisition Act*[824] is the enabling legislation that governs the process. As regards the legal right of the President, the Act empowers the President to acquire any land for any estate or term where such land is required for any public purpose.[825] The Act has categorised "public purposes" to include, for example, where land is required for exclusive Government use, general public use, and agricultural development, provision of industrial and agricultural sites, commercial development, social services and housing.[826] Currently, we have witnessed several cases of land acquisition to enable activities such as mining operations, road construction, tourism, industrial installations and many similar activities to be conducted.

---

822 Section 118 (1).

823 Section 118 (2).

824 [Cap. 118 RE 2002]. According to the long title to the Act, the Act is there to provide for compulsory acquisition of lands for public purpose and in connection with housing schemes.

825 Section 3.

826 Section 4 (1). See the whole section for other categories of public purpose.

The case of *Attorney General v Sisi Enterprises Ltd*[827] is on all fours with the point on "public interests." The facts of the case are that the respondent company instituted a suit in the High Court[828] seeking, *inter alia*, a declaratory order that the acquisition of its piece of land comprised in certificate of title No. 16395, popularly known as Drive in Cinema, was unlawful. It argued that it was the holder of that land since 1966 in a 99 years lease, which it developed by constructing a building complex, "Drive in Cinema." It explained, further, that in 1999 it signed a letter of intent with the Department of State of Government of the United States of America to enter into an exclusive option to sell the land at a consideration of USD 3,000,000/=. Before this deal could materialize, the Government of Tanzania acquired the land under the provisions of section 4 of the *Land Acquisition Act*, 1967 and offered it to the Embassy of the United States of America. In return the government offered to compensate it at a sum of Tshs. 602, 363, 000/=. The company declined to accept the offer which, it considered inadequate and, it instead filed a suit against the Government. On the part of the government it was argued that the acquisition was lawful as it proceeded under the *Land Acquisition Act*, that the President had issued a notice of acquisition vide Government Notice number 469 of 1999, and that the land was required for public interests. Three issues were framed at the trial: first, whether there was proper and sufficient notice for acquiring the suit land under the *Land Acquisition Act;* secondly, whether the purpose in which the land was purportedly acquired was a public purpose under section 4 of the *Land Acquisition Act*, and, whether the proposed compensation offered by the government is adequate having regard to the circumstances of the case. The trial court (Ihema, J.- as he then was) answered all issues in the negative. He then ordered compensation of USD 3,000,000/= with interest at the market price under section 3 (1) (g) (vii) of the *Land Act*. The appellant was aggrieved, hence he appealed to the Court of Appeal of Tanzania.

---

827 [2006] TLR 9.

828 As Civil Case No. 47 of 2001.

In the opinion of the Court of Appeal, the most important dispositive issue was whether the acquisition for purpose of the American Embassy was public interest. It answered the issue in the negative regard being that "public interest" or "public purpose" must include a purpose, that is to say, an aim or object in which the general interest of the community is concerned or involved as opposed to the particular interest of individuals or institutions.[829] It was the Court's observation that acquisition in this case was not within the ambit of section 4 of the *Land acquisition Act* whose "spirit was, and indeed still is, to acquire land for public purpose and not for any other use". In a word the court found the acquisition to be not legally supported and the respondent to be the lawful owner. However, since the American embassy had already built on the land, common sense was to award the respondent compensation for exhausted improvement at the value of Tshs. 998, 467, 000/=.

As regards the question of the procedure involved, the Act requires the Minister, when the President resolves that land is required for public purpose, to give a notice of the intention to acquire land to the person interested in or claiming to be interested in such land or to the person entitled to sell or convey the same.[830] In this notice, or in any other subsequent notice, the Minister is required to direct the receiver of the notice to yield possession of such land after the expiration of the period specified in the notice, which is generally six months, except where it is made shorter by the President.[831] It is also a requirement that the notice be published in the official Government gazette after the same has been served to the holder of the right of occupancy.[832] At the expiry of the period so specified, the President or any other persons authorised by him shall enter into possession of such land accordingly.[833]

---

829 The Court of appeal reached this definition of "pubic interest" by reference to the definitions in *Agro Industricries Ltd v Attorney General* [1994] TLR 43, *BP Bhatt and another v Habib Rajan* [1958] E.A 536 and *Hawabai Franjee v Secretary of State for India* [1915] 39 BOM. 279.

830 Section 6.

831 Section 7 (1).

832 Section 8 (3).

833 Section 7 (2).

When it comes to the rights of the original holder of the right, the law imposes a duty to the Minister to pay compensation to the original owner, which is either agreed upon or determined in accordance with the *Land Acquisition Act*.[834] Again the President may grant a new public land not exceeding in value and upon the same terms and conditions as for the land he held in lieu of or in addition to any compensation.[835] Compensation is payable for "unexhausted improvements" which, according to the Act, means any quality permanently attached to the land directly resulting from the expenditure of capital or labour by a person holding under a right of occupancy or Government lease, or any person acting on his behalf or holding under him for a term of years, and increasing the productive capacity, utility or amenity thereof, but does not include the results of ordinary cultivation other than standing crops or growing produce.[836] In case of a land in rural areas which is used for agricultural or pastoral purposes, the same is compensated except if it has not been in use for twelve months immediately before the publication of the intention to acquire it for public purposes.

The process to, and the ultimate acquisition of land may, and has more often than not, led to some litigations among the parties in their move to challenge, *inter alia:* the right of the government to acquire land; the legality of the procedures in land acquisition; the right to compensation on acquisition; the amount of compensation payable; identity of persons entitled to be compensated; and the apportionment of compensation between the parties entitled to the same. Whenever litigation arises, and the parties fail to settle it within six months from the date of publication of the notice, the Minister or any other person holding or claiming any interest may institute a suit in the court for the court to determine the dispute[837]. This is what, for instance, happened in the cases of *Mulbadaw Village Council and 67 Others v National and Agricultural Food*

834 Section 11 (1)

835 Section 12 (2).

836 Section 12 (7).

837 Section 13 (1).

Corporation[838], *National Bank of Commerce v Suleiman Nassoro Ally,*[839] and *Mtumwa Shahame Baya Kondo & 111 Others v Principal Secretary, Ministry of Works & Attorney General*[840] and many others on a long list.

In the *Mulbadaw* case the plaintiffs' land was forcefully taken by the Government and allocated to the defendant, NAFCO. The plaintiffs went to court to challenge the right of the defendants to take the land claiming, *inter alia*, that the process involved was illegal for non conformity with the provisions of the *Land Acquisition Act*. On the part of the defendant, it was argued that the Act did not apply to lands held under customary law. The High Court of Tanzania at Arusha ruled in favour of the plaintiffs by saying that where someone is in lawful occupation of the land, no valid right of occupancy can be offered to anyone else over the same land unless the provisions of the *Land Acquisition Act* have been complied with. The decision was affirmed by the Court of Appeal of Tanzania, when NAFCO appealed against the decision of the High Court.[841] Specifically, the Court of Appeal of Tanzania was of the view that, "If the villagers who had testified could establish that as natives they had right of occupancy by virtue of customary tenancies, then the view of the judge that such villagers in this case could only be evicted or dispossessed under the provisions of the *Land Acquisition Act* No.47 of 1967 is sound."

In the *National Bank of Commerce* case, the President acquired land held by the respondent. Notice of intention to acquire was accordingly issued and published in the official gazette. Later on, the respondent sued the appellant for trespass and succeeded in the lower courts after the court had observed that the appellant had not registered the land after being allocated the same. The Court of Appeal of Tanzania allowed the appeal, the reasoning being that the *Land Acquisition Act* does not consider the requirement of registration as the prerequisite to

838 [1984] TLR 15 (HC).

839 [1989] TLR 67 (CA).

840 High Court of Tanzania (Land Division) at Dar es Salaam, Land Case No. 31 of 2004.

841 See *National and Agricultural Food Corporation v Mulbadaw Village Council ad 67 Others*, [1985] TLR 88 (CA).

the completion of acquisition. The Court was of the view that the fact of acquisition will already have been established by the expiry of the period indicated in the notice published in the gazette. In other words, the Court was saying that the respondent had time to file his objections before the expiration of six weeks but he did not do so, and could, therefore, not be heard to complain.

Of all the problems arising out of the process of land acquisition, matters of compensation have turned out to form the most serious problem. Very frequently the media has been replete with the complaints of the land holders against the Government. Even the parliamentary sessions have, occasionally, been dominated by complaints over the right to compensation in most cases of land acquisition by the government. The problem on compensation stems from the failure of the government to offer adequate and prompt compensation. The most recent example about people's dissatisfaction for the compensation payable in the process of land acquisition has been the case involving the Kipawa residents in Dar es Salaam and the Government. In 1992 the Government acquired the land occupied by the residents (about 1200 *kayas*) with the intention of extending the then Dar es Salaam International Airport (now renamed the Mwalimu Nyeyrere International Airport). However, no compensation was paid to the occupants. As a result, the occupants continued to reside in their lands pending compensation, until 2009 when the government undertook to pay them and ask them to vacate. The government move was met with severe objections from some of the resident who challenged the amount of compensation offered. In essence, the residents wanted to be paid compensation under the *Land Act*, but the government insisted in paying the same under the *Land Acquisition Act*. Of course, at the end of the day the government succeeded for some technical reasons. It is submitted that had the government paid compensation promptly at the time the land was acquired this kind of sad relationship between the government and its citizens would have been avoided.

Chapter Five

Succession and the Law of Inheritance in Tanzania

Inheritance is legal succession of property that occurs on a person's death. Its purpose is to ensure continuity of disposal over property. Inheritance is a basic human right and any restriction to it is a contravene of constitutional law.

- Dr. Andrea Polgar[842] -

842 See "The Law of Inheritance" in Dr. Hidas and Partners Law Office Newsletter, Budapest, November 2001. The paper was accessed through the web, http//: www.hidasi.hu. (April 2007).

This topic covers one of the most controversial areas of land administration in Tanzania since it answers the difficult, but relevant question: what should be done with a person's estate when he or she dies? James and Fimbo observe that this is a question which can never be avoided in any system of law.[843] The immediate and appropriate answer to this question is that the property or the interests therein is distributed to the survivors. However, the bone of contention has always been on the determination of persons who are entitled to the distribution of the estate; the mode of distribution, and; the rights of other persons, say creditors if any, who may happen to have interests in the property of the deceased person. It becomes a serious problem if the deceased died intestate. In such a situation the law of inheritance is normally resorted to, as an essential tool to resolve the controversy formally and conclusively. As to how this branch of law works, Alun A. Preece observes, in summary, that there are three fundamental ways in which the law governs the distribution of property on death, that is to say: by will of the deceased (testator); by the model prescribed by law as on intestacy, and; through family provisions legislation under which the courts may vary the provisions of the will of the deceased, if insufficient provision is made for a spouse, children or other dependants of the deceased. This limits the testator's freedom of testation.[844] Basically, there are four main issues of great significance which need to be considered by whoever undertakes to address the above questions, namely: whether the deceased person has written a will (testacy) or not (intestacy); the issue on the applicable law; whether or not all the necessary procedures have been followed in administration of the deceased's estate, and; the issue concerning the court with competent jurisdiction to hear and determine matters arising out of the process of administration of estate. The rest of the discussion in this chapter is pegged on these four issues. They are conversed elaborately with a professional echo so as to enable the audience to understand them by heart and, therefore, be able to follow the law on succession along its appropriate course.

---

843 JAMES, R.W and FIMBO, G.M, *op cit,* at p. 165.

844 PREECE, Alun A., " The Impact of the Law of Inheritance on the Family", A Paper Presented at the 7th Australian Institute of Family Studies Conference, Sydney Convention and Exhibition Centre, Darling Harbour Sydney, 24-26 July 2000, at p. 3.

Testacy, Intestacy and Freedom of Testation

Testacy and Intestacy Defined

When a person writes a will disposing his estate to one or many persons of his own choice, such as his survivors, and dies later, then we say, in law, that he has died testate. Immediately the word "testacy" comes into use in respect thereof. The deceased is called a testator and the person to whom the property in the deceased's estate reverts is a "devisee" or "legatee", depending on the nature of the property in the estate[845]. In contrast, if a person dies leaving no will, or leaving a defective will, then we say he has died intestate, calling for the term "intestacy" to come in use in addressing the event.

The most significant note that we should make is that none of the two situations of testacy and intestacy has been free from some legal wrangles. They have, more often that not, been issues of great concern and at times they have brought the legal minds to cross-roads. With respect to testacy, especially, two legal questions have always occupied the minds of lawyers: (1) what is a will? , and (2) what is a valid will in law? We can define a will in simple terms to mean a legal declaration by a person of his intention to dispose his property according to his own desires. However, a legal definition appears, for example, under the Rules on Will[846] which define a "will" as an attestation made freely by a person in his life time showing his intention as to how he would like his property to be distributed after his death.[847] From this definition we note that a will is legally valid and therefore enforceable if it meets the following characteristics: (a) it must be a legal declaration by the person who is competent to make it, meaning that, a will made, for example, by a minor[848] or a person of an unsound mind[849] will be invalid and, therefore, unenforceable; (b) there must be an *animus testandi*, that is an intention to dispose the estate in the mind of the testator, lack of it

845 The English law recognizes a devise as being a disposition of freehold land contained in a will, and legacy or bequest as being disposition of any other property. It is from this categorization that we get "devisees" and "legatees".

846 Third Schedule to the Local Customary Law (Declaration) (No.4) Oder, GN 436/ 63.

847 See Rule 1, *ibid*.

848 See, for example, section 9 of the English *Wills Act*, 1837 which speaks in clear terms that, "No will made by any person under the age of [eighteen years] shall be valid". The Act is available in KENNY, Phillip H. and HEWITSON, Russell, (1994): *Property Law*, London, Dublin, England: Butterworths.

849 Rule 26 of the Rules on Inheritance, GN 436/63 provides that, "Any person male or female and who is not of unsound mind can make a will except those under the age of 21 years".

will obviously invalidate the will; (c) the will must express the intention to depose property, meaning that if the declaration pretends to dispose something other than the testator's property then it will not be a valid will, and; (d) the declaration must be to the effect that it is to be operative after the death of the testator[850]. The case of *Ramnik Vaghella v Mahendra Vaghella*[851] states, in clear terms, the general principle about the validity of the will. The parties to this case were uterine brothers. Upon the death of their mother, the Respondent applied for and was granted probate by the High Court of Arusha. In the application he had annexed a will of the deceased. The Appellant challenged the appointment on grounds, among others, that the will was invalid as it was made at the time the deceased was so physically and mentally incapacitated that she could not understand the contents of the will. The Trial judge found the will valid and granted probate as applied. On appeal to the Court of Appeal of Tanzania, the Court established the principle by stating (at page 227 of its judgment) that:

> *It is settled that in order for a will to be legally enforceable it has to be valid, and its validity in turn derives from the capacity of the testator and the circumstances attending its making. A lunatic cannot make avalid will during subsistence of his insanity and a will obtained by fraud or one improperly executed cannot count for a valid testament.*

The will speaks from the time of death, not before. Above all, a valid will can be executed and be enforced in the court of law if it is signed by the testator or someone in the testator's presence and direction, express or implied. When the signature is not that of the testator himself, but of another person on the testator's behalf, then it is a matter of evidence for the court to satisfy itself as to whether the testator had knowledge of the content of his will at the time of its execution. Equally important, the will must be attested by at least two witnesses and in the presence of a testator[852]. In addition, the legal requirement is for the witnesses to sign the will after the testator has signed his part. We note, again, that it is not an absolute rule that the will must always be written. It is possible to have an oral will.[853] There are various authorities to support this

---

850 The word "***testator***" is ordinarirly used to refer to a deceased male, and the word "***testatrix***" refers to the deceased female.

851 [2000] TLR 223 (CA).

852 See appendix 4 which is a specimen of a legal will below at p. 296.

853 Rule 2 of the Rules on Will, provide that "A will can take two forms: an oral will and a written will".

proposition. For example, we have on record a law stating that, "Probate may be granted of the content of an oral will, if it can be established by evidence"[854]. Note that there are certain situations that may necessitate the dispensation of the legal formalities of a will and bless, for example, unwitnessed wills. A case may arise where a person, say a soldier in active service (war), wishes to execute a will in a situation where there is no pen, papers or witnesses. Whatever such a person executes will be taken as valid even if it departs from a formal will. Under the English law, this is taken care of by the *Wills (Soldiers and Sailors) Act*, 1918.

Where customary law is involved, it is a legal requirement that the will shall be attested to by special witnesses who must be present at the same time.[855] Apart from the special witnesses the will should also be witnessed by the wife or wives of the testator who live with him. [856] If the testator is literate, at least two special witnesses, one being a relative of the testator must attest the will, and if the testator is illiterate, the number must at least be four, two being the relatives of the testator.[857] The witnesses are required to witness the testator sign, and must also put their signatures on the will.[858] The case of *George A Mmari and Anande A Mmari v Afra Fuime*[859] is founded on the validity of a will. In this case it was alleged that the deceased, one Anael Kikoka Mmari, wrote a will, bequeathing his property (including the disputed house) to the respondent, one of his wives and a stepmother to the appellants who are the two children of the deceased. The appellants raised an action challenging the validity of the will for want of a clan member to witness. They also argued that the will was written under the undue influence of the respondent while the deceased was sick. The court (Mwaikasu, J.- as he then was) observed that the will was attested by the respondent (the wife) and a doctor in contradiction to Rule 5 and 19 of the Rules on Wills, according to which a will drawn by a literate person is valid only when attested, besides the wife (wives) by at least two persons of whom one must be a relative of the deceased. The court's conclusion was that since the requirement was not complied with, then the will was defective for want of proper

854 See section 25 (3) of the *Probate and Administration of Estates Act*, [Cap. 352 R.E 2002].

855 Rule 3 of the Rules on Wills.

856 *Ibid*, rule 5.

857 *Ibid*, rule 19.

858 *Ibid*, rule 21.

859 [1995] TLR 146 (HC).

attestation and that in the circumstances the deceased was to be taken to have died intestate and for the administration of his estate to be done in accordance with the applicable law as if he had died intestate. Under the same law, if the will is made by a person who is illiterate, that is to say, one who does not know to read and write, then, it must be attested by four members, whereby two of them must be relatives of the deceased.

Similarly, in the case of *Jackson Reuben Maro v Hubert Sebastian*[860], the Court of Appeal of Tanzania invalidated the will purported to be executed by one Sauli, but which was not attested to neither by special witnesses nor by the wife of the deceased. The rationale behind this requirement is to safeguard the estate against fraud. This is what we learn through Msumi J (as he then was) in the case of *John Ngomoi v Mohamed Ally Bofu.*[861] The brief facts of the case are that the respondent petitioned before a primary court to be granted letters of administration in respect of the estate of the deceased which included a house along Uhuru Street in Dar es Salaam. The appellant filed an objection claiming that the house belonged to him by way of a will, which, he claimed, was executed in his favour. Both the Primary and District courts were not satisfied with the genuineness of the will for none of the four witnesses to it was a relative of the deceased. They equally dismissed the appellant's claim. On appealing to the High Court of Tanzania, an advocate for the appellant argued that since the deceased had no relatives, it was quite proper for her to choose any person to witness the will. The Court dismissed the argument by saying that it was not true that the deceased did not have relatives. Essentially the court was of the view that even if the deceased had no relatives at the material time, her ten cell leader ought to have been included as among the witness to the alleged will. Stating the rationale of having witnesses who are relatives to the deceased, the court stated that the requirement that at least half of the number of witness to a valid will executed under customary law must be related to the testator is intended to act as safeguard against any possible fraud against the testator as well as against the lawful heirs of the estate. It is important to note that the ordinary rules of signature apply to the attestation of wills, that is to say, minors and persons who

---

860 Court of Appeal of Tanzania at Arusha, Civil Appeal No. 84 of 2004 (Unreported).

861 [1988] TLR 63 (HC). There is on record a litany of cases in which the validity of a will has been challenged for want of proper attestation. These include: *Ferdinand s/o Lumboyo v Ngeiyamu s/o Kajuna*, [1982], TLR 142; *Abdul Sadiki v Wilfred Rutakinikwa*, [1988] TLR 167 (HC), and; *Thomas Matondane v Didas Rwakalila and Others*, [1989] TLR 210 (HC).

are *non compos mentis* (persons of unsound mind) should not attest the will. However, the rules of will do not apply to Islamic wills. Fias Badrudin Tyabji writes[862] :

> *A Muslim is not obliged to observe any special formality in making his will, and his intentions with respect to his property which he desires to be carried out after his death in whatever form they are declared, may operate as a will, provided that they are declared with sufficient clearness to be capable of being ascertained. In particular, the will need not to be framed or worded in any technical form or language; it need nnot be in writing, if in writing, it need not be signed by the testator, or attested by witnesses; and if oral, no specific number or classes of witnesss need be present at the time of the declaration.*

The Doctrine of Freedom of Testation

"Avoid unnecessary conflicts: Write a will." The statement stands as a motto for the recent campaign launched by the Tanzania Women Lawyers Association (TWLA), to sensitise people on the importance of writing a Will before one dies.[863] In the Tanzanian experience, practice has revealed that most individuals are still reluctant to write wills. The repercussion of the omission cannot be overemphasized, for, most hostilities leading to prolonged litigations over the right to inheritance, and at times to bloody struggle, arise out of intestacy. The truth of this assertion is quite supported. According to the Editor:[864]

> *In the willless eventuality, hostility has replaced harmony in families, and court cases have been triggered due to wrangling over a scramble for assets. This stems from a lack of wills that would have spelt out who deserves which share of the assets. Matters are also complicated by the emergence into the scene, of sideline wives and children who claim a share of the assets. They are complicated*

---

862 (1919): *Principles of Mohamedan Law in British India*, Second Edition, Butterworths & Co., at page 806. The learned author was cited with approval by the High Court of Tanzania in *Asha Shemzigwa v Halima A. Shekigenda* [1998] TLR 254 which rightly observed that Islamic Law requires no special formality in making a will. The Court was challenging the Appellant's contention challenging the oral will of her deceased husband for want of a proper witness which, according to the Court, could not be supported by the Court.

863 The said campaign was launched on 16th March, 2008 by the said TAWLA and graced by the learned Chief Justice of Tanzania, His Lordship, Justice Augustino Ramadhani at the TAWLA Head Office, Dar es Salaam.

864 See The Editor, "Will writing as a Culture" in *Sunday Observer*, February 25, 2007. See also an account by MUSHI, P., "Elderly Widows Need Training on Inheritance Rights", *The Guardian*, Monday, March 17, 2008.

> *even further by greedy, inconsiderate in-laws who dispossess, actually rob widows of the assets, usually in execution of outdated wills, or customs or spur-of-the-moment creations meant to suit their selfish interests. The sufferers, in the end, are widows, widowers, children and other close relatives of the deceased persons.*

It is the Editor's inevitable call that people must cultivate the culture of writing wills, because the repercussions of their absence apparently translate into disturbance of the spirits of the departed. "Wills are the surest guarantors against confusion, tension, conflicts, and in extreme cases, deaths and injuries".[865] In short there are very good reasons to avoid intestacy and encourage testacy because the latter provides a rather smooth path to inheritance by avoiding the rigorous rules and procedures behind the distribution of an intestate's estate; it avoids doubt and uncertainty which may exist after a person's death as to who should inherit; it allows the testator to enjoy the right to the freedom of testation in disposing the estate to a person or the persons of his or her own choice, due regard being to the wife or wives and children.

In our humble opinion, will writing may not be a successful exercise unless people are made to know the importance of the will, this knowledge being backed up by what lawyers understand to be the doctrine of freedom of testation. In order to explain this doctrine and make it workable, we ought to answer two basic questions: what is the nature and extent of freedom that is available to the testator when he writes a will?; can the testator's will be altered, added to, revoked or disregarded? The answer to the first question is that the law on wills gives every person the right to freely write a will and devise, bequeath or dispose all real estate and all personal estate which he shall be entitled to at the time of his death.[866] The freedoms envisaged in this sense, include the freedom to write or not to write a will; the freedom to devise, bequeath or dispose the estate to the heirs (beneficiaries) as he desires, and; the freedom to appoint the executor or executors of the will of the person's own choice. The only legal limitations of this type of freedom pertains to age and state of mind of the testator, meaning that a minor or person of unsound mind cannot be allowed to write a valid will, and that the testator cannot appoint a minor or person of unsound mind to be the executor of the will[867].

---

865 *Ibid.*

866 See section 3 of the English *Wills Act*, 1837.

867 Section 23 of [Cap. 352 R.E 2002] states: "Probate and letters of administration shall not be granted to any person who is a minor or of an unsound mind."

As regards the second question, the answer varies depending on the time when the will is said to be altered, added to, revoked or disregarded. At the first level and before the testator's death, a will can be altered, added to, or revoked, at any time as long as the testator survives and, of course, only by the testator. Alteration or addition to a will may be made by way of a *codicil*, while revocation may be made by writing another will, a *codicil* or by destruction thereof. In short a "codicil" means an instrument made in relation to a will, and explaining, altering or adding to its dispositions[868]. The available record has elaborately described a codicil as follows:

> *A codicil is of similar nature to a will, as regards both its purpose and the formalities relating to it but in general it is supplemental to and considered as annexed to a will previously made, and executed for the purpose of adding, varying, or revoking the provisions of that will. A codicil is nevertheless capable of independent existence, so that revocation of a will does not necessarily affect the revocation of a codicil thereto.*[869]

The point of departure is that a codicil must be executed under the same principles and formalities as a will itself. The advantage enjoyed by testator in respect of his freedom to change will is that it allows him the flexibility to change the previous will as much as he desires in response to change of circumstances. However, one consequence that is most likely to occur as a result of the testator's freedom to change wills is that, parties may find themselves litigating on the basis of a series of wills executed by the testator in his lifetime. If this happens, wisdom will always favour the last will of the deceased in terms of the date of its making, whether or not the executor of it states his intention to revoke the previous will.

At a second level, once a will is dully made and meets all the legal prerequisites, the general rule is that such a will must be respected to the letter and spirit after the death of the testator. This is a clear case of, "Once a Will always a Will". In short, the basic advantage attached to the freedom of testation is that it ensures flexibility. On the one hand, it empowers a person to dispose the property to the heirs of his own choice including both male and female heirs evenly and without discrimination. One the other hand, it allows a person the freedom to consider the needy and also to command respect among the potential heirs.

---

868 See section 2, [Cap. 352 R.E 2002].

869 See *Halsbury's Laws of England*, 3rd Edition at p. 842.

The legal question that has, more often than not, tasked the minds of the legal profession has been whether freedom of testation at the second level is absolute. In other words, the legal issue is whether a testator's will can, in law, be altered, added to, revoked or disregarded upon the testator's death. There is no "yes" or "no" answers to this question except that each case will be determined according to its circumstances, depending on the nature of the property itself, that is , whether it is self-acquired or is clan land, and consideration of better title between two competing rights[870]. Two judicial decisions may be examined to illustrate the point. The first is the Tanzanian case of *Celestina Paulo v Mohamed Hussein.*[871] The facts of the case were that the deceased had executed a will, naming the appellant as an administrator of her estate where the beneficiary was her eight year-old daughter. The respondent challenged this appointment in that he was the father of the beneficiary and therefore entitled to administer the estate. He further argued that the appellant was from a different clan and belonged to a different religion (a Muslim). The Primary Court considered the adduced evidence and confirmed the appointment of the appellant as the administrator of the deceased's estate. In the District Court the honourable magistrate reversed the decision and appointed the respondent. The appellant was aggrieved by the decision, hence her appeal to the High Court of Tanzania. The court (Mushi, J.- as he then was) held that it is a known fact that an ascertained will of the deceased must be respected in both letter and spirit and that the District Court's decision was a regrettable one. The Court further considered the nature of the property bequeathed by the deceased and found that it was her personal property that had nothing to do with her clan. In other words, the Court observed that the deceased had, before her death, the absolute right to choose the beneficiary and

870 Rule 34, Rule on Wills provides, for example, that, "Any person who intends to deprive the heir of his inheritance must clearly say so in his will and must give reasons". It follows that if the heir is disinherited without any justification property will pass to him under the discretion of the court. In the case of the Haya, paragraph 48 of the CORY, H. and HARTNOLL M.M., (1945): *Customary Law of the Haya Tribe*, Tanganyika Territory, Frank Cass, London, lists 8 reasons of disinheritance as including (1) assault of a man by his heir; (2) sale of a man's cattle without his consent by his heir; (3) neglect of a sick man by his heir; (4) undertaking a long journey by the heir against the will of a testator; (5) adultery by the heir with one of his father's wives; (6) civil action taken by the heir against his father; (7) transgression of the rules of marriage restrictions; and (8) general misbehaviour. Paragraph 41 is even more protective of the family since it requires that if a will contains a change of the rule and disinherits the family, appointing a man outside the family as an heir, at least 10 witnesses must be called.

871 [1983] TLR 291 (HC).

the administrator of her own choice. The Court found no reasonable ground that entitled the magistrate to purport to tell the deceased what she should have done against her clearly expressed wish. The second and oldest case is the American case of *Riggs v Palmer*[872], which has dominated the literature in jurisprudence. The facts of the case are as follows. The testator, one Mr. Francis B. Palmer, made his last will and testament, in which he gave small legacies to his two daughters, Mrs. Riggs and Mrs. Preston (the plaintiffs in this action) and the remainder of his estate to his grandson Elmer E. Palmer, the defendant. Elmer lived with him as a member of the family. He, at the age of sixteen, knew the provisions made in his favour in the will and formed an intention of preventing his grandfather from revoking such provisions. He therefore sought to obtain a speedy enjoyment and immediate possession of the property by wilfully murdering his grandfather by poisoning him. He then claimed the right to property in that the testator was dead, the will was made in due form and admitted to probate and was accordingly of effect to its letters. The plaintiffs challenged the claim in the court of law. The legal issue before the court was whether the defendant was entitled to inheritance as per the will.

Earl, J.- as he then was leading the majority decision of the Court disinherited the defendant on two principal grounds. In the first he invoked the doctrine of equitable construction of the statute which requires a judge to place himself in the position of an upright and reasonable man in deciding a case, and not to be bound by the general language contained in the laws. This is what has been referred to as the mischief rule of statutory interpretation under which the Court is required to find out the intention of the legislature when making certain legislation and apply that intention to the case. In other words, the Court found that it could not have been the intention of the legislature that a murderer should inherit the estate of the person that he kills intentionally. In the second place, the Court made a reference to what it called the fundamental maxim of the common law that no one shall be permitted to benefit by his own fraud, or to take advantage of his own wrong, or to found any claim upon his own inequity, or to acquire property by his own crime.

Gray, J.- as he then was led the dissenting minority decision of the court. He was of the opinion that the Court was bound by the rigid rules of law as passed by the legislature, and within the limits of which the determination of the question was confined. To him the issue for

---

872 Court of Appeal of New York, decision of October 8, 1889.

determination by the Court was whether a testamentary disposition can be altered, or a will revoked, after the testator's death through an appeal to the courts, when the legislature has, by its enactments, prescribed exactly and how wills may be made, altered and revoked. His worry was that, by the majority decision, the Court was practically asked to make another will for the testator when the laws do not warrant this judicial action.

What we read from the case is the doctrine of none absoluteness of freedom of testation and the importance of judicial intervention in the administration of Wills, especially so when it happens that the rights to inheritance of the vulnerable groups such as women and children are put in severe jeopardy by the unscrupulous and greedy individuals who have the power to influence the execution of wills in their favour. To day, courts are in a position of invoking the human rights language in guarding the interests of these vulnerable groups. The case of *Dillon v Public Trustee of New Zealand*[873] is our point of reference, especially where the Court states emphatically and in clear terms that:

> *It is the object of the legislation to secure, on grounds of public policy, that a man who dies, leaving an estate which he distributes by will, shall not be permitted to leave widows and children inadequately provided for, if the Court thinks that the distribution of the estate should be altered in their favour, even though the testator wished by his will to bestow benefits upon others, and even though he has framed his will as he has contracted to do.*[874]

It is in that sense the English *Inheritance (Provision for Family and Dependants) Act*, 1975, for example, protects the right of the family members, such as, the wife, husband, children and dependants by conferring on them the right to apply to the court for a judicial remedy on the grounds that the disposition of the deceased's estate effected by his will or the law relating to intestacy is not such as to make the reasonable financial provision to him or her.[875] The court has the power to make the necessary orders[876] after taking into consideration general factors including[877]: the financial resources and financial needs which the

873 (1941) A.C 294.

874 Page 303-4.

875 Section 1 (1).

876 Section 2

877 Section 3(1).

applicant has or is likely to have in the foreseeable future; any obligations and responsibilities which the deceased had towards the applicant; the size and nature of the net estate of the deceased; any physical or mental disability of the applicant, and; any other matters that the court will consider relevant. When the applicant is a wife, husband, former wife or former husband, the court will, in addition, consider the age of the applicant and the duration of the marriage and the contribution made by the applicant to the welfare of the family of the deceased including any contribution made by looking after the home or caring for the family[878]. This means that the court has the power to interfere with the deceased's will or the rules of inheritance for the sake of an applicant applying under the provision of this law.[879]

Laws of Inheritance and their Scope of Application

As we discuss inheritance in Tanzania, we are quite aware of the multiplicity of the legal systems that govern the subject. The point we should emphasize, however, is that understanding these systems is not only important but also highly encouraged because, more often than not, the different legal systems have a tendency of creating some internal conflict of laws. It means, therefore, that whoever is faced with a matter of inheritance born out of intestacy, the choice of the law to apply in the circumstances becomes of utmost importance. The legal systems that are currently in place are discussed here below.

Statutory (State) Law

The relevant law in place is the *Indian Succession Act, 1865* which was made applicable in Tanzania vide the *Indian Acts (Application) Ordinance*[880]. It is still recognised as such by the Judicature and Application of Laws Act.[881] However, not all provisions of the Act have an application in Tanzania, part XXIX-XL and section 333 are excepted[882]. The Act applies in the distribution of property in all cases of intestacy and, according to the Act, a person dies intestate in respect of all property of which he has

---

878 Section 32 (a) and (b).

879 See the decisions of the court in *Re Andrews* [1955] 1 WLR 1105; *Re Callagham* [1983] 3 WLR 1076, and; *Re Leach* [1985] 3 WLR 413.

880 Cap. 2.

881 [Cap. 358 R.E, 2002].

882 *Ibid*, item (a) of the Second Schedule.

not made a testamentary disposition.[883] However, in law intestacy may be classified into two classes. One, total intestacy and this entails the two scenarios: where one has not written a will, and; where the document is held to be a defective will. Two, partial intestacy, meaning a scenario where one has bequeathed only part of his estate, leaving another part indisposed. A simple dissection of the Act has revealed the following to be its salient features:

The first feature concerns the applicability of the Act. The Act does neither apply to the estate of a member of a customary community, where resort is made to customary law, nor that of the deceased Muslim which is subject to Islamic law. In other words, the Act applies in respect of the estate of the deceased Christians and to all those of European origin. Our memory must take us back to the famous case of *Re-Innocent Mbilinyi*[884], in which the court found the Indian Succession Act to be the applicable law. In this case, a husband, a Roman Catholic and a member of the Ngoni tribe married a wife, also Roman Catholic and Chagga by tribe under Christian marriage protocols. The husband died intestate, whereby dispute over inheritance arose between the wife and the relatives of the deceased, who had to compete for the administration of the deceased's estate. As the dispute was before the court, the relatives argued that the Ngoni customary law was applicable in the administration of the estate. The wife, then a widow, objected to this argument saying that the deceased had not wished to have any of his estate regulated by customary law and that the deceased had told her that she was the beneficiary of the principal asset in the estate. The court held that on the available evidence, the deceased had abandoned the customary way of life in favour of the Christian, non-traditional law. As a conclusion, the court held that the Indian Succession Act, then, was the applicable law.

The second feature concerns the persons who are entitled to inherit the estate. In short the Act provides that where a person dies intestate, the property devolves upon a wife or husband or upon those who are the kindred of the deceased.[885] The point of emphasis, here, is that the Act protects the welfare of the deceased's immediate family members and dependants, and that unlike customary law or Islamic law, the widow has a strong hand on the deceased's estate.

---

883 See section 24.

884 (1969) HCD 283.

885 Section 26. As regards to the mode of distribution, see sections 27-30.

The third feature concerns the issue of degree of inheritance. The Act is inclined towards equality of protection over the distribution of the estate among heirs of the same degree. For example, the Act does away with the distinction between male and female children of the deceased. These two groups inherit equal shares under the law. Looking at it with the prism of human rights, our fair comment is that the Act enhances the principle of non discrimination on ground of sex, which is equally enhanced by the International Bill of Rights.[886]

The fourth feature is on the principle of exclusion. Like all legal systems governing inheritance, the Act excludes illegitimate children from inheriting in the estate of their fathers. However, the Act recognises the right to inherit available to such children in respect of the estate of their mothers.

Customary Law

It is very important to note, at the outset, two basic facts about customary law of Tanzania. The first fact is that customary law is not uniform in all customary communities across the country. This is because of the nature and form in which it exists. Customary law may be written or unwritten, declared or undeclared, provided it is recognised and proved by the community in which it is used as having the force of law. However, the customary law that applies in most communities in Tanzania, especially in matters of inheritance, exists in a codified form, that is, the Rules of Inheritance, which appear in the Second Schedule to the Local Customary Law (Declaration) (No.4) Order, 1963.[887] In some communities, the code is supplemented by other documented customs. Taking Kagera as our example, I record the Rules of Inheritance by Female Heirs of 1944, which according to the Court of Appeal of Tanzania[888], "are statutory rules promulgated by the chiefs of Bukoba by virtue of powers contained in section 15 (1) of the Native Authority Ordinance" as well as the rules documented by the writers[889], which again, are applicable in the Haya Communities of Kagera Region. The second fact, is that the customary law as codified and applied through

886 Readers are referred to a detailed discussion of the International Bill of Rights in Chapter One above.

887 G.N 463/63.

888 *Deocras Rutabana v Deus Kashaga*, [1981] TLR 122, at p. 125.

889 See CORY, H. and HARTNOLL, M.M., *op cit.*

the decades has proved to be insufficient and, at times, it has been held to have failed the test of time and, therefore, is repugnant to the principles of justice and human rights. The two basic facts above compel us to approach customary law with great caution. [890]

The common and salient features of customary law, in matters of inheritance, are summarised below.

In terms of application, customary law applies in respect of the estate of the deceased, who is a member of a certain customary community, and in respect of which, customary law is meant to apply. In terms of who is entitled to inherit, customary law applies discriminately, in that it treats male heirs differently from female heirs, for example, rule 31 of the Rules of Inheritance provides that a female cannot inherit the family land which she is allowed to use for her life but with no power of sale.[891] Equally, rules 20 and 31 are of the effect that a woman can inherit her deceased father's landed property except for the family or clan land, which she can use for her life but with no power of sale. According to the rules, if there are no males in the clan, a female, then, can inherit the land absolutely. As to the degree of heirs, rule 25 of the Rule of Inheritance recognises three categories in the degree of heirs. In the first degree, the heir is usually the eldest son from the first house and takes the biggest share in the estate. In the second, heirs include all other sons and they inherit a relatively large share. Finally is the third degree of which heirs are the daughters of the deceased and who are entitled only to a small share. Rule 29 provides that if there are no sons, the eldest daughter of the first house will be the main heir. According to the Haya customs, for example, the three classes of heirs are known

---

890 Hon. Mwakasendo, Ag, J. (as he then was) happened to have his own approach toward customary law. Deciding the case of *Mbaruku v Chomonyogoro* (1971) HCD No. 406, the learned judge expressed his approach thus, "Speaking to myself, I believe that customary rules are like the reignless wild horse which only the expert horseman can mount and control but if left to the uninitiated, it can do deadly harm. I believe too, that it is the duty of the courts at this momentous period of our history to assist the growth and promotion of equitable customary rules. We should be failing totally in this respect, if we are to abide without reflecting or common sense, by the unchanging and changeless traditions of the past, as if they were priceless medieval relies".

891 See the discussion in Chapter Five below.

to include (1) the *Musika*, a primary heir, (2) the *Mainuka*, a secondary heir, and (3) the *Kyagati*, a minor heir[892]. Four, as regards the rights of the widow and widower, rules 27 and 28 provide to the effect that a widow has no share in her husband's estate if there are issues of the union and that the husband cannot inherit from his wife who dies intestate, unless the wife left no children or any member of her own family. Finally, rule 43 provides that illegitimate children cannot inherit patrilineally except under the will. The case of *Violet Kahangwa and Jovin Mutabuzi v The Administrator General and Mrs Eudokia Kahangwa*[893] is an interpretive device when it comes to the right to inheritance of illegitimate children. The background of the case was that the deceased Bruno Kahangwa died intestate. He was survived by the widow, Eudokia Kahangwa with whom he had celebrated a monogamous Christian marriage, and one female child of that marriage. However, at the time of his death, the deceased had separated with Eudokia and was living or cohabiting with another woman, Violet Ishengoma with whom he contracted a customary marriage evidenced by a marriage certificate. Immediately after Bruno's death Eudokia made an application to court asking the court to appoint an Administrator General to administer the deceased's estate and the application was accordingly granted. The appellants, Violet Ishengoma and Jovin Mutabuzi, the brother of the deceased, then applied to the High Court praying for the orders of revocation of the appointment of the Administrator General. At the time of hearing the application, they abandoned this prayer and asked the court to determine only two issues: whether the customary law of the Bahaya should govern the distribution of estate, and; whether the children of the deceased by Violet would qualify for a share in the estate. The Court (Mapigano, J.- as he then was) answered the first issue in the positive by saying that the customary law of the Bahaya applied. As regards the second issue the view of the court was that since the second marriage involving Violet was contracted during the subsistence of the first marriage, that marriage was a nullity

892 See paragraph 2 of CORY H. and HARTNOLL M.M. See also *Didas Rwakalila and 3 Others v Thomas Matondane* [1992] TLR 314 (CA).

893 [1990] TLR 72 (CA).

and the children born to it were illegitimate, hence were not entitled to a share in the deceased's estate. The appellants were aggrieved by the High Court's decision, specifically about the right to inheritance of the illegitimate children. On their appeal to the Court of Appeal of Tanzania, the Court speaking through Kisanga, J.A,- as he then was, had the following to say about the issue:

> *Paragraph 43 of the law expressly prohibits illegitimate children from inheriting from the father's side where the father died intestate. Thus the facts of the case fall squarely within that provision: the two children Reynold and Diana were obviously illegitimate and it is common ground that their father died intestate. There is nothing vague, ambiguous, inconsistent or incomplete about paragraph 43 which having regard to the facts of the case, would call for interpretation.*

As to what should be done to promote the rights of illegitimate children in matters of inheritance in similar situations, the Court's advice, which advise we consider to be very correct, was that:

> *It is perhaps appropriate to observe here that it seems advisable that in cases like this where a father feels that he owes a moral obligation towards his illegitimate child or children he should seek to honour that obligation by leaving a will. That would go some way to alleviate the hardship often facing illegitimate children; it would make easier the task of the Courts in handling such cases when they came to Court and it would serve to put the conscience of the putative father at some ease.*

It is my opinion, as point of departure, that the discriminatory character of customary law of inheritance against females should be seen as an important factor in the ongoing land law reforms which are being adopted as safeguards against the vice.

Islamic Law

Islamic law (also known as Mohamedan Law or Shari'a) [894] is the law recognised by members of the Islamic community as having a force of law and, therefore, governs various matters to include family law and inheritance.[895] The application of Islamic law, albeit, in matters of succession is well recognised by the laws of Tanzania.[896] When a Muslim dies, there are four duties which follow immediately in respect of his estate. The duties include: payment of the funeral expenses; payment of debts; execution of the will, if any, and; distribution of the remaining estate amongst the heirs according to the law. The last two duties will depend on whether the deceased has died testate or intestate. Islamic Law regulates both cases of testacy and intestacy. Indeed, Islamic experience tends to show that writing a will (*wasiyya*) is regarded as a duty for every believer, and that not writing it is a serious breach of this noble duty. This is what we learn through one of the *hadith:*

> *It is the duty of a Muslim who has anything to bequeath not to let two nights pass without writing a will about it.*

Islamic Will

A general principle is that once a person (a Muslim or non-Muslim) has written a will the will shall prevail over any claim over inheritance which is a mere sham, that is, not founded on and supported by the will. The case of *Tatu Abdallah v Waziri Musa* [897]supports this point. In

---

894 Reference is made to a unified body of moral and legal principles derived from both the Quran (the literal and final word of God) and Sunna (a body of information on statements and actions of the Prophet as he elaborated on the meaning of the Quran and supplemented its rulings).

895 A deceased's estate may not be subjected to Islamic Law for example where the deceased person had through a written or oral declaration provided that customary law should apply, or where the deceased person through his life had acted with the intention that his estate should be administered in accordance with Customary Law. It is, therefore, a matter of evidence to prove that the deceased had asked that his estate be governed in accordance with Customary Law. See the case of *Musa Makono v Rehema Hassan* (1967) HCD 159. This was a case in which the parties were all Wangoni and Muslims by religion and the court (Georges, C.J.- as then he was) held that there was nothing in the circumstances to show that the parties intended their religious law to apply as their personal law, but their tribal law.

896 See the *Succession (Non-Christian Asiatics) Act*, [Cap. 28 R.E 2002], section 6 (1); the *Judicature and Application of Laws Act*, [Cap. 358 R.E 2002], section 11 (1) proviso (ii); the *Magistrates Courts Act*, 1984 [Cap. 11 R.E 2002], section 18 (1) (a) (i).

897 [1975] LRT 7.

this case, the deceased had a house in Dar es Salaam and when he died, left no issue. The appellant claimed inheritance on the ground that he was willed, while the respondent claimed his entitlement to the same by virtue of his blood relationship to the deceased, as a nephew. The court was of the view that although both parties were Muslims but in the event of existence of a will it makes no difference which religion or relationship one professes for the will takes priority. However, in this case, the Court dismissed the appellant's claim on two main grounds: one, that no will was proved to exist; two, that the respondent's claim took priority because his relationship to the deceased was by blood, as he was the deceased's nephew, while between the appellant and the deceased there was no consanguinity, the appellant being the deceased's friend's daughter. It was further observed by the Court that as long as the appellant was not related to the deceased she could take the house if it was a gift made in her favour by and during the lifetime of the deceased. There was no evidence to show this. It was the Court's conclusion that the evidence is clear that the respondent was the relative of the deceased, and as there was nobody else, the respondent was entitled, under Islamic law, to inherit the property.

The case of *Juma Goboka v Halima Mohamed*[898] is authoritative in all cases where claims of title over the deceased's estate are established not by will but by way of a gift *inter vivos*. In the case, the appellant claimed, and was proved to be the cousin of the deceased. On the other hand, the respondent was proved to be the daughter of the deceased's boyfriend, one Mohamed, and that she was brought up by the deceased from the time she was 4 years of age. It was further observed by the Court that the property in the two houses was transferred by the deceased to the respondent by way of gift. It was the Court's firm observation that under the Islamic Law, a Muslim man or woman may give away his property either in his life time or under a will. The Court went on to note that there are three laid down rules governing the validity of a gift: one, there must be a manifestation of the wish to give on the part of the donor; two, there must be an acceptance of the gift by the done, which is either implied or express, and; there must be the taking of the subject matter of the gift by the donee either actually or constructively. It was the Court's further observation that there was no evidence to show that the disease affecting the deceased had rendered her so weak that she could not talk

898 [1975] LRT No 1.

or that it had also affected her mental capacity so that she was not in full control of her faculties so as to know the nature of her action at the time when she made a gift to the respondent and that the gift was valid. The Court conclusion that the appellant's right was to inherit all the property of the deceased except the two houses which the deceased had, during her lifetime, transferred to the respondent as gift (*hiba*) and that the respondent's right was to retain the two houses.

The two decisions above show that a Muslim has two ways in which he can dispose his property freely to any person of his or her own choice, and that is by giving it as a gift during his lifetime; and by Will. However under the Islamic law, the testator's freedom of testation is subjected to Islamic Law limitations, in that, a person has power to dispose by Will only one-third of the estate after payment of funeral expenses and debts, leaving the remaining two-thirds to be administered according to Islamic Law principles[899]of intestacy. Moreover, if the disposition by Will exceeds the limit (one-third), or if it is made to the legal heir without the consent of the rest of heirs, it is considered to be invalid under the law.[900] The case of *Waziri Maneno Choka v Abas Choka*[901] explains this limitation. In the case the respondent, elder brother of the deceased Maneno Choka, applied for letters of administration in a primary court of Bagamoyo and the appellant, son of the deceased, successfully resisted the application. The evidence showed that Maneno Choka left a will bequeathing all the property to the appellant. So the court found that it was the appellant who was entitled to be appointed administrator of the estate. The respondent was dissatisfied and he appealed to the District Court. The court affirmed the decision of the primary court in respect of the appointment of the appellant but said he was a stranger (illegitimate child) of his mother, one Salima Mbaraka, who lived with the deceased without solemnising any marriage, and that he was, in that capacity entitled only to one third of the testator's estate. The appellant appealed unsuccessfully against that decision in the High

899 See MWAIPOPO, Rita Alice, "Gender and the Law in Tanzania: Aspects of the Position of Women on Land and Property" in BINCHY, William and FINNEGAN, Catherine, (eds.), (2006): *Human Rights, Constitutionalism and the Judiciary: Tanzanian and Irish Perspectives*, Clarus Press, pp. 93-109, at p. 101.

900 See also COULSON, N.J., (1971): *Succession in the Mulsim Family*, Cambridge: Cambridge University Press.

901 Court of Appeal of Tanzania at Dar es Salaam, Civil Appeal No. 51 of 1999 (Unreported).

Court, hence, his appeal to the Court of Appeal of Tanzania. His only ground of appeal was that the courts below erred in denying him the right to the whole of the estate when the deceased father had, by a properly executed will appointed him as heir of the estate. The only issue before the Court was whether the appellant should be entitled to the whole estate in accordance with the will of the late Maneno Choka. The Court upholding the High Court's decision and, therefore, dismissing the appeal said:

> *We have had the occasion to study the works of various authors on Mohamedan Law. Those whom we have studied, all agree that testamentary disposition may not exceed a third of the estate. This applies irrespective of whether the disposition is to the heir recognised under Mohamedan Law or a stranger.*

The Court came to the conclusion that, even if the appellant was not an illegitimate child, still he could not be entitled to the whole of the estate as long as the will was governed by Islamic Law.

We are informed, again, that through the authority of the case of *Said Selemani Masuka v Anwar Z. Mohamed,*[902] that the "one third rule" of inheritance under the Islamic will has been openly challenged in a court of law as being unconstitutional and attracted tense reactions from both the reformist and non-reformist camps. The facts of the case show that the respondent (a son of the deceased by another man) was granted letters of administration of estate of one Rukia Ahmed by the Court in Probate and Adminstration Cause No. 44B of 1995. The Appellant (a husband of the deceased) objected the appointment by filing a caveat, and producing a Will of the deceased bequeathing to him all her property. The High Court of Tanzania dismissed the caveat on two grounds: (1) the Will is invalid because it bequeathed more than the one-third permissible by Islamic Law, (2) the disposition by Will was not consented to by other heirs of the deceased. The case records that in the cause of arguing before the High Court and in support of the Applicant's case, Justice Korosso attacked the constitutionality of Islamic Law by arguing that the law restricting the amount of a property a person could dispose by a Will should be ignored as it infringes the constitutional right of a person to own property and to dispose it as he wishes. Reacting to this argument, Msumi, J. had the following to say:

---

902 Court of Appeal of Tanzania at Dar es Salaam, Civil Application No. 5 of 1997 (Unreported). A summary of the ruling of the Court appears in FIMBO, G.M., (2010): *The Land Law of Tanzania*: A Case Book, Dar es Salaam (Unpublished), pp. 129-131.

> *In his submission the learned counsel for the applicant Justice Korosso urged the court to ignore this rule of Islamic Law because it infringes the constitutional right of a person to own property and to dispose it in a manner he wants. I must say that I was utterly astonished by this submission. The Islamic rules of inheritance are part of religious tenets enshrined in the Quran. It is mandatory that the estate of a deceased Muslim must be administered in accordance with these rules. Hence any attempt with interpolation of these rules amounts to amending the Quran. I don't think that anybody wishing good of this country can encourage a court of law to entertain such a move.*

The Applicant was aggrieved by the High Court's decision dismissing his caveat and applied successfully for leave to appeal against it to the Court of Appeal of Tanzania. In allowing the application, a single judge of the Court of Appeal (Justice Ramadhan,- as he then was) stated, *inter alia*, that:

> *Before MSUMI, J., Justice Korosso (retd) argued that the Islamic Law rule restricting the amount of property a person could dispose by a will should be ignored as it infringes the constitutional right of a person to own property and to dispose it as she wishes. Justice Korosso (retd) reiterated that submission before me. Ms Sheick argued that Islamic Law is part of the laws of the United Republic. I agree with her. But still the argument of Justice Korosso (retd) stands. Other laws of this country have been challenged on the same ground that they infringe the constitutional rights of the individuals. So we need this matter to be decided once and for all. Advocates belonging to the same school of thought as Justice Korosso (retd.) might come with this issue again... We need legalistic grounds, rather than religionist or patriotic, for rejecting the submission that Islamic Law rules, which are part of the laws of this country in matters of inheritance, do or do not violate the constitutional rights to property.*

It is important to note, that until now the constitutionality of Islamic Law rules of inheritance has not been decided by any court of law. The day will come when daring advocates may test the wisdom of the court by raising this issue again at the appropriate time.[903]

---

903 See comments by MAKARAMBA, Robert, "The Secular State and the State of Islamic Law in Tanzania" in JEPPIE, S. *et al.*, (eds.), (2010): *Muslim Family Law in Sub-Saharan Africa: Colonial Legacies and Post-Colonial Challenges*, Amsterdam University Press.

Islamic Intestacy

It is a subject of great interest to learn that property relations under Islam are founded on the Holy Quran, which provides for the rules of intestate inheritance, the rules which cannot be subjected to human revision. Going through the facts and decision of the court in the case of *Sofia Said and Yusuf Mohamed Musa v Awadh Ahmed Abeid and 3 Others,*[904] we learn two features that are most salient in the Islamic law of intestate inheritance. One is that Islamic Law distinguishes three classes of heirs, namely: the class of "Sharers" or "Koranic heirs", which comprises all the family members including spouses and children as well as parents; the class of "Residuaries" comprised of closest relatives such as nephews; and the class of "Distant Kindred," that is those who are not closely related to the deceased. The other feature is that Islamic law accommodates the rule of exclusion based on the principle of proximity. It means that individuals nearer in degree (proximity) to the deceased exclude others who are remote within the same class, for example, sons exclude grandsons, and full-blood relatives exclude half-blood relatives. It follows, therefore, that residuaries are called to succession only where there are no sharers or where the inheritable estate is not exhausted by sharers, while distant kindred are called to succession only where there are no sharers and residuaries. Apart from the above two features, Islamic Law also has rules of disqualification which excludes people in the category of the non-believers, homiciders and illegitimate children[905].

The point we should emphasize, here, is that Islamic Law, unlike, customary law confers a right of inheritance to a surviving spouse of a lawful marriage under Islamic Law and other female relatives of the deceased person. This has been regarded by some scholars as a fundamental change in the jurisprudence of Islamic Law, which was introduced by the Quran.

> *The Quran introduced fundamental changes on the laws of inheritance. The Arabian society being overly patriarchal did not accord any right of inheritance to females. And even among the males, the right to inherit was limited to those whose connection with the deceased was through a male relative. Entitlement to share in the inheritance was therefore solely a preserve of the agnatic relatives of the deceased. The Quran changed all*

904 [1992] TLR 29 (CA). See also *Salima Hussein v Hussein Ibrahim Sadiki & Sons*, Court of Appeal of Tanzania at Dar es Salaam, Civil Appeal No. 55 of 2000 (Unreported).

905 For the proposition that illegitimate children cannot inherit under Islamic Law, see *Amina Tratibu Mbonde v Selemani Ahmed Mtalika,* [2000] TLR 56 (HC).

> *this by admitting for the first time into ranks of entitled heirs female relatives as well as other male relatives who would not have otherwise been entitled under Arabian customary law.*[906]

We read from the record the following principles to be applicable in the distribution of the estate of a Muslim who dies without writing a will[907]: the first principle is that, where a man dies and leaves a widow and children, his estate shall be divided into eight shares and the widow shall be entitled to one eighth of the estate.[908] Secondly, where the deceased leaves a widow with no children, the widow is entitled to one quarter of the husband's estate and the reminder passes to the other heirs. Conversely, where a wife dies and is survived by no children, the husband is entitled to half of the property of the deceased wife. If there are children, the widower shall be entitled to one quarter of the deceased wife's estate[909]. Thirdly, where a man leaves behind more than one widow, their collective share shall be one quarter if there are no children and one eighth if there are children. The portion allocated to the widows is divided equally amongst them. Fourthly, where there are daughters of the marriage, these shall be collectively entitled to two-thirds of their deceased father's estate only if there are no male children and where there is only one child who is a daughter, she is entitled to half of her father's property. Fifthly, where there are sons and daughters, each son is entitled to a portion equal to that of two females. If there is only one child who is a son, he shall be entitled to two thirds of his deceased father's estate. Such a model of division, though commended by some scholars as having liberated women Muslims in matters of inheritance, is seen by others as an impediment as long as it discriminates against women by awarding them a lesser share compared to their male counterparts.[910] Bina Agarwal sees this model as an expression of the "Quranic injunction" against women.[911]

---

906 See CHUWA, Goodluck and MURUKE, Zainab., "Marriage and Spousal Relationship under Islamic Law" in The Tanzania Lawyer, Vol. 1 No. 3, (2007), pp. 27-42, at p. 29.

907 See, for example, MWAIPOPO, Rita Alice, *op cit*, at p. 102.

908 See *Leila Jalaludin Haji Jamal v Shaffin Jalaludin Haji Jamal*, High Court of Tanzania at Dar es Salaam, Civil Case No. 373 of 2001 (Unreported), in which the plaintiff successfully sued to recover her Koranic one-eighth of the estate of her deceased husband.

909 See *Sofia Said and Yusuf Mohamed Musa v Awadh Ahmed Abeid and 3 Others*, [1992] TLR 29 (CA) which the Court of Appeal of Tanzania confirmed that the right of the widower, one Mgeni Hemed, to inherit half of his deceased wife's estate, when the deceased left no children, did not attract any objection.

910 See AN-NA'IM, Abdulaah Ahmed, "Human Rights in the Muslim World" in HAYDEN, Patrick (ed.), (2001): *The Philosophy of Human Rights*, 1ST Edition, Pagagon House, pp. 315-335.

911 See AGARWAL, Bina, (1994): *A Field of Ones Own: Gender and Land Rights in South Asia*, Cambridge, Cambridge University Press, at p. 157.

Rules of Procedure in the Administration of Estate

Immediately after a person's death there follows the administration of his estate, which is done by the personal representative (s) of the deceased. These may appear either as executor (s) or as administrator(s) depending on whether that person has died testate or intestate. Where a person dies testate he will have appointed, in a will, a person to administer his estate upon his death. Such an appointee is called an executor[912]. He derives his powers to act from the will. However, it is a legal requirement that his position must be approved by the Court of law when there is an application for grant of probate[913] made to the court by the person who is so appointed in the will.

Since the executor is appointed by the testator in his last will, it means that when a person dies intestate, no executor is appointed in the circumstance. Under the provisions of section 2 (1) of the *Probate and Administration of Estates Act*, an "administrator" is defined to mean "a person appointed by the court to administer the estate of the deceased person when there is no executor or where no executor is able and willing to act." The administration of estate in all cases of intestacy is, therefore, done by the administrator. The court's appointment is made following an application for the letters of administration by one or more of the interested parties.

The real problem, however, has always been on the determination of a person or persons entitled to apply for the letters of administration. Where State law is applicable, the law suggests that if the deceased left a widow, administration shall be granted to the widow unless the court sees cause to exclude her, either on ground of some personal disqualification, or because she has no interest in the estate of the deceased.[914] However, the issue is more complicated in all cases of customary and Islamic intestacies, especially so in polygamous marriages involving a widow, a stepmother, children, and other family or clan members. Although the usual practice is for all family or clan members to meet under the guidance

---

912 A statutory definition of the term appears under section 2 (1) of the *Probate and Administration of Estate Act*, [Cap. 352 R.E 2002] that: "executor" means a person to whom the execution of the last will of the deceased person is, by the testator's appointment confided.

913 Probate, a term derived from the Latin word "probatum" or simply "proved" means nothing other than an official acceptance by the court that the will appointing an executor is genuine, and that the executor's right to administer the estate is officially sanctioned. The *Probate and Administration of Estate Act*, defines "probate" to mean the copy of a will, or in case of oral will, a statement of the contents thereof, certified under the seal of the court, with a grant of administration to the estate of the "testator".

914 See Section 219 (a) of the *Indian Succession Act*..

of the elder members to choose a legal representative or representatives who may later apply for the letters of administration in a court of law, the reality is that, more often than not, the majority of family members tend to turn hostile against the innocent widows and daughters.

It is for this reason that all Human Rights lawyers are invited to support the two decisions, that is, one by the East African Court of Appeal in the case of *Re Kibiego*[915] and another by the High Court of Tanzania in the case of *In the Matter of the Late Rabiuzima Matiro Mboro and in the Matter of An Application for Letters of Administration by Adeline Rabiuzima*[916]. All are inclined towards recognizing, respecting, protecting and promoting the rights of widows to be pointed as administrators of their deceased husbands' estates in all cases of intestacy. *Kibiego's* case involved a matter of administration of estate where a widow had applied for letters of administration in the High Court of Kenya. Her application was objected to, and the issue for determination was whether a widow was capable of making such application. The High Court of Kenya observed that there was a custom that on intestacy the family elders will always appoint the eldest son of the deceased as an administrator. On appeal to the East African Court of Appeal, the Court was confident to rule that:

> *I am of the opinion that in today's Kenya, in the absence of a valid reason such as grave instability, a widow of whatever race living in this country is entitled to apply to the court for grant of the letters of administration, more so when children, as in the instance case, are minors. A widow is the most suitable person to obtain representation to her deceased husband's estate. In the normal cause of events she is the person who would rightfully, properly and honestly safeguard the assets of the estate for herself and her children. It would be going back to a medieval conception to cling to a tribal custom by refusing her a grant which is obviously insisted to a progressive society of Kenya in the year of grace.*

Also in *Adeline's* case the applicant, a widow, applied to the High Court seeking to be appointed the administrator of estate of her deceased husband. The application was bitterly objected to by the deceased's brother on grounds that he was the one appointed by the clan members to take over its administration. When litigating this dispute it was discovered that the clan had decided to disinherit the widow and two sons of the deceased on the grounds that they had murdered the

---

915 (1972) E.A 179.

916 High Court of Tanzania at Moshi, Probate and Administration Cause No. 2 of 1998, (Unreported).

deceased. The court decided the application in the favour of the widow on grounds that: the decision to disinherit the widow was illegal because it was made in her absence; that is, she was condemned unheard, which is a violation of the rules of natural justice; the allegation of killing the deceased was never true and was not proved in court since the widow was not even charged with murder, and; the widow was the co-owner of the matrimonial property, which was labelled as the deceased's estate. As we may all note from the above cases, Tanzania, as seems to be the case in Kenya, the legal safeguard in favour of the greedy and inconsiderate relatives who are apt to tread on the widows' toes upon the death of a husband, is reflected in the statutory law that requires, in case of an application for grant of letters of administration under the *Probate and Administration of Estate Act,* that the application be supported by written consent of all those who, according to the rules for the distribution of the estate of an intestate applicable in case of the deceased, would be entitled to the whole or part of the estate[917]. Apart from the requirement of consent, the law also mandates the court to issue an order of citation insisting that the application be published[918], for example, in local newspapers inviting any person to object to the grant where there are good reasons to do so[919]. Despite the fact that there are cases on record which tend to show that widows are capable of, and have in some occasions been granted letters of administration[920] many people tend to take advantage of the procedural rules to object against a widow's right in the administration of estate. Thanks to the courts that tend to sympathise with innocent widows!

However, as to the other side of the coin, the legal safeguard, again, has always helped individual widows to enter a caveat[921], or appearance against the grant of letters of administration whenever their rights to

---

917 Rule 71 (1), Probate Rules.

918 Rule 73. See also rule 5 (4) of the Primary Courts (Administration of Estate) Rules G.N No. 49/1971 which provides for the advertisement of the application for grant of letters of administration made before a primary court.

919 For the purpose of learning, a citation inviting the interested parties in the local news paper would appear as appendix 5 below.

920 See, for example, *Young Wook Youn v Yum Hun Hwa*, Probate and Administration Cause No. 20 of 2001 (Unreported).

921 Section 59, [Cap. 352 R.E 2002], and rule 82 (4) of the Probate Rules. A caveat may be defined to mean an official request that a court should not take a particular action without issuing a notice to the party lodging the caveat and without affording an opportunity of hearing him. According to the decision of the Court in *Nuru Hussein v Abdul Ghani Ismail Hussein* [2000] TLR 217, the filing of a caveat in probate or administration proceedings changes the proceedings into an ordinary suit, the petitioner becoming the plaintiff and the caveator becomes the defendant. Also according to the decision in *Kijakazi Mbegu and 5 Others v Ramadhani Mbegu* [1999] TLR 174, the Court has a duty to determine the caveat before it can grant probate or letters of administration.

their husbands' estate have been downtrodden. On many occasions, for example, widows of the deceased would appear to object to the grant of letters of administration by advancing many reasons including, for example, claims:

> *That there was no clan meeting which appointed the petitioner (s) to petition for Letters of Administration and/or if there was any, I being the wife of the deceased, was not involved howsoever.*
>
> *That the asset which was referred to by the Petitioner, house No. 2 situated on Plot X, Dar es Salaam, is a matrimonial home where I and other members of the family are residing.*
>
> *That the Petitioner and a few other members of the family are not trustworthy and responsible as their intention is to deprive me of my matrimonial home, which was jointly acquired with my late husband.*

Such complaints are expected to be more prevalent in customary and Islamic communities, which tend to disregard the rights of women to property than in cases where State law applies. The old case of *Re The Estate of the Late Suleman Kasundwa*[922] is an aid to widows who are on the verge of being excluded from inheritance of their deceased husband's estate. In this case, the first respondent, an Administrator-General, was granted letters of administration of the estate of the deceased, an African Muslim. The will was annexed, which purported to give the estate to the deceased's nephew while the name of the applicant who was one of the four widows of the deceased was not included in the list of the beneficiaries of the estate, the reason being that she was not known to the Administrator-General at the time of the grant. The widow was not served with the notice of citation, nor did she give her consent to the grant as required by law.[923] So when she was made aware of the grant, she applied to Court for two alternative remedies, that is, either for the revocation of the grant or for an order that her name be included in the list of beneficiaries. She won her case. The court qualified the grant by declaring that the provision of the annexed will should only be limited to the one-third of the property which the deceased was, under Islamic law of inheritance, entitled to dispose. This means the nephew was entitled only to one-third and the rest of the estate would be distributed to the other beneficiaries including the applicant.

---

922 [1965] E.A. 247.

923 That is section 5 (2) of the then *Administrator- General's Ordinance*, Cap. 27. It is now cited as *The Administrator General (Powers and Functions) Act*, [Cap. 27 R.E 2002].

Courts and their Jurisdiction in Probate and Administration Proceedings

It should be clearly understood that whoever is faced with a matter involving the administration of the deceased's estate, identification of a court of competent jurisdiction[924] to hear and determine it becomes a matter of great significance. This is because of the relevance attached to jurisdiction of courts in the overall administration of justice. It means that any matter stands to be dismissed if it is instituted in a court of law which has no jurisdiction to determine it, and should such a court proceed to determines it, the whole of the proceedings and decision will be nullified on appeal to a superior court in the hierarchy of courts.[925] There are basically three classes of courts with concurrent jurisdiction to hear and adjudicate on matters involving the administration of estates, namely Primary Courts, District Court and, the High Court. The jurisdictional mandate of each of these courts is discussed, albeit, summarily as hereunder:

Primary Courts: as a general rule, a primary court has the jurisdiction to entertain all proceedings of civil nature where the law applicable is Customary or Islamic Law.[926] However, as far as the powers of the primary court in administration proceedings are concerned, the law states that the jurisdiction of the primary court in administration of the deceased's estates, where the law applicable to the administration or distribution of the estate is customary or Islamic law, may be exercised in cases where the deceased at the time of his death, had a fixed place of abode within the local limits of the court's jurisdiction[927]. It follows, therefore, that since most of the administration of estate involve customary and Islamic law,

---

924 See a discussion on the concept of jurisdiction in Chapter Six below.

925 The doctrine of jurisdiction of courts is elaborately discussed in Chapter Six of this book. We have cited, in this part as our examples, the cases of *Lucia Paulo v Lenna Ndege*, High Court of Tanzania (Land Division) at Dar es Salaam, Misc. Land Appeal No. 48 of 2006 (Unreported) and *Mtumwa Ally Said and Another v Mwamtoro Ally Said*, High Court of Tanzania (Land Division) at Dar es Salaam, Land Appeal No. 48 of 2006 (Unreported), in which the proceedings were nullified for the reason that they were entertained by the Land Courts established by the *Land Dispute Courts Act*, [Cap. 216 R.E 2002] instead of courts with jurisdiction to deal with matters founded on the administration of estates.

926 Section 19 (1) (c), *Magistrates' Courts Act*, [Cap. 11, RE 2002]. In the case of *Sofia Njati v Mire Artan Ismail and Another*, High Court of Tanzania at Dar es Salaam, Civil Revision No. 82 of 2003 (Unreported), the Court (Mandia, J.) nullified the proceedings and grant of letters of administration in Probate and Administration Cause No. 112 of 1998 in the Court of Resident Magistrates at Kisutu, Dar es Slaam, for lack of jurisdiction under the provisions of section 19 (1) (c) of the *Magistrates Courts Act* read together with the Fifth Schedule thereto which vests in the Primary Court, jurisdiction to administer customary and Islamic Law estates.

927 Section 1 (1), Fifth Schedule of Cap. 11.

and since, unlike in normal civil suits, the issue of pecuniary jurisdiction does not bar a primary court from entertaining administration matters and granting probate or letters of administration, primary courts in Tanzania have been heavily occupied with administration proceedings. The legal issue which seem to have disturbed the minds of lawyers in land law, but which has been finally settled, was whether a primary court has jurisdiction to entertain administration cases in respect of the estate of the deceased where it involves registered land under the *Land Registration Act*. Earlier before the decision of the Court of Appeal of Tanzania, in the case of *Scolastica Benedict v Martin Benedict*[928], many of the courts' decisions tended to suggest that the primary court lacked jurisdiction in administration cases involving registered lands,[929] and only a few decisions upheld a different view[930].

The facts of *Scolastica's case* were that: the appellant's husband, one Benedict Katanyebile died intestate in 1971. He was survived by two wives, (the appellant being a second wife) and a number of sons and daughters. The husband left to his heirs substantial property, including the disputed house on plot Nos. 17 and 19 Block "D" in Bukoba township, whose title was registered under the then Land Registration Ordinance. The Urban primary court at Bukoba appointed administrators to administer the estate, who on the guidance of the clan council distributed the property to the heirs according to the Haya Customary Law whose effect was to exclude the two wives. The disputed house was allocated to the respondent who later sought to evict the appellant from the house in which she had been living with her deceased husband. The appellant refused to hand over the house, she decided to appeal against the administration proceedings in the primary court arguing, as one of the grounds, that the primary court under which the estate of the appellant's husband was administered had no jurisdiction over registered lands. The Court of Appeal of Tanzania, after making a thorough examination of the law, observed that the Magistrate Courts' Act did not specify the particulars of the jurisdiction of primary court in the administration of estate, but empowered the Chief Justice to specify such jurisdiction. The Court went on to note that by an order published in the Gazette as Government Notice No 320 of 1964, the Chief Justice did specify such

928 [1993] TLR 1 (CA).

929 See for example *Salmin Mohamed v Abdu Mohamed* [1986] TLR 251 (HC); *Bibi Makongoro v Issa* (1970) HCD 192; *Mohamed Yusufu v Tunda Kassim* (1968) HCD 487.

930 See *Manungwa Lutalamila and Two others v Martha Lutalamila* [1982] TLR 98.

jurisdiction in that under rule 2 of that order it was stated that, "Every primary court shall have jurisdiction in the administration of estate of a deceased person, if (a) the deceased, at the time of his death, had a fixed place of abode within the area of the jurisdiction of the court, and; (b) the law applicable to the administration or distribution of, or the succession to, the estate is customary law or Islamic and the estate is not one to which the provisions of the Marriage, Divorce and Succession (Non-Christian Asiatics) Ordinance apply".

The Court came to the conclusion that, "It is evident from this order of the Chief Justice that all primary courts have been given jurisdiction in matters of administration of estate regardless of whether the subject matter is land registered under the Land Registration Ordinance, provided the applicable law is Customary or Islamic Law."

From the above analysis, it follows that the primary court's jurisdiction in administration cases is limited by two factors: the applicable law which need be Customary or Islamic Law[931], and; the place of abode of the deceased, which need be in the local jurisdiction of the court. Once the jurisdiction of the primary court is established, the primary court exercises its powers as conferred to it by the provisions of the Fifth Schedule to the Magistrates' Courts Act, including the power to appoint an administrator[932] or an officer of the court or some reputable and impartial person able and willing to administer the estate either together with or in lieu of an administrator appointed under section 2 (a)[933], and the power to revoke the appointment when there are good reasons to do so[934]. In no circumstance is the court empowered to distribute the estate to the heirs. In the case of *Samson Kishosha Gabba v Charles Kingongo Gabba*[935], a primary court was faulted when, apart from appointing the Ward Secretary to administer the deceased's estate, went on to distribute the estate to the heirs by making a decision about the shares the heirs were entitled to. Allowing the appellant's appeal, Mwalusanya, J.- as he then was) stated that:

931 The grant of administration by the primary court in *Ibrahim Kusaga v Emmanuel Mweta* [1986] TLR 26 (HC) was faulted by the High Court of Tanzania in that the court had acted outside of its jurisdiction since the estate of the deceased included a partnership property which is not covered under Customary Law or Islamic Law.

932 Section 2 (a), Fifth Schedule, [Cap. 11 R.E 2002].

933 Section 2 (b).

934 Section 2 (c).

935 [1990] TLR 133 (HC). See also the case of *Ibrahim Kusaga v Emmanuel Mweta* (1986) TLR 26 (HC).

> *The appointment of a Ward Secretary as the administrator of the deceased's estate was quite correct. However, the trial court had no power to distribute the estate of the deceased to the respective heirs: that power of distribution is given to the administrator of the deceased's estate. So the primary court usurped the power it does not have under the law...In this case the trial court was wrong to decide the ownership of the houses on plots No. 125 and No. 33 Block A when the distributor had yet to distribute them.*

Note that administration proceedings commenced in a primary court may be transferred to a superior court under the provisions of section 47 of the Magistrates' Courts Act, if there are good reasons to do so. For example, a request by the party to engage an advocate[936] may constitute a good cause for the court to allow transfer of the proceedings to a superior court where advocates are allowed to appear. The matter in *Mwanahawa Muya v Mwanaidi Maro*[937] had started in the primary court, from where it was transferred to the district court as the appellant (then a petitioner) had indicated that she was employing an advocate.

District Court: the legal jurisdiction of a District Court (including a Resident Magistrates Court) in dealing with administration cases appears not to be very clear. Read very carefully, the *Magistrates Court Act* provides in part that:

> *A court of a resident magistrate shall have and exercise jurisdiction in all proceedings in respect of which jurisdiction is conferred by the Second Schedule to this Act and any law for the time being in force on a court of a resident magistrate or on a district court presided over by a resident magistrate or a civil magistrate, in the exercise of its original jurisdiction.* [938]

The Second Schedule to the Act confers jurisdiction to resident magistrates in respect of matters coming under the whole of the *Probate and Administration of Estates Act.* It means that on the right of the above provision, a resident magistrate whether, sitting in the District Court or a Court of a Resident Magistrate, has jurisdiction to entertain administration matters, provided that the law applicable is not Customary or Islamic Law (which is administered in primary courts),

936 Note that advocates are debarred from appearing in primary courts under the provisions of section 33 (1) and (3) of the *Magistrates' Courts Act, 1984*..

937 [1992] TLR 78 (CA).

938 Section 41 (1).

and also that the deceased had a place of abode in the court's local area of jurisdiction and the courts acts within its pecuniary jurisdiction regarding the subject matter. At best, we are all witnesses to the fact that many administration proceedings have been commenced in the Resident magistrates Court all over the country. However, the Probate and Administration of Estates Act brings in the concept of a "District Delegate", meaning, "a resident magistrate appointed as a District Delegate under section 5 of the Act. [939] The point of interest is on what has been the court's interpretation of this provision in the case of *Shomary Abdallah v Abdallah Hussein and Another.*[940] In this case, there was a probate cause initially instituted in the primary court, and later transferred to the District Court of Ilala at Kisutu, in which the grant of administration was made by the resident magistrate. Being dissatisfied, the appellant appealed to the High Court of Tanzania. Before deciding the appeal, the Court (Kyando, J.- as he then was) sought to know if the magistrate who granted the application was a "District Delegate" duly appointed under section 5 of the Act. It was to the court's satisfaction that the magistrate was not, as she had no instrument of appointment to be a District Delegate. Nullifying the proceedings of the District Court, the learned judge was of the observation that:

> *According to the Ordinance (now the Act) the general jurisdiction under it is conferred on the High Court; the District Courts and District Delegates have only limited jurisdiction; the exercise by resident magistrates of powers relating to probate and administration of deceased's estate is not automatic; these magistrates have to be appointed District Delegates under section 5 in order to be vested with such powers, and; the appearance of the Ordinance (Act) under the Second Schedule to the Magistrates Courts Act must have been an oversight on the part of the drafters of the schedule.*

---

939 Section 5 of the *Probate and Administration of Estates Act* provides that:

(1) The Chief Justice may, from time to time, appoint such resident magistrates as he thinks fit to be District Delegates.

(2) A District Delegate shall have jurisdiction in all matters relating to probate and administration of estates with power to grant probate and letters of administration of estates if the deceased, at the time of his death, had his fixed place of abode within the area for which the Delegate is appointed–

(a) in non-contentious cases;

(b) in contentious cases, if the Delegate is satisfied that the gross value of the estate does not exceed fifteen thousand shillings, or the High Court authorises the Delegate to exercise jurisdiction in such circumstances as are specified in subsection (3).

940 [1991] TLR 135 (HC).

Following the decision in the above case, one would not hesitate to conclude that the District Court and Resident Magistrates Court have no jurisdiction to deal with administration matters except where a presiding magistrate is appointed as a District Delegate, or where the Court acts under the provision of section 6 of the Act, which confers powers to a district court in respect of administration of small estates. The position taken by the court in the interpretation of the law in this case, and the practical reality that administration cases are always flooding the resident magistrates' courts, without any evidence as to whether the magistrates of these courts are District Delegates, suggest that the powers of the District Courts in administration of estates in Tanzania are subjected to great scrutiny. As if reacting to rectify this practical problem, the Chief Justice has issue Circular No. 1 of August 2008 which appoints all resident magistrates who have been in practice for a period of one year to qualify as District Delegates.

The High Court: the general rule is that the powers of the High Court in all civil and criminal matters are full and unlimited[941]. So in matters of administration of estate, section 3 of the Probate and Administration of Estates Act provides clearly that, "the High Court shall have jurisdiction in all matters relating to probate and the administration of deceased's estates, with power to grant probates of wills and letters of administration to the estates of deceased persons and to alter or revoke such grants," while section 4 provides that, "The High Court shall have jurisdiction to re-seal grants of probate and letters of administration made by a court of probate in any part of the Commonwealth in accordance with the provisions of Part X of this Act. Re-sealing of probate or letters of administration is required in the following scenario. Suppose Mr X, a Ugandan who happened to live in Tanzania dies in Uganda. He leaves an estate of immovable property both in Uganda and in Dar es Salaam, Tanzania. Y, Mr. X' son applies for and is granted the letters of administration of his deceased father's estate by the High Court of Uganda. The letters so granted cannot have a force of law in respect of the property in Tanzania, unless there is an application made to the High Court of Tanzania for re- sealing (with the seal of the court) of the letters. Once re-sealed the letters attain a force of law as if they were granted by the court of Tanzania.

941 See section 2 (1) of the *Judicature and Application of Laws Act*, [Cap. 358 R.E 2002].

Procedural Requirement in Probate and Administration Proceedings

The procedure that applies in all matters of administration of estate are, by and large, dependent on a number of factors such as: the applicable law; the court involved, and; the basis of the proceedings, that is to say, whether the proceedings are founded on testacy or intestacy. As far as the factor on the applicable law is concerned, administration proceedings are regulated by two bodies of law depending on the type of the court in which such proceedings are instituted. On one hand, there are the provisions of the Fifth Schedule to the *Magistrates' Courts Act*[942] and the Primary Courts (Administration of Estates) Rules[943], all of which provide for the practice and procedure of administration of estate in Primary Courts, and on the other hand there are the provisions of the *Probate and Administration of Estate Act* and the Probate Rules made thereto, which provide for the procedure and practice involved in courts other than the Primary Courts.

In all cases where the *Probate and Administration of Estate Act* applies, administration proceedings are commenced by a petition made by the executor (in all cases where application is for grant of probate) or by a party who, according to the rules applicable in the distribution of the estate of the intestate deceased, would be entitled to the whole or part of such deceased's estate (in all cases where application is for the grant of letters of administration), to the court of competent jurisdiction. The legal requirement is that when a person applies for a grant of probate, the application must be accompanied by a will appointing him to administer the estate[944]. Failure to attach a copy of the will is a contravention of the procedure, and the application shall be dismissed. This is the gist of the case of *Hamson D. Ghikas v Ludwina G. Ghikas*[945]. The facts of the case are that the respondent petitioned for, and was granted probate by the High Court of Tanzania in respect of the estate of her late father. The appellant, also a child of the deceased father, applied for revocation of the grant, which application was refused by the same court. On appeal to the Court of Appeal of Tanzania, the Court's observation was that the petition by the respondent was not accompanied by any will, and there was no mention of any will left by the deceased. The Court went on to nullify the grant of probate by saying that:

942 [Cap. 11 R.E 2002].

943 GN No. 49/1971.

944 See sections 24 (1) and 33 (a), [Cap. 352 R.E 2002].

945 [1992] TLR 288 (CA).

> *In the circumstances, therefore, it seems plain to us that the petition for probate by the respondent was grossly misconceived and the purported grant of the same was simply null and void...In the result we set aside the purported grant of probate as being null and void and as this is entirely a family matter we make no order for costs.*

Besides the requirement to attach the will, the petition must also state:[946] the date and place of the testator's death; the statement that the writing annexed is the last will and testament; the amount and nature of assets which are likely to come to the petitioner's hands; the names and addressees of all executors named in the will, stating also that the petitioner is an executor named in the will, and; the statement that no similar proceedings have been commenced in any other court of law.

Where the petition is for the grant of letters of administration the requirement, then, is that the petitioner shall state the following in his petition[947]: the date and place of the deceased's death; the family and other relatives of the deceased and their prospective residence; the rights in which the petitioner claims; the amount and nature of the assets which are likely to come to the petitioner's hands; a statement that a diligence search has been made and no valid will has been found; and a statement that no any proceedings for grant of letters of administration of the estate has been commenced before any other court.

Accordingly, the effect of omitting any of the above requirements is to render the petition defective and, where grant of probate or letters of administration has been granted on the basis of a defective petition, that grant will be nullified on appeal. The case of *Mwanahawa Muya v Mwanaidi Maro*[948] authoritatively supports the point. The appellant in this case applied for and was granted letters of administration by the Resident Magistrates Court of Arusha after the respondent's objection in these proceedings had been dismissed. Later on, the respondent applied in the High Court for grant of letters of administration in respect of

---

946 Section 55 (1). The section need be read together with rule 33 (1) of the Probate Rules made under section 9 of the Act.

947 See section 56 (1), [Cap. 352 R.E 2002]. See also Rule 39 of the Probate Rules.

948 [1992] TLR 78 (CA).

the same estate. She deposed in her petition that there had been no proceeding for grant of letters of administration regarding the estate. The High Court granted the same, in ignorance of the fact that such letters had already been granted to the appellant. The appellant was dissatisfied and she objected against the second grant to the respondent. The High Court, instead of addressing the issue of the validity of the second grant, invoked its revisional powers to declare that the proceedings in the RM's court were null and void. The appellant was, again, dissatisfied, hence her appeal to the Court of Appeal of Tanzania. Allowing the appeal, the Court stated:

> *The respondent's blatant lies that there had not been previous proceedings regarding grant of probate or letters of administration while she was in fact the objector in the RM's Court which letters of administration were granted to the appellant, amply demonstrated that she was bent to defraud other interested parties in the estate.*

The Court's main concern was that the High Court was misled in the petition and that it could not have granted the said letters of administration if it had been aware of all the information relevant to the respondent's petition.

Powers and Duties of Administrators of Estates

The powers of an administrator of the estate are statutorily provided for, depending on the nature of the administration. In cases of administration effected at the primary court level, the powers of administrators as are outlined under part II of the Fifth Schedule to the *Magistrates Courts' Act*. Under the provision of section 5, for example, the administrator appointed by a primary court has the power, with reasonable diligence, to collect the property of the deceased and the debts that were due to him, to pay the debts of the deceased and the debts and costs of the administration and, thereafter, to distribute the estate of the deceased to the persons entitled thereto. In carrying out his duties, the administrator needs to give effect to the directions of the primary court.

Where administration is made under the *Probate and Administration Act*, then the powers of an administrator are as appear under the provisions of part XI of the Act. The general rule is that an administrator is a legal representative of the deceased for all purposes, and all the property of the deceased vests in him[949]. As such he has numerous powers including: the power to sue in all causes of action that survive the deceased and to recover all debts due to the deceased at the time of death[950]; the power to dispose of the property as he thinks fit, including the power of sale,[951] and the power, with reasonable diligence, to collect the property of the deceased and the debts that were due to him, to pay the debts of the deceased and the debts and costs of administration, and to distribute the estate to the persons entitled to the same or to trustees for such persons in accordance with the provisions of this Act, as the case may be.[952]

One of the serious problems that the administrator or executor is likely to encounter, especially in the course of paying the debts which a creditor, or some creditors may be owing to the deceased, concerns the dilemma in which he may find himself when the debt (s) exceed the total value of the deceased person's estate. In that scenario, the law requires the executor or administrator to pay the debts in accordance with their order of priorities[953] and that only the debts that are known to the executor or administrator are paid equally and rateably as far as the assets of the deceased extend. Meanwhile, there is a possibility for some debts to be claimed when the estate has passed to the heirs. In that scenario the liability to pay shifts to the heirs and, as a general principle of the English law, is limited to assets of the estate which he or she received from the deceased. This is a restatement of the Court of Appeal of Tanzania in the case of *Maagwi Kimito v Gibeno Werema*,[954] in which the Court observed that:

> *Under the principles and rules derived from English Law an heir's liabilities are limited to the assets of the estate which he or she received from the deceased.*

949 Section 99.

950 Section 100.

951 Section 101.

952 Section 108 (1).

953 Section 109 (2).

954 [1985] TLR 132 (CA).

However, the rules of customary law seem to provide to the contrary when it comes to the heir's liability to pay debts. These rules, which appear under the Second Schedule to the Local Customary Law (Declaration) Order, 1933 and whose English translations are made in R.W. James and G.M. Fimbo[955] read that:

> *11. If the intestate's property is not sufficient to pay the deceased's debts important debts will be paid first and the rest will be paid proportionately.*
>
> *12. The rest of the debt is satisfied by the heirs from their own property.*
>
> *Claims and debts are inheritable.*

Of all the tree rules, rule 12 appears to be an unjust rule as it requires the heir to pay the debts to which he is not a party, even from his own property if the deceased's estate is insufficient to discharge the debt. Notwithstanding, it was considered to be a good rule of customary law by the Court of Appeal of Tanzania, a Court whose decisions, according to the doctrine of precedent, are authoritative and binding upon the lower courts in the judicial hierarchy. Specifically, the Court of appeal said that:

> *It is clear from these rules, especially rule 12, that an heir is liable to pay in full the debts where the deceased's estate are insufficient to pay all the debts in full. It is clear from the provisions of rules 11, 12 and 13 that a three-stage procedure will be involved in satisfying the liabilities. Firstly, payment in full is made in respect of important debts. Secondly, if the important debts are fully discharged from the assets, the remainder of the debts is paid out proportionately. Thirdly, in any event, the balance of the debts is paid out in full by the heirs from their own property.*

As to whether the rule imposing an obligation to the heir to pay even from his own property was unjust, the Court was of the view that it is not since a person is not compelled to become an heir to a deceased. But once the person accepts to be an heir, the responsibility described above devolves upon that person.

According to the record, of all the powers available to the executors or administrators of estate, the power of sale has been the most contested, and has, therefore attracted most litigation in the court of law in which

---

955 See JAMES, R.W. and FIMBO, G.M., *op cit*, paragraph 166.

some interested parties have had the courage to challenge the sale or to claim some rights under the sale, as reflected in the respective cases of *Aziz Daudi Aziz v Amin Ahmed Ally* & *Selemani Wagharibu*[956] and *Mohamed Hassani v Mayasa Mzee & Mwanahawa Mzee*[957], both cases coming before the Court of Appeal of Tanzania.

The facts in Aziz's case were that the appellant, Aziz, sued the two respondents for having alienated the property of his late father, that is, house No. 2 of Kariakoo Street in Dar es Salaam. His main claim was that the second respondent had secretly and fraudulently sold the house to the first respondent and that the house belonged to the appellant's late father Daudi who inherited it from his aunt, one Katija Aziz. The available evidence indicated that the second respondent was appointed as an administrator of the estate of Katija Aziz when the latter died, and had sold the house in his capacity as an administrator long before the death of the appellant's father. In dismissing the appeal for lack of merits, the Court of appeal said that:

> *Once the administrator of the estate of the deceased was properly appointed whatever steps he took in dealing with the property of the deceased should be considered as part of his undertaking he gave on his appointment that he would faithfully administer the estate by paying all the debts of the deceased and distributing the property to all the legal heirs of the deceased".*

The Court went on to say, "Once an administrator of the estate is appointed then the name of the deceased-owner of the property is changed in all documents and that of the administrator is substituted and it is left to his discretion to administer the estate in the best way he can. The sale of this house being legal, the sale price should accordingly be distributed to the heirs".

In Mohamed Hassani's case the facts were that the appellant successfully sued the respondents and one Mfundo Omari (deceased at the time the case reached the court of appeal), claiming the return of the house on plot No. 2 Block 86 Central Ngamiani area in Tanga. The house had been sold to him by Mfundo Omari in his capacity as an administrator of the estate of the late Mzee Risasi. The appellant won the case in the Resident Magistrates' Court of Tanga, but lost in the High

956 Court of Appeal of Tanzania, Civil Appeal No. 36 of 1990 (Unreported).

957 [1994] TLR 224.

Court, where the Court held that Mfundo's appointment was void and that he had, therefore, no power to dispose the property by selling it to the appellant.

Aggrieved by the decision, the appellant found his way through the Court of Appeal of Tanzania. His three grounds of appeal were that: first, that the learned judge erred in law when he held that the primary court had no power to appoint Mifundo Omari as administrator of the estate of the late Mzee bin Risasi and that he was not properly appointed according to Rule 2 (a) of the Fifth Schedule to the Magistrate's Courts Act. Secondly, that the learned judge erred in fact when he held that the sale of the suit house was arbitrary and did not take the interests of the estate when there was ample evidence to prove that the suit house was at stake. Thirdly, that the learned judge erred in law in holding that there was no consent of the beneficiaries to sell the suit house when in fact the authority to sell was vested in the administrator by the operation of the grant under which he was appointed. Addressing the first ground, the Court was of the view that the evidence indicated that the primary court had revoked Mayasa's appointment after receiving complaint from other beneficiaries of the estate and appointed Mfundo under Rule 2 (b) as a "reputable and impartial person able and willing to administer the estate." As for the second ground, the court's view that in the circumstance of this case, selling the house and distributing the proceeds among the various contending heirs was the only sensible option open to the administrator for the record showed that there were two hostile contending groups among the heirs of the late Mzee bin Risasi. The heirs were grouped according to their mothers. There was absolutely no way of reconciling the two groups. "We are therefore satisfied that the decision to sell the suit house was not arbitrary, in fact it was in the best interests of the estate and all the heirs", the court remarked. Finally, the court addressed the third ground by going back to Aziz's case in which it was held that the administrator had power to sell even without the consent of the beneficiaries.

It is important that in this case, the appellant won all the grounds of his appeal, but the court ordered the property to be resold by public auction after it was found that the sale to the appellant was executed in two documents indicating different prices.

The Role of an Administrator-General in Administration of Estate

The law in Tanzania[958] gives powers to the Minister, for the time being responsible for legal affairs, to appoint an Administrator-General and Assistant Administrator- General as may be required.[959] When it comes to matters of administration of estate, the law also provides that where it appears to the court that circumstances of the case require, for reasons recorded in its proceedings, the court may, of its own motion or otherwise, grant letters of administration to the Administrator-General or to any other person notwithstanding that there are persons who in the ordinary course, would be legally entitled to administration.[960]

The reasons that may compel the court to grant letters of administration to the Administrator-General include, but are not limited to the following: where a testator has indicated in his last will that his estate be administered by the Administrator-General; in the absence of an interested person, a relative of the deceased, to apply for letters of administration; the unwilling of the person appointed to administer the estate, and; mismanagement of the administration process by the person appointed to administer the estate. The case of *Issa Batenga v Kheri Batenga and Another*[961] is one of the cases, which the points to the role of an Administrator-General. The facts of this case show that the respondents were granted letters of administration of the estate of the deceased, their brother. Upon an application by the son of the deceased, the High Court revoked the appointment of the respondents and substituted the appointment of the Administrator-General. The respondents applied to a single judge of the Court of Appeal for stay of execution of the decision pending an appeal to the Court. The application was granted, hence this reference by Issa Batenga to the full bench of the Court. To support the reference it was argued for the applicant that the appointment of the respondents as administrators of the estate was not consented to by the heirs of the deceased as required by law, and that in handling the estate the respondents are shown to have been guilty of mismanagement of the estate, for instance, by failing to file an inventory with the court and to account for the proceeds of sale of part of the estate. The Court of Appeal affirmed the decision of the High Court in revoking the appointment of the respondents when it said at p. 3 that:

958 Reference is made to the *Administrator General (Powers and Functions) Act*, [Cap. 27 R.E 2002].

959 Section 4.

960 See the Proviso to section 5(1).

961 Court of Appeal of Tanzania at Dar es Salaam, Civil Reference No. 6 of 1995 (Unreported).

> *Indeed the High Court found that by their own admission the respondents had failed to give a full account of their administration of the estate for the period of four years since their appointment as administrators to the date of the High Court decision, and that they had equally failed to account for the proceeds of sale of part of the estate. The learned judge found that was not faithful administration of the estate. We think that such view was justified, and there is nothing in Dr. Lamwai's submission to fault it.*

With that view in mind the Court said the Administrator-General must proceed with the administration of the estate pending the determination of the respondent's intended appeal. However, his responsibility for the time being was limited only to collecting and maintaining the estate. The distribution of the estate could not be effected until the intended appeal was determined.

Again, in the case of *Violet Ishengoma and Jovin Mutabuzi v The Administrator- General and Mrs Eudokia Kahamba* (cited and discussed above) where the appointment of the Administrator-General in the administration of estate, especially where customary law applied and the supervising court being Primary Court, the Court of Appeal of Tanzania explained the role of the Administrator- General as follows:

> *In administering the estate the Administrator-General does not have to appear in the Primary Court for any purpose. For, he is not acting as an advocate representing a particular party. All that is required of him is to distribute the estate to all those who qualify for distribution. In determining who qualifies for what share he, as a lawyer, is to apply the customary law of the Bahaya, and in case he runs into a difficulty he may turn to the High Court for directions.*

Chapter Six

Women and the Right to Land in Tanzania

Then God blessed them and God said to them "Be fruitful and multiply; **fill the earth and subdue it**, have dominion over the fishes of the sea, over the birds of the air and over every living thing that moves on earth". (Emphasis added).

- Genesis 1: 28 -

The International Law Jurisprudence on Women's Right to Land

The question of women's right to property, including in this sense landed property, is very old and of an international character. Whoever undertakes to discuss it successfully, therefore, is advised to have, in the first place, a reflection over the above quote from the Scripture. The idea behind this need is to enable him to appreciate how John Locke, the first political thinker in feminist jurisprudence, relies on the quote to reach a conclusion that, in the beginning God granted a "joint title" to both man (Adam) and woman (Eve). Locke begins his interpretation of the above provision by asking what seems to be a rhetorical question.

> *If it be said that Eve was subjected to Adam, it seems that she was not to him as to hinder her dominion over creatures, or property in them, for shall we say that God ever made a joint grant to two, and one only was to have the benefit of it?*[962]

To Locke, any interpretation that disqualifies women from property rights is untenable for it contradicts the Scripture, which to him, "speaks not nonsense"[963]. That being so, the question from the Human Rights camp is therefore: what then took away the original right of the woman to "fill the earth and subdue it"? To Locke, the truth is in the prejudices of our ill-grounded opinions that authorise man to understand the Scripture contrary to the direct and plain meaning of the words.[964] Going by this line of reasoning, then, a conclusion must be that denying women their right to landed property is a direct consequence of man turning away from the word of God. It is not only the biblical doctrines that address land as a common property, but even the S*haria* is inclined towards that reality. We learn through Yakubu M.G that:

> *In sharia, land is considered as indispensable to individual and social life just like water, air, light, and fire and no person will have an exclusive power of control over it expect for the part he uses... Land is a gift from Allah (God) and everybody has usufructory right to it.*[965]

Whatever reason may be advanced to explain the misfortune created by the deliberate denial of the right to land of women, the reality is that the right of women to access land and enjoy the fruits thereof has turned

962 See Locke, *op cit*, Book I p. 31 at paragraph 29.

963 *Ibid*, p. 23, at paragraph 31.

964 *Ibid*, p. 26, at paragraph 37.

965 See YAKUBU, M.G., (1985): *Nigerian Land Law*, London: Macmillan, at p. 8.

out to be a human rights agenda both in the national and international arenas. In the end, the conclusion seem to favour the truth that male bias has, for quite long, tended to crack the very foundation of the rights of women, including property rights. Many efforts have been in place to address the problem and the fight continues to date.

According to the available records, Olympe De Gouge is probably the first women in the feminist camp to speak overtly for the rights of women. She, having been dissatisfied by the revolutionary French Declaration of the Rights of Man and Citizen of 1790 which did not recognise women, wrote what she called the *Declaration of the Rights of Woman of 1791.* Articles II and XVII of this declaration are relevant for the purpose of this discussion and, therefore deserve full quotation as hereunder:

Article II

> *The purpose of any political association is the conservation of the natural and imprescriptible rights of woman and man; these rights are liberty, property, security, and especially resistance to oppression.*

Article XVII

> *Property belongs to both sexes whether united or separate; for each it is an inviolable and sacred right, no one can be deprived of it, since it is the true patrimony of nature, unless the legally determined public need obviously dictates it, and then only with a just and prior indemnity.*

In this Declaration, Olympe was calling for the State to respect not only the right of women to land, but also the parallel right to a just and fair compensation, when their lands are taken for public interests. However, as one would expect the state of affairs in the reign of the rule of the jungle, De Gouge's devotion to speak out foe the rights of women caused her to pay the ultimate price! She was charged with treason under the rule of the National Convention. She was arrested, tried, and later, in November of 1793, executed.[966]

Another equally important figure from the same camp is Mary Wollstonecraft (1700-1800) who also invoked the human rights language to speak openly in favour of the women's right to land, among other rights. Writing in 1792, of course on the strength of the experience of her times, Wollstonecraft saw the necessary link between property and evil.

966 For the full story, see LEVY, D.G., *et al.* (eds.), (1980): *Women in Revolutionary Paris, 1789-1795*, Urbana, University of Illinois Press.

> *From the respect paid to property flow, as from a poisoned fountain, most of the evils and vices which render this world such a dreary scene to the contemplative mind...One class presses on another; for all are aiming to procure respect on account of their property: and property, once gained, will procure respect due only to talents and virtue.*[967]

With that in mind, Wollstonecraft was very critical of the society that embraced the inequality of men and women in property rights. She therefore recommended that there must be more equality established in society or morality would never gain ground, and this virtuous equality would not rest firmly even when founded on a rock, if one half of mankind (she meant women) was chained to its bottom by fate.[968] We read her stern atitude towards emancipation of women in matters of property rights when she says:

> *A truly benevolent legislator always endeavours to make it the interest of each individual to be virtuous; and thus private virtue becoming the cement of public happiness, an orderly whole is consolidated by the tendency of all the parts towards a common centre. But, the private or public virtue of woman is very problematical; for Rousseau, and a numerous list of male writers, insist that she should all her life be subjected to a severe restraint, that of property. Why subject her to property-blind property, if she be capable of acting from a nobler spring, if she be an heir of immortality?*[969]

In the final, Wollstonecraft warns the world by an assertion that by denying them equality of property rights women are in chains. She therefore makes a humble promise that if the rights of women are respected and protected, they (women) would be more beneficial to the society not only as good mothers but also as good citizens.

> *Would men but generously snap our chains, and be content with rational fellowship instead of slavish obedience, they would find us more observant daughters, more affectionate sisters, more faithful wives, more reasonable mothers- in a word, better citizens*[970].

---

967 See WOLLSTONECRAFT, Mary, (2004): *A Vindication of the Rights of Women*, Penguin Books, at p. 175. The book is taken to be the first declaration of feminist independence, and its author the mother of modern feminism.

968 *Ibid.*

969 *Ibid*, at p. 180.

970 *Ibid*, at p. 186.

Wollstonecraft's call was not a cry in the wilderness! History tends to show that it was out of Wollstonecraft's voice that the English *Married Women Property Act* was promulgated in 1882 and that other international efforts towards the emancipation of women in property relations followed that course. The tide of historical developments have recorded some positive steps through which the international community has undertaken to address the moot issues about the rights of women to land. To our best knowledge, there are several specific international instruments of human rights both binding and persuasive, which tend to address the question of women's right to land in the most clear and admirable terms. Some of the most relevant instruments, on a long list, include: the General Assembly Resolution 2263 (XX11) of November 7, 1967 which requires states to undertake legislative measures to ensure that women, married or unmarried, get equal rights as men in matters of civil law especially to acquire, administer, enjoy, dispose and inherit property, including property acquired during marriage.[971] Another instrument is the General Assembly Resolution 2542 (XXIV) of December 11, 1969, which requires the establishment of forms of land ownership and of means of production, which preclude any kind of exploitation of man, ensure equal right to property for all and create conditions leading to genuine equality among people in order to attain the true social progress.[972] In a similar sense there is the International Convention on Elimination of All Forms of Discrimination against Women (CEDAW), 1979, which imposes a positive duty to member States to adopt all appropriate measures to abolish gender discrimination of whatever form[973]; to accord to women equal treatment with men, and legal capacity to conclude contracts and administer property[974]. The Convention also requires states to eliminate discrimination against women in all matters relating to marriage and family[975], and to ensure that, on the basis of equality of men and women,

971 Article 6 (1) (a), Unite Nations General Assembly Declaration on Elimination of Discrimination against Women, 1967.

972 See Article 6, United Nations General Assembly Declaration on Social Progress and Development.

973 Article 2.

974 Article 15 (1) and (2).

975 Article 16 (1).

both spouses have rights in respect of the ownership, acquisition, management, administration, enjoyment and disposition of property.[976] Lastly, but not least in importance, is the Commission of Human Rights' Resolution 2000/13[977], by which the Commission raises its voice very high, admitting: that it recognises that laws, policies, customs and traditions that restrict women's equal access to credit and loans, also prevent women from owning and inheriting land, property and housing, and exclude women from participating fully in development process, are discriminatory and may contribute to the feminization of poverty; that it affirms that discrimination in law against women with respect to acquiring and securing land, property and housing, as well as financing for land, property and housing, constitute a violation of women's human rights, and; that it encourages Governments to support the transformation of customs and traditions that discriminate against women and deny women security of tenure and equal ownership of, access to, and control over land and equal right to property and to adequate housing and to ensure the right of women to equal treatment in land and agrarian reforms as well as in land resettlement schemes and in ownership of property and in adequate housing, and to take other measures to increase land and housing availability to women living in poverty, particularly female heads of households.

Despite all the international efforts enumerated above, the big question that has always been have always been posed from the human rights camp, is whether or not the principles enshrined in the above international instruments have successfully promoted,and protected women's rights to land in their respective countries. We dare to say that emancipation of women has remained the most difficult task to fulfil, especially in most of our traditional communities, which are pegged on the patriarchal system ofhuman relations (*mfumo dume*). Whether or not Tanzania has successfully applied the above global principles to address women's rights to land in accordance with our local circumstances is the subject of considerable discussion in this chapter.

---

976 Article 16 (1) (h).

977 Adopted by the 52nd meeting on April 17, 2000 as a Resolution on Women's Equal Ownership of, Access to and Control Overland and the Equal Rights over Property and to Adequate Housing.

The Domestic Jurisprudence on Women's Right to Land before the Land Acts

The history about women and their access to land in Tanzania has rather been a very dolorous. Women in particular have been considered as inferior and not of equal status with men. As such they have remained vulnerable and marginalised as victims of discrimination, both directly and indirectly, in various areas including, *inter alia*, education, finance and property ownership. However, with the advent of the international language of human rights, Tanzania has not remained an island unto herself. She has learnt, albeit at a slow pace, to speak in the human rights language when addressing the human rights of women, particularly the right to land. There have been in place various measures undertaken by the Government to ensure that women's right to land is recognised, respected, promoted and protected at all levels. Of all the measures on record, I have chosen to discuss only the legislative as well as judicial measures for the simple reason that from the legislature and the judiciary we get legal principles which are not only well documented and therefore easily accessible, but are also authoritative and binding on whoever places his hand in the administration of land law in the country.

Legislative Measures in Respect of Women's Right to Land

It is not surprising to learn that in Tanzania, as has been the case in other countries in Africa and the world at large, the recognition of women's right to land has taken a substantially slow pace; that is, from a state of non-recognition to the state of recognition and protection by law. What has been achieved to date in respect of the right of women to land is, indeed, a result of great efforts through legislative and judicial reforms, of course, in a gradual process. As far as legislative measures are concerned, Tanzania's first effort in the process was to enact the *Law of Marriage Act*[978] in 1971, to at least recognise and protect property rights of married women[979] including: equal right of a woman and man to acquire, hold and dispose of property, whether movable or immovable;[980] equality of rights and status of wives in a polygamous marriage;[981] the right of a spouse to acquire separate property[982] and;

978 [Cap 29. R.E 2002].

979 See Part IV of the Act.

980 Section 56.

981 Section 57.

982 Section 58.

the right of a spouse to a matrimonial home during the subsistence of marriage.[983] As to second, similar effort, in point of time, Tanzania recognised and ratified all international legal instruments of importance on the rights of women, such as the Women's Convention, of 1979 which provides, *inter alia*, for the right to equality of spouses, men and women, and for the right against discrimination on grounds of, among others, sex.[984] As to the third effort, Tanzania incorporated a Bill of Rights in its Constitution[985] in 1984 in which she introduced all the international principles on human rights, including: the principle of equality of all persons before the law,[986] the principle of non-discrimination on grounds of, *inter alia*, gender;[987] and; the principle of the right to property.[988] The fourth effort saw Tanzania formulating a national Policy on Women and Development, "the women policy" of 1992, to cater for the specific rights of women in Tanzania.[989] The policy statement clearly recognised the rights of women in respect to property as it stated that:

> *Tanzania believes in equality of rights of each person. This belief is enshrined in the constitution of the United Republic of Tanzania of 1977 as amended in 1984. The constitution emphazises the equality of each person, respect for each person's humanity and the right to justice before the law. Implicitly it safeguards gender freedom, security of life,* ***right to ownership of property and productive resources...***[990] *(The emphasis is mine).*

The women policy admits that majority of women still lack protection and, therefore, highlights customs and traditions which discriminate against women as the main constraint in the effort to emancipate women in Tanzania.[991] Also of importance, the women policy considers the eradication of all forms of discrimination against women as being

983 Section 59.

984 Tanzania ratified the Convention on July 17, 1980.

985 See the Constitution of the United Republic of Tanzania, 1977 as amended from time to time. The Bill of Rights was introduced in the Constitution through Act No. 16 of 1984.

986 Article 13 (1).

987 Article 13 (4) and (5).

988 Article 24 (1).

989 UNITED REPUBLIC OF TANZANIA, (1992): *A Policy on Women in Development in Tanzania*, Ministry of Community Development, Women Affairs and Children.

990 *Ibid*, paragraph 1.

991 *Ibid*, paragraph 7 (1).

an issue of great priority and, therefore, calls, *inter alia*, for immediate measures to enable women to have a right to own and inherit resources and implements for production and the right to own the income accrued from their own labour.[992] Of all the rights, the right to acquire and own land through purchase in the market is the surest way for women to enjoy their right to land although the same is limited as it is only available to the economically able women. Speaking about women's right to purchase land in Cameroon, Patrice Bigombe Logo and Elise H. Bike have noted, a note which women in Tanzania are advised to make a reflection on, that:

> *The transformation of land is also perceptible as a result of the process of commoditization of land. Land is no longer a heritage or a resource. It has become a marketable good with monetary value. It can be bought and sold. One can buy land as long as he has money. Women are also free to buy land and those who have money do so. Women are becoming land owners...Purchasing enables them to counter discrimination and inequality. Women buy land either to farm or build houses, demonstrating that they are capable of taking lives into their own hands.*[993]

Judicial Measures in Respect of Women's Right to Land

Women and the Right to Self-Acquired Land

As we have already stated above, the *lex specialis*, apart from the general principles on human rights[994] providing for the right of married women to acquire property in Tanzania, movable or immovable, is the *Law of Marriage Act*.[995] The Act begins by establishing the equality of rights of a man and woman to acquire, hold and dispose property; to contract, and; to sue or be sued on a contract or in tort.[996] It goes on to provide for the

---

992 Paragraph.

993 See BIKIE, Elise H. & LOGO, Patrice Bigombe, "Women and Land in Cameroon: Questioning Women's Land Status and Claims for Change" in WANYEKI, Muthoni (ed.), (2003): *Women and Land in Africa: Culture, Religion and Realizing Women's Rights*, Zeb Books Limited, London, New York, David Philip Publishers Cape Town.

994 See the right to property as envisaged in Article 24 of the Constitution of the United Republic of Tanzania, 1977 and other International Instruments on Human Rights.

995 See the provisions of Part IV of the Act. The Act as a whole should be read in the light of its Preamble which reads as "*An Act to regulate the law relating to marriage, personal and property rights as between husband and wife, divorce and other matrimonial reliefs and other matters connected therewith and incidental thereto.*"

996 Section 56.

right of a spouse to acquire, own and dispose property in his or her own name before or after marriage.[997] Finally, the Act makes it a rebuttable presumption that a property is presumed to belong to a spouse in the exclusion of the other, if it is acquired in the name of that party during the subsistence of marriage,[998] or to belong to both if it is in the name of the husband and wife jointly.[999] Going by the above provisions one would expect unimpeded access of women to property during marriage. However, the practices on the ground tend to prove the contrary due to societal attitudes and perceptions that group women as inferior subjects and, therefore, incapable of enjoying the rights entailed in the above provisions of the Act. This phenomenon has deep roots in history as Irene Mwakilema observes:

> *Discriminatory behaviour is an historical phenomenon, as traditionally men were seen to be stronger than women. This is because the then nature of life forced men to engage in farming or animal keeping or hunting and gathering, while women were left to prepare food and look after the family. The fact which to date, though circumstance changed, yet in most societies, women are still regarded as [an] inferior group which can neither own nor acquire property of their own.*[1000]

Mwakilema's submission suggests no more than the traditional belief that while the role of women is in the kitchen, the role of men is that of a "bread winner". Worse still, there are some of us who tend to argue in favour of the inferiority of women by seeking guidance in the Scripture, which invites believers to believe that the inferiority of women has been sanctioned by God![1001] The effect of this belief has, in practice, been that of denying women the right to land even where the law grants those rights in unambiguous terms. Thanks to courts of law which have stood firm to protect the rights of women, especially, over a self-acquired land. The two cases of *Regina A. Kalukwa v Zubail Katumwa*[1002]

---

997 Section 58.

998 Section 60 (a).

999 Section 60 (b).

1000 See MWAKILEMA, I.T., "Right to Property: Study of the Law of Marriage Act 1971 and Widows Inheritance of Matrimonial Property Upon Their Spouses Deaths", Advanced (LL.M) Coursework Paper, University of Dar es Salaam, (Unpublished), at p. 3.

1001 "I will intensify the pangs of your childbearing; in pain shall you bring forth children. *Yet your urge shall be for your husband, and he shall be your master*". (Emphasis added). See Genesis 3: 16.

1002 [1988] TLR 85 (HC). This case has formed part of the literature in MASHAMBA, Julius Clement, "Preempting Justice: The Repugnancy of Customary Law in Tanzania" *The Tanzania Lawyer*, Vol. 2, No. 1, 2008, pp. 59-79, at p. 77.

and *Celestina Paul v Mohamed Hussein*[1003] (discussed in Chapter Four above) are momentous and straight to the point. Regina's case records the following facts: the appellant, a widow and her deceased husband, one Andrew Katumwa, occupied a piece of land, the disputed *shamba* for quite sometime before death took the husband. Immediately after his death the respondent, then, a brother of deceased sued the appellant for vacant possession of the *shamba* and a house in it which was under the occupation of the widow, alleging that it was the deceased who had bought the *shamba* and built a house in it. The appellant won the case in the Primary Court at Rubale, but lost it on appeal by the respondent to the District Court. She was aggrieved and preferred an appeal to the High Court of Bukoba. His argument, at all levels, was that she had herself bought the *shamba* from one Omari and built the house in it with the help of her relatives, and that the said *shamba* was not liable to clan inheritance. She won the case on the strength of the evidence (Munyera, J.- as he then he was). Part of the record is reproduced to show how the appellant appeared to be brave and responsible in ensuring the security of her self-acquired property:

> *The question before the court was the ownership of the suit property as between the deceased and his widow. The key witness was Ahmad Omari from whom the property was bought. Some months before this suit was filed, probably the appellant guessed something sinister would befall her, she went to Ahmad and told him she had lost the sale document concerning the shamba; she wanted something to protect her. Ahmad agreed to accompany her to Bukoba town and there he swore an affidavit before an advocate (Rutakelezibwa) to the effect that on 15/5/71 he sold the shamba to the appellant for Shs. 8550/=. She produced the affidavit in the trial court as Exh. B. Ahmad repudiated the affidavit as false. The trial court was not duped, it held the affidavit a genuine document if it were not, then Ahmad should have produced his own genuine document on which the sale to the deceased was recorded. I am inclined to agree with the trial court. The fact that the respondent did not call Ahmed to give evidence on his side suggests that he feared the witness would speak the truth as to whom he sold the shamba. It did not matter that Ahmad turned hostile to the appellant, his affidavit and his admission in court that he handed the shamba to the appellant not to the deceased supported the appellant's case. For that reason I disagree with the decision of the District Court.*

1003 [1983] TLR 291 (HC).

Celestina's case, again, is a case in which the deceased person had appointed, through a valid will, the appellant to administer her estate for the benefit of the deceased's eight-year old daughter. The respondent challenged the appointment saying that the appellant was disqualified by his religion and clan membership, which differed from that of the deceased. Allowing the appeal, the court was of the view that the property which she bequeathed was her personal property and had nothing to do with the clan, and that she had the right to choose her beneficiary and also an absolute right to choose the administrator of her own choice. Apart from this case there are many other instances in which the courts have come in aid to protect the rights of women to self-acquired land including the rights against unlawful disposal of the same by unscrupulous joint owners.[1004]

Women and the Right to Matrimonial Property

This is another area in property relations of married women that has been developing quite encouragingly. Traditionally, the right of women to a share in the matrimonial property was unknown. However, it may be said without hesitation that the *Law of Marriage Act* came to cure the vice. In the first place, the Act establishes the want of consent from a spouse before his or her partner undertakes to disposes a matrimonial home by way of sale, gift, lease, mortgage or any other similar undertaking.[1005] Secondly, the Act gives a right to a spouse to have a share in the matrimonial property in all cases of divorce and if the property is jointly acquired.[1006] It is ideal to note that these two areas of law have attracted serious litigations among spouses or between a spouse and a third party, where some courageous women have dared to approach the court of law to demand their property rights created by marriage. The list of such litigations is depressingly long. Suffice it to name and discuss just a few cases, being our case study to show the progressive and protective role of the court in safeguarding women's property rights through judicial interpretation of the law. The case of *Bi Hawa Mohamed v Ally Sefu*[1007] has been and continues to be the authoritative case in all cases involving women's rights to matrimonial

1004 See, for example the case of *Mtumwa Rashid v Abdallah Iddi and Salum Omari*, Court of Appeal of Tanzania at Dar es Salaam, Civil Appeal No. 22 of 1993 (Unreported). In this case the Court nullified the sale of the house which a husband had fraudulently sold without involving a wife who was a co-owner by virtue of her monetary contribution in purchasing it. See a full discussion of the case in Chapter Three above.

1005 Section 59 (1).

1006 Section 114.

1007 [1983] TLR 32 (CA).

property. The brief facts of the case are that the parties had married in accordance with Islamic Law in 1971, in Kenya before they shifted to Dar es Salaam in Tanzania, in 1975. The husband, Ally had bought a house in Dar es Salaam in 1974 where they lived until they divorced under the court's decree in 1980. Bi Hawa applied for the distribution of the matrimonial property under the provision of section 114 (1) of the *Law of Marriage Act*, which provides, *inter alia*, that:

> *The court shall have power, when granting or subsequent to the grant of a decree of separation or divorce, to order the division between the parties of any assets acquired by them during the marriage by* ***their joint efforts*** *or to order the sale of any such asset and the division between the parties of the proceeds of sale. (Emphasis is mine)*

In the District court and later the High Court of Tanzania, the applicant lost the claim, the reason being that since she did not earn income, and did not contribute her money in the acquisition of the house, her domestic duties did not amount to her "joint effort" and, therefore, could not be regarded as contribution in the acquisition of the matrimonial property, including the matrimonial house in Dar es Salaam. Another line of reasoning by the two courts was that since traditionally the looking after the household and caring for the children is the occupation and responsibility of a wife, just as the feeding and clothing of the family is the occupation and responsibility of the husband, then that should not be considered as a contribution or joint effort in terms of the above named provision. Dissatisfied, Bi Hawa appealed to the Court of Appeal of Tanzania.[1008] The court invoked the principle of equality, one of the principal pillars of human rights, to determine the matter, when it said:

> *The mischief which the Law of Marriage Act, 1971 sought to cure or rectify was what may be described as the traditional exploitation and oppression of married women by their husbands. It is apparent that the Act seeks to liberate married women from such exploitation and oppression by reducing the traditional inequality between them and their husbands in so far as their respective domestic rights and duties are concerned. Although certain features of traditional inequality still exist under the Act, such as polygamous marriages, these do not detract from the overall purpose of the Act as an instrument of liberation and equality between the sexes.*[1009]

1008 This is the final court and the court of the last resort in all matters.

1009 See the case in Peter, C.M., at p. 403.

On the basis of this reasoning the Honourable Court of Appeal of Tanzania concluded that domestic works of the wife should account as her contribution towards the acquisition of the matrimonial property. The Court aptly said:

> *Guided by this objective of the Act, we are satisfied that the words "their joint efforts"...have to be construed as embracing the domestic "efforts" or "work" of a husband and wife.*[1010]

The Court's decision marked the birth of a new era in the administration of matrimonial justice in Tanzania in that the rights of married women over the matrimonial property would, since then, be protected and guaranteed. It is a decision that has been commendably welcomed by every person who would like to see the rights of women promoted and protected. We learn this from writers and researchers like Idd Ramadhani, who has the strongest confidence to tell us that:

> *This decision thus stands as a milestone in attempts to alleviate social injustices that were inflicted on women in this country.*[1011]

Another important case is the case of *Letisia Bugumba v Thadeo Magoma and Another.*[1012] In this case, the facts show that the appellant and the first respondent had cohabited together and lived as husband and wife without having contracted a formal marriage since 1976. In 1985 the first respondent decided to desert the family, leaving behind the appellant wife and their two children. He then formed an opinion to sell (and actually sold) the house to the second respondent. The purchaser took an action to evict the appellant and the rest of the occupiers. The appellant raised an action that she had an interest in the house and could, therefore, not be evicted. The issue in the court of the first instance and on appeal was whether the appellant woman had an interest in the house. The appellant lost the case in the District court on the ground that there was no evidence to show that she was, in law, the wife of the first respondent, their marriage having not been formalised. In the High Court, she won the case on the ground that her marriage was protected

1010 *Ibid.*

1011 See RAMADHANI, Idd, "The Court of Appeal of Tanzania: Its Positivistic Policy and Justice", LL.M Dissertation, UDSM, at p. 5.

1012 High Court of Tanzania at Mwanza, Civil Appeal No.8 of 1989 (Unreported). The case is also reproduced in Peter, C.M. and Bisimba, H.K. *op cit* at pp. 410-417.

under section 160 (1) of the *Law of Marriage Act*, 1971, which provided for the presumption of marriage.[1013] The court also relied heavily on the precedent set by the Bi Hawa's case to hold that the appellant had, by her domestic duties, jointly contributed to the acquisition of the disputed house, thus she had interest and could not be evicted as such. The following extract from the decision of the Court is worth quoting.

> *It was the appellant's case at the trial that the house in dispute was built by joint efforts. The trial court held that as the woman made no monetary or physical contributions towards building the house, then the house was the property of the man alone. He was wrong apparently because he is not aware of the decision of the Tanzania Court of Appeal in the case of Bi Hawa Mohamed v. Ally Seif. The case stands for the proposition that performance of domestic duties by a house wife (like cooking food and looking after children) is sufficient contribution towards a house that is build by the husband alone. So joint contribution is not limited to direct contribution by a spouse by way of money, property and work to the acquisition of that asset but housekeeping and raising children do count.*

Hemed S.Tamim v Renata Mashayo[1014] is another case that we must mention. The facts of the case were that the parties cohabited together as husband and wife for eight years. When their relationship turned sour, the respondent sued in the primary court for divorce and division of assets in the form of a dwelling house. The primary court granted all the prayers. The appellant was aggrieved and appealed to the District court. The court found that the marriage was rebutted under section 160 (1) of the *Law of Marriage Act*, 1971 and, therefore, that there was no marriage to dissolve, and the division of assets did not arise. The respondent appealed to the High Court which ruled that although the presumption of marriage had been rebutted, the respondent had some residual rights to property under section 160 (2). The appellant sought leave to appeal to the Court of Appeal on a point of law, that is, "Whether the respondent was entitled in law to a share of assets in the circumstances of this case". Dismissing the appeal, the Court of Appeal had the following to say:

1013 The presumed marriage is sometimes referred to as a common law marriage. It means couples live together as for a certain specified period of time (two years in Tanzania) and attain the status of a husband and wife.

1014 [1994] TLR 197 (CA).

> *Both the District Court and the High Court found that the presumption under s 160(1) had been rebutted but the High Court held correctly that following this rebuttal the court had the power and jurisdiction to make the same consequential orders as in the dissolution of marriage or separation. The order for division of matrimonial assets is one such order, consequently the learned judge ordered equal division of the house at Kiwalani which was acquired by the parties during or in the course of their relationship. However, having found that the parties were not duly married, the learned judge should not have ordered the restoration of the Primary Court order regarding the dissolution of marriage, for quite obviously there was no marriage to dissolve. Consequently the order of dissolution of marriage upheld by the High Court is set aside.*

What the Court meant was that the right to matrimonial property was available to a wife even if there was no formal marriage between her and the husband, provided, that all criteria under section 160 (1) are: cohabiting together, for two years or more, and attaining a reputation as husband and wife. This decision of the court has been invoked as a judicial principle to fall back on whenever the rights of women have been in issue[1015].

Finally, we have on record the case of *Mwajuma Mohamed Njopeka v Juma Said Mkorogoro*[1016], whose decision has been pegged firmly on the human rights language. The background of the case is that parties thereto were married under Islamic law but remained childless for about nine years. As their marriage tasted sour, the husband pronounced the Islamic *talak*, divorcing his wife. The wife successfully applied for the judicial divorce at the local primary court. When deciding the matter, the court granted divorce as prayed for and ordered the husband to pay the wife Tshs. 500,000/= to be what is known in the Islamic law as "parting gift". Dissatisfied by part of the decision, the wife appealed unsuccessfully to the District Court. On her further appeal to the High Court, the court switched to the human rights language to arrive at the just decision. In other words, the court invoked Articles 9 (f) and 13 (1) of the national Constitution which provide for the fundamental principles

---

1015 See, for example, *Martin Mbujilo v Elizabeth Lucas*, High Court of Tanzania at Tabora (PC) Civil Appeal No. 6 of 2003 (Unreported). In this case the High Court of Tanzania awarded wife an amount equivalent to 40% of the value of a house on Plot No. 31 Block C Tabata area, Dar es Salaam which was jointly acquired by the parties during their cohabitation as husband and wife.

1016 High Court of Tanzania at Dar es Salaam, (PC) Civil Appeal No. 6 of 2001, (Unreported).

of the state policy on equal protection before the law, and; also Article 7 of the Universal Declaration of Human Rights, 1948 and Article 2 of the United Nations Convention on the Elimination of All Forms of Discrimination Against Women, 1979. For this reason alone, the court quashed the orders of the two courts below on grounds that they were made when the courts had not given weight to the contribution of the appellant for her nine years in marriage; that the orders left her without shelter, and; that the lower courts' decision was discriminatory and in contravention of the law. At the end of it all, the court ordered that the appellant be entitled to one of the two matrimonial houses and the husband to retain the remaining house.

Women and the Right to Inheritance over Land

Again, the history of the women's right to inheritance in Tanzania is rather agonising. The reason is attributed to the socio-cultural factors which have inclined towards the exclusion of women, or towards according them inferior status compared to men in all spheres of life including matters of inheritance[1017]. These societal and cultural practices, otherwise referred to as customs, existed in isolation, that is to say, each particular community had its own customs until 1963 when these were codified through the Declaration of Customary Law Order of 1963. As stated earlier in Chapter Five above, when customary law is involved, matters of inheritance are governed by the "Rules of Inheritance", appearing in the Second Schedule of the Customary Law (Declaration) (No. 4) Order, 1963, while in an Islamic Community they are governed by the Islamic Law (*sharia*). The rules on inheritance, customary or Islamic, have attracted a protracted attention within the courts of law such that while some activists in the judicial hierarchy have stood by the rules to deny women the right to inherit property, others have invoked the principles of justice and fairness as enshrined in the Constitution and other international human rights instruments to depart from the rules of customary law. A discussion on the rights of women in this part targets two groups: daughters and widows.

1017 It is on record that, "Under the customary law of many patrilineal communities in Tanzania such as the Chagga, the agro-Maasai (Larusa), Sambaa and Pare, daughters are completely barred from inheriting clan land and sometimes their own father's land. The assumption is that girls marry away from their parental base, as such they are not entitled to inherit land, lest they transfer the land outside the clan or family through marriage". See KAPINGA Wilbert B.L., "Some Reflections on the Presidential Commission Report and National Land Policy" in *Change*, Vol. 5, First Quarter, 1997, pp. 9-17, at 14.

Daughters: We have noted earlier[1018], that under rule 25 of the customary Rules of Inheritance, daughters are positioned in the third degree in the order of inheritance. It means that, under customary law, daughters are entitled to inherit the estate of their deceased father only after the distribution has been made satisfactorily to sons in the first and second degrees respectively. In other words, under customary law, daughters are entitled to inherit the "leftovers" of their father's estate. The only exception to this rule is when there are no sons to survive the deceased.[1019] Equally, rule 20 and 31 are of the effect that a woman can inherit her deceased father's landed property except for the family or clan land,[1020] which she can use for her life without selling it and that if there are no sons, then, she can inherit it absolutely. Of all the rules, rule 20 has been challenged as being discriminatory toward women in a number of cases,[1021] attracting both conservative and liberal attitudes of the court. The rule gives to a woman the right to inherit clan land and use it for her life but without powers to dispose it. The rule treats females differently from their counterpart males who may inherit clan land and dispose it on condition that they get consent of the clan members. At one point in history, the High Court of Tanzania (Katiti, J.- as he then was) had the courage to say, without, hesitation that the rule is bad in law. He therefore predicted for its elimination in our legal system when he said:

> *But I would like to add, may be in passing that at any one time, we may have bad as well as good law, and I venture to say without qualms, that this piece of customary law is bad, it discriminates against women, encourages expansionist greed on the part of males against female relatives and deprives females of important resources for self assistance...So much for the ugly aspects, but what is encouraging is that the grave for the same is being dug, for the contemptuous burial of the same for the sake of equality, when the Fifth Constitutional Amendment, 1984 takes its rightful place in 1988*[1022].

1018 See Chapter Five above.

1019 See rule 29 that entitles the eldest daughter of the first house to be the main heir.

1020 According to Mwalusanya, J.- as he then was) in the case of *Jibu Sakilu v Petro Miumbi* [1993] TLR 75, (HC), "clan land" is a land which has been inherited successfully without interruption from the great fathers or from a great father by members of the same clan.

1021 See for example Bilimbasa Zacharia v Jervas John [1983] TLR 67 (HC) and Leonce Mtalindwa v Mariadina Edward [1986] TLR 120 (HC).

1022 *Leonce Mtalindwa v Mariadina Edward* [1986] TLR 120 (HC).

In the long list of cases founded on rule 20, it suffices to name and discuss the two cases of *Angelo Bisiki v Antonia Bisiki and Others,*[1023] and *Bernado Ephrahim v Holaria Pastory and Another*[1024]. The facts in the case of Angelo Bisiki were that the appellant claimed to redeem a clan land which was sold by the first respondent, a daughter, to the second respondent without the consent of the clan members. In the court, the issue for determination was whether the sale was valid. Invalidating the sale, the court (Mushi, J.- as he then was) was of the view that, on the footing of the Court of Appeal of Tanzania in the cases of *Deocras Lutabana v Deus Kashaga,*[1025] and *Rutakuba Ntemi v Bi Julia Hassan and Gervas Baruti,*[1026] the Bahaya female heir, having inherited clan land, has no more than a life interest in the land which she could neither sell nor bequeath to any person whosoever, even with the clan consent. The effect of this decision was to nullify the sale and declare that such sale did not pass any title to the second respondent. In the case the court's conclusion was that:

> *In the result, I allow the appeal, quash and set aside the decisions of both courts below, and hereby declare that the transaction of sale by first respondent to second respondent, and by second respondent to third respondent were, and still are, invalid. The first respondent is ordered to refund the purchase price of Tshs. 140, 000/= to the second respondent who, in her turn, is ordered to refund the purchase price of Tshs. 300.000/= to the third respondent. The first respondent to pay to the third respondent compensation for unexhausted improvements, if any, to be determined by the trial Primary Court as stated earlier in this judgment. The appellant to have his costs in this court and the courts below.*

In Holaria's case, however, a different decision was reached by the court guided by the principles of human rights. The facts in the Holaria's case were that a woman, Holaria Pastory had inherited a clan land from her father by a valid Will. Finding that she was getting old and senile and that there was no one to take care of her, she decided to sell that land to one Mr. Gervasi Kaizilege, who was not a member of that clan.

1023 [1989] TLR 225 (HC).

1024 High Court of Tanzania at Mwanza, Civil Appeal No. 70 of 1989. Reported in [1990] LRC (Const) 757.

1025 Civil Appeal No 5 of 1981. Reported in (1981) TLR 122.

1026 Civil Appeal No. 19 of 1986 (Unreported).

The appellant, Bernado filed a suit in the court of law, challenging the sale and praying for the declaration that the sale was null and void, for the simple reason that under the Haya[1027] customary law, a female had no power to sell clan land[1028]. The appellant won the case in the Primary court; he lost it in the District Court, hence an appeal in the High court of Tanzania. The most admirable part of the court's (Mwalusanya, J.- as he then was), decision reads:[1029]

> *What is more is that since the Bill of Rights was incorporated in our 1977 Constitution vide Act No. 15 of 1984 by Article 13 (4) discrimination against women has been prohibited. But some people say that, that is a dead letter. And the Universal Declaration of Human Rights, 1948 which is part of our Constitution by virtue of Article 9 (1) (f) prohibits discrimination based on sex as per Article 7. Moreover Tanzania has ratified the Convention on the Elimination of All Forms of Discrimination Against Women, 1979. That is not all. Tanzania has also ratified the African Charter on Human and People's Rights, 1981 which in Article 18 (3) prohibits discrimination on account of sex. And finally Tanzania has ratified the International Covenant on Civil and Political Rights, 1966 which in Article 26 prohibits discrimination based on sex. The principles enunciated in the above named documents are a standard below which any civilised nation will be ashamed to fall. It is clear from what I have discussed that the customary law under discussion flies in the face of our Bill of Rights as well as the international conventions to which we are signatories.*

The court finally outlawed the customary law that was discriminatory against women and made a commendable call to all women in Tanzania to consider themselves as of equal rights as men in matters, albeit, of inheritance:

> *From now on, females all over Tanzania can at least hold their heads high and claim to be equal to men as far as inheritance of clan land and self-acquired land of their father's is concerned. It is part of the long road to women's liberation.*[1030]

1027 The Haya are the inhabitants of the Western Part of Lake Victoria in Tanzania bordering Uganda in North West and Rwanda in the South West. The author is, in fact, a Haya.

1028 Reference was being made in relation to section 20 of the Customary Rules of Inheritance which allowed men to inherit clan land and to dispose it at will, but which allowed women only to inherit clan land and to use it for their benefits, but not to sell it.

1029 See Peter, C.M., *op cit* at p. 388.

1030 *Ibid*, at p.395.

The Holaria case has bred new seeds of hope in the jurisprudence of the rights of women to inherit land in Tanzania. The decision from the case has been positively welcomed by everyone in the human rights camp. This is what we learn from the resource persons in the legal profession like Kapinga, who states in clear terms that:

> *Holaria Pastory is a juridical landmark in that it has created a legal framework in which females just like males can rightfully inherit clan land or self-acquired land of their fathers and dispose the same in any manner howsoever. Thus the disposal of clan land to strangers without the consent of the clan is only subject to the old rule that any other clan member may redeem the land on payment of the purchase price to the buyer. This rule originally operated only in favour of transactions by male clan members.*[1031]

Widows: of all categories of women, widows form the most marginalized and, therefore, vulnerable group when it comes to property relations of many societies. Their immediate experience at the death of their husbands has been dispossession of whatever they have, and eventual eviction from their matrimonial homes by the male relatives of the deceased person. The most unlucky ones have even suffered death at the hands of the greedy and monstrous murderers who decide to eliminate them to safeguard some interests in the property of the departed. Let me record one, touching story about the fate of the widows in Tanzania. The story is about the criminal case of *Republic v Daudi Mdee*[1032], in which the accused, together with his brother (who died in remand) killed their in-law, a widow, who demanded a share over the landed property, including two houses, left by her deceased husband in Makamba "A" area, Kilosa District in Morogoro. All the evidence as tendered in court led the sitting judge to conclude that the motive for the killing was the vying for the interest in the property left by the deceased. This is what we learn as we read the judgment at p. 8 that:

> *The motive for the murder is not far to fetch. The deceased wanted a share of her husband's properties of which the accused was the administrator. The accused refused to give her anything. This is evidenced by the caution statement "P2" and corroborated by PW7 evidence that at the family meeting in Moshi held in*

1031 See KAPINGA, Wilbert B.L., *op cit* at p. 15.

1032 High Court of Tanzania at Morogoro, Criminal Session Case No. 8 of 1999, Judgment dated 11/12/2003 (Unreported).

December 1996, the deceased demanded a portion of her late husband's properties at Makamba but the accused refused and she was barred from visiting Makamba. Further corroboration is provided by DW 1's testimony that he did not wish to involve the deceased in running the business because of her low level of education and that she was more suitable in household chores.

The sufferings of widows over their rights of inheritance are not the talk of the day only in Tanzania. One of the writers on women affairs has recorded narrative experiences of one woman from Tanzania and another from Kenya, which reflects the common experience of most, if not all, widows of our societies. From Tanzania, the narration of a victim widow goes as follows:

I was very well off before my husband died. I ran a restaurant business. However, after the death of my husband, since I was childless, his children whom I had brought up evicted me from the matrimonial home...I wasn't even allowed to enter the restaurant. This restaurant, which I had bought together with my husband, is no longer in my control. As I no longer have a means of earning an income, I am now begging from relatives[1033].

On the other hand, a record of a narration from Kenya reads that:

The night my husband died, his brothers...came into the house and ransacked it to find the money...They took away all our household possessions...even the blanket and the bed. They left nothing. When I tried to stop them they beat me and the children, and threw us out of the door...Now I have nowhere to live and my children are ill and have no education. They accuse me of having poisoned him, using witchcraft.[1034]

Reading the above extracts we note that the position of the widow in respect of the law of inheritance has never been encouraging, especially under customary law. This is because, under the provisions of rule 27 of the Rules of Inheritance, a widow has no share of the inheritance if the deceased left relatives of his own clan. The widow's share is to be cared for by her children just as she cared for them. Similarly rule 66A

1033 See HHOJA, Monica E. Magoke, "Impact of Customary Inheritance on the Status Widows and Daughters in Tanzania: A Challenge to Human Rights Activities" in BOND, Johanna, (ed.), (2005): Voices of African Women: Women's Rights in Ghana, Uganda and Tanzania, Carolina Academic Press, Durham, North Carolina, pp. 255-266 at p. 255.

1034 *Ibid*, at p. 261.

of the First Schedule, "Law of Persons"[1035] provides that a widow is free to choose a relative of the deceased husband to live with as his wife or to remain with her children in the house of the deceased husband as an independent member of the family. The case of *Scolastica Benedict v Martin Benedict*[1036] is a case in point to address the rights of the widow at the death of the husband. To repeat what has been discussed in Chapter Five above but for a different purpose, the facts of this case were that: the appellant's husband, one Benedict Katanyebile died intestate in 1971. He was survived by two wives, (the appellant being a second wife) and a number of sons and daughters. The husband left to his heirs substantial property, including the disputed house on plot Nos. 17 and 19 Block "D" in Bukoba township, whose title was registered under the then Land Registration Ordinance. The urban Primary Court at Bukoba appointed the administrators to administer the estate, who were guided by the clan council in distributing the property to the heirs according to the Haya Customary Law. In so doing they excluded the two wives. The disputed house was allocated to the respondent who later sought to evict the appellant from the house in which she had been living with her deceased husband. The appellant refused to hand over the house, and decided to appeal against the administration proceeding. One of her grounds of appeal was that the administrators appointed by the court erred in depriving the appellant of her matrimonial right of residence in the house of her deceased husband. Dismissing the appellant's claim, the Court of Appeal of Tanzania had the following to say:

> *Furthermore, we are satisfied that even if the appellant had properly challenged the administration of the estate of her late husband, she would not have succeeded, since her matrimonial right of residence upon death of her husband is under customary law concomitant with her right to live with her children in a house of her deceased husband. It is so stated under Rule 66A the Customary Law Declaration Order 1963 published as Government Notice No 279 of 1963 and was applied to the Bahaya community by Government Notice 605 of 1963. That customary rule states in Kiswahili: Mjane anayo haki ya kumchagua ndugu mmoja wa marehemu na kuishi naye kama mume wake, au anaweza kudai kuishi na watoto wake katika nyumba ya marehemu na atakuwa mmojawapo katika jamaa ya marehemu.*

1035 Government Notice No. 279 of 1963.

1036 [1993] TLR 1 (CA).

> *The relevant part is italicised by us for purposes of clarity. A free translation into English of that part reads as follows: `Or she may claim her right to reside with her issue in a house of the deceased, and thus become one of the deceased's kinsfolk.' Bearing in mind that under customary law, the residence of the issue of the deceased is determined to a great extent by rules of inheritance, it follows that a widow who elects to reside with her issue, elects to reside where her issue are entitled to reside by rules of inheritance. In the present case, the appellant's daughter was entitled to reside at Kanoni Shamba and not in the house on plot Nos 17 and 19 Block `D' in Bukoba township. The appeal before us cannot therefore succeed as it has no legal legs upon which to stand.*

Of all the widows, the childless widows' position in the course of death of their beloved has even been the worst. Rule 77 of the Law of Persons[1037] provides in sub-rule (1) and (3) to the effect that, the movable and immovable property acquired during the married life shall be divided into two after the debts have been paid. The widow shall receive a twentieth part of one half for every year of married life, and that regarding the immovable property she shall receive part of the land in the same proportion and shall enjoy the usufruct thereof until she remarries or dies. Equally, sub-rule (4) provides to the effect that all immovable property shall revert to the deceased husband's family when the widow remarries or dies. The above rules were successfully challenged in the case of *Masunga Musobi v Ndege Lukuba.*[1038] In this case, a childless widow refused to be remarried by one of her late husband's relatives. She instead filed an action in Innonelwa Primary Court, seeking, *inter alia*, a share of her deceased husband's estate. The court ruled in her favour, but the District court reversed the decision on the ground that childless widow had no right to inherit under the Sukuma customary rules of inheritance. In the High Court, Katiti, J.- as he then was held that where a widow with her late husband have jointly acquired property, she should be entitled to inherit that property or part thereof. Still, the best literature about the childless widow's right

1037 See The Law of Persons, First Schedule Local Customary Law (Declaration) Order, G.N No. 279 of 2963.

1038 High Court of Tanzania at Mwanza, Civil Application No. 67 of 1984, (Unreported).

of inheritance over the deceased husband's property has been recorded by the High of Tanzania under the aid of the human rights language in the case of *Elizabeth Mtawa v Hassan Mfaume Risasi.*[1039] The simple facts of this case were that at the death of the husband, the Primary Court of the area permitted the widow (the appellant in the High Court) to continue to reside in a matrimonial home until her death or remarriage under Rule 77 (3). The District Court set aside the order. On appeal to the High Court, it was noted that Rule 77 (3) and (4) did not provide for any possibility of a married woman asserting ownership over real property as she is only given usufruct rights. Further, the court observed that the effect of this rule was discrimination against the woman on the basis of her sex and which, according to the court, contravened Articles 2 and 17 of the Universal Declaration of Human Rights, the Tanzanian Constitution as well as section 3 (2) of the *Land Act*, 1999. As another line of its reasoning, the court cited Bi Hawa Mohamed's case by saying that although Bi Hawa concerned division of matrimonial assets on divorce, the principle in that case is also relevant when considering distribution of a deceased's estate where he is survived by a widow. In conclusion, the court was of the view that the appellant was entitled to half share of the disputed matrimonial home by virtue of her contribution to the welfare of the family. The other half share went to the children of the deceased.

Having seen the legal position in respect of the women's rights over inheritance I am of the firm belief that the problem of disinheriting widows and daughters of the marriage can only be resolved at least in part by encouraging the husbands to write wills and specify therein the shares of their wives and daughters respectively. Although this may not resolve the problem wholly and finally, in the end, it is the surest way to go by. I may, indeed, not explain this idea better than Winnie Bikaako and John Ssenkumba, who, when making a critical study on gender and land rights in Uganda, made some monumental observations which, I believe, reflect a similar trend in the property relations of most Tanzanian communities. In the first place the duo have observed that:

1039 High Court of Tanzania at Dodoma, Civil Appeal No. 12 of 2001, (Unreported). The case is also discussed in RWEZAHURA, Bart and WANITZEK, Ulrike: "The Constitutionalization of Family Law", *Open University Law Journal*, Vol. 1, No. 2, December 2007, pp. 110-131.

> *As insurance against the vagaries of marriage, parents are finding it increasingly necessary to reserve shares for each daughter. To strengthen the protection of their daughters' land rights, parents are forced to specify what they have given to their daughters (and sons) while they are still alive, so that there are as many witnesses to such transfer as possible. This is important in the light of rampant tampering with wills, often through forgery*[1040].

In yet another observation these members of academia have noted that:

> *Wills, whether oral or written, have offered some protection to the widows and children of deceased husbands. Families, therefore, depend on the goodwill of the deceased husbands to protect their property from in laws. The research findings indicate that most wills are respected. In some cases, where wills seem to favour widows, in-laws either change the will to suit their interests or hide them so that the contents are not disclosed. Tampering with wills is more common where widows are barren, or are given more property than other dependants, or where poor relations exist between widows and in laws*[1041].

National Jurisprudence on Women's Right to Land under the Land Acts

Any land lawyer shall certainly agree with us that, as a matter of law, the *Land Acts* have concluded the race on women's emancipation in matters of property relations. The history immediately before the *Land Acts* were enacted, and the salient features of thereof need be recounted with a nuanced appreciation of the great efforts of many people, individually and collectively. It all began with the Shivji Commission Report[1042], in which the Commission addressed the question of gender and succession by recording three important observations:[1043] that gender inequality and biases against women, particularly under customary systems render land inaccessible to women in terms of ownership and control even though they work it; that discriminatory laws of inheritance embedded

---

1040 BIKAAKO, Winnie and SSENKUMBA, John, *op cit*, at p 250.

1041 *Ibid*, at p. 261.

1042 See a discussion on the Report in Chapter Two above.

1043 p. 124.

in customs and culture work against the interests and welfare of widows and daughters, and; that traditional male domination and female subservience result in practically all major decisions on land being made by men or an assembly of men. As to its recommendation, the Commission's view was, among others, that a permanent solution to the issue of gender inequality and problems of female succession required further research.[1044]

The Report was immediately followed by the National Land Policy[1045] The relevant part of the Policy on women access to land is the observation that under the customary law, women generally have inferior land rights relative to men, and their access is indirect and insecure and that in allocating land, village councils have been guided by customs and continue to discriminate against women by allocating land to heads of household who are usually men.[1046] From this, the Policy statement reads:

> *In order to enhance and guarantee women's access to land and security of tenure, women will be entitled to acquire land in their own right not only through purchase but also through allocation. However, inheritance of clan land or family land will continue to be governed by custom and tradition provided they are not contrary to the Constitution and principles of natural justice[1047].*

Over and above the Shivji Commission's Report and the National Land Policy, individual persons and institutions who were accorded the opportunity to air out their views as part of their contribution to the content of the present *Land Acts* spoke very positively in favour of the women's rights to landed property.

As a result we have the *Land Acts,* which speak very clearly about the rights of women to land. A cursory survey of the laws has identified the following areas in the *Land Acts* as directly addressing the right to land of the women in Tanzania. We have, under the *Land Act*, 1999, a provision that states that, "The right of every adult woman to acquire, hold, use, and deal with land shall to the same extent and subject to the same restrictions be treated as a right of any man."[1048] We have, as

1044 p. 249.

1045 See a discussion about the policy in Chapter Two above.

1046 Paragraph 4.2.5.

1047 Paragraph 4.2.6.

1048 Cap. 113, Section 3 (2).

well, provisions that require a spouse to consent before a disposition of a matrimonial property takes place.[1049] As regards the *Village Land Act*, 1999, there is a provision which provides that, "The right of every adult woman to acquire, hold, use, deal with and transmit land by or obtain land through the operation of a will, shall be to the same extent and subject to the same restrictions as the right of every adult man".[1050] Equally, the law provides for the application of the customs, traditions and practices of the community concerned in the administration of the village land, provided that the same are consistent with the fundamental principles of the National Land Policy and of any other written law. It means that a rule of customary law or any decision in respect of land held under customary tenure shall be void and inoperative, and shall not be given effect to by any village council or village assembly, of any person or body of persons exercising any authority over village land or in respect of any court or other body, to the extent to which it denies women lawful access to ownership, occupation or use of any such land[1051].

Again, when it comes to decision making in land matters, *Village Land Act* and the *Land Dispute Courts Act* require the decision-making bodies such as the Village Land Council and the Ward tribunal to be constituted by members that shall include women. Similarly, women are given the opportunity to sit as assessors of the court in the District Land and Housing Tribunal as well as the Land Division of the High Court.

Reading the above provision in letter and spirit, any serious person will note that commendable efforts are in place to formulate a law that not only guarantees women's access to land in Tanzania, but also gives them decision-making powers in matters affecting land.

However, it is one thing to have a legal protection of the women's rights and another thing for the same women to realise their rights in practice, for while the law may be progressive in its provisions, the enforcement of that law may deliver different results. There are a number of factors that have always obstructed women to realise their land rights which are likely to remain despite the new law. These include: the economic disempowerment of women, which limits their power to purchase land freely in the market; deep-rooted traditions and customs, including male resistances, prejudices and stereotypes against women, which tend to discourage women in their struggle to access land; women's adoptive

1049 *Ibid*, Sections 114 (1) and 161 (3).

1050 Cap. 114, Section 3 (2)

1051 *Ibid* Section 20 (2).

preferences which make them to believe that they are inferior and, therefore, that they are too low in status to own or enjoy land rights; lack of awareness on the part of women about their legal rights; fear and lack of courage to pursue their rights in courts; the negative role of male-dominated courts to support women in their struggle to demand their land rights; fear of retaliation in that women are likely to be subjected to serious hatred by their families or communities if they prefer legal actions against other members of the family in claiming land rights, and; corruption in the rights enforcement machinery which places women to many disadvantages.

Before I conclude this part, I wish to put in on record that the effect of disowning women in matters of property relations is very obvious. First and primarily, disowning women of their land or limiting or restricting their access thereto, exposes them to the risk of extreme poverty and food insecurity, especially so for women of the rural communities. This aspect has been succinctly documented in the literature in that:

> *The negative relationship between the risk of rural poverty and land access is well established. Land can provide both direct and indirect benefit. Direct advantage can stem from growing crops or fodder or trees. Indirect advantage can take various forms: owned land can serve as collateral for credit or as mortgageable or sellable asset during crisis*[1052].

Secondly, disowning women has the likelihood of encouraging them to seek for alternative means of survival including prostitution and some other criminal preoccupations. The current research tends to suggests that landless women are more exposed to unsafe commercial sex activities which, at the end, makes them vulnerable to HIV/AIDS infection[1053].

It means, therefore, that any effort to encourage women to realise their land rights, whether by the individuals, NGOs, private and public institutions, or the Government, should be geared towards addressing the basic obstructions against women's access to land. We ought to record our appreciation to the great role that is being played by different NGOs in sensitizing women to know their land rights and lobbying to

---

1052 See AGARWAL, Bina, "Gender and Land Rights Revisited: Exploring New Prospective via the State, Family and Market" in RAZAVI, Shahra (ed.), (2003): *Agrarian Change, Gender and Land Rights*, Blackwell Publishing, pp. 184-224 at p. 194.

1053 See RWEGASIRA, Abdon, (2006): "Human Rights, Law and HIV/AIDS Infection: A Focus on the Vulnerability of Women in Tanzania", Advanced LL.M Course Paper, University of Dar es Salaam.

ensure that such rights are realised. A survey of some of NGOs on record brings us to: the Legal and Human Rights Centre (LHRC); the Tanzania Women Lawyers Association (TAWLA); the Tanzania Media Women Association (TAMWA); the National Organisation for Legal Assistance (NOLA), and; the Tanzania Gender Networking Programme (TGNP), and Women in Law and Development in Africa (WILDAF).

Apart from sensitization, these NGOs also engage in research, advocacy and litigation. In the same spirit our appreciation go to the individual persons such as members of the academia and researchers whose role is, again, in sensitizing women's awareness of their land rights and also assisting them to realise the same. Their efforts in this endeavour needs to be commended and encouraged[1054]. I am, thus, assured that through legal consultation, advice, assistance and publicity offered by the above named as well as the unnamed NGOs, it is expected that women's passivity and docility will gradually be replaced by activism and progressive assertiveness. At the centre of all efforts lies the human rights language which, when known, and spoken by all-persons and institutions- the vice of stripping women of their right to, or to access, land shall be nipped in the bud. I share the observation on the ideal solution to the age-old problem of women's right to land with many others in the human rights camp. Suffice it to quote from Winnie Bikaako and Ssenkumba John who also believe that:

> *To establish women's land rights requires not only removing gender inequalities in statutory law, but also ensuring that law is implemented. Women's ability to claim and retain their land rights, including effective control over lands, needs to be strengthened. The complexity of noted obstacles and their contextual variability preclude simple prescriptions and specific strategies. These will evolve through localised campaigns. In such campaigns, the compelling force of human rights could play a pivotal role.*[1055]

1054 See for example, MIGIRO, Mtengeti Rose, "The Division of Matrimonial Property in Tanzania", Journal of Modern African Studies, Vol. 28 No. 3 1990, pp. 521-526; MANJI, Ambreena, "Gender and the Politics of Land Reform Processes in Tanzania", Journal of Modern African Studies, Vol. 36 No. 4 1998 pp. 645-667; MHOJA, Monica E. Magoke, " Impact of Customary Inheritance on the Status of Widows and Daughters in Tanzania: A Challenge to Human Rights Activities" in BOND, Johanna (ed.), (2005): *Voices of African Women: Women's Rights in Ghana, Uganda and Tanzania*, Carolina Academic Press, Durham, North Carolina.

1055 See BIKAAKO, Winnie and SSENKUMBA, John, *op cit*, at p. 277.

Chapter Seven

The Right to Land of the Indigenous Minorities in Tanzania

> In Kenya and Tanzania, the establishment of National Parks has caused tremendous land alienation and eviction and restriction of local communities from resources that were critical for their survival. This has affected many pastoralists, not least the Maasai. The creation of all the National Parks: Manyara, Tarangire, Ngordoto, Serengeti, Mkomazi in the case of Tanzania, and Amboseli, Maasai Mara and others in the case of Kenya, has led to the eviction of indigenous Maasai from their ancestral land without compensation, supposedly in the national interest.
>
> -African Commission of Human and Peoples' Rights[1056]-

1056 AFRICAN COMMISION ON HUMAN AND PEOPLES' RIGHTS (ACPHR): Report of the African Commission's Working Group of Experts on Indigenous Populations/Communities, 2005, as adopted by the African Commission of Human and Peoples Rights at its 28th Ordinary Session. The document is available at www.achpr.org and www. iwgia.org.

General Comments

The right to land of the indigenous minorities in Tanzania has been reasonably written on and succinctly addressed by resource persons of academia.[1057] My limited contribution in this book is simply to add my own voice to their work through a different style of presentation in terms of form and content, the emphasis being on the international law standards that have been developed to address the right to land of the indigenous and the minority people. It is my considered opinion that before I undertake to discuss the specific jurisprudence on the right to land of the indigenous minorities in Tanzania, logic compels me, in the first place, to analyse this right as articulated by, and protected in the jurisprudence of international law generally. The analysis also gives a brief account of the necessary distinction between indigenous peoples and the minorities.

International Concern on the Right to Land of Indigenous and Minority People

Indigenous People

As a matter of history, researchers, both in and outside the legal profession, know well that the indigenous people's movement is an age-old phenomenon that has disturbed great minds in the international human rights camp. The problem of the indigenous people dates back to the pre-19th century movement of the native people in America, following the gradual European occupation of their ancestral lands and the forced evictions against them that ensued.[1058] However, until the middle of the 20th century the problem of the indigenous people had remained localised following the absence of the collective international movement on the rights of indigenous people which, again, is explained by the absence of the international language of human rights at that

---

1057 See for example: MADSEN, Andrew, (2000): The Hadzabe of Tanzania: Law and Human Rights of a Hunter Gatherer Community, IWGIA; TENGA, Ringo W., "Minority Rights in Tanzania", in FINNEGAN, Catherine, and BINCHY William, (eds), (1995): *Human Rights, Constitutionalism and the Judiciary: Tanzanian and Irish Perspectives*, Clarus Press, pp. 71-91; TENGA, Ringo W., "Legitimizing Dispossession: The Tanzanian High Court's Decision on the Eviction of Maasai Pastoralists from Nkomazi Game Reserve", *Cultural Survival Quarterly*, Issue 22.4 January 33, 1999; LOBULU, Ben, "Dispossession and Land Tenure in Tanzania: What Hope from the Court," *Cultural Survival Quarterly*, Issue 22.4 January 31, 1991; and, PETER, Chris Maina, "Human Rights of the Indigenous Minorities in Tanzania and the Courts of Law", A Paper presented at the University of Bergen, Norway, February 2007.

1058 This occupation found support in the doctrine of "discovery" whereby Europeans claimed to have discovered a new land in America, which they alleged was a *terra nullius*, i.e, a land without an owner.

time. In other words, the indigenous movement was confined within the boundaries of the respective national states. It was a time when no international law jurisprudence on the rights of indigenous people was in place; a time when no people would raise their voices high to claim their rights as indigenous people, and; a time when such people were not aware of the similar sufferings of other peoples beyond the national borders.

It can be said that the international concern for the rights of the indigenous people featured in the international legal system, especially in the middle of the 20th century, following the birth of the international human rights movement generally, and the rise of institutions advocating and lobbying for the rights of indigenous people specifically. It all began with the formulation and adoption of the various international human rights documents including: the Universal Declaration of Human Rights of 1948; the International Covenant on Civil and Political Rights of 1966 and; the International Covenant on Economic Social and Cultural Rights of 1966, all of which speak openly about the rights of the people to self-determination including the right to own land and dispose the natural resources.[1059] This means that Indigenous people would later invoke the language of "rights" to organise themselves and strategically air out their claims on various rights, especially so on the international platform through conferences.[1060]

The second development is in relation to the creation of some international bodies and institutions to support the global indigenous movement. We have, for example, the General Assembly of the United Nations, which has greatly stretched its hand to influence the affairs of the indigenous peoples, particularly their rights to land and resources. In 1983, the Assembly created the United Nations Working Group on Indigenous People (UNWGIP), whose role is to set standards for the rights of Indigenous peoples and also to monitor the implementations of these standards. The group took an active part in the drafting of the

1059 See for example, the common Article 2 to the International Covenant on Civil and Political Rights, 1966 and the International Covenant on Economic, Social and Cultural Rights, 1966.

1060 We have on record the examples of the 1975 World Council of Indigenous Peoples, which met in Canada and in which participants from North and South America, Europe, Asia and the Pacific adopted a Declaration of Principles on the Rights of Indigenous Peoples; and the 1993 First World Summit of Indigenous Peoples, which was held in Guatemala and in which the participants from all corners of the world adopted the so-called B'okob Declaration of the World's Indigenous Peoples.

United Nations Draft Declaration on the Rights of Indigenous People of 1994[1061], which is meant to bind State Parties when they sign and/or ratify this Declaration. Of all rights of the indigenous people which the document tends to recognise and protect, the right to land is the most extensively addressed since it is covered by four distinct articles, that is, article 25, 26, 27 and 28, which are reproduced here for quick reference:

Article 25

Indigenous peoples have the right to maintain and strengthen their distinctive spiritual and material relationship with the lands, territories, waters and coastal seas and other resources which they have traditionally owned or otherwise occupied or used, and to uphold their responsibilities to future generations in this regard.

Article 26

Indigenous peoples have the right to own, develop, control and use the lands and territories, including the total environment of the lands, air, waters, coastal seas, sea-ice, flora and fauna and other resources, which they have traditionally owned or otherwise occupied or used. This includes the right to the full recognition of their laws, traditions and customs, land-tenure systems and institutions for the development and management of resources, and the right to effective measures by State to prevent any interferences with, alienation of or encroachment upon these rights.

Article 27

Indigenous peoples have the right to the restitution of lands, territories and resources which they have traditionally owned or otherwise occupied or used, and which have been confiscated, occupied, used or damaged without their free and informed consent. Where this is not possible, they have the right to just and fair compensation. Unless otherwise freely agreed upon by the people concerned, compensation shall take the form of lands, territories and resources equal in quality, size and legal status.

1061 See UN Doc. E/CN.4/Sub.2/1994.1.20 April 1994. The full document is reproduced in TENGA, Ringo W., "Minority Rights in Tanzania," *op cit* at p. 88.

Article 28

> *Indigenous peoples have the right to the conservation, restoration and protection of the total environment and the productive capacity of their lands, territories and resources, as well as to assistance for this purpose from States and through international cooperation. Indigenous peoples have the right to determine and develop priorities and strategies for the development or use of their lands, territories and other resources, including the right to require that States obtain their free and informed consent prior to approval of any project affecting their lands, territories and other resources, particularly in connection with the development, utilization or exploitation of mineral, water or other resources. Pursuant to agreement with indigenous peoples concerned, just and fair compensation shall be provided for any such activities and measures taken to mitigate adverse environmental, economic, social, cultural or spiritual impact...*

Secondly, the Assembly declared the year 1993 to be an International Year for the World's Indigenous Peoples.[1062] It also declared the 14th day of August each year to be the International Day of the Indigenous Peoples[1063], and; finally it declared the 1995-2004 decade to be an International Decade of the World's Indigenous Peoples.[1064] Other bodies include the International Labour Organisation (ILO) which, in its efforts to address the problems of the indigenous peoples, did, among other things, adopt Conventions No. 107 of 1957[1065] and No.169 of 1989[1066] which speak loudly about the rights of indigenous and tribal peoples in independent countries, including the right to their traditional lands. There is also in place the International Human Rights Committee, which is the principal watchdog against States' violations of the rights of the indigenous peoples. The Committee does its work through research

1062 See the United Nations General Assembly Resolution 48/163 of December 21st, 1993.

1063 See the United Nations General Assembly Resolution 49/214 of December 23rd, 1994.

1064 See the United Nations General Assembly Resolution 50/157 of December 21st, 1995.

1065 The Convention Concerning the Protection and Integration of Indigenous and Other Tribal and semi-Tribal Populations In Independent Countries, as Adopted by the International Labour Organization on June 26th, 1957.

1066 See The ILO Convention No 169, Concerning Indigenous Peoples and Tribal Peoples in Independent Countries, adopted in Geneva, Switzerland on June 27, 1989.

and standard setting.[1067] We also note the role of the International NGOs which have been at the forefront in addressing and lobbying for the rights of indigenous peoples.[1068]

The third development has been the role of the free and impartial courts of law, both international and local, which have stood for the rights of indigenous people. We have on record: the International Court of Justice, which held that the *Saharawi* people of Western Sahara have the right to their traditional land;[1069] the High Court of Australia which held in favour of the *Meriam* people,[1070] and; the South African Constitutional Court which held in favour of the *San* people.[1071] Of the cases listed above and many others not listed, the two cases of *Mabo and Others v Queensland* and *Richtersveld Community v Alexkor Limited and the Government of the Republic of South Africa* are the most important to discuss at the moment for the relevance which is attached to the jurisprudence that grew from them.

The brief facts of the Mabo case were as follows: [1072]Britain took over Australia (the British called it Queensland) as her colony, and she immediately passed the *Queensland Coastal Island Act,1879*, in which it was declared, *inter alia*, that "after the 1st day of August 1879 the Islands described in the schedule shall be annexed to and become part of the colony of Queensland and shall be and become subject to the laws in force therein." The schedule included the plaintiffs' land which was located in the Torres Strait between Australia and Papua New Guinea.

1067 We have a well-documented literature about the global violations of the rights of Indigenous Peoples, which is known as the Martinez Cobo Report of 1983. The document got its breath at the sole initiative of the Committee.

1068 We have nn record, for example, the Statement by the International NGOs issued at the Conference on Indigenous Peoples and Land, held in Geneva, Switzerland on September 15-18, 1981; and Agenda 21 adopted at the Rio Conference on Environmental and Development, all of which speak loudly about the rights of the indigenous peoples, including the basic right to land.

1069 See the *Western Saharan Case*, Advisory Opinion ICJ Reports, 1975.

1070 *Mabo and Others v Queensland* (No.2) [1993] LRC 194.

1071 See the *Richtersveld Community v Alexkor Limited and the Government of the Republic of South Africa*, Judgement of the Constitutional Court 2003.

1072 See some commentaries about the case in RICHARD, Barlett, "The Mabo Decision", *Australian Property Law Journal*, Vol. 1, No. 3, December 1993, pp. 236-261 and PETER, Butt, "Native Title Takes Off", *Australian Law Journal*, Vol. 69, No. 1 January 1995, pp. 8-12.

The obvious effect of the Act was to extinguish the native title to land of the plaintiffs, who were indigenous people of the Murray Islands, "the Meriam people." The customary right to their traditional land remained extinguished until 1992, when they went to court to seek for a declaration that they (Meriam people) are entitled to the Murray Island as owners, as possessors, as occupiers or as persons entitled to use and enjoy the said Island.

The main issues that were framed for determination by the court were: whether the Meriam people did have traditional rights and interests in the land of the Murray Islands, and if so, whether Australian law would protect them, and; if native title is recognised, whether indigenous people are entitled to compensation if their land is taken.

The defendants' argument was grounded on two main reasonings. In the first place, they invoked the international law doctrine of *terra nullius*, to argue that the Crown had annexed the land which was then a *terra nullius*, that is to say, a land which belonged to no one. In the second, they invoked the doctrine of the exclusive Crown ownership of land to argue that when the territory of a settled colony became part of the Crown's domination, the law of England so far as applicable to colonial conditions became the law of the colony and that by that law, the Crown acquired the absolute beneficial ownership of all land in the territory so that the colony became the Crown's demesne and no right or interest in any land in the territory could thereafter be possessed by any other person (including the plaintiffs) unless granted right of occupancy by the crown.

The court's reasoning, which ultimately assisted it in deciding the case in favour of the plaintiffs was grounded on the international language of human rights as reflected in the various international legal instruments and the local Australian legislation, that is, the *Racial Discrimination Act* of 1975, which condemned discrimination in its different forms. In principle the court was of the majority view that the fiction by which the rights and interests of the indigenous inhabitants in land were treated as non-existent was justified by a policy which has no place in the contemporary law of the country, and that whatever the justification advanced in earlier days for refusing to recognise the rights and interests in land of the indigenous inhabitants of settled colonies, an unjust and discriminatory doctrine of the kind could no longer be accepted. The court attacked the common law, then in place, by saying that:

> *The common law does not necessarily conform with international law, but international law is a legitimate and important influence on the development of common law, especially when international law declares the existence of universal human rights. A common law doctrine founded on injustice and discrimination in the enjoyment of civil and political rights demands reconsideration. It is contrary both to international standards and the fundamental values of our common law to entrench discriminatory rule which, because of the supposed position on the scale of social organisation of the indigenous inhabitants of a settled colony, denies them a right to occupy their traditional lands.*

The Court went on to observe that:

> *The common law of this country would perpetuate injustice if it were to continue to embrace the enlarged notion of terra nullius and to persist in characterizing the indigenous inhabitants of the Australian colonies as people too low in the scale of social organisation to be acknowledged as possessing rights and interests in land.*

Furthermore, the court was of the view that the preferable rule supported by authorities was that the mere change of sovereignty did not extinguish native title to land. According to the court, the Meriam people asserted an exclusive right to occupy the Murray Island and, as a community, held a proprietary interest in the Islands for they had maintained their identity as a people and observed customs which are traditionally based. In conclusion, the court declared that the Meriam people were entitled as against the whole world to the possession, occupation, use, and enjoyment of the land of Mer. Their title was subject to the power of the Parliament of Queensland and the power of the Governor in Council of Queensland to extinguish that title by valid exercise of the respective powers, provided any exercise of those powers was not inconsistent with the law of the commonwealth.

It is submitted that the importance which is attached to the judgment in the Mabo case is threefold. In the first place the judgment altered the foundation of land law in Australia by overturning the doctrine of terra nullius just as did the decision of the International Court of Justice in the Western Sahara's case. In the second place, the judgment introduced new land law reforms, especially the doctrine of native title into the Australian land law since it was immediately followed by the enactment of the *Native Title Act* of 1993, which officially recognised the natives' title to land. In the third place, the judgment became home to the principle that native title of all indigenous peoples exists where it has not been formally extinguished.

As regards the Richtersveld Community case, the background and facts of the case were as follows:[1073] in its Interim Constitution of 1993 and the Constitution of 1996, South Africa made a provision that, "a person or community dispossessed of property after 19 June 1913[1074] as a result of past racially discriminatory laws or practice is entitled, to the extend provided by an Act of Parliament, either to restitution of that property or to equitable redress"[1075]. The Interim Constitution was followed immediately by a legislation, the *Restitution of Land Rights Act 22* of 1994 which, again provided, in part, that a person shall be entitled to restitution of a right to land if "it is a community or part of the community dispossessed of the right in land after 19 June 1913 as a result of past racially discriminatory laws and practices."[1076]

Following this legal development, the respondents, Richtersveld Community[1077] and Others, instituted a case in the Land Claims Court of South Africa[1078] claiming the restitution of their land under the *Restitution of Land Rights Act*. They lost the case in the Court and appealed successfully to the Supreme Court of South Africa[1079], which granted the leave to appeal, set aside the order of the trial Court and granted reliefs to the respondents.

Aggrieved by the Supreme Court's decision, the appellants found their way to the South African Constitution Court, whose decision is the core of the discussion in this part. In the Court, the issues for determination

---

1073 See some commentaries on this case in HITCHCOCK, Robert and VINDING, Diana (eds.), (2004): *Indigenous People's Rights in Southern Africa*, IWGIA, Document No. 110, Copenhagen, and WACHIRA, George Makundi, "The Role of Courts in Protecting Indigenous Peoples' Rights to Land and Resources in Kenya and South Africa" in the *East African Journal of Peace and Human Rights*, Vol. 13 No. 2, 2007, pp. 240- 269.

1074 19th June 1913 was the effect date when the Native Lands Act 27 of 1913 came into force. The effect of the Act, as we have stated in Chapter One above, was the deprivation of black South Africans of their rights to own lands, and rights in land in the vast majority of the South African Land mass.

1075 As per section 27 (7) of the Constitution of 1996.

1076 Section 2 (1) (d) of the Act.

1077 Richtersveld is situated on the north-western corner of the Northern Cape Province of South Africa.

1078 See *Richtersveld Community and Others v Alexkor and Another* 2001 (3) SA 12 93 (LCC).

1079 See *Richtersveld Community and Others v Alexkor and Another* [2001] (4) All SA563 (LCC).

included: whether the respondents were a Community; whether they were dispossessed of their land after 19 June 1913, and; whether the dispossession was a result of racially discriminatory laws and practices. It was argued for the respondents that all the issues answered squarely in favour of the respondents while, on part of the appellants, it was argued that their rights over the subject land ceased way back in 1847 when the British Crown annexed the land, and, alternatively that the dispossession of the subject land was not the consequence of racially discriminatory laws or practices.

The Court observed, in the first place, that the determination of the real character of indigenous title to land and its content involves the study of the history of a particular community and its usages.[1080] Applying this principle to the case before it, the Court went on to observe that the real character of the title that the Richtersveld Community possessed in the subject land was a right of community ownership under indigenous law, and that the content of that right included the right to the exclusive use of land by members of the community. By virtue of this right, the community had the right to use its water, to use its land for grazing and hunting and to exploit its natural resources above and beneath the surface. In other words, the Court found that prior to annexation, the Community had a right of ownership in the subject land under indigenous law, which ownership included communal ownership of the minerals and precious stones.

As regards to events after annexation in 1847 until and even after 1913, the Court was of the view that looking at the Annexation Proclamation and other relevant conduct of the British Crown as legislative acts or acts of state, there is nothing either in the events proceeding the annexation of Richtersveld or in the language of the Proclamation which suggests that the annexation extinguished the rights of the Community. Stated otherwise and in the Court's opinion, after the annexation, the right of the Community to indigenous law ownership could have been extinguished and the Community could have lost its indigenous land ownership if: the laws of the Crown expressly distinguished the community's customary law ownership of land; the laws of the Crown applicable to Richtersveld

1080 Reference was made to the case of *Amodu Tijani v The Secretary, Southern Nigeria* (1921) 2A.C 399 in which the Privy Council of the House of Lords had come to the same observation.

rendered the exercise of any of the material incidents of the indigenous law rights to ownership unlawful; the Community was granted limited rights in respect of the land by the Crown in the circumstances where the reasonable inference to be drawn is that the rights of indigenous law ownership were extinguished, or; the land was taken by force. None of the above had taken place! The Court's conclusion on this point was that the evidence proved that the community had been in occupation of the subject land at the time of annexation and continued to be until its eviction after the discovery of diamonds in the 1920s. In all that time the Community occupied the whole of the Richtersveld including the subject land, it used the said land, let it and granted mineral rights in respect of it, and exercised other rights to which it was entitled in accordance with its indigenous law on ownership of the land.

As regards to what happened after 1913, the Court found that by virtue of the *Precious Stones Act 44* of 1927, which came as a direct consequence of the discovery of diamonds in the subject land and the Proclamation Orders of 1928, 1929, 1931 and 1963, the state subsequently treated the subject land as its own, required the community to leave it, exploited it for its own account and later transferred it to Alexkor. All these happened after 1913 and effectively dispossessed the Community of all its rights in the subject land: the right to occupy and exploit the subject land, including its minerals.

Finally, as to whether the laws and practices were racially discriminatory, the Court observed that owners whose ownership was registered in the deeds office and on which State alluvial diggings were established were treated differently from those who held them according to indigenous law, where no system of registration was required, and registered owners were allowed to have access to land, to keep their homesteads and to share in the mineral wealth of the land. Such a trend was nothing but racial discrimination where almost all registered owners were whites.

The totality of the above developments in respect of the rights of the indigenous people makes scholars believe that the indigenous people's movement is now an international concern which everyone in and outside the human rights camp must acknowledge and appreciate. This is what we learn from Johansson Dahre who notes that:

> *Today indigenous people are part of international law but as passive objects and not as equal, political subjects. Indigenous peoples all around the world still struggle to be acknowledged as equal to other peoples. They must also gain equal participation in the decisions that affect them.*[1081]

One important thing that may be noted is that there is no one and binding definition in the international legal system for the term "indigenous people or peoples". However, we read from the Report of the African Commission's Working Group of Experts on Indigenous Populations/Communities[1082] that the traditional test that has been in place for determination of indigenous status of the people, especially so during the decolonisation processes, has been the *aboriginality* of the people or peoples concerned. That is to say, it has traditionally been considered as enough, using this test, to establish that these people were in occupation of a defined territory before the same was encroached by foreigners, and that, therefore, they are indigenous. The Report recounts the point very clearly that:

> *The initial approaches considered indigenous peoples to be aboriginal peoples of a given land who have become marginalised after having been invaded by colonial powers or invaders who settled there and are now politically dominant over the earlier occupants.*

However, modern researchers and writers[1083], including the African Commission's Working group of experts, tend to agree that the aboriginality test is no longer the only test, and that indigenous status of the people must be established by looking at what constitutes common characteristics of the people considered to be protected in this movement. According to the group of experts, particularly, these characteristics include the following: one, their cultures and ways of life differ considerably from the dominant society and their cultures are under threat in some cases to the extent of extinction; two, in most cases, the survival of their particular way of life depends on access and rights

1081 See DAHRE, Johansson, *op cit* at p. 14.

1082 See the 2005 Report of the African Commission's Working Group of Experts on Indigenous Populations/ Communities, as adopted by the African Commission of Human and Peoples Rights at its 28th Ordinary Session.

1083 See for example, GALATY, John G., "Losing Ground: Indigenous Rights and Recourse Across Africa", *Cultural Survival Quarterly*, Issue 22.4 January 31, 1991.

to their traditional land and natural resources therein; three, they suffer from discrimination as they are being regarded as less developed and less advanced than other more dominant sectors of society; four, they often live in inaccessible regions, often geographically isolated, and suffer from various forms of marginalization, both politically and socially, and; fifth, they are subjected to domination and exploitation within national, political and economic structures that are commonly designed to reflect the interests and activities of the national majority. In other words these are the elements which, together, constitute dispossession and denial of their human rights. Denial of rights in this category has, for example, been experienced by the *Sami* of Northern Scandinavia in Eastern Europe, the *Indians* of America, the *San* of Southern Africa, the *Batwa* or *Pygmies* of Rwanda, Burundi, Uganda and eastern region of the Democratic Republic of Congo, *Ogiek* of Kenya, *Ogoni* of Nigeria, the *Nuba* of Sudan, *Hadzabe,Barbaig, Ndorobo, Sandawe, Iraqw* and *Maasai* of Tanzania.

The most serious problem in the international jurisprudence on Indigenous People is that most states have taken too long to recognise the presence of indigenous people in their respective territories and to undertake to protect their rights. The record show that at least in Europe some positive steps have been undertaken by States to recognised the presence of indigenous peoples in their territories. [1084] However, there is yet a long way to go in Africa, where according to the available record, almost all African States have declined or desisted to entertain claims of the indigenous people in their territories, the reason being the States' non admission of the existence of indigenous peoples in their territories, [1085] and the absence of legislative measures at state level to cater for the rights of indigenous people.

1084 It is to our understanding that Canada and New Zealand, for example, officially recognised the presence of indigenous peoples in their territories in 1998 and 1995 respectively, and took some policy steps to address their rights.

1085 We learn from HICHCOCK, Robert and VINGING, Diana, op cit at p. 8 that "Most African Governments have until now maintained that all their citizens are indigenous or, alternatively argued that there is no such thing as indigenous group in their country". This means that indigenous peoples in Africa have been left to cry in the wilderness! No single African country is a member of the ILO Convention 169. We think that the Report of the African Commission on Human and Peoples Rights of November 2003 on Indigenous Peoples and Communities is a positive and step towards recognising the rights of indigenous peoples in Africa.

Minorities

It is difficult to mark the exact birthday of the international law jurisprudence concerning the rights of the minorities (or the minority people).[1086] However, my quick research has brought me to the German-Polish Upper Silesian Convention of 1922[1087] as the first document to mark the beginning of the international movement for the protection of the rights of the minorities in the inter World Wars era. This means, therefore, that the United Nations Resolution 217 C (III) of 10th December 1948 was yet another expression of the international community over its concern for the rights of the minorities after the Second World War. Later developments focusing on the rights of minorities are: the Convention Concerning the Protection and Integration of Indigenous and other Tribal and semi-Tribal Populations in Independent Countries, (ILO Convention No. 107) of 1957;[1088] the International Covenant on Civil and Political Rights of 1966;[1089] the Convention Concerning Indigenous and Tribal Peoples in Independent Countries, (ILO Convention No. 169) of 1989;[1090] the United Nations Declaration on the Rights of Persons Belonging to National or Ethnic, Religious and Linguistic Minorities;[1091]

1086 The Advisory Opinion on the Greco-Bulgarian Convention, 1930 P.C.I.J Rep. Series B, No.7, p.19 and the Case Concerning the Question of Minority Schools in Albania 1935 P.C.I.J Series A/B, No. 64, p.17, for example, suggest that the issue concerning the minority rights pre-dates the Second World War. Similarly, the establishment of the United Nations Sub-Commission on Prevention of Discrimination and Protection of Minorities suggest that the international community's move towards the realization of the minority rights is an on-going process of the post World War era.

1087 This Treaty was concluded in Geneva on May 15, 1922. It is for that reason, sometimes, referred to as the Geneva Convention of May 15, 1922. For a brief discussion of the Treaty, see KOROWICZ, Marek St., "The Problem of International Personality of Individuals" *The American Journal of International Law*, Vol. 50, No. 3 (Jul., 1956), pp. 533-562. According to this writer, the clear protection of the Upper Silesian minorities was expressed in the provisions of Articles 147-157 of the Treaty. That is to say, when their rights had been infringed by the State, the members of the minority had to submit a petition to the Minorities Office in the State Party to the Convention. Then the Minorities Office would forward the petition to the President of the Mixed Commission for his opinion, and in case, it [Minorities Office] was not satisfied, it would then appeal to the Council of the League of Nations.

1088 Adopted by the International Labour Organization on June 26th, 1957.

1089 Adopted by the General Assembly of the United Nations on December 16th, 1966.

1090 Adopted by the General Conference of the International Labour Organisation on 27 June 1989.

1091 Adopted by the General Assembly of the United Nations as Resolution 47/133 of December 1992.

the Framework Convention for the Protection of National Minorities,[1092] and; the Lund Recommendations on the Effective Participation of National Minorities in Public Life.[1093]

A quick survey of all these instruments indicates that the basic goal of the instruments is the protection of all human rights of the minority people including, of course, the right to their traditional lands. As we read these instruments we will note, for example, that the International Covenant on Civil and Political Rights, 1966 provides in Article 27 that:

> *In those States in which ethnic, religious, or linguistic minorities exist, persons belonging to such minorities shall not be denied the right, in community with the other members of their group, to enjoy their own culture, to profess and practice their own religion, or to use their own language.*

Again, the ILO Convention No 169, though it does not employ the use of the term "minorities", intends to protect, apart from indigenous people, the rights of tribal peoples. According to the Convention "tribal peoples" are peoples in independent countries "whose social, cultural, and economic conditions distinguish them from other sections of the national community, and whose status is regulated wholly or partially by their own customs or traditions or by special laws or regulations"[1094]. The Convention addresses, quite substantially, the right to land of the protected people. It obliges State members, firstly, to recognise the peoples' rights of ownership and possession of the lands which they traditionally occupy;[1095] secondly, to consult the people and negotiate terms if their land is to be acquired for public interest, including paying them fair compensation;[1096] thirdly to seek the free consent of the people if they should be reallocated to other places as an exceptional measure;[1097] and to reallocate them areas with lands of quality and legal

---

1092 Signed by States Members of the Council of Europe, at Strasbourg, on February 1st, 1995.

1093 Adopted by the Internationally Recognised Independent Expert, at Lund, May 9th 1999.

1094 See Article 1 (1) (a).

1095 Article 14 (1).

1096 Article 15 (2).

1097 Article 16 (2)

status equal to that of lands previously occupied by them.[1098] Finally, the Convention prevents persons not belonging to these peoples from taking the advantage of their customs or lack of understanding of the laws to secure ownership, possession or use of land belonging to them.[1099]

Apart from the international legal instruments of relevance in respect of the rights of the minority people as listed above, we also have on record various writers at the international level whose role in the development of the international law jurisprudence on minority rights cannot be said to be insignificant.[1100]

As it has been the case of the indigenous people, there is no one and binding definition of the term "minorities" or "minority people" in international law. Of all who have attempted to define the term, Francesco Capotorti who has been a Special Rapporteur to the United Nations Sub-Commission on Prevention of Discrimination and Protection of Minorities, has the best impression as he defines the term to mean:

> *"a group which is numerically inferior to the rest of the population, whose members possess ethnic, religious or linguistic characteristics which differ from those of the rest of the population and who, if only implicitly, maintain a sense of solidarity, directed towards preserving their culture, traditions, religion or language".*[1101]

The immediate problem of the lack of a binding definition of minorities in international law is that most states, not to mention the African States, tend to deny the existence of the minority people in their territories, and as such they make no any effort to protect their rights, including the right to land. This is what we learn from Jay A. Sigler who observes that:

1098 Article 16 (4).

1099 Article 17 (3).

1100 See, for example, CAPOTORTI, Francesco, (1991): *Study on the Rights of Persons belonging to Ethnic, Religious and Linguistic Minorities,* New York: United Nations; JOHNSSON, Christina, (2002): *National States and Minority Rights: A Constitutional Analysis*, Uppsala: Universitet; PENTASSUGLIA, Gaetano, (2002): *Minorities in International Law: An Introductory Study*, Strasbourg: Council of Europe Publishing; THORNBERRY, P., (1991): *International Law and the Rights on Minorities*, Oxford: Clarendon Press; WRIGHT, J., "The OSCE and the Protection of Minority Rights" in *Human Rights Quarterly* Vol. 18, 1996, pp. 190-205.

1101 See Capotorti's report on the Study on the Rights of Persons Belonging to Ethnic, Religious and Linguistic Minorities, 1977, UN Doc. E 91.XIV.2.

> *The very existence of minority group is often denied by political leaders of national-states. This refusal to acknowledge the presence of a minority group is an easy way to deny that group any claim of right.*[1102]

As we may observe from the above discussion, aboriginality and number are the key characteristics of the indigenous people and minorities respectively. For that reason alone a group of people can come forward and claim protection as indigenous people if it can establish, among others, that it is comprised of aboriginal people who have occupied a specific territorial area from time immemorial (regardless of their number) in comparison with the rest of the people in the state. On the other hand a group is entitled to protection as a minority group if it can establish that it is numerically smaller in number when compared with the rest of the population of the state and that it has occupied a given territorial area for a long time in accordance with its own customs. Other factors such as self- identification of the group in terms of ethnicity, culture, religion and language, and domination by the rest of the population are common features of both groups. The point of emphasis, here, is that both groups need protection from the state against any violation of their rights and especially their right to land. The next part of this chapter looks at how Tanzania has lived this noble obligation in the light of the international standards.

The Tanzanian Jurisprudence on the Right to Land of the Indigenous Minorities

In Tanzania we have some ethnic groups, which have both attributes as indigenous people (aboriginality) and as minority people (smaller in number when compared with the rest of the population). It is for this reason that our preference is to refer them as indigenous minorities. These include the Maasai who dominate the Northern part of Tanzania especially in the regions of Arusha and Manyara, the Hadzabe who live as hunters and gatherers in the regions of Shinyanga, Dodoma, Arusha and Singida, the Ndorobo who also live as hunters and gatherers in Arusha and Manyara, the Barabaig in Arusha, Singida, Shinyanga and Dodoma, and the Mbulu of Mbulu District in Manyara. There are reasons to believe that these are indigenous minorities in that they comprise groups of people who are considered inferior due to their cultural heritage, which they have been fighting, tooth and nail, to preserve.

1102 See SIGLER, Jay A., (1983): *Minority Rights: A Comparative Analysis*, Westport, Connecticut and London: Greenwood Press, at p. 3.

However, there is on record a negative history about the land rights of these people for reasons attributed partly to the nature of the tenurial systems of land ownership under the Tanzanian land law which classifies all land in Tanzania as being public land vested in the President for the benefit of all Tanzanian citizens[1103], partly to the widespread migrations and resettlements of the said communities, which tends to deprive them the status of being aboriginal and distinct, and partly to the absence of specific law to protect their interests, particularly in respect of land ownership and control. The first fact has the effect of giving precedence to the public interests at the expense of the individual or group interests; the second fact has the effect of making it hard for any community involved to raise its voice and prove that it has occupied a specific area from time immemorial, and; the third fact has the effect of making it hard for these people to find refuge in the legal system. It is on the light of these facts that most communities have unsuccessfully gone to court to claim rights in land, and that there is little prospect, or none at all, for any community to claim land rights successfully in the future.

We have earlier (Chapter Two above) discussed how the Barbaig people of the Hanang District in Arusha were illegally and brutally evicted from their land after the same had been allocated to the investor, NAFCO, by the government of Tanzania. They were aggrieved by this move but lost their action in court for technical reasons, including that of failure to establish their status as natives.[1104] Much may be said about the most recent eviction of the *Maasai* of Loliondo (Chapter One) and an attempted eviction of the *Hadzabe* of Yaeda Chini Valley, in Mbulu District[1105]. In this chapter we go further to record the case of *Likengere Faru Parutu Kamunyu and 53 Others v Minister for Tourism,*

1103 This position was set by the provisions of section 3 of the Land Ordinance and had been maintained under section 4 (1) of the *Land Act, 1999*, [Cap. 113 R.E 2002].

1104 Reference is made in relation to the cases of *National Agricultural and Food Corporation (NAFCO) v Mulbadaw Village Council and Others*, (1985) TLR 88 (CA). See also TENGA, Ringo W. and KAKOTI, George, "The Barbaig Land Case: Mechanism of State Organised Land Grabbing in Tanzania" in HANNE, Veber *et al.* (eds.) (1993): Never Drink from the Same Cup: Proceedings of the Conference on Indigenous Peoples in Africa, Tune. Denmark: IWGIA Doc. 74.

1105 See a brief account of the government's move to dispossess the *Hadzabe* of their traditional land in LEGAL AND HUMAN RIGHTS CENTRE, Tanzania Human Rights Report, 2007, at p. 49.

Natural Resources and Environment & 3 Others.[1106] The background of this case was that the appellants, who were basically nomadic Maasai, were in 1988 evicted from land comprising the Mkomazi Game Reserve along the Pangani/ Ruvuma rivers in the Kilimanjaro-Tanga province in mainland Tanzania, so as to give room to the tourist industry. The available record shows that the eviction against the appellants was carried out inhumanely by the government machinery and in total violation of the appellants' right to dignity as human beings:

> *...game scouts and militiamen effecting the eviction assaulted pastoralists, harassed their families, mothers with newly born babies had to be carried and dumped into the bush in the rush of the eviction; cattle, donkeys and calves strayed into the wilderness where they were lost or devoured by beasts; bomas, huts, kraals, cattle, domestic articles, food stuffs, veterinary medicines, cash and ornaments got lost or razed down by the fires the game scouts started. Families were dislocated and broken up. In short the plaintiffs were seriously inconvenienced, put to a great crisis and thrown out of the reserve without assistance for resettlement in terms of alternative land.*[1107]

At the end of it all, these humble citizens were seriously aggrieved by the said eviction and decided to knock on the door of the High Court of Tanzania at Moshi where they instituted a suit against the government[1108] for wrongful interference of their legal rights by: forceful eviction of the plaintiffs and their families from their ancestral lands; burning down homesteads and dwellings and destroying livestock and property thereby, and; breaking down of the Maasai way of life and precipitated emigration of their numbers to Kenya and to towns. The appellants moved the court for a numbers of remedies including: a declaration that they were still the residents of the disputed land (which

---

1106 [2000] TLR 288 (CA).

1107 An extract from the High Court decision as reproduced in TENGA, Ringo W., "Legitimizing Dispossession: The Tanzania High Court's Decision on the Eviction of Maasai Pastoralists from Mkomazi Game Reserve" *Cultural Survival Quarterly*, Issue 22.4 January 31, 1999.

1108 See High Court of Tanzania at Moshi, Consolidated Civil Case No.33 of 1994.

they locally knew as *Alaililai Lemwazuni*); a declaration that the forceful eviction or otherwise removal of pastoralists from the area was not done in accordance with the law, and; an award for compensation. They partly won the case before the High Court after the Court had found that they were entitled only to a part of the area known as Umba Game Reserve and, for that reason, that they were entitled to an alternative land and compensation. The High Court decision has been commented by Ringo W. Tenga who observes that:

> *The Mkomazi case is one step forward in that the recognition of customary resource rights in game reserves has been established and that extinction of such rights must follow due process based on Constitutional safeguard.*[1109]

However, the appellants/ plaintiffs were not satisfied by the court's finding for the reasons that: the Court failed to order restitution when it had found that the eviction was illegal and unprocedural; the Court ruled in their favour for alternative remedy but the remedy was unpractical as it was to be realised on a self-help basis and had no time frame set, and; the Court gave them damages of Shs. 300,000/=, which was small in terms of the actual loss. They appealed against the judgment and order of the court to the Court of Appeal of Tanzania. One of the main issues for determination by the Court was whether the Maasai community of which the appellants were members had an ancestral customary land title over the whole of the Mkomazi Game Reserve.

The Court reached its decision based on two lines of reasoning. It was the court's first line of reasoning, on evidence, that the Maasai Community or tribe in question was not the first tribe to arrive in the geographical area, the subject of the case, but were preceded by other tribes such as Pare, Shambaa and even the Kamba, and that they, as nomadic tribe, began to reach the area in the second half of 1940s, and their presence was still scanty at the time the Mkomazi Game Reserve was established in 1951. Thus, the Court, speaking through Nyalali, C.J- as he then was, was of the following observation at page 17:

1109 TENGA, Ringo W., "Legitimizing Dispossession: The Tanzania High Court's Decision on the Eviction of Maasai Pastoralists from Mkomazi Game Reserve" *Cultural Survival Quarterly*, Issue 22.4 January 31, 1999.

> *That being the position, we are bound to hold that the Maasai Community in question did not have ancestral land title of over the whole of the Mkomazi Game Reserve. We are aware that the learned trial Judge found that such title existed in a portion of the Game Reserve, that is, Umba Game Reserve. The Respondents have not cross-appealed against that finding, but since such finding of the learned trial judge is inconsistent with our overall finding, we have to invoke our revisional jurisdiction provided under Section 4 (2) of the Appellate Jurisdiction Act, 1979 as amended by Act No. 17 of 1993 so as to set aside such finding which is inconsistent with ours. We do so accordingly, and find that no such title existed in Umba Game Reserve.*

As its second line of reasoning, the Court considered the Tanzanian land law and the nature of the title which the appellants could have had before they were evicted and came to the following observation, also at page 7:

> *As a matter of land law, it is indisputable that all land on the mainland of Tanzania is PUBLIC LAND as stated under section 3 of the Land Ordinance, CAP 113. The land is vested in the President on trust for the benefit of the Tanzanian indigenous population as stated under section 4 of the Ordinance. Because of this position of land under the Land Ordinance, no individual person or group of persons can have rights in land which are superior to public title. The nature of title available to persons or group of persons cannot be anything but a right to use public land. Since the appellants are members of the Tanzanian indigenous population, like many other Tanzanians, it follows that the appellants were using the Mkomazi Game Reserve as beneficiaries of public land, subject to legal regulations made for proper land use.*

Another equally important issue for determination by the Court was the issue of the reliefs which the appellants were entitled to. The Court, having observed as above, and guided by the provisions of the *Wildlife Conservation Act, 1974,*[1110] said that the appellants fell into two categories,

1110 Act No. 12 of 1974.

that is to say, those who were ordinary residents before 1951[1111] or their descendants, and those who failed to tell the Court how they came to the Reserve. In that respect, it was the Court's view that for the 27 appellants who were ordinary resident in the area before 1951, their right to land was protected[1112] and they were, therefore, entitled to compensation at the tune of Shs. 300,000/= each and to re-allocation to an alternative grazing land of comparatively the same standard as that used by other pastoralists in the country within 6 months from the date of the decision. As to those who failed to prove how they came to the Reserve, the Court saw no option other than leaving them empty- handed.

The discussion in this chapter has shown very clearly that the international and national jurisprudence on the right to land of the indigenous and minority people is growing very encouragingly. With the Mkomazi case on record, we are convinced that the future of the protected groups in Tanzania is turning brighter. The international standards on consultation, compromise and/or compensation of the people whenever their right to land is at issue are the surest ways toward this hope. The challenge ahead is on questions of tolerance on the part of the State, vigilance and courage on the part of lawyers who are called to litigate for the interests of the these people, and righteousness on the part of the courts of law.

1111 This is the year of establishment of the Mkomazi Game Reserve.

1112 Article 24 of the *Constitution of the United Republic of Tanzania, 1977* and the provisions of the *Land Acquisition Act, 1967.*

Chapter Eight

The Right to Compensation

Finally, it is a fundamental human right that no man shall be deprived of his property without adequate compensation. That right is inalienable and is recognised by every civilised society including our own. Some societies insist not merely on adequate compensation but adequate and prompt compensation. In theoretical terms the right to compensation may be traced to the concept of ownership.

- Judge Kahwa K. Lugakingira[1113] -

1113 *Berabera Ujamaa Village v Abubakari Bura* [1983] TLR 219 (HC)

Of all the rights that accrue from the right of occupancy (including any derivative right thereof), the right to compensation in Tanzania appears to be a thorn in land administration. Let it be on record that the right to compensation has a long history both in the international law, and national law jurisprudence. It is, therefore, very unfortunate to note that, despite the global and local standards in respect of this right, the same has been observed more in violation than promotion even in Tanzania, where cases of evicting people from their lands without compensation, or with inadequate and unreasonable compensation have been top on the agenda of our formal and informal discussion about the land administration system. Thanks to Justice Lugakingira who openly perceived the right to compensation as a "fundamental human right" that must be jealously recognised, promoted, and protected; to the government whose effort through legislation of the Land Acts has successfully set the standards to guide the awarding of compensation, and; to the courts of law which have stood for the right to compensation, especially the victims of illegal evictions where the same has been denied by the some actors in land administration.

The Right to Compensation in International Law

To my own understanding through legal research, the right to compensation in all cases of land deprivation and/or acquisition has a philosophical foundation in the thinking of the early political thinkers such as John Locke (1632-1704) and many others who believed in three things: that God has given the world to men in common; that He also has given them the reason to make use of it to the best advantage of life and convenience; that man puts the labour of his body and the work of his hand to convert what is common to his own use and benefit by tilling a piece of land, improving it, cultivating and planting it as his own property, and using the products from it for his own welfare, and; that whoever, therefore, takes that property must pay him for the labour spent to effect the said improvement.

It has earlier been noted (in Chapter 1) above, that the origins of international human rights lie in the philosophical discussions evolved through the centuries. It is no wonder, then, to note that the coming of the language of human rights in the international sphere brought with it a bundle of property rights, including the right to compensation which was initially the domain of political thinkers. It is now trite law that the right to compensation is a human right, and is recognised, promoted and protected as such by many state members of the international community. The legal framework on the right to compensation, at the international level, is traced from the *Universal Declaration of Human Rights, 1948*; though it does not expressly mention compensation as a right, it altogether prevents arbitrary deprivation of one's property[1114]. Arbitrary deprivation in the legal sense means a deprivation which departs from due process of law, including payment of compensation.

At the regional level there is, for example, *Protocol 1 to the European Convention for the Protection of Human and Fundamental Freedoms, 1952*, which also prevents deprivation of "possessions except in public interest and subject to the conditions provided for by law and the general principles of international law"[1115]. Similarly, the *American Charter on Human Rights, 1969*, is very particular in this aspect since it also prevents deprivation of one's property except "upon payment of just compensation, for reasons of public utility or social interest, and in the cases of and according to the forms established by law"[1116]. Akin to the above named instruments, the *African Charter on Human and Peoples' Rights, 1981* also guarantees the right to property and prevents its encroachment except "in the interest of public need or in the general interest of the community and in accordance with the provisions of appropriate law"[1117].

Apart from the international and regional instruments providing for the right to compensation, there are also other instruments which provide for the right of compensation to specific category of people. We have already recorded, for example, the ILO *Convention Concerning Indigenous and Tribal Peoples in Independent Countries, 1989* which, on one hand, prohibits removing indigenous people from their traditional lands and relocating them in another land, and on the other hand, provides that if such a relocation is necessary, they shall be provided "with lands of quality and legal status at least equal to that of the lands previously occupied by them, suitable to provide for their present needs and future development", and that "where the people concerned express a preference for compensation in money or in kind, they shall be so compensated under appropriate guarantees"[1118].

1114 Article 17 (2).

1115 Article 1, para. 1.

1116 Article 21 (2).

1117 Article 14.

1118 Article 16.

All the above instruments collectively provide the best evidence that the right to compensation is indeed a fundamental human right which all owners of property are entitled to. Three things may be learnt about these instruments. The first is that some instruments provide for the right to compensation not only in respect of landed property, but also in respect of all other forms of property including, but not limited to, intellectual property rights. The second is that some of them provide for the right to compensation in all cases of deprivation, without any direction as to the form, extent of time for, compensation. Thirdly, we find that yet some other instruments simply state that deprivation of property shall not be arbitrary, but shall be in accordance with the "appropriate" laws of the state, and "the principles of international law". All these mean one basic fact that state parties to these instruments are required to enact their own appropriate national laws which shall recognise, promote and protect the right to compensation, and through which the aggrieved parties can accordingly enforce this right in the courts of law. This point brings us to another long discussion as to what is the place of compensation in the jurisprudence of land law in Tanzania.

Compensation and the Law in Tanzania

Sometimes it is hard to believe that the right to compensation is part of the Tanzanian land law. We say so because of the prevalence of violations of this fundamental right, the government being the principle perpetrator. There is on record a sad history of evictions or attempted evictions of the land holders from their lands without compensation at all, or without adequate, just and prompt compensation. Evictions of this nature cover the old Meruland Case of 1950s, the Mulbadaw Village Case of 1980s, and the recent Maasai eviction sage of July 2009, among many others on record, whose horrendous consequences in society, including loss of property, homelessness, breach of peace and social disharmony have not been insignificant. There are two factors behind this state of affairs: one is the history and nature of the law on compensation which has been developing at different phases and is changing in terms of form and content, and; two, is disregard of the law on the part of actors in the machinery of land administration and control.

Compensation before the Bill of Rights

Before independence there was no law in Tanzania that spelt the right to compensation in clear and binding terms. The first document in point of time to spell out the right compensation was the Government Circular No. 4 of 1953, which tended to extinguish customary titles in urban areas and which, for that reason, empowered the District Commissioners to compensate customary holders of land for the loss of their rights of occupancy in the said urban areas. Towards independence, the philosophical foundation of the right to compensation was then elucidated by Mwalimu Nyerere in what came to be called the "Nyerere's doctrine of land value"[1119]. The post independence period covering the entire of 1960s, 1970s and the early years of 1980s (when there was, finally, the incorporation of the Bill of Rights in the country constitution) witnessed only few legislative measures in an attempt to recognise the right to compensation. This was reflected, particularly, in the Preamble of the *Interim Constitution of the United Republic of Tanzania, 1965* and the *TANU Constitution* all of which spelt the right of all men to the "just return of their labour" and the *Land Acquisition Act, 1967*[1120] which described a right to compensation to a land holder whose land was compulsorily acquired by the government for public interest. Compensation payable under this Act is limited to "unhexausted improvements" only.

The point of emphasis, here, is that in the entire period before the incorporation of the Bill of Rights in the country's constitution, the right to compensation was hardly considered to form part of the fundamental rights of citizens as long as there was no law in place to recognise it as such. However, the courts turned to the above named-documents and Nyerere's doctrine of land value as legal tools in the course of adjudicating for the rights of land holders who knocked at the court's door to seek protection against illegal evictions and deliberate denial of their right to compensation. Note that some serious violations of the rights of people in respect of land occurred during the "Operation Vijiji", in which people were arbitrarily dispossessed of their land by the government in the move to develop planned villages including Ujamaa Villages. The cases of *Lalata Msangawale v Henry Mwamlima*[1121], *Berabera Ujamaa Village v Abubakar Bura*[1122] and *Ntiyahela Boneka v Kijiji cha Ujamaa Mutala*[1123] are referred to as our case study.

1119 See a full account of the doctrine in Chapter Two above.

1120 A detailed discussion of the Act, including the scheme of compensation under the Act, appears in Chapter Four above.

1121 [1979] LRT no. 3.

1122 [1983] TLR 219 (HC).

1123 [1988] TLR 156 (HC).

In the *Lalata Msangawale* case, for example, the appellant, who had cleared a virgin land and developed it by planting crops was arbitrarily deprived the same by people who acted on behalf of the Nziga Ujamaa village. He instituted and won a case in the Primary Court for the return of his *shamba* [farmland] or payment of compensation in lieu thereof. The respondents successfully appealed before a District Court of Mbozi, which reversed the judgment and order of the trial court. The appellant won the appeal in the High Court of Tanzania, at Dodoma where the court did not hesitate to rule as it did that:

> *In the instance case the appellant had successfully proved before the trial Court that he had occupied the land in dispute when the same was virgin and unoccupied. Therefore even if the villagers considered it expedient to grab that piece of land in order to enlarge the adjacent shamba of the wajamaa, the appellant, at the very minimum was entitled to be paid compensation by those wajamaa who wanted to, and who in fact did, take his shamba and crops thereon.*
>
> *In this country we still respect the law on individual ownership of property and since the appellant had invested his labour on that piece of land those other people who took it over should have paid him compensation as rightly decided by the trial Court.*

Compensation after the Bill of Rights

The incorporation of the Bill of Rights in the Constitution in 1984 brought with it a bundle of rights including the right of owners of property to be paid compensation which is commensurate to the value of the property whenever a property is nationalised or taken for any other purpose.[1124] So, it is axiomatic that from the date of the incorporation of the Bill of Rights the right to compensation acquired the constitutional status of being a fundamental human right, meaning that the state was then obliged to recognise it, promote it, and protect it. However, despite the constitutional articulation about the right to compensation, there were two notable and practical problems that hindered the proper realisation of this right. One; apart from the *Land Acquisition Act, 1967* whose application was also limited, there was no law in place that provided for matters affecting compensation including the time of compensation,

1124 See Article 24 (2).

nature, and amount of compensation payable. Two; the government was prepared to discourage promotion of the right to compensation and, at times, did what was best at its disposal to curtail or limit the right to compensation through legislative measures. Thanks are due to the courts of law, which took the position of a watchdog against violation of the right to compensation.

The case of *Attorney General v Lohay Akonaay and Another*[1125], is cited in support of the government attitude on the matter. The case reports one of the saddest components in the history of land administration in Tanzania. This is the fruitless effort which the government took to enact a law[1126] where it intended, among other things, to extinguish customary rights in land in certain areas and prohibit the payment of compensation for such extinction. The respondents were the immediate victims of the law because they had been deprived of their land without compensation, and the law was purposely enacted to bar them from claiming compensation. For this reason, they successfully challenged it in the High Court of Tanzania at Arusha.[1127] The Court considered it to be unconstitutional, *null* and *void*, and went on to order that it be struck off from the statute book. The government was badly aggrieved by this decision and appealed to the Court of Appeal of Tanzania. In the trial Court, as well as the Court of Appeal of Tanzania, the respondents' incisive argument was simple. They submitted that as they [respondent] had improved the land, they were, by reason that reason alone, entitled to compensation in the manner stipulated in the Constitution and that compensation was payable before their rights in land could be extinguished.

On the part of the government, it was submitted that the respondent could not seek protection under the provisions of the Constitution because they were holders of customary right of occupancy whose interests did not constitute "property". The respondent won the appeal in respect of the right to compensation. Precisely, the Court of Appeal came to a conclusion which deserves a long quote as it formed the basis of the law on compensation that came a few years later:

1125 [1995] TLR 80. The case is discussed at length in Chapter Two above.

1126 Reference is made to the *Regulation of Land Tenure (Established Villages) Act, 1992* [Act No.22 of 1992].

1127 See Miscellaneous Civil Cause No. 1 of 1993.

> *For all these reasons therefore we have been led to the conclusion that customary or deemed rights in land, though by their nature are nothing but rights to occupy and use the land, are nevertheless real property protected by the provisions of art 24 of the Constitution. It follows therefore that deprivation of a customary or deemed right of occupancy without fair compensation is prohibited by the Constitution. The prohibition of course extends to a granted right of occupancy. What is fair compensation depends on the circumstances of each case. In some cases a reallocation of land may be fair compensation. Fair compensation however is not confined to what is known in law as unexhausted improvements. Obviously where there are unexhausted improvements, the constitution as well as the ordinary land law requires fair compensation to be paid for its deprivation. We are also of the firm view that where there are no unexhausted improvements, but some effort has been put into the land by the occupier, that occupier is entitled to protection under art 24(2) and fair compensation is payable for deprivation of property. We are led to this conclusion by the principle, stated by Mwalimu Julius K Nyerere in 1958 and which appears in his book 'Freedom and Unity', published by Oxford University Press, 1966.*

We find the judgment in this case to be watermark for the obvious: it is through this judgment that the Court of Appeal of Tanzania recognised all holders of a right of occupancy including holders of customary or deemed rights of occupancy to have a right to fair compensation which is well stipulated by Article 24 (2) of the Constitution of the United Republic of Tanzania, 1977. It is also through this judgment that the Court affirmed that the right to compensation is founded on the philosophical principle and that it is payable as a return to a person's labour which was spent in the course of improving the land. Furthermore, the Court recognised various forms of compensation including reallocation of the land; and finally the Court affirmed that the right to compensation extends beyond the so-called "unexhausted improvements" and covers every effort that has been spent no the land by the occupier.

Compensation under the Land Acts[1128]

As can be grasped from the discussion above, the law on compensation was not free from some black spots until the coming of the Land Acts. Problems rose here and there in the overall administration of land law. It means, therefore, the *Land Acts* came to smooth the platform

1128 The Acts need to be read together with the Land (Assessment of the Value of Land for Compensation) Regulations, 2001.

by addressing the area on compensation more sufficiently and in the clearest terms, covering matters such as: entitlement to compensation; form, time and manner of compensation; and establishment and management of a Compensation Fund. So, in the first place, and as fundamental principle of the National Land Policy, the Acts recognise the right to a full, fair and prompt compensation of any person whose right of occupancy or recognised long-standing occupation or customary use of land is revoked or otherwise interfered with to his detriment by the State under the *Land Act* or under the *Land Acquisition Act*, and call upon all persons exercising powers under, applying or interpreting the Acts to have regard to this principle.[1129] In the second place, the *Land Act, 1999* provides for the criteria to be used in assessing the compensation payable which include: the market value of the real property; disturbance allowance; transport allowance; loss of profit or accommodation; cost of acquiring or getting the subject land, and; interest at the market rate[1130]. In the third place, the *Land Act, 1999* states the nature and mode of compensation payable to the holder of a right of occupancy. However, the Act strictly limits compensation to unexhausted improvements made in accordance with the terms and conditions of the right of occupancy at the time of revocation, and subject to deductions as the law directs.[1131] In the fourth place, the *Land Act, 1999* establishes the Land Compensation Fund[1132], whose object and purpose is to provide compensation to any person who suffers any loss or deprivation or diminution of any rights or interest in land[1133] at the hands of the Government or any public or local authority.

1129 See Section 3 (g) of, *the Land Act, 1999* and section 3 (h) the *Village Land Act, 1999*. See also section 34 (3) of the *Land Act, 1999*, which protects the rights of customary holders who occupy land that forms a subject matter of a granted right of occupancy, including the right to be relocated only when it is necessary to enable the purpose for which the right was granted and subject to paying them full compensation for loss of any interest in land and any other losses that may be incurred due to any move or interference with the occupation. Equally important, Section 14 (2) of the *Village Land Act, 1999* protects the rights of customary holders whose land may be acquired under the *Land Acquisition Act, 1967* [118 R.E 2002] or declared a planning area under the provisions of the *Town and Country Planning Act, 1956* [Cap. 355 R.E 2002].

1130 See the proviso to Section 3 (h).

1131 Section 49 (3).

1132 Section 173 (1).

1133 Section 173 (4).

Grey Areas in the Realization of the Right to Compensation

There is no doubt that the right to compensation in Tanzania is now well established under the law, both the Constitution and ordinary laws. However, there is much doubt if this right is really enjoyed by the people. One luminary in matters of land control and administration in Tanzania belives that there is still many problems on the realization of the right to compensation and pointed his accusing finger directly to the government by recording that:

> *Both the Constitution and Land laws state that land shall be expropriated according to the due process of the law, and that fair and prompt compensation should be paid. The compensation package in the case of appropriation has been improved and made clear under the Land laws to include value of land, disturbance, transport assistance and loss of profit. However, there is universal complaint against compulsory acquisition of land because the process of determining the rates used in determining the amount of compensation is not transparent and the affected always complain that they are being underpaid. Complaints against compensation usually do not succeed and the government has proceeded with project implementation even where there are cases pending in courts. Compensation is in most cases not paid on time and no remedial measures are taken as provided for under the law. The government, which is the one appropriating land determines the rates to be used, carries out and approves the valuation. The valuation is not sufficiently vetted. There are many disputes relating to dissatisfaction with compensation.*[1134]

It has been pointed out that the right to compensation in Tanzania is still a thorny issue for the reason that it is being violated quite often, even by the government, which seems not to learn from the past. The fact that we still witness illegal evictions, sometimes resulting in stiff resistance and/ or protracted litigation in the courts of law, tells clearly that the road to full realization of the right to compensation, in the proper meaning of the word, is still poorly paved. Despite the clear and sufficient law in the statute book today, there are still some grey areas that cannot go without a comment, if the right to compensation is to be fully enjoyed in practice and as a human right. These include, for example, the issue on entitlement to compensation, time of compensation, and the amount of compensation payable to the right holder.

1134 See KIRONDE, Lussunga J.M., "Improving Land Sector Governance in Africa: The Case of Tanzania", Paper Prepared for the workshop on "Land Governance in Support of the MDGs: Responding to New Challenges", Washington DC, March 9-10 2009.

Entitlement to Compensation

It was earlier noted that the right to compensation is premised on the philosophical doctrine of a "just return for a person's labour". However, since the law on compensation is not there to protect trespassers or to encourage any act of trespassing into another person's land, it follows, therefore, that any person is entitled to compensation if he establishes that he has invested his labour in the form of energy, or talent, or money to improve the land, and if he establishes further that at the time of carrying out such improvements he had apparent justification for doing so.[1135] It means that a person is not required to be the owner of the granted right of occupancy in order to qualify for entitlement to compensation. He may as well be a holder of a customary or deemed right of occupancy, an occupier in a recognised long-standing occupation or even an occupier of land under a valid licence. The issue of entitlement to compensation has turned to be the greyest area in respect of the right to compensation and has formed endless causes of action in many of the cut-throat litigations in the courts of law. The case of *Mtumwa Shahame, Baya Kondo & 111 Others v Principal Secretary, Ministry of Works and The Attorney General*[1136] is cited in support of the point. In this case, the first respondent formed an opinion that the plaintiffs, the residents of Mivinjeni, Mtoni Mtongani and Mtoni Kwa Azizi Ally along Kilwa Road area in Dar es Salaam, were trespassers in the Kilwa Road Reserve and in 2002 issued a notice under the provisions of the *Highway Act, Cap. 167*, ordering the plaintiffs and hundreds others not in court, to demolish their houses and vacate the area. The said residents resisted the order as they claimed for their right to compensation. The first defendant took the extra measures of employing a bull dozer to demolish the houses, forcing the residents to go to a court of law to claim their right to compensation.

In the court, it was argued for the residents that they were lawful and long time occupiers of the area and, therefore, were entitled to be compensated by the government before the move to evict them. On the part of the defendants, it was argued that the 1967 Highway Roads Act specified the Kilwa Road to have a width of 75 feet on either side, that the widening of the road was done in 1967 to the extent of 45 feet,

1135 See *Alli Mangosongo v Chrispina Magenje* [1977] LRT No. 18.

1136 High Court of Tanzania (Land Division), at Dar es Salaam, Land Case No. 31 of 2004 (Unreported).

leaving the reminder to the future, and that those who occupied land at that time were compensated, meaning that the plaintiffs' claim was not valid, and that they had been trespassing since 1967. It was further submitted for the defendants that the plaintiffs did not prove ownership of the land or the unexhausted improvements.

The court ruled in favour of the plaintiffs on the strength of the following reasons: first, the court found that the plaintiffs were not disproved in court to have been in continuous occupation of the land as customary holders who are protected under section 2 of the Highway Act; second, the court observed that the evidence adduced in court clearly showed that at no time since the first expansion of the Kilwa Road Highway did the defence take note of the new occupiers of the land by the road (including the plaintiffs) and if any action was taken by the defence to remove them from their acquired land for the future development, and; finally, the court found that the defence failed to tender in court the particulars of compensation they alleged to have paid in 1967 and this denied the court an opportunity to know who had been paid and left out.

The case teaches us one important aspect in the administration of land law that is to say; matters of entitlement to compensation, more often than not, carry some serious issues to be resolved by courts of law and on the weight of evidence to be adduced in court. It is, therefore, contrary to law when a government official, say a District Commissioner in the cases of Nyamuma and Loliondo evictions discussed earlier, or any other natural or artificial person such as the Tanzania Portland Cement Company Limited in the case of Wazo Hill Residents eviction case, raises his voice and says that someone is a trespasser on a certain land and undertakes to issue and execute eviction orders, sometimes at gun-point, without involving a court of law, and without regard to the duty to pay full, fair and prompt compensation.

It has been stated, above, that a person is entitled to the just return of his labour if he has made improvements on the land, and if at the time of effecting such improvement he had apparent justification or reason to do so. An occupier may be said to have apparent justification who, for example, buys and develops the land in good faith but later it transpires that the seller had in fact no title to such land which he could pass to the buyer. This doctrine of "apparent justification" is, however, another controversial area in land law. The doctrine suggests that not every improvement in the land is a subject of compensation. An occupier of the land may be disqualified from entitlement to compensation if he did not have apparent justification to carry out such improvement at a time when he did so. This is the position, for example, in the cases of *Ghina Abass v Peter Sylvester*[1137] and *Anna Benedict v Mrisho*[1138].

In the *Ghina Abass case*, the facts tell that the appellant had by an agreement licensed his farm to the respondent for a fixed term and on certain specific conditions, including a clause prohibiting the respondent from building permanent structures or planting permanent trees in the said farm. The respondent failed to honour the agreement by planting some permanent tress. When the term of the license expired, the appellant demanded his farm back but the respondent refused to vacate by insisting that he had the right to be compensated. The parties referred the matter to the Ward Tribunal of Msongola Ward which decided in favour of the appellant, that is, by ordering the respondent to vacate the land within six months, and made no order as to compensation. The respondent successfully appealed in the District Land and Housing Tribunal of Ilala, Dar es Salaam[1139], which reversed the decision by ruling that the respondent should be compensated by the appellant because the former had developed the land extensively. On the appellant's appeal in the High Court of Tanzania (Land Division), the Court allowed the appeal by disqualifying the respondent from entitlement to compensation. In essence the Court of Appeal's right reasoning was that the respondent had developed the land in contravention of the terms and conditions of the licence, he had overstayed after the expiry of the term of the licence, and the trial court had properly considered him by allowing him to reap the fruits which he had in the *shamba* (farmland).

The *Anna Benedict* case on the other hand records the following facts: a committee allocated a plot of land to the respondent when the same was already allocated to the appellant, Anna Benedict. The appellant filed a suit in the Resident Magistrates' court, claiming ownership of the land. The court held that the land belonged to her and ordered the respondent to vacate. However, the court upon declaring the appellant as a rightful owner of the land, ordered her to pay compensation to the

1137 High Court of Tanzania (Land Division), at Dar es Salaam, Misc. Land Appeal no. 5 of 2006 (Unreported). The facts, reasoning and decision of the High Court in this case are on all fours with the facts, reasoning and decision in the case of Alli Mangosongo v Chrispina Magenje [1977] L.R.T no. 18. The decisions from both cases tend to discourage people who undertake to develop the land, e.g, by growing permanent crops, in bad faith. Such people are not entitled to any compensation in respect of those crops.

1138 East African Court of Appeal, Civil Appeal No. 41 of 1976 (Unreported).

1139 Reference is made to Land Appeal No. 14 of 2005.

respondent for the improvements he had put on land. The appellant was aggrieved by the order of the court directing him to pay compensation to the respondent and appealed against that order to the High Court of Tanzania[1140] and later to the East African Court of Appeal. The argument in favour of the appeal was that the responded went on to build on the land even after he had notice that the land was in dispute. Both higher courts submitted to the general principle that a party should not reap the benefits of the improvements to the land affected by the opposite party without paying for such benefit and compensating the opposite party for this expenditure in so improving the value of the land[1141]. However, in this case, the East African Court of Appeal did not find it reasonable to force the appellant to take up a building which she might not have wanted to build in such a fashion since she might want to build a less expensive building altogether. The court was of the opinion that the most reasonable thing to do was to order the respondent to demolish his building and take away all his building materials within a certain, specified period.

The two cases above make it clear that a party who, being aware of some encumbrances upon a land, undertakes to develop it does so at his own peril. In a case of his being required to give a vacant possession to the rightful owner, he may not be heard to claim the right of compensation. He will be constrained by the doctrine of "apparent justification". A summary statement about entitlement to compensation made by the High Court of Tanzania in the case of *Ramadhani Kambi Mkinga v Ramadhani Said*[1142]:

> *Where A knowingly or recklessly enters upon B's land in circumstances that amount to a trespass, and B promptly (i.e. at the earliest possible opportunity) makes protests against his entry, A is not legally entitled to be paid any compensation by B for any of the improvements he might have effected on the land in the course of the trespass.*

It is submitted that this graphic presentation on entitlement to compensation is very important in two singular aspects: it disallows a trespasser from benefiting from the fruits of his illegal trespass, and it

1140 The case before the High Court of Tanzania is reported as *Anna Benedict v Seif Mrisho and Another* [1977] LRT No. 36.

1141 This principle has a base in the "equitable doctrine of unjust enrichment" and was articulated for the first time by the High Court of Tanzania in *Hamisi Sinahela v Assan Mbele* [1974] LRT No. 28.

1142 [1985] TLR 140 (HC).

imposes a duty upon the lawful owner of the land to protest against trespass at the earliest possible opportunity. Failure of this duty on the part of the owner might give right to compensation to the trespasser who enters the land and develops it for a long time without being disturbed.

Time of Payment, Nature and the Amount of Payable Compensation

It has been noted above that the law on compensation gives a right to compensation to an occupier of land when he is deprived of his land. The law dictates that such compensation must be *full, fair* and *prompt*. A close look at the legal scheme on the right to compensation shows that although the law provides for the right to full, fair and prompt compensation, it does not define what constitutes "fair" and "prompt" compensation. The reality on ground indicates that there have been numerous incidences of evictions, especially at the instance of the government, which involved payment of untimely and unfair compensation.

As regards "fair compensation" there are two questions which may be posed: what constitutes *fair* compensation? and, what is the standard measure of a *fair* compensation? Before the adoption of the *Land Acts,* it seems fair compensation was determined in the light of the "unexhausted improvements" found in the land at the time of deprivation or acquisition[1143]. However, a progressive departure from this position was plausibly articulated by the Court of Appeal of Tanzania[1144] when it stated that:

> *What is fair compensation depends on the circumstances of each case. In some cases a re-allocation of land may be fair compensation. Fair compensation, however, is not confined in what is known in law as enexhausted improvements. Obviously where there are unexhausted improvements, the Constitution as well as well as the ordinary law requires fair compensation to be paid for its deprivation. We are also of the*

1143 Note that the term "unexhausted improvement" is defined differently by the *Land Acquisition Act, 1967* [Ca. 118 R.E 2002] and the *Land Act, 1999* [Cap. 113 R.E 2002]. The former defines the term narrowly in section 12 (7) that "unexhausted improvements" means any quality permanently attached to the land directly resulting from the expenditure of capital or labour by a person holding under a right of occupancy or Government lease, or any person acting on his behalf or holding under him for a term of years, and increasing the productive capacity, utility or amenity thereof, but does not include the results of ordinary cultivation other than standing crops or growing produce". The latter's broad definition in section 2 is that, "unexhausted improvement" means any thing or any quality permanently attached to the land directly resulting from the expenditure of capital or labour by an occupier or any person acting on his behalf and increasing the productive capacity, the utility, or the sustainability of its environmental quality and includes trees, standing crops and growing produce whether of an agricultural or horticultural nature."

1144 See *Attorney General v Lohay Akonaay* (supra).

> *firm view that where there are no enexhausted improvements, but some effort has been put into the land by the occupier, that occupier is entitled to protection under Article 24 (2) and a fair compensation is payable for deprivation of property...*

The *Land Act, 1999*, for its part, limits compensation to be equal to the value of unexhausted improvements made in accordance with the terms and conditions of the right of occupancy, in the event of land being revoked for breach[1145]. It means that in any other cases determination of a fair compensation may consider other matters including the market value the real property; disturbance allowance; transport allowance; loss of profit or accommodation; cost of acquiring or getting the subject the land, the subject matter; any other cost, loss or capital expenditure incurred to the development of the land, and; interest at the market rate.

Yet, another acceptable method of determining a fair compensation has been the replacement method. By employing this method, one takes into account the type and age of the structures on the land and decides to pay compensation which is sufficient enough to facilitate the materials for putting up a similar structures elsewhere, including costs for getting another plot of land, transportation, inconvenience and loss of profit and accommodation for specified period.[1146]

That which is discussed above in relation to fair compensation leads to one general conclusion: that fair compensation is a matter to be decided by the circumstance of each case. It may take the form of money or re-allocation to an alternative land or both. To be accepted as fair, compensation must not be something to be unilaterally decided by a strong hand and arbitrarily imposed on the part of the weaker, but it must be evaluated with the most possible transparency and must, at the end of the day, be reasonable in the mind of any right thinking member of the community. Reflecting about the Tabata Dampo Demolition Saga (discussed at length in Chapter One above), for example, it is debatable as to whether the flat compensation at a rate of 20mil (Tshs.) for every demolished house, in addition to reallocation of the residents in Mbuyuni, was fair compensation or not. One thing is certain about this case: that the residents of the Tabata Dampo area had developed their respective pieces of lands differently depending on the economic

1145 See section 49 (3).

1146 The replacement method was affirmed as correct in the circumstance by the High Court of Tanzania in *Mtumwa Shahame, Baya Kondo &111 Others v Principal Secretary, Ministry of Works and Attorney General* (supra).

capacity of each occupier, meaning that some had temporary structures, others semi-permanent structures and still others permanent and well-furnished structures. So to have a flat compensation at the stated rate meant healthy and unexpected harvest, hence more than fair compensation to some of the occupiers, while to others this meant nothing but unfair compensation, which did not answer to the value of the capital invested in the demolished houses.

As regards "prompt compensation", again, the question is: what amounts to *prompt* compensation? It has already been pointed out that the legal scheme on the right to compensation does neither define the term prompt nor does it provide any time frame within which compensation is payable. So, whether the requirement of promptness is met in practice for the purpose of "prompt" compensation or not, this is another debatable issue and it depends, largely, on the definition that one may assign to the term "prompt". However, the legal and guiding principle is that a person ought not to be deprived of, or evicted from, the land until his interest in the land has been extinguished first[1147]. It follows that compensation shall be said to be "prompt" if it is paid in full immediately after the evaluation of the improvements in the land and before deprivation or eviction of a person from the land.

There is another area of great concern which needs to be considered in the area of legislation in future if we are to promote and protect human rights especially the right to housing (shelter). This is about the time frame between the date of extinguishing the occupier's interest in the land (paying full and fair compensation including reallocation of new lands) and vacation or eviction from the acquired land. Following the absence of any legal provision to provide for a reasonable time frame, the modern practice has shown that occupiers of land are asked "to pack their belongings up and go" in the soonest time immediately after (or even before) they are fully compensated. In other words, the modern practice does not give occupiers any reasonable time to establish themselves in the new areas, for example, by building new houses to secure their right to shelter, safety and security. The very recent case involving the Kipawa residents in Dar es Salaam is cited for reference. In this case, the government had formed an intention to acquire the land then under the occupancy of some residents (about 1,200) in Kipawa area, Dar es Salaam for the purpose of extension of the Mwalimu Nyerere International Airport. To effect its intention, the Government

1147 *Mtumwa Shahame, Baya Kondo and 111 Others v Principal Secretary, Ministry of Works and the Attorney General* (supra).

evaluated the land way back in 1997 and promised to compensate the affected residents for the value of their land plus the compound interest of 6% under the provisions of the Land Acquisition Act, 1967. However, nothing followed until 4th Febuary 2000 when it issued Government Notice No. 23/ 2000 vesting the said land to the President. However, the matter remained in a coma until late 2009, when Tanzania Airport Authority issued a 45 Notice to vacate to the Kipawa residents. In the said Notice the government not only committed itself to pay compensation and reallocate the residents new lands, but also ordered them to leave the area immediately, before it employed the bulldozer to demolish all the houses in the acquired area. Following the event, a substantial number of residents were not satisfied with the amount of compensation paid to them and the most courageous decided to institute a case in the court of law, claiming that they were denied the right to adequate compensation under the provisions of the *Land Act.* On the other hand, there some residents who obeyed the order and left as required only to find themselves in face to face with serious problems of resettlement in the new areas including land conflicts with some other people who claimed also to have prior interests in the allocated plots, insecurity and lack of social services in the areas of resettlement. As if this were not enough, some months later, the government, speaking through the District Commissioner of Ilala District, confirmed that some residents (about 195) did not get alternative land, and that the process was underway to reallocate them. One thing is certain, that until the resettlement was complete, there were some residents who were denied the right to fair compensation while others were denied their right to housing, at no fault of their own making. This case and others of a similar nature compel us to recommend that the law on compensation needs to be revisited in order to address the issue of time for compensation. This will allow all persons who suffer from deprivation of their land reasonable time to resettle to the new lands if problems of reallocation are to be avoided.

Chapter Nine

Land Disputes, Litigation and the Role of Courts in Tanzania

> Our democratic order requires an orderly and fair resolution of disputes by courts or other independent and impartial tribunals. This is fundamental to the stability of an orderly society. It is indeed vital to a society that, like ours, is founded on the rule of law.
>
> - Ngcobo, J.[1148] -

1148 *Barend Petrus Barkhuizen v Ronald Stuart Napier,* Constitutional Court of South Africa, Case No. CCT 72 of 2005, paragraph 31.

General Overview on Land Disputes and the Role of Courts in Tanzania

The term dispute can simply be defined to mean a disagreement on a point of law or fact or a conflict of legal view or interest. It was once stated by the International Court of Jutice that in order to establish the existence of a dispute, "it must be shown that the claim of one party is positively opposed by the other".[1149] In this context, the Court of Appeal of Tanzania defines "land dispute" to mean "complaints on ownership or occupation of land, which includes buildings and other structures permanently affixed to land"[1150]. A land dispute may arise, for example, if X claims that he is the legal owner of a piece of land over Plot No. 000, Block B, along Ubo Street in Dar es Salaam and Y, who disputes X's claim by saying that the land in question belongs to him instead. A cursory perusal of records, especially through the decided cases reveals that most land disputes arise in the context of various claims, the most common being: claims over or against the right to acquire land[1151]; claims based on the right of ownership of land (title) especially where there is double allocation[1152]; claims against the trespass of one person into the land of another[1153]; claims over the right to compensation in cases of unlawful and illegal evictions[1154]; claims based on non performance of contractual obligations by one part where there is a disposition[1155]; claims

---

1149 See *South West Africa Case*, (Preliminary Objection), Judgment, ICJ Reports, 1962, p. 328.

1150 See *Mariam Ghahae v Fatuma Ghahae*, Court of Appeal of Tanzania at Dar es Salaam, Civil Appeal No. 43 of 2009 (Unreported).

1151 See *Shaffique A.S. Dhiyebi v Presidential Parastatal Sector Reform Commission*, High Court of Tanzania (Land Division) at Dar es Salaam, Land Case No. 46 of 2004 (Unreported).

1152 See *Simon Byanyuma v A.E Halday*, High Court of Tanzania (Land Division) at Dar es Salaam, Land Case No. 27 of 2004. (Unreported), and; *Mohamed F Dossaji v Frederick Lwezaula*, High Court of Tanzania (Land Division) at Dar es Salaam, Land Case No. 25 of 2004, (Unreported).

1153 *Patrick Kimilo v Sheweji Ulinda and Another*, Court of Appeal of Tanzania at Dar es salaam, Civil Application No. 99 of 2001 (Unreported).

1154 See *Mtumwa Shahame Baya Kondo & 111 Others v Principle Secretary, Ministry of Works and Another*, High Court of Tanzania (Land Division) at Dar es Salaam, Land Case No. 31 of 2004, (Unreported).

1155 See *Rashid Halfan v Pendael Singa and National Housing Tribunal*, High Court of Tanzania (Land Division) at Dar es Salaam, Land Case No. 173 of 2004 (Unreported); *Beno Chelele t/a General Intergrated Firm v National Housing Corporation and 2 Others*, High Court of Tanzania (Land Division) at Dar es Salaam, Land Case No. 96 of 2004. (Unreported); *Shaidu Juma v Seleman Mussa*, High Court of Tanzania (Land Division) at Dar es Salaam, Land Case No. 18 of 2006, (Unreported), and *Riziki Habibu v Fatuma Juma*, High Court of Tanzania (Land Division) at Dar es Salaaam, Land Case No. 102 of 2004, (Unreported).

based on the right to inheritance of the deceased person's estate[1156], and claims over the right to matrimonial property.[1157]

Whenever a land dispute erupts, the hostile relationship is automatically born between the parties at dispute. In such a situation, and in order to avoid the fights and the consequences that might arise out of the hostile relationship, the law comes in rescue. Essentially, the law gives parties to a dispute the chance to settle their dispute by way of a suit. It is at this point, when the parties to a suit are in court, that we talk of litigation. In other words, there is a civil litigation or the *litis contestatio*, when there is a contested dispute involving two parties or two rival groups, one claiming some rights and the other opposing the existence of those rights, and when the contested right is a legal right as opposed to a moral right. In practice, parties in a dispute tend to approach the matter, in the first place, by way of negotiations before going to court. Therefore, courts are, more often than not resorted to when negotiations fail to harmonise parties or to deliver mutual satisfaction.

By courts of law, reference is made to those institutions which have been established by law and conferred the legal powers (jurisdiction) to administer justice according to law. This is the noblest duty of all courts of the land, and for this reason, courts of law are sometimes called the courts of justice or, as Mwesiumo, J.- as he then was puts it, "temples of justice"[1158]. It means that when all other amicable means of resolving the dispute cannot bear fruits parties find themselves compelled by law to seek the guidance of the court and the court has the duty to assist them to settle the dispute according to law. In societies where the rule of law is cherished such as in Tanzania, the courts of law are known and respected as being the only institutions which are mandated to determine the rights of all persons according to law. We see this very clearly in our Constitution, which states in black and white that courts are the final institutions with the final say in the determination of the

1156 For example, in *Tatu Mohamed v Maua Mohamed*, Court of Appeal of Tanzania at Dar es Salaam, Civil Appeal No. 31 of 2000 (Unreported).

1157 See, for example, *Hemed Tamim v Renata Mashayo* (1994) TRL 197 (CA); *Martini Mbujilo v Elizabeth Lucas*, High Court of Tanzania at Tabora, Civil Appeal No. 6 of 2003 (Unreported).

1158 In *Lalata Msongawale v Henry Mwamlima* (1979) LRT No. 3, the learned judge elegantly described the courts of law to be temples of justice when he said,"However, the courts of law in this country, just as is the case in any other country where the rule of law is cherished and enshrined by all concerned, are temples of justice in which it is expected by all reasonable members of the community that justice will not only be done but will be manifestly seen to be done".

rights of citizens (including the right to land) in the United Republic of Tanzania .[1159] With this legal mandate and in the event of a land dispute, courts are expected to receive a person's claim over his interest in land, proceed to determine the rights of the parties in that dispute in accordance with the rules of evidence and procedure, and make a decision and issue orders without fear or favour. The parties have a legal duty to respect the courts' orders in letter and in spirit in order to make the role of the courts meaningful. The opposite is to encourage endless disputes and litigations in courts and social disharmony or breach of peace in society. For this reason, we think that it is very important for all citizens to know the Tanzanian court system and the way it operates in the administration of land law. This knowledge does not only assist citizens to appreciate the role of the courts in the administration of land law, but it instils in them confidence and respect of the rule of law as opposed to the rule of whim and caprice.

Establishment, Composition and Powers of Land Courts

It is important to note that until the adoption of the *Land Act 1999*; all ordinary courts of competent jurisdiction (Ward Tribunal[1160], Primary Court[1161], District and Resident Magistrates Courts[1162], the High Court[1163], and the Court of Appeal of Tanzania[1164]) had the power to determine land disputes according to law. However, at one point immediately prior to the enactment of the *Land Act 1999*, these courts proved to be very inefficient in the adjudication of land disputes. Possibly due to population pressure and the importance attuned to land at the time, the Government, through the 1995 National Land Policy, and as a way of implementing the recommendation of the famous Shivji Commission, decided to create a distinct and efficient machinery for the purpose of handling the ever- increasing land disputes. The decision materialised when a new legislation, the present time *Land Act, 1999* was born. Section 167 of the Act introduced a special system of courts to deal with land matters. These courts operate hierarchically on the down-up basis

1159 See Article 107 A (1) & (2).

1160 Established by the *Ward Tribunals Act, 1985* [Cap. 206 R.E 2002].

1161 Established by the *Magistrates' Courts Act, 1984* [Cap. 11 R.E 2002].

1162 *Ibid.*

1163 Established by the *Constitution of the United Republic of Tanzania, 1977*, [Cap. 2. R.E 2002]

1164 *Ibid.*

and include the Village Land Councils, the Ward Tribunals, the District Land and Housing Tribunal, the High Court of Tanzania, and the Court of Appeal of Tanzania. The Land Act introducing this new system of courts was immediately followed by a specific law, the *Land Disputes Courts Act, 2002*[1165], which, according to its long title came "to provide for the establishment of land dispute settlement machinery and for matters incidental thereto".

The Village Land Councils

A Village Land Council, "the Council" is established in every village under section 60 (1) of the *Village Land Act, 1999*. The Council is composed of seven members, three of whom must be women, who are nominated by the Village Council and approved by the Village Assembly[1166]. The *Village Land Act, 1999* insists that members of the Council must be persons of integrity and knowledge of the customary land law[1167]. The main function of the Council is to mediate between and assist parties in a dispute to arrive at a mutually-acceptable solution on any matter concerning the village land. The Village Land Council performs its duties by receiving a complaint from a party, arranging for and calling a meeting with the parties to a dispute and mediating and assisting the parties accordingly. Three things are very important to note as regards the rights of the parties who seek the assistance of the Council: first, seeking the service of the Council is voluntary and for this reason, no person is compelled to refer the matter to the Council[1168]; second, parties or any of them has the liberty to refer the matter to a court of competent jurisdiction if he is dissatisfied by the decision of the Council or when he wishes to cease to make use of the service of the Council,[1169] and; third, the Council's role is mediatory as opposed to adjudicatory. It means that the duty of the Council is to assist the parties to settle the dispute amicably and therefore, it cannot make binding decisions or issue enforceable orders.

1165 [Cap. 216 R.E 2006]. The Act came into force on 1st October 2003.

1166 Per section 5 (1) of the *Land Disputes Courts Act*, 2002 [Cap. 216 R.E 2002]

1167 Section 60 (4).

1168 Section 61 (1) (2) (6) of the *Village Land Act, 1999* [Cap. 114 R.E 2002].

1169 Section 62 (1). According to section 9 of the *Land Disputes Courts Act, 2002* [Cap. 216 R.E 2002] a Court of competent jurisdiction, in this case, is the Ward Tribunal.

The Ward Tribunals

Ward Tribunals are established in every Ward under the provisions of section 3 of the *Ward Tribunals Act, 1985* and are vested with adjudicatory powers, as courts, to deal with matters under the Land Acts[1170]. The Tribunal's composition is the minimum of four and maximum of eight members, three of whom must be women.[1171] The functions of the Tribunal are twofold. In the first place, and as its primary role, the Tribunal performs a mediatory function of securing peace and harmony by mediating between and assisting the parties to a dispute to arrive at a mutually acceptable solution.[1172] In the second, the tribunal, as a competent court of law, determines land disputes arising out of the Land Acts.[1173] The Tribunal's jurisdiction, in all proceedings of civil nature, is limited, pecuniarily, to subject matter (land) whose value does not exceed three million[1174]. However, as it is not easy, sometimes, to prove on evidence, that a certain property is valued at three million, some Ward Tribunals have had the privilege of adjudicating on disputes involving subject matters whose face values have been apparently above three million. The case of *Lweshabura Mzinja v Julieta Jacob*[1175] truly underscores this proposition. In this case the appellant lost the case before the Ward Tribunal. He appealed and lost the appeal both in the District Land and Housing Tribunal and the High Court of Tanzania (Land Division) at Dar es Salaam. The main ground of his appeal in both appellate courts was that the Ward Tribunal erred in law and in fact by deciding the case, the subject matter of whose value was more than Tshs. 15 million. In other words, it was the appellant's argument that the Ward Tribunal decided the case when it had no pecuniary jurisdiction to do so. The High Court (Rugazia, J.) dismissed the appellant's ground of appeal in these words:

1170 See Section 10 (1) of the *Land Disputes Courts Act, 2002* [Cap. 216 R.E 2002]

1171 *Ibid*, Section 11.

1172 *Ibid*, Section 13 (1).

1173 .*Ibid*, Section 13 (2).

1174 *Ibid*, Section 15.

1175 High Court of Tanzania (Land Division) at Dar es Salaam, Misc. Land Appeal No. 7 of 2005 (Unreported).

> *...the respondent challenged the assertion claiming that it cannot hold water in the absence of a proper valuation. I think the respondent has a point in that, in the absence of a Valuation Report any attempt by any of us to attach value of the property is nothing but conjectural. Even the photographs annexed to the submission (unfortunately without court leave), cannot be of any assistance because I cannot dare, let alone attempt, to possess any expertise in the field of evaluation.*
>
> *This leg of ground one has to fail because we cannot estimate the value of the subject matter on speculation.*

The court's decision underscores one important point, that any person who wishes to challenge the pecuniary jurisdiction of the Ward Tribunal can successfully do so on the basis of a Valuation Report of an expert in the field of valuation. Over and above the issue of jurisdiction, there are some other important issues which, if not well known to the court or the parties to a suit, or when not properly observed, tend to create good grounds of faulting the Ward Tribunal's decisions on appeal, and consequently to prolong litigations in courts.

One of such matters is the issue of quorum of the Tribunal. Essentially, the law requires the Tribunal to be properly constituted by stating very clearly that, "The Tribunal shall in all matters of mediation consist of three members at least one of whom shall be a woman"[1176]. We learn two things from this provision. First, the law requires the quorum in matters of mediation to be three members including at least one woman. Second the law is silent on the required number of the members to form a quorum in a full trial. It means that reference need be made to section 11 of the Land Disputes Courts Act, 2002, which provides for a general composition of the Tribunal to be of four members, minimum and eight members, maximum. What is important is for the Tribunal to ensure that it is properly constituted to be able to form a legal decision or else the decision shall be faulted on appeal. The case of *Ameleck Ngajilo v Nuru Mohamed*[1177] supports this observation. The history of the case is founded on the application by the respondent before the Ward Land Tribunal for Charambe, in the district of Temeke, claiming to have been unlawfully dispossessed of her land by the appellant. The Tribunal heard

1176 Section 14 (1) of the *Land Disputes Courts Act, 2002*, [Cap. 216 R.E 2002].

1177 District Land and Housing Tribunal for Temeke District at Temeke, Land Appeal No. 33 of 2006 (Unreported).

the matter and decided it in favour of the respondent. The appellant was dissatisfied and appealed. One of the grounds of appeal was that the Ward Tribunal was improperly constituted. The District Land and Housing Tribunal found that the judgment of the Ward Tribunal was signed by the chairman and the secretary, but no quorum was indicated to evidence how many members heard the case. Allowing the appeal, the court (S. K. Mwandu) said:

> *Therefore the proceedings of the Ward Tribunal are nullified. The Ward Tribunal to write quorum on each attendance so as to ensure proper composition of the Ward Tribunal.*

The second issue concerns appearance before the Tribunal. As regards appearance, advocates are not allowed to appear before the Ward Tribunal.[1178] It means a party who knocks upon the doors of a Ward Tribunal must be prepared to state the case on his own without assistance from a recognised lawyer. Even parties to a case who wish to transfer cases form a Ward Tribunal to the District Land and Housing Tribunal in the desire to engage an advocate cannot be allowed to do so. This is what we learn at best from the case of *Fans William Muze v Kalumela Mlula*[1179] . In this case, the appellant faulted the decision of the trial Chairman of the District Land and Housing Tribunal of Kinondoni on the ground that the learned "Chairman erred in law and in fact in holding that a case from the Ward Tribunal cannot be transferred to the District Tribunal while there is a clear provision in the law that Advocates are not allowed to appear in the Ward Tribunal". In other words, it was the appellant's staunch argument that a person who wishes to engage an advocate must be allowed to transfer his case from the Ward Tribunal to the District Tribunal where advocates have a *locus standi*. The High Court (Rugazia, J.) dismissed this ground of appeal by saying that, "A case should not be transferred from the Ward Tribunal on the only ground that a party has engaged an advocate. This ground alone should not be acceptable". However, possibly due to the importance that the law attaches on right to representation, a relative or member of the household is allowed to appear before the Tribunal and

---

1178 Section 18 (1), *Land Disputes Courts Acts, 2002* [Cap. 216 R.E 2002]

1179 High Court of Tanzania (Land Division) at Dar es Salaam, Misc. Land Appeal No. 3 of 2005 (Unreported).

represent a party to a case[1180]. This position of the law tends to assist those parties who find themselves to be tongue tied, to be able to engage family members who are not shy to appear and defend a case in a court of law.

When it is properly constituted, and after observing any other procedural requirements, the Ward Tribunal has powers, as any other court, to order the recovery of possession of the disputed land, to order specific performance of contracts, to make orders in the nature of injunctions both mandatory and prohibitive, to award the amount claimed, compensation, costs and any other orders which the Tribunal may deem just[1181]. If the judgment debtor has failed to comply with Tribunal's orders, the Tribunal shall refer the matter to the District Land and Housing Tribunal for enforcement.[1182] An appeal to the District Land and Housing Tribunal is available to any party who is dissatisfied by the Tribunal's decision within forty-five days from the date of the decision. A second appeal goes to the High Court of Tanzania from the decision of the District Land and Housing Tribunal and it is filed in the High Court as a Miscellaneous Land Appeal.

The District Land and Housing Tribunals

The law empowers the Minister (responsible for legal affairs) to establish in each district, region or zone, a court to be known as the District Land and Housing Tribunal[1183], hereinafter referred to as the District Tribunal or simply the Tribunal, which exercises jurisdiction within the district, region or zone in which it is established[1184]. The functions of the court are governed, largely, by the provisions of the *Land Disputes Courts Act, 2002*[1185]; the Land Disputes Courts (The District Land and Housing Tribunal) Regulations, 2003[1186], "the Regulations", and by virtue of section 51 (1) of the Land Disputes Courts Act, *2002*; the *Civil Procedure Code*, 1966[1187] and *the Evidence Act, 1967.*[1188]

1180 *Ibid*, section 18 (2).

1181 See section 16 (1), Land Disputes Courts Act, *2002*, [Cap. 216 R.E 2002].

1182 *Ibid*, section 16 (3).

1183 *Ibid*, section 22 (1).

1184 *Ibid*, section 22 (2).

1185 [Cap. 216 R.E 2002].

1186 G.N No. 174 of 2003.

1187 [Cap. 33 R.E 2002].

1188 [Cap. 6 R.E 2002].

As far as composition is concerned, the District Tribunal is composed of the Chairman[1189] and not less than two assessors.[1190] Assessors are appointed by the Minister in consultation with the Regional Commissioner, the number being not more than seven for the court, with at least three of them being women[1191]. Assessors are supposed to be persons with knowledge on land and housing matters and customs and norms of the area in which the tribunal is established.[1192] Once appointed the assessors must subscribe to the Code of Conduct for Assessors[1193]. The role of assessors is to assist the Chairman to reach a just decision in the case. According to law, assessors are required to give their opinion before the Chairman reaches a judgment.[1194] However, the Chairman, though being legally required to take into account the opinion of the assessors, is not bound by it. Once he differs with their opinion, he must give reasons in the judgment for differing with the opinion of the assessors.[1195]

As regards matters of jurisdiction, the District Tribunal have original jurisdiction which is pecuniarily limited to fifty million, being the value of the property if the matter is about recovery of immovable property and forty million in other proceedings in which the subject matter is being capable of estimation at money value. [1196] The Tribunal also enjoys appellate[1197] as well as revisional[1198] jurisdictions over matters coming from the Ward Tribunals. From the time District Land and Housing Tribunals were established until the very recent High Court

---

1189 According to section 25 (1) Cap. 216, the Chairman is appointed by the Minister from amongst legally qualified persons, and by virtue of section 25 (2) of the same law, as amended by Act No. 12 of 2004, a Chairman of the Tribunal is required, before holding office, to take an oath before a judge of the High Court. A Chairman can be removed from office under the by the Minister after holding an inquiry under section 18 (2) of the *Land Act, 1999*, [Cap. 113 R.E 2002]. See Regulation 34 of the Regulations.

1190 Section 23 (1), [Cap. 216 R.E 2002]

1191 *Ibid*, section 26 (1).

1192 Per Regulation 33 (1) (a) the Regulations.

1193 T he Code of Conduct for Assessors appears in the Fourth Schedule to the Regulations.

1194 Section 23 (2), [Cap. 216 R.E 2002].

1195 Section 24, [Cap. 216 R.E 2002].

1196 Section 33 (2). The Tribunal enjoys unlimited jurisdiction only in all matters under the *Customary Leasehold (Enfranchisement) Act*, Cap. 377 and the *Regulation of Land Tenure Established Villages) Act, 1992*. [Cap. 267 R.E 2002].

1197 See section 34.

1198 Section 36 (1).

decision in the case of *Olam Tanzania Limited Property International v Baraka Mkondola*[1199], District Tribunals used to hear and determine land matters arising out of or affecting all categories of land. However, coming to the decision in Olam's case, the High Court of Tanzania (Chingwile, J.), decided that District Land and Housing Tribunals have no original jurisdiction to adjudicate matters concerning land registered under the *Land Registration Ordinance, Cap. 334*. In the High Court's reasoned opinion, in interpreting section 37 (1) (c) and (e) of the Land Disputes Courts Act, 2002, such jurisdiction resides exclusively in the High Court (Land Division) of Tanzania. Immediately after the decision of this case, all disputes involving registered lands and pending before the District Land and Housing Tribunals in the whole of Tanzania were halted in the course of waiting for a proper interpretation of the law by the Court of Appeal of Tanzania. Thanks to the Court of Appeal of Tanzania which, in exercising its powers under section 4 (3) of the Appellate Jurisdiction Act, has revised the Olam case and finally stated its position at page 17 of its ruling[1200] that:

> *...subject to territorial and pecuniary limits and the restrictions imposed by section 37 (1) ofthe Land Disputes Courts Act, District Land and Housing Tribunals have jurisdiction to hear and determine all land disputes arising under the Land Act, regardless of whether the said land is registered or not.*

As regards matters of procedure, proceedings in the Tribunal are commenced by the party or his representative (a relative or an advocate) who files an application in a prescribed form[1201] to the Tribunal. Once this is done other normal procedures such as issuing summons to the respondent;[1202] submission of Written Statements of Defence;[1203] hearing

---

1199 High Court of Tanzania (Land Division) at Mtwara, Land Appeal No. 14 of 2007 (Unreported), judgment delivered on 25 September 2009.

1200 See *Olam Tanzania Limited and 3 Others v Seleman S. Selemani and 4 Others*, Court of Appeal of Tanzania at Mtwara, Consolidated Civi Revisions No. 2, 3, 4, 5, & 6 of 2010, ruling made on 11th October 2010 (Unreported).

1201 See Form No. 1 in the Second Schedule to the Regulation.

1202 Regulation 5.

1203 Regulations 7 and 8.

of the case,[1204] and; delivering of judgment and issuing of the decree,[1205] follow. The Tribunal's judgement must satisfy all the provisions of Order XX Rule 4 of the *Civil Procedure Code, 1966,* that is to say, it must contain a concise statement of the case, the points for determination, the decision thereon and the reasons for such decision. In *The Registered Trustees of the Masjid Al-Kadiria v Ali Muhidini & 6 Others*[1206] the decision of the Land and Housing Tribunal for Temeke was faulted for failure of the Chairman to write the reasons for the decision made.

The Tribunal has powers to execute its own decrees and orders[1207]. The law gives the decree holder the right to apply for execution of the decree as soon as practicable after the pronouncement of the judgment or ruling.[1208] The decree holder's right to apply for execution goes hand-in-hand with the judgment debtor's right to object to the execution within fourteen days after an order is made against him requiring him to comply with the decree or order to be executed[1209], or to appeal against the decision of the Tribunal to the High Court[1210] and, by way of an interlocutory application, to apply for stay of execution.[1211]

The High Court of Tanzania

The High Court of Tanzania is, generally speaking, a constitutional creature, having been established by Article 108 (1) of the Constitution of the United Republic of Tanzania, 1977. Until the recent amendments, it was only the Land Division[1212] of the High Court, which had jurisdiction

---

1204 Regulations 11-17.

1205 Regulations 18-21.

1206 High Court of Tanzania (Land Division) at Dar es Salaam, Land Appeal No. 9 of 2006 (Unreported).

1207 Section 33 (3), [Cap. 216 R.E 2002].

1208 See Regulation 23 (1) of the Regulations. Application for execution is made in a prescribed form, that is, Form No. 3 to the Second Schedule of the Regulations.

1209 Regulation 23 (3) and (4).

1210 Regulation 24.

1211 Regulation 25 (1).

1212 Section 167 (1) (b) of the *Land Act*, 1999 read together with the High Court Registries (Amendment) Rules, 2003, Government Notice No. 301 of 2003, dated 19 September, 2003.

to entertain land matters. However, in his move to curb the problem of a shortage of judges sitting in the Land Division, and the obvious consequences of congestion of land cases in court, the Chief Justice of Tanzania (Hon. Augustine Ramadhani) has appointed all judges of the High Court to be judges of the High Court (Land Division). It means that from the date of appointment[1213], land matters can be filed in, and adjudicated by any judge of the ordinary registry of the High Court. This administrative move by the Chief Justice has been followed by the Written Laws (Ammendments) Act No. 2 of 2010 which amends Section 167 (1) (b) of the *Land Act, 1999* by deleting the words "Land Division" and conferring powers to the ordinary registry of the High Court to hear and determine land disputes. The High Court has unlimited jurisdiction. When it comes to land matters specifically, the High Court has the exclusive original jurisdiction to entertain, among others[1214], proceedings for the recovery of possession of immovable property whose value exceeds fifty million; other proceedings where the subject matter is capable of being estimated at money value exceeding forty million; proceedings under the *Tanzania Investment Act, 1997*, the *Land Act, 1999* and *Land Acquisition Act, 1967* involving the Government, and; proceedings involving Public Corporations specified in the Rent Restriction (Exemption) (Specified Parastatals) Order, such as the National Housing Corporation.[1215] The Court also has appellate as well as revisional jurisdiction over decisions of District Land and Housing Tribunals[1216]. According to the law[1217], the High Court when hearing appeals under section 38 shall be constituted by a single judge sitting with two assessors. This suggests that sitting with assessors in any other proceedings, other than appeals under section 38 of the Land

1213 The letter of appointment was issued by the Chief Justice on 1st December, 2009.

1214 Section 37 (a) (b) (c) and (d).

1215 Section 37 (2) of the Land Disputes Courts Act as amended by Act No. 11 of 2005 provides that where the Land Division of the High Court is not operational within any district, the Land and Housing Tribunal shall have the jurisdiction to determine a dispute involving public corporations specified under subsection (1) (d).

1216 See section 38 for appeals originating in the Ward Tribunal and section 41 for appeal against the decision of the District Land and Housing Tribunal when exercising original jurisdiction.

1217 Section 39 (1), [Cap. 216 R.E 2002].

Disputes Courts Act, is optional. The cases of *Simon Byanyuma v A.E Halday*[1218] and *Fatuma Ghahae v Mariam Ghahae and National Housing Corporation*[1219] offer some examples in which the court made good use of assessors. In Simon Byanyuma's case the trial judge (Honourable Kileo, J.- as she then was) sat with the two assessors and she repeatedly fell back on the assessors' opinion in delivering her judgment, for example when she said:

> *Both assessors were of the opinion that the extraordinary speed with which the plaintiff obtained the title raises many questions. I entirely agree. I cannot help but think that the circumstances of this case strongly suggest that there was some dishonesty somewhere, which led to the plaintiff being offered plot no 46 while the same plot had previously been offered to the defendant*[1220].

In Fatuma Ghahae's case, again, the trial judge (Honourable Longway, J.- as she then was) sat with assessors but, unlike Kileo, J. above, decided to differ with assessors when she said:

> *I do see that the honourable assessors hold the view that favours the plaintiff and her recommendations, but viewing as I do the evidence technicality, I am unable to agree with them. The complaint lacks proof for it to be proven.*[1221]

In matters of procedure, the court is governed by the provisions of the Land Disputes Courts Act, 2002; the Civil Procedure Code, 1966 the Evidence Act, 1967 and any other procedural law whose application in the High Court is unlimited. As regards other rights of the parties, parties have a bundle of rights in the Court, including the right to apply for execution of decrees and orders of the Court by the successful party and the right to object such execution, to apply for stay of execution pending, for example, appeal, and other interlocutory orders may be

---

1218 High Court of Tanzania (Land Division) at Dar es Salaam, Land Case No. 27 of 2004, Judgment of 13th October, 2005 (Unreported).

1219 High Court of Tanzania (Land Division) at Dar es Salaam, Land Case No. 261 of 2004, Judgment of 6th March 2006 (Unreported).

1220 See page 6 of the judgment.

1221 See page 10 of the judgment.

sought in the court in accordance with the relevant rules of evidence and procedure. An appeal by the party who is aggrieved by the decision of the High Court (Land Division) in the exercise of its original, revisional or appellate jurisdiction goes to the Court of Appeal.[1222]

It is not surprising to learn that, at times, parties have decided to refer disputes on some land matters to the Commercial Division of the High Court, instead of the Land Division. The reason is that the [1223]law confers powers to the High Court (Commercial Division) to adjudicate on land matters of commercial nature. When the case of *NBC Holding Corporation v Shirika la Uchumi na Kilimo (SUKITA) and 63 Others*[1224] was filed in the Commercial Court, the defendants objected, among other things, to the jurisdiction of the court to entertain the suit. The Court (Dr. Bwana, J.- as he then was) overruled the objection by saying that the this case falls in the class of commercial cases which, according to R.2 of the Rules, GN 141/ 1999, are civil cases involving a matter considered to be of commercial significance including but not limited to "the contractual relationship of a business or commercial organisation with our bodies or persons outside." A good number of cases on land matters that have been adjudicated by the Court have been those cases arising out of breach of mortgaged contracts.[1225]

The Court of Appeal of Tanzania

The Court of Appeal of Tanzania, being the highest Court of the land in the judicial hierarchy, and having the final appellate and revisional jurisdiction in all matters, landed and non-landed matters, union and non union matters, and being placed in the top position of the judicial ladder to set precedents and binding principles to all other courts subordinate to it, is the Court that has, most exhaustively, attracted the attention of researchers and writers in and outside the legal profession. It is, to say the least, the Court on whose shoulders rests a heavy load

1222 Section 47 (1), [Cap. 216 RE 2002].

1223 Rule 2 of the High Court Registries (Amendment) Rules, G.N 141 of 1999.

1224 High Court of Tanzania (Commercial Division) at Dar es Salaam, Commercial Case No. 24 of 2001 (Unreported).

1225 See Chapter Three, above.

of literature, both for the better and for the worse.[1226] The focus of the author in this book is, therefore, limited just to some matters of relevance in relation to the role of the Court in the administration of land law. Like the High Court of Tanzania, the Court of Appeal is also a constitutional creature. Article 117 (1) of the Constitution establishes the Court of Appeal of Tanzania and confers upon it the jurisdiction of the Court of Appeal in accordance to the Constitution and any other law. That other law, in matters concerning land in Tanzania Mainland include the *Land Disputes Courts Act*, and the *Appellate Jurisdiction Act*[1227] under which

1226 See, for example, RAMADHANI, Idd, (2007): "The Court of Appeal of Tanzania: Its Positivistic Policy and Justice", LL.M Dissertation, UDSM; MFALILA, Lameck. M. S., " Twenty Five Years of the Court of Appeal and the Independence of the Judiciary" in BISIMBA, H.K. & PETER, C.M., (2007): *Law and Justice in Tanzania: Quarter a Century of the Court of Appeal*, Dar es Salaam, Mkuki na Nyota Publishers, p. 81; LUBUVA, Z., " The Court Structure and the Need for the Establishment of an Appellate Court above the Court of Appeal" in BISIMBA, H.K. & PETER, C.M., *ibid*, p. 99; NGALO, Colman, " Rules of the Court of Appeal of Tanzania" in BISIMBA, H.K. & PETER, C.M., *ibid*, p. 113; FIMBO, G.M., "Customary Tenure in the Court of Appeal of Tanzania" in BISIMBA, H.K. & PETER, C.M., *ibid*, p. 139; NGULUMA, Alex T., "The Court of Appeal of Tanzania and the Development of Insolvency Law in Tanzania: A Historical Perspective" in BISIMBA, H.K. & PETER, C.M., *ibid*, p. 173; RAMADHAN, Augustino S.L., Twenty Five Years of the Court of Appeal of Tanzania and the Establishment of the East African Court of Justice" in BISIMBA, H.K. & PETER, C.M., *ibid*, p. 223; PETER, Chris Maina, "The Contribution of the Court of Appeal of Tanzania in the Maintenance and Safeguarding of the Rule of Law and Human Rights" in BISIMBA, H.K. & PETER, C.M., *ibid*, p. 237; COURT OF APPEAL OF TANZANIA, (2004): *The History of Administration of Justice in Tanzania*, Dar es Salaam: Mathews Bookstore & Stationers; JESSE, J., (1999): "The Role of the Court of Appeal of Tanzania in Educating and Guiding the Legal Profession: Reflection of the Last Ten Years (1988-1998)", LL.B Dissertation, UDSM; BAHROOM, (1993): The Role of the Court of Appeal of Tanzania: With Particular Reference to Cases on the Right to Liberty", LL.M Dissertation, UDSM; BAHATI, A., "The Court of Appeal and Development of Laws Relating to Commercial Transactions", Volume 16 No. 2 *Eastern Africa Law Review*, 1989, p.89; FIMBO, G.M., "The Court of Appeal of Tanzania: Tasks of Educating and Guiding the Legal Profession", Volume 16 No.2 *Eastern Africa Law Review* 1989, p.44; FIMBO, G.M., "The Court of Appeal of Tanzania: A Decade of Land Law Development", Volume 16, No. 2 *Eastern Africa Law Review* 1989, p. 101; FIMBO, G.M., "The Court of Appeal of the United Republic of Tanzania: A Descriptive Essay", Volume 16 No.2 *Eastern Africa Law Review*, 1989, p. 229; MAPUNDA, A.M., *et al.*, "Reflection on the *Stare decisis* on the Court of Appeal of the United Republic of Tanzania", Volume 16 No. 2 *Eastern Africa Law Review*, 1989, p. 1; MKUDE, T.L. and FIMBO, G.M., "The Court of Appeal of Tanzania on Civil Practice and Procedure", Volume 16 No.2 *Eastern Africa Law Review*, 1989, p. 24; NDITI, N.N.N., " The Court of Appeal of Tanzania and the Development of Commercial Law", Volume 16 No. 2 *Eastern Africa Law Review*, 1989, p. 66; RWEZAHURA, B.A., "Court of Appeal of Tanzania and the Development of the Law of Domestic Relations", Volume 16 No. 2 *Eastern Africa Law Review*, 1989, p. 146; WAMBALI, M.K.B., "The Court of Appeal of Tanzania and the Development of the Law of Torts", Volume 16 No. 2, *Eastern Africa Law Review*, 1989, p. 213; NGONYANI. G., (1988): "The Nature of the judicial Process in the Post Independence era in Tanzania: An Analysis on the Role of the Court of Appeal of Tanzania", LL.M Dissertation, University of Dar es Salaam.

1227 [Cap. 141 RE 2002].

are made the Court of Appeal Rules which provide for the procedure to be followed when litigating land matters before the Court.

The Court is conferred jurisdiction to hear and determine appeals from the High Court (Land Division).[1228] However, there are two basic requirements that go with appeals to the Court: Leave of the High Court (Land Division) is one such basic requirement before one can appeal to the Court.[1229] Also, for appeals originating from the Ward Tribunal, a Certificate of the High Court (Land Division) certifying that there is a point of law involved in the appeal is another such requirement.[1230] Once an appeal is properly filed in the Court, Court enjoys all the powers of an appellate court to allow or not to allow the appeal, and to make any other consequential orders, as the Court may deem fit.

It is well on record that the position of the law on the requirement of leave by the High Court (Land Division) to appeal to the Court of Appeal was, in one instance, considered to be bad law, but was saved by the Court of Appeal of Tanzania on technical grounds. This was in the case of *Dero Investment Ltd v Heykel Berete*.[1231] Briefly, the facts of the case were that the appellant, having been aggrieved by the ruling of the High Court Land Division at Dar es Salaam (in Land Case No. 6 of 2004) appealed to the Court of Tanzania, but, without first seeking leave of the Court to appeal as required under section 47 (1) of the Land Dispute Courts Act. The Respondent, through his legal Counsel, filed a notice of preliminary objection in that although the appeal lies against a decree of the High Court (Land Division) in its original jurisdiction, the appellant ought to have sought leave from the court as required under section 47 (1) of the Land Dispute Courts Act. It was argued for the appellants, *inter alia*, that section 47 (1) is inconsistent with section 5 (1) of the Appellate Jurisdiction Act under which appeals against original decrees of the High Court do not require leave. The Counsel for the respondent also conceded that the section is problematic and even unconstitutional as it unnecessarily curtails the right to appeal especially where leave might be refused. The Court considered the submission by the Counsel and observed that:

1228 See section 48 (1), [Cap. 216 R.E 2002].

1229 *Ibid*, section 47 (1).

1230 *Ibid*, section 47 (2).

1231 Court of Appeal of Tanzania at Dar Es Salaam, Civil Appeal No. 92 of 2004 (Unreported).

> *There is no clue in the Act or in section 47 why all appeals from decisions of the Land Division of the High Court, except in a case originating in the Ward tribunal, need leave of that Division of the High Court. In particular, it is not the norm that appeals from decisions of a division of the High Court in its original jurisdiction should require leave of that division of the High Court. To that extent section 47 (1) of the Act may be said to be an anomaly.*

Despite this Court's observation the Court went on to hold that:

> *Our reading of section 47 (1) of the Act gives us a firm conviction that Parliament, curiously, intended every word of that provision. In other words it intended the departure from the provisions of section 5 (1) (a), of the Appellate Jurisdiction Act, 1979.*

In conclusion the Court was of the view that:

> *It may well be that in restricting appeals to the Court of Appeal from decisions of the High Court (Land Division) in its original jurisdiction Parliament was curtailing the constitutional rights of the litigants. If it is thought so however, an aggrieved party or parties may wish to argue it before the High Court in a constitutional case. It cannot be argued and decided in the first instance in this Court. We therefore uphold the preliminary objection and strike out the appeal as incompetent for non-compliance with section 47 (1) of the Land Disputes Courts Act, 2002.*

Of the many decision that the Court of Appeal of Tanzania has made in the course of handling land disputes, the decision of the Court in *Haruna Mpangaos & Others v Tanzania Portland Cement Company Limited*[1232] deserves our attention. A bloody dispute arose between the residents and the Cement Company over the right to land, the former claiming customary rights in the land nearing the factory premises in the Wazo Hill area, Dar es Salaam and the latter claiming granted rights of occupancy over the same land. The resident lost the case in the High Court of Tanzania[1233] but decided to appeal in the Court of Appeal. They applied for the order of stay of execution pending the determination of their appeal but lost badly before a single judge[1234]. They applied for and

1232 Court of Appeal of Tanzania, Civil Reference No. 3 of 2007 (Unreported).

1233 This was Civil Case No. 173 of 2003.

1234 Civil Application No. 171 of 2006.

won in a reference before the three justices of appeal who sympathised with the fate of the residents if execution were not to be stayed. The reasoning of the three justices of appeal was heavily founded on the right to housing which, as we noted earlier, is a human right per se.

> *The question is, as between the applicants and the respondent, which one would be more inconvenienced if a stay order is not granted? Execution of a decree would mean that the houses in which the applicants are accommodated with their families will have to be demolished giving way to quarrying activities. The applicants would of necessity have to be evicted from their homes. We are of the firm view that the applicants would suffer greater injury if a stay is refused than the respondent will suffer if it is granted...We order that the execution of the decree of the High Court be stayed while the parties await the outcome of the appeal.*

Legal Technicalities Affecting a Person's Right to Land

The reality about rights, both legal and human, is that, it is one thing to have a certain right, and quite another thing to realise that right both in law and in practice. The reason is that there are several technical and practical factors that tend to limit wholly or partly, a person's right to land. Some of these may appear in the form of deliberate denial of a person's right to access land, for example, by way of illegal evictions; others may be attributed to socio-economic realities including extreme poverty that tend to limit the person's purchasing power over lands in the market and societal attitudes and perceptions through which certain categories of persons (such as women) are denied the right to acquire land, and; yet others fall in the category of legal technicalities by which a person's right to land is affected because of failure to comply with legal requirements in the course of claiming the right to land through the courts of law. Such a failure may result out of practical difficulties or mere ignorance of the rules of evidence and procedure. This part discusses in details some of the legal technicalities that tend to affect a person's right to land.

Legal Limitation of Actions

It is a cardinal principle of law that any person who has a legal claim against another must present it in a court of law by way of a civil suit within a prescribed period of time, counted from the time when the cause of action[1235] accrued. This simply means that, if a person has a legal claim (including claims over the right to land) against another, but does not present it to court within the the period prescribed by law, he will lose it. The rationale behind the philosophy on the law of limitation of actions is best explained by the South African Court of law in the case of *Mahlomi v Minister of Defence*[1236] that:

> *Rules that limit the time during which litigation may be launched are common in our legal system as well as many others. Inordinate delays in litigation damage the interest of justice. They protract the dispute over the rights and obligations sought to be enforced, prolonging the uncertainty of all concerned about their affairs. Nor in the end is it always possible to adjudicate satisfactorily on cases that have gone stale. By then witnesses may no longer be available to testify. The memories of ones whose testimony can still be obtained may have faded and become unreliable. Documentary evidence may have disappeared. Such rules prevent procrastination and those harmful consequences of it. They thus serve a purpose to which no exception in principle can cogently be taken.*

We need not dig deep into the history of the law of limitation in this work; suffice to record that the first law of limitation was the English statute enacted in 1623-24 which made limitation period for recovering land to be twenty years.[1237] In our present time, we have legislation on limitation of actions in all Western legal systems, such as the English Limitation Act[1238], the Indian Limitation Act[1239], and the Tanzanian Law of *Limitation Act, 1971*[1240]. In all these pieces of legislation, there are three basic and essential elements for consideration as we undertake to discuss limitation of actions, namely: the length of the period of limitation; the

---

1235 The term "cause of action" may simply be defined to mean all facts or circumstances that give a plaintiff a right to sue the defendant. See *MIC (T) v Tanzania Telecommunications Company Ltd (TTCL)*, High Court of Tanzania (Commercial Division) at Dar es Salaam, Commercial Case No. 146 of 2002 (Unreported) and *Ramadhani Mussa v Francis Migilimo and Another*, High Court of Tanzania at Tabora, D.C Civil Appeal No. 13 of 2002 (Unreported). The courts have, in both cases, explained at length the meaning of the term cause of action.

1236 1997 (1) SA 124 (CC) at p. 11.

1237 BURKE, Barlow *et al.*, (2004): Fundamentals of Property Law, Second Edition, at p. 107.

1238 1980.

1239 1908.

1240 [Cap. 89 R.E 2002].

time when a course of action is said to accrue, and; the effect of lapse of time. All Acts provide for the period of limitation in an action to recover possession of land to be twelve (12) years[1241], meaning that any action to recover land, which is instituted after the expiry of this period is said to be time barred and must, as a consequence, fail under the law.[1242] As to when time starts to run, this is an area of law that requires a detailed discussion. According to the legal provisions, commencement of time is counted from the date on which the right of action accrues.[1243] In an action for recovery of land, for example, time is said to accrue when there is an act of dispossession of the land of the claimant by a trespasser.[1244] The twelve years rule under the Limitation Act applies in respect of all matters which are commenced in the District Land and Housing Tribunal and the High Court (Land Division).[1245] In other words, the Law of Limitation Act applies only in these institutions. A similar rule applies in relation to suits commenced in the Ward Tribunals but under a different law.[1246]

There are certain exceptions to the rule in which a person can institute a suit when the period of limitation has expired. One category involves the exclusion of certain periods in computing the time. For example, if a person is under disability at the time when the course of action accrues, computing time shall start when that person ceases to be under disability or when he dies.[1247] The second category involves the extension of time by half of the period described by law by the Minister responsible for legal affairs by virtue of the powers conferred upon him by the law.[1248] However, the Minister may only exercise this power when he is of the opinion that it is just and equitable to grant extension of time, and after he has consulted the Attorney General and if he acts under his own hand.

1241 See item No. 22 to the First Schedule of the Limitation Act, [Cap. 89 R.E 2002].

1242 Section 3 (1) of the *Limitation Act, 1971* [Cap. 89 R.E 2002] provides for the dismissal of proceedings instituted after the period of limitation.

1243 Section 4.

1244 See the details in Section 9.

1245 See section 52 (2), [Cap. 216 R.E 2002].

1246 The Customary Law (Limitation of Proceedings) Rules, GN No. 311 of 1964, item 6 of the Schedule to the rules.

1247 Section 15, [Cap. 89 R.E 2002].

1248 *Ibid*, section 44.

Apart from the institution of suits which must be within a given time of limitation, other proceedings, including appeals and other applications are equally limited by time. The time being much shorter for such application (normally in terms of days) than time fixed for suits. There are various procedural laws that govern limitation of action in matters of applications including the Law of Limitation Act, the Land Disputes Courts Act,[1249] the Civil Procedure Code, the Appellate Jurisdiction Act and Court of Appeal Rules made thereto. The power to extend time to make applications other than to institute a suit is a discretionary power to be exercised by the court[1250] which either issued a given order or which has appellate jurisdiction, and when it [court] is requested to do so by a party to a suit. This is the gist of section 14 (1) of the *Law of Limitation Act* which states very clearly that:

> *14-(1) Notwithstanding the provisions of this Act, the court may, for any reasonable or sufficient cause, extend the period of limitation for the institution of an appeal or an application, other than an application for the execution of a decree, and an application for such extension may be made either before or after the expiry of the period of limitation prescribed for such appeal or application.*

The point we wish to undeline, here, is that not being aware of, or deliberate failure to comply with, the law on limitation of actions has turned to be a legal obstacle for most people to realise their right to land. There is on record a litany of cases in which parties have lost their claims over the right to land due to simple reason that their actions before the courts of law are barred by time. In *Mohamed Hassan Hole v Keya Jumanne Ramadhani*[1251] which is of such cases, the parties thereto disputed over a piece of land. The facts of the case were that the appellant filed a suit against the respondent claiming an acre of land which was occupied by the respondent. He argued that the land had belonged to his father, one Hadji Hassan Hole. Hassan Hole died in 1977 and his son, the appellant, was appointed to administer his deceased father's estate. Another piece of evidence, in opposition, showed that earlier on that piece of land had been allocated to the respondent during operation vijiji in 1974. The appellant lost the suit to recover the land from the respondent in all courts, that is, the Primary Court of Bereko, Kondoa

1249 [Cap 216, R.E 2002].

1250 See the relevant provision of law, such as Section 14 (1), [Cap. 89 R.E 2002].

1251 Court of Appeal of Tanzania at Dodoma, Civil Appeal No. 19 of 1992 (Unreported).

District Court, the High Court of Tanzania at Dodoma, and finally the Court of Appeal of Tanzania, on point of limitation. Dismissing the appeal, the Court of Appeal of Tanzania (speaking through Mnzavas, J.A- as he then was, said:

> *However we fail to understand why the appellant was so dilatory in pursuing his claim after his father's death in 1977. If the record is anything to go by he filed his claim against the respondent in 1989 about 13 years after his father's death. This was after the respondent had developed the land and planted seasonal and permanent crops and erected a permanent building on the land.*[1252]

As regards limitation of actions in appeals and applications, the case of *Abdulrasul Ahmed Jaffer and 2 Others v Parin A. Jaffer and Another*[1253] offers the best legal position. In the case, the respondents, a son and his father, made an application in the High Court[1254] for the rectification of the Land Register[1255], arguing that the lease in respect of Plot no 2254 Block 83 Mwisho/Zaramo Street in Dar es Salaam, was wrongly granted to the 1st respondent, and further that the entry of his name in Land Register was obtained by fraud or under a mistake. The application was met with objections on several points of law, one of them being the limitation of time under item 21, part III of the First Schedule to the Law of Limitation Act, which requires all applications under the Civil Procedure Code, the Magistrates' Courts Act or other written law for which no period of limitation is provided in the Act or any other written law, to be made within sixty days. The applicants' application was made in gross excess of this period and without moving the court for the order to grant extension of time. In its ruling, the High Court (Mapigano, J.- as he then was), granted the extension of time *suo motu* on the basis of the reasons advanced by the court that, "Provisions which give exceptions to the operation of the statute are, in principle, to be interpreted liberally", and also that, "All High Courts in India are now in agreement that for the purpose of section 14 ignorance or bonafide mistake of law may be

1252 See p. 3 of their Lordship's judgement. In its judicial reasoning, the Court cited with approval the cases of *Shabani Nassoro v Shabani Simba* (1967) HCD 233 and *Simon Osita v Adrianus Serere* (1968) HCD No. 21.

1253 Court of Appeal of Tanzania at Dar es Salaam, Civil Appeal No. 5 of 1994 (Unreported).

1254 See Misc. Civil Cause No. 48 of 1992.

1255 The application was made under section 99 (1) (b) (d) and (f) of the Land Registration Ordinance (Act), [Cap. 334 R.E 2002], as well as section 95 and Order 43 rule 2 of the Civil Procedure Code, 1966.

taken into consideration in determining whether the discretion ought to be exercised". The appellants were severely aggrieved by the ruling pronounced by the High Court, hence they appealed against it in the Court of Appeal of Tanzania.

The Court of Appeal, guided by section 14 (1) of the *Law of Limitation Act*, faulted the learned trial judge and allowed the appeal by stating emphatically at page 7-8 that:

> *The Court's discretion under section 14 (1) reproduced above should be exercised only upon an application being made to the Court in that behalf, and both sides have been given the opportunity of being heard. Such approach puts the court in a position where it can properly determine whether or not reasonable or sufficient cause has been disclosed for extending the time, and serves to ensure that the court's discretion is exercised judicially. In the instance case no such application was made and, therefore, the learned judge wrongly invoked the provisions of the section.*

The Court reached this conclusion after it had expressed its fear that, "Where the Court, acting on its own initiative, proceeds to extend the time this may bring about an undesirable or anomalous situation". It should be noted that in this case, and many similar others, courts, not to mention the Court of Appeal of Tanzania, have been very strict whenever limitation of time has been in question. In *Godwin Ndewesi and Another v Tanzania Audit Corporation*[1256], the Court of Appeal of Tanzania (Mnzavas, J.A- as he then was) struck out, as incompetent, the notice of appeal which was filed one day after the expiry of the period of limitation. Also in *MT 11168 Corporal Kafuku Kandusi v The Minister of Defence and Attorney General*[1257] the application filed in court out of time was mercilessly dismissed after the Court (Kalegeya, J.- as he then was) had reached the conclusion that:

1256 Court of Appeal of Tanzania, at Dar es Salaam, Civil Application No. 57 of 1994 (Unreported). Other cases where the Courts were very strict on points of limitation include *Edward Msango v Aga Khan Sports Clube*, High Court of Tanzania at Dar es Salaam, Civil Application No. 15 of 2002 (Unreported) in which the court said ignorance of law on limitation constitutes no good reason to move the court to grant extension of time, and *Abdallah Salanga & 63 Others*, Court of Appeal of Tanzania at Dar es Salaam, Civil Application No. 4 of 2001 (Unreported) in which the Court held that the inability of the applicants to raise money to engage an advocate, if it results in delay to file an application, does not make it good cause to move the court either.

1257 High Court of Tanzania at Dar es Salaam, Civil Application No. 107 of 2007 (Unreported).

> *It is trite law that when it comes to limitation of time the court cannot extend even a grain however sympathetic it may be to the applicant/ litigant. Limitation of time is a merciless monster that entertains no spek of sympathy whatsoever unless the leeway is provided by law.*

From all the above, we learn that limitation has a direct negative effect against a person's legal rights in that whenever limitation of time is successively raised as a point of preliminary objection against a suit or proceedings instituted by the claimant in a court of law, it renders such suit or proceedings incompetent, and the court remains with no option but to have the same dismissed, even without going to the merits of the claim.

However, as human rights lawyers, we share much with Chipeta who admirably asserts that, "Rules of Civil Procedure are not there to hinder the due administration of justice"[1258]. With that in mind we find it important to give a caution that the law of limitation, especially, in applications must not be construed very strictly in all cases but due consideration needs to be made in each and every particular case. We think that the principles developed by the Court of Appeal of Tanzania in the case of *Yusufu Same & Hawa Dada v Hadija Yusufu*[1259] are ideal and ought to persuade other courts when similar situations arise. The facts of the case are that the respondent was the wife of the late Juma Abdallah Samanya who died intestate in 1979, leaving landed properties in Dar es Salaam, including the disputed house No. 44 on Plot No. 9 Block 33 Mafia Street, Kariakoo area. In 1981 Haruna Juma Abdallah, one of the deceased's children, applied successfully in the primary court of Kariakoo to be appointed the administrator of the deceased's estate. However, before the appointment he, with another child, sold the disputed house to one Omari and one Salimini and the two sold it later to the appellants. Unaware of the first appointment, the respondent applied successfully in the High Court[1260] to be appointed the administratrix. The appointment was later revoked by the same High Court on application by the appellants. Aggrieved, the respondent sought leave to appeal to the Court of Appeal. Her application was dismissed for being time barred. She did not give up but applied for extension of time within which to file a leave to appeal to the Court of Appeal. The High Court

---

1258 CHIPETA, B.D., (2002): Civil Procedure in Tanzania: A Student's Manual, Dar es Salaam University Press, at p. xxiii.

1259 Court of Appeal of Tanzania at Dar es Salaam, Civil Appeal No. 1 of 2002, judgement of 19/10/2006, (Unreported).

1260 This was the Probate Cause No. 64 of either 1991 or 1992.

(Kalegeya, J.) granted the application. The appellant were dissatisfied and appealed to the Court of Appeal of Tanzania. The Court, speaking through Munuo, J.A. developed the following principle, which we consider to be guidance to all courts below in the judicial hierarchy. At one time the Court said:

> *It is trite that an application for extension of time is entirely in the discretion of the court to grant or to refuse to grant it. This discretion however has to be exercised judicially and the overriding consideration is that there must be sufficient cause for so doing. What amounts to "sufficient cause" has not been defined. From decided cases a number of factors have to be taken into account, including whether or not the application has been brought promptly; the absence of any or valid explanation for the delay; lack of diligence on the part of the applicant.*

At another time the Court said:

> *It should be observed that the term "sufficient cause" should not be interpreted narrowly but should be given a wide interpretation to encompass all reasons or causes which are outside the applicant's power to control or influence resulting in delay in taking any necessary step.*

Applying these principles in this case and considering the respondent's advanced reason of financial constraint, the Court concluded that:

> *We are aware that financial constraint is not sufficient ground for extension of time...But in the circumstances of this case at hand, where the respondent was a widow, depending on legal aid, her plea of financial constraint cannot be held to be insignificant. Like the learned judge of the High Court (Kalegeya J) we are satisfied that the delay from 29.11.1996 to 3.1.1992, about one month and five days, was with sufficient cause.*

As it was earlier noted, limitation of actions is a significant obstruction when it comes to the realisation of rights through a court action. For this reason, some daring people in certain jurisdictions have approached the Court of law to challenge the constitutionality of some limitation clauses on grounds that the clauses infringe the constitutional right of access to court to seek judicial redress. It suffices to record the two cases of *Mahlomi v the Minister of Defence* [1261]and *Barend Petrus Barkhuizen*

1261 (1997) (1) SA 124 (CC).

v Ronald Stuart Napier,[1262] both from South Africa. In Mahlomi's case, the applicant successfully challenged the constitutional validity of time limitation in section 113 of the *Defence Act 44 of 1957*, which required any legal action against the Defence to be instituted within six months from the time when the cause of action arose and to give one month's prior notice before the commencement of the legal action. However, in Barend's case the applicant lost action against the constitutionality of the limitation clause in an insurance policy between him and the insurance company, which required service of summons against the insurer to be done within 90 days of repudiation of the insured's claim by the insurer.

Exclusive Jurisdiction of Courts

Jurisdiction of courts has been defined to mean "the extent to which, or the limits within which a particular court can exercise its powers and what powers"[1263]. The legal effect for the court to entertain a suit without jurisdiction to do so is the nullification of the entire trial by a superior court on appeal or revision. There is a long list of cases in which superior courts have exercised their powers to nullify the proceedings in the subordinate courts where the same were conducted by courts devoid of jurisdiction[1264]. Suffice to record the case of *Tanzania Tractors Manufacturing Co Ltd/ PSRC v Gracious Mwanguya and Another*[1265] in which the High Court (Luanda, J.- as he then was), allowing an appeal against the decision of the Resident Magistrates Court, had the following to record:

> *All in all the trial court had no jurisdiction to entertain this case. It follows therefore that the trial is a nullity. The proceedings are quashed and the judgment and decree set aside.*

When it comes to land matters, there are, presently, special courts, "the land courts", which are vested with exclusive jurisdiction to handle litigations whose subject is founded on disputes concerning land.[1266] The

---

1262 Constitutional Court of South Africa, Case No. CCT 72 OF 2005, judgment delivered on 4th April 2007.

1263 See CHIPETA, B.D., (2002): *Civil Procedure in Tanzania: A Student's Manual*, Dar es Salaam University Press Ltd, at p. 4.

1264 See, for example, *Michael Leseni Kweka v John Eliafe*, Court of Appeal of Tanzania, Civil Appeal No. 51 of 1997 (Unreported) and *Issa Omary v Masood Issa*, High Court of Tanzania at Dar es Salaam, Misc. Civil Cause No. 4 of 2001 (Unreported).

1265 High Court of Tanzania at Dar es Salaam, Civil Appeal No. 203 of 2001 (Unreported).

1266 See a discussion on land courts in 9.2 above.

knowledge on the exclusivity of jurisdiction vested in land courts is very important to a lawyer for three reasons. First, it is trite that ordinary courts are denied jurisdiction to try land cases. Secondly, it is also trite that non land matters have no room in the land courts. Thirdly, it is trite that even land courts themselves have different jurisdiction based, for example, on their respective geographical locations (territorial jurisdiction) and the monetary value of the subject matter of the case (pecuniary jurisdiction). We learn, in law, from the wording of subsection (1) in section 167 of the *Land Act, 1999*, that, "The following courts[1267] are hereby vested with exclusive jurisdiction, subject to the provisions of this Part, to hear and determine all manner of disputes, actions and proceedings concerning land", meaning courts not mentioned in this provision of the Act lack the legal powers to adjudicate any landed matter.

Equally we learn, in practice, about the exclusive jurisdiction of land courts in the cases of *Mtumwa Ally Said and Another v Mwamtoro Ally Said and Another*[1268] and *Lucia Paulo v Lenna Ndege.*[1269] In both cases, matters concerning the administration of estate have been said to be non land matters and, as such, they fall outside the jurisdiction of land courts. In Mtumwa Ally's case, the 1st Respondent, acting in the capacity of an administrator of estate duly appointed by a primary court, sold a house on plot No. 28 Block J, IIala which had belonged to the deceased, one Said Salum Sela. The appellants filed a case in the District Land and Housing Tribunal of Ilala challenging the sale of the property. They lost the case in the Tribunal as well as the appeal in the High Court on point of jurisdiction of the court to entertain the matter. Dismissing the appeal, the court (Longway, J.- as she then was) had the following to say:

> *I have studied the proceedings on record of the lower Tribunal, especially the submissions upon which the ruling now sought to be impugned is based. Looking at the pleadings of the application by the appellants at the District Land and Housing Tribunal, Ilala, shows that the sale complained about was a process done by the 1st Respondent in his capacity as an Administratrix of the estate of Said Salum Sela. According to paragraph 6 (a) and (b) in my considered view, those are particulars related*

1267 Reference is made to the Village Land Councils, Ward Tribunals, District Land and Housing Tribunals, High Court of Tanzania (Land Division) and the Court of Appeal of Tanzania.

1268 High Court of Tanzania (Land Division) at Dar es Salaam, Land Appeal Case No. 48 of 2006. (Unreported).

1269 High Court of Tanzania (Land Division) at Dar es Salaam, Misc. Land Appeal No. 48 of 2006. (Unreported).

to the said Administratrix's misconduct in the administration of Said Salum Sela's estate...This is clearly a misconduct of an administrator and the appointing court, an issue best dealt with by that court in review or may be revision of a higher forum.

This higher forum was not the Tribunal nor this court, for the simple reason that the complaint is not a landed matter.

Similarly in Lucia Paulo's case, the parties, a grandmother and her granddaughter respectively, had a dispute over the ownership of the house which formally belonged to one Magret Said, who died and in respect of whom the appellant was appointed the Probate Administratrix. The respondent contested the probate administratorship. The Ward Tribunal found in favour of the appellant as the owner of the house in question. The matter went through the District Land and Housing Tribunal, which decided that both parties should get a share, and landed, finally, in the High Court. The High Court, (Longway, J.- as she then was) dismissed it for want of jurisdiction. Her Ladyship, the judge observed that:

But in my considered view, in as far as the issue dividing shares of the deceased person's property are concerned the same does not fall within the realm of the courts under the Land Acts or land matters...

The subject matter even if narrow, was within the ambit of the normal courts to determine. The proceedings are therefore declared a nullity. As a consequence the parties are advised to seek redress afresh in the competent magistrate's court.

Hannah Swahiba Shoko v Savings & Finance and Others[1270] is another important case on point of jurisdiction. The background to the case is that the plaintiff's husband guaranteed repayment of an overdraft facility extended by the defendant to a third party. On failure to repay the loan, the first defendant successfully moved against the guarantor, and obtained *ex-exparte* judgment and order of attachment and sale of his house located on Plot No. 403, Ursino North within the city of Dar es Salaam. The house was accordingly attached and sold to the second defendant.[1271] The plaintiff instituted this case seeking a High Court's declaration that the house was a matrimonial home, and not a subject

1270 High Court of Tanzania (Land Division) at Dar es Salaam, Land Case No. 298 of 2008 (Unreported).

1271 See *Savings Finance Commericial Bank v Moses Maira and Another*, Resident Magistrate's Court of Dar es Salaam at Kisutu, Civil Case No. 79 of 2004 (Unreported).

of attachment by a court's order under Section 48 (1) (e) of the *Civil Procedure Act, 1966*. The suit was strongly resisted by the defendants' counsel, who insisted that the Court lacked jurisdiction to entertain the suit on the first reason that the High Court (Land Division) is not in the judicial hierarchy with the Magistrate's court which issued an execution, and on the second reason that the plaintiff could have moved a competent court by appeal or revision, not by filing a fresh suit on matters which had aready been determined and decided by the RM's court. In its judgment dismissing the suit, the High Court (Hon. Nchimbi, J.) had this to say, at p. 8 of the typed script:

> *The plaintiff took a defeatist view that this court is empowered to entertain the suit because it involves a dispute over land. I have found that this court has no jurisdiction over this case because the plaintiff has circumvented the matter by way of a fresh suit when, in fact, she is challenging the sale of property in question, subject of mortgage, and is further asking the court to nullify the said sale. I should repeat such a claim is not maintainable for the law does not allow that. I have also observed that the plaintiff is challenging sale of property effected in execution of a decree in an ordinary civil case before Resident Magistrate's Court. In effect, therefore, she is opposing the whole execution process. This cannot be a subject of fresh suit because if allowed it would be like entertaining appeal or revision…This court has no jurisdiction over the case and the procedure adopted by the plaintiff to challenge the sale is not known to law. In the upshot the suit is ordered dismissed with costs.*

This decision reminds us of two basic principles on procedure: first, that a person can challenge the execution orders of a subordinate court only by appealing or seeking a revision in the High Court, provided the High Court is in the same judicial hierarchy with the subordinate court which made the orders. Second, a person can only institute a fresh suit in the capacity of an objector and under the provision of Order XX1, Rule 62 of the *Civil Procedure Act, 1966*.[1272]

In certain instances parties have even dared to approach criminal courts to seek judicial remedies from these courts for matters which are landed in nature. In *Kibwana Mohamed v Republic*[1273], *Ismail Bushaija*

1272 See also *Presidential Parastatal Sector Reform Commission v Data Machine Limited & 3 Others*, High Court of Tanzania (Land Division) at Dar es Salaam, Land Case No. 248 of 2004.

1273 [1980] TLR 321 (HC).

v Republic[1274] and *Silvery Nkangaa v Raphael Albertho*[1275], among many others, the court commonly held that a criminal court is not the proper forum for determining the rights of those claiming ownership of land. Only a civil court via a civil suit can determine matters of land ownership.

The point of emphasis is that, like limitation of actions, the issue of jurisdiction of courts in dealing with land matters is another serious obstacle that tends to affect a person's realization of the right to land, for if it is objected to successfully, it has the effect of nullifying the proceedings. There is a long list of court decisions[1276] which have affirmed that lack of jurisdiction of courts is a fundamental defect that is not curable at all. Also there is a long list of decisions[1277] that affirm that the issue of jurisdiction may be raised at any stage of the proceedings since it goes to the root of justice. We all know that litigation is a very costly process both in terms of time and money. It follows, therefore, that once proceedings are nullified at a later stage, any of the following consequences may follow the event: one, the affected party may despair and abandon the claim and, therefore, lose his right to land; two, the losing party may be sued for costs, a fact which will add salt into that person's wound, and; three, a losing party may be sued for damages for malicious prosecution, if he had moved the court criminally. The case of *Partick Kimilo v Shaweji Ulinda & Another*[1278] should not escape our attention on this point. In this case, there was a dispute between the applicant and the respondent over a piece of land. The respondent reported the matter to the police accusing the applicant of trespass. The police arrested the applicant, detained him instituted a criminal case against the applicant which was dismissed for want of prosecution. The applicant was found to have no case to answer, was acquitted and he instituted a suit against the respondents for malicious prosecution. He lost the case both in the court of the Resident Magistrates of Kibaha and Kisutu, Dar es Salaam, the latter having been presided over by a Resident

---

1274 [1991] TLR 100 (HC).

1275 [1992] TLR 110 (HC).

1276 See, for example, *Issa Omary v Masood Issa*, High Court of Tanzania at Dar es Salaam, Misc. Civil Cuase No. 4 of 2001 (Unreported); *William Rajabu Mallya and two Others v Republic* [1991] TLR 83; *John Agricola v Rashid Juma* [1990] TLR 1.

1277 See, for example, *Michael Leseni Kweka v John Eliafe*, Court of Appeal of Tanzania, Civil Appeal No. 51 of 1997 (Unreported) and *Issa Omary v Masood Issa*, High Court of Tanzania at Dar es Salaam, Misc. Civil Cause No. 4 of 2001 (Unreported).

1278 Court of Appeal of Tanzania, at Dar es Salaam, Civil Application No. 99 of 2001 (Unreported).

Magistrate with Extended Jurisdiction. He sought the leave of the High Court to appeal to the Court of Appeal but the leave was denied. This attracted a second chance whereby the applicant applied for the leave to appeal in the Court of Appeal. In granting the leave, the Court of Appeal stated an important principle which is quoted in extenso:

> *Both parties had a claim of right over the disputed parcel of land. It should have been realised by the respondents, therefore, that if they needed to take any action against the applicant who appeared to them to be making a false claim to the disputed land it was for them to seek to establish ownership. It should have been realised also that where there is a rival claim of ownership of property one does not go to a criminal court to prove one's claim of ownership. One goes to a civil court. Once the civil court decides on who rightfully owns the property, the party against whom the decision is given cannot lawfully take or remain in possession of the property without permission from the adjudged owners. In the case of land he would be considered a trespasser and could be prosecuted for trespass. What I am trying to say is that where there is a rival claim of ownership of land one of the parties will not be entitled to prosecute the other for trespass unless he has first established his title to it in a civil court...*
>
> *But one of the important issues which the Principle Resident Magistrate with extended jurisdiction did not consider was whether in the absence of a court decision unequivocally declaring the second respondent as the rightfull owner of the disputed piece of land the two respondents could set in motion the criminal process against the applicant. It was not enough that the respondents believed the applicant was a greedy land grabber and rushed to the police who then took action against the applicant. I think, therefore, that the question whether the respondents had reasonable and probable cause to prosecute the applicant for trespass, which is a legal point, needs to be considered by the Court of Appeal.*

From all that is stated above, parties are emphatically advised and encouraged to first find out about the competence of a court in the nature of its jurisdiction to entertain a suit before knocking at its doors for assistance. The advice is given at the instance of the consequences that parties can be subjected to when a suit is dismissed or a judgment nullified for want of jurisdiction.

Appearance and the Right to Legal Representation

It is one of the cherished fundamental rights for every person to approach a court of law or tribunal to seek judicial redress whenever his rights have been infringed.[1279] In Tanzania, appearance varies according to the level of the court involved in the determination of the dispute. For example, if the matter is before a primary court (in all cases of probate and administration of estates) or a Ward Tribunal (in landed matters other than probate and administration of estate) the law gives the right to a party to a dispute to appear and defend his case, without the assistance of a lawyer. But the court can allow a relative or member of the household of any party to the proceedings, upon the request of that party to appear and act for such party.[1280] Again, if the matter is in the courts higher than the primary courts and Ward Tribunals in the judicial hierarchy, appearance may be made by the party to the proceedings, or his recognized agent, such as a person holding powers of attorney[1281] or by an advocate[1282] duly appointed by such party to act or appear on his behalf.[1283]

More often than not, appearance and the right to legal representation by a professional lawyer (advocate) become obstacles to the realization of right to land for the obvious reasons. In societies where poverty and illiteracy abound-the conditions that isolate the people they handicap from the mainstream of law-most persons who have been injured are either unaware of or are poorly informed about their legal rights to land and what they should do in order to enforce them. Access to the professional advice and assistance that they need so sorely is often difficult for financial or geographical reasons.

1279 Article 13 (3) of the *Constitution of the United Republic of Tanzania, 1977.*

1280 See section 33 (2) of the *Magistrate Court's Act*, [Cap. 11 RE 2002], and section 18 (2) of the *Land Disputes Courts Act*, [Cap. 216 RE 2002]. Note that advocates are barred from appearing in primary courts (section 33 (1) of the Magistrates' Courts Act) and in a Ward Tribunal (section 18 (1) of the *Land Disputes Courts Act*, [Cap. 216 R.E 2002]).

1281 A power of attorney has been defined to mean "a formal instrument by which one person empowers another to represent him or act in his stead for certain purposes". Per Mapigano,- as he then was, in *Parin A.A Jaffer and Another v Abdulrasul A Jaffer*, High Court of Tanzania at Dar es Salaam, Misc. Civil Cause No. 48 of 1992, at p. 2.

1282 Reference is made to a person whose name is entered in the Roll of advocates in accordance with the provisions of the *Advocates Act*, [Cap. 341 RE 2002].

1283 The authority of persons, other than a party to the proceedings, to make appearance is provided by Order 3 rule 2 of the *Civil Procedure Code*, [Cap. 33 R.E 2002].

Appearance in Person

As we have noted earlier above, the reasons attributed to poverty, illiteracy and geographical disadvantages have compelled most parties to land disputes to go it alone, that is, to appear in courts in person without representation. The majority have dared to do so and unaware of technical issues, including limitation of actions, jurisdiction of courts, and other procedural matters such as framing of suits, joinder of parties and the rules of pleadings. Yet, some other people have even approached the courts of law without knowing the nature of the remedies to which they are entitled. The consequences of such anomalies have been, to mention only a few: prolonged litigations; summary dismissal of actions on points of law and liabilities to pay costs, and; failure of some parties to realize their land rights, which they might have been entitled to, but they fail to realize them on point of legal technicalities. The following cases are of great help in illustrating this reality.

In *Atuganile Mwaitege v Timoth Mwakalinga*[1284] the parties disputed over the ownership of a piece of land where the appellant claimed that the disputed land was given her by the late Asubisye Mwakalinga while the respondent claimed that it was part of the estate of his brother, the late Asubisye Mwakalinga which he was entitled to administer. The dispute was referred to the Kipawa Ward Tribunal which entered judgment in favour of the appellant. Accordingly the parties where informed of their right to appeal against the decision within 30 days, if aggrieved. The respondent was aggrieved but, instead of appealing against the decision of the Kipawa Ward Tribunal, he filed a fresh suit in the Primary Court of Buguruni, in Dar es Salaam, in total contravention of the clear provisions of the *Ward Tribunal Act, 1985*.[1285] The Primary court Magistrate, either in ignorance of the law or intentionally, accepted the fresh case and decided in favour of the respondent on ground that the appellant had no documentary evidence to prove that she was given the piece of land by the deceased. The appellant was aggrieved and appealed unsuccessfully in the District Court which affirmed the Primary Court's decision on similar ground. The appellant sought the assistance of the Legal Aid Committee of the University of Dar es Salaam to appeal to the

---

1284 High Court of Tanzania at Dar es Salaam, PC Civil Appeal No. 34 of 1999 (Unreported).

1285 Section 20 (1) of the Act provides that, "Subject to sub-section (2), a person aggrieved by a decision of the Tribunal may appeal in writing to the Primary Court".

High Court against the decision of the District Court. The High Court (Manento, J.- as he then was) held that the appeal was incompetent on two points of law. In the first place, the court said that the Primary Court and District Court lacked jurisdiction as there was no appeal by the respondent to the Primary Court against the decision of the Ward Tribunal[1286]. In the second place, the court held that there was no appeal on point of law to the District Court whose decision would have been final without the right to further appeal to the High Court[1287]. In conclusion the Court stated that:

> *In the circumstances, the proceedings in Buguruni primary court Civil Case No. 38/98, the Ilala District Court Civil Appeal No. 42/98 and the High Court Appeal No. 34/99 are all declared to be a nullity for reasons stated above and the decision of the Kipawa Ward Tribunal is declared to be the right decision on the matter in issue.*

Immediately after the Court's decision, the respondent, aggrieved by the decision, made an application to the same court for, among other orders, the court to issue a certificate as to point of law to refer the appeal to the Court of Appeal of Tanzania. The High Court (Manento, J.- as he then was) refused to issue the certificate on ground that there was no "legal point to be determined by the Court of Appeal worth or warranting the High Court Court to issue a certificate on point of law".

The point we want to make is that the decision in this case would have been different if the parties had been properly and professionally advised. The other sad part of the story in this case is that despite that the decision of the Kipawa Ward Tribunal was confirmed as the valid decision, the appellant failed to apply for execution of that decision for reasons related to ignorance of the law at a time of enforcing the decision of the Ward Tribunal. Until todate, the dispute between the parties or their assignees over the same piece of land is still going on.[1288]

1286 Section 20 (1) of the *Ward Tribunal Act* (Act No. 7 of 1985) invoked.

1287 Section 20 (2) of the Act provides that, "Except on points of law where the appeal lies to the District Court, a decision of the Primary Court on any appeal made to it shall be final and conclusive".

1288 It was just in the middle of the year 2007 when the appellant, Atuganile Mwaitege came back to the Legal Aid Committee of the University of Dar es Salaam to seek assistance in the execution of the decision of the Kipawa Ward Tribunal, almost nine years after the same was made.

In *Mohamed Hassan Hole v Keya Jumanne Ramadhan*[1289] the parties disputed over ownership of a piece of land. The appellant, who had instituted a suit initially in a Primary Court of Bereko, Kondoa, lost the Appeal to the District Court of Kondoa, the High Court of Tanzania at Dodoma and, finally, this appeal before the Court of Appeal of Tanzania at Dodoma on point of limitation of action, which he had filed about 13 years since the accrual of time of his action. During the hearing of the appeal before the Court of appeal, the appellant, who was now represented by an advocate, prayed to be declared a lawful owner over the disputed land. Alternatively he prayed for an order that the case be remitted to the primary court for determination on the question of compensation to be paid to the appellant. The Court of Appeal rejected all the prayers for the reasons that the first prayer was overtaken by an event, that is, barred by time and because the second prayer was not made in the courts below.

> *As Dr. Lamwai, learned Counsel for the appellant, will no doubt agree on reflection the question of compensation was directly and substantially in issue in the case before Bereko Primary Court but such question was not raised. Nor was it raised in the district court or the High Court. That being the position we do not see how we can issue an order regarding compensation a matter which did not feature in any of the three lower courts.*

Aware of the proposition that the right to compensation for one's labour is well known and cherished in Tanzania[1290], we believe that the decision of the Court would have been different if the appellant had been properly and professionally advised to make compensation one of his prayers in the proceedings in the courts below, that is at the earliest possible time.

Presently there is a legal aid scheme through which the needy litigants get free legal assistance. We record the great role that is being played by some units in this scheme, including: the Legal Aid Committee (LAC) of the University of Dar es Salaam;[1291] the Tanzania Women Lawyers

1289 Court of Appeal of Tanzania at Dodoma, Civil Appeal No. 19 of 1992 (Unreported).

1290 See a detailed discussion on the Right to Compensation, especially as stated in the cases of *Lalata Msangawale v Henry Mwamlima* (1979) LRT No. 3; *Ntiyahela Boneka v Kijiji cha Ujamaa Mutala*, High Court of Tanzania at Tabora, (PC) Civil Appeal No. 21 of 1987 (Unreported); *Attorney General and Another v Lohay Akonay and Another* (1995) TLR No. 95.

1291 See *Atuganile Mwaitege v Timoth Mwakalinga*, High Court of Tanzania at Dar es Salaam, (PC) Civil Appeal No. 34 of 1999 (Unreported), in which the Committee represented the appellant.

Association (TAWLA);[1292] the Legal and Human Rights Centre (LHRC) and the Magomeni Legal Aid Clinic;[1293] the National Organization for Legal Assistance (NOLA);[1294] and the Land Rights Research Institute (LARRI or HAKIARDHI) among others. However, we are afraid that the service offered by these units through the legal aid scheme is very limited for the following reasons: one, their operation is geographically limited-they being urban centred-thus inaccessible by the handicapped rural dwellers who form the majority of the Tanzania population. Two, majority of units, if not all, are donor-funded and, thus, their functions are dependent on the good will of the donors. Three, these units tend to recruit inexperienced younger lawyers who are insufficiently exposed to the intricacies of litigation, including legal and procedural technicalities, the worst being those who, as President Mkapa was once worried[1295], have joined the legal career, not for its professional nobility, but for its social mobility. Finally, the aid offered by these units is limited to paper work, especially that of drafting pleadings and submissions, and not appearance in courts. The conclusion that we can draw from the above on-going discussion is that much is still required to assist the litigants to access justice, especially so when land claims by the poor and illiterate are on the stage.

Appearance Through an Advocate

Let it be pointed out clearly that while all advocates are lawyers, not all lawyers are advocates. An "advocate," according to law[1296], "means any person whose name is duly entered as an advocate upon the Roll" and the "Roll" means "the list of advocates kept in accordance with the provisions of Part IV" of the Advocates Act. Being an advocate is not an automatic virtue upon attaining a law degree. Some other steps are required for a lawyer to become an advocate of the High Court and the subordinate courts thereto. These include: petitioning to the Chief

---

1292 See *Paul Michael Simbaine v Asia Hassan Ramadhani*, High Court of Tanzania at Dar es Salaam, Civil Appeal No. 150 of 1999 (Unreported) in which TAWLA offered the applicant a limited legal assistance by drawing a written submission in support of a memorandum of review.

1293 See *Edward Msango v Aga Khan Sports Club*, High Court of Tanzania at Dar es Salaam, Civil Appeal No. 15 of 2002, in which the two units assisted the applicant in his application for leave to file an appeal out of time.

1294 The Organisation, formally established in Dar es Salaam, has now extended its services in other regions to include, among others, Dodoma, Iringa, and Kigoma.

1295 See MKAPA, Benjamin William, "The Legal System Should be rore Accessible and Affordable to more Tanzanians" in BISIMBA, H.K. & PETER C.M., *op cit*, pp. 33-41, at p. 37.

1296 See section 2 of the Advocates Act, [Cap. 341 R.E 2002].

Justice for consideration to be admitted as an advocate of the High Court of Tanzania; satisfying the Council of Legal Education that one has sufficient knowledge of the laws of Tanzania as well as the practice and procedure in courts; being admitted as an advocate of the High Court of Tanzania and the subordinate courts thereto, except primary courts and ward tribunals; and obtaining a practicing certificate[1297].

The law allows advocates, when duly appointed by a party to litigation, to appear and act on his behalf[1298]. Appearance by advocates is, indeed, very important for the obvious reasons. An advocate is a lawyer who is, no doubt, acquainted with sufficient knowledge of the laws of the land as well as the practice and procedure in courts, and as such, he is not expected to be caught by the horns and lose the case on technical grounds, as would do any person who appears on his own behalf. Should it happen that he loses, then that should be on merits since he has all the rules as arms at his disposal. Chipeta[1299] puts it very correctly that:

> *The rules of Civil Procedure may well be intricate and, possibly, sometimes make "dull" reading. But the inevitable truth is that no practicing lawyer can make much headway in civil litigation without a sound working knowledge of those "intricate" rules. To him those rules are his compasses and roads that guide him and are as indispensable to him as a torch light is to a man walking in darkness.*

An advocate is also an officer of the court, as such he has the duty to assist and guide the court (not to mislead it) to administer justice. He has a corollary duty to his clients with whom he has fiduciary relationship and to whom, therefore, he must demonstrate his ability to manage the client's case, and to the legal profession, which demands observance of the rules of etiquete and professionalism. This position places an advocate in the highest esteem and reputation with the expectation that he will undertake to apply all his faculties to deliver the best result of his client's case. No advocate, we believe, is courageous enough to stand challenged by the court as it was directed against fellow advocate in the

---

1297 See the Advocates Act, [Cap. 341 R.E 2002], section 8, the Advocates (Professional Requirements) Regulations, G.N No. 395 of 1963; MAPUNGA, Angelo M., "Standardising the Criteria for Admission to Practice Law in East Africa" in BISIMBA, H.K. & MAINA, C.P., *op cit*, at p. 277, and TWAIB, Fauz, (1994): *The Legal Professional in Tanzania*, Dar es Salaam University Press.

1298 Order 3 rule 1 of the Civil Procedure Act, [Cap 33 R.E 2002].

1299 See CHIPETA, B.D., *op cit* at p. xxiii.

case of *Joshua Maswi & 145 Others v B.P Tanzania Ltd & 2 Others.*[1300] In this case there were two applications in the court, one for the leave to apply for orders of certiorari and mandamus and another for the said orders. The court granted the leave sought and ordered the parties to file their written submissions in favour of the substantive application. Very surprisingly, the Counsel for the applicant filed a submission in support of the application for leave, a stage that was already passed, instead of filing a submission in favour of the substantive application. The court found the submissions to be irrelevant to the Application before it. Mihayo, J.- as he then was, found this to be "a high degree of carelessness on the part of the counsel, not knowing what was before the court and arguing it". He not only directed a challenge against the learned counsel, but went on to dismiss the application for lack of arguments to support it:

> *An advocate is an officer of the court and he is therefore deemed to know what he submits before the court he is appearing. If he submits on irrelevancies, he does so at his own peril. This court ordered the submission on the main application. If submissions do not address the issue before me, I have nothing in support of the evidence in the affidavit of Joshua Maswi. An application like this one would be lost or won on the legal arguments advanced for or against. Those arguments are not there. Because no legal arguments have been advanced, all I can say is that I have nothing before me to rule in favour or against it...I find no merit in this application and dismiss it with costs.*

The point we want to emphasize is that the role of advocates in litigation cannot be over-emphasized. However, the reality on the ground is that not every person can access the professional assistance of an advocate. There are at least obvious reasons to explain this. First, the number of advocates on the Roll, especially, the practicing advocates, is very low compared to the potential clients in the field. Secondly, the cost of engaging an advocate is too high to be afforded by the ordinary members of the society. This is a problem that happened to attract the attention of Benjamini William Mkapa, the third phase government President of Tanzania, who once said:

1300 High Court of Tanzania at Dar es Salaam, Misc. Civil Cause No.9 of 2003 (Unreported).

> *The majority of our people are poor, and if access to justice is determined by ability to afford professional legal counsel, the majority of taxpayers who sustain our judicial system will be the very ones to be shut off from it. In other words we will tax the majority of Tanzanians to provide justice to the minority who can afford it. This, of course, is a universal problem. The best legal counsel is expensive, and is available only to those who can afford it. Not even in the United States can everyone afford the legal counsel that was retained by O.J Simpson! But a line has to be drawn, a threshold determined, below which no citizen should find him or herself unable to access justice in a free and democratic country. Legal discrimination on the basis of economic status is not right*[1301].

Thirdly, most firms of advocates are urban based, a fact which curtails the rural dwellers from services of these legal professionals. At the end of it all, it is the poor and illiterate majority of our people who remain obstructed in their struggle to realize their right to land.

1301 MKAPA, Benjamini William, "The Legal System Should be More Accessible and Affordable to More Tanzanians" in BISIMBA, H.K. & PETER C.M., *op cit*, pp. 33-41, at p. 39.

Conclusion

I must emphasize here that whoever is given authority to deal with land he must exercise extreme care and diligence considering its sensitivity and the important role it plays in the development of the citizens. Strict adherence to the provisions of the law is vital not only in order to avoid problems that occurred in land administration in the past, which resulted in the reform of our land laws, but also to do away with loopholes that may give room to corruption, which is an evil that we must employ every weapon at our disposal to fight.

- Judge E.A Kileo[1302] -

1302 *Shaffique A.S Dhiyebi v Presidential Parastatal Sector Reform Commission*, High Court of Tanzania (Land Division) at Dar es Salaam, Land Case No. 46 of 2004, pp. 13-4.

We have carefully followed the land law of Tanzania along its line of historical development. All what we have discussed from the first page of the book to the last one brings us to the conclusion that all Tanzanians are, now, placed in a better position to realise their right to land compared to when they were subjected to the law and practice of the past two or three decades. The dark chapter on land law and practice of the past has been closed by the *Land Acts* complemented by the International Bill of Rights, which set the basic standards on rights, and the right to land in particular. However, we know that we live in a world of human beings, in which the full realisation of rights may be limited in some instances by the human factor. Salmond has correctly cautioned that, "Law is the theory of things as received and acted upon within the courts of justice, and this theory may or may not conform to the reality of things outside. The eye of the law does not infallibly see things as they are. Partly by deliberate design and partly by errors and accidents of historical development, law and practice; legal theory and the truth of things may fail in complete coincidence.[1303]

It means, therefore, that the way forward must be for all of us to stand by the challenge amidst us to ensure that all citizens access and enjoy the right to land. Guided by the fundamental principles of the national land policy generally[1304], and the above quote by the learned judge in particular, each of us must be extremely careful and diligent in dealing with land matters. In that endeavour, the President, who holds all land in trust on behalf of all the citizens[1305] must employ all his legal and moral fortitude to eliminated severe cases of homelessness and landlessness and make land be accessible to all, in addition to advocating for better and sufficient housing. Such a move is possible only if the President is willing, for example, to revoke titles and/or acquire lands of the landed few, who have curved bigger lands than they actually need for redistribution to those who need land but do not have it. However, such a move would be justified only if it is for that purpose, and in accordance with the law,[1306] and; when full, fair and prompt compensation is paid to the affected persons.[1307] It has been reported over the media that

1303 Salmond, (1957): *Jurisprudence*, 11th Edition at p. 57.

1304 See section 3 common to the Land Act and the Village Land Act.

1305 *Ibid*, section 3 (1) (a).

1306 .Section 4 of the Land Acquisition Act and section 45 of the Land Act.

1307 Section 3 (1) (g) of the Land Act.

the incumbent President, Jakaya Mrisho Kikwete, has expressed his willingness to walk that talk:

> *According to the reports, the President has announced far-reaching reforms under which the government could seize expansive tracts of land owned by wealthy individuals and distribute them to poor, landless people as a way of forestalling a land ownership crisis.Tanzanian law stipulates that all land in the country is public property held in trust by the President on behalf of wananchi, and President Kikwete has stated that he will revoke any land title deed, if that would be in the interests of the poor and the nation.*[1308]

To other personnel involved in land administration in the Ministry of Lands, Housing and Human Settlement Development, that is: the Minister[1309]; the Commissioner for Lands[1310] and other officers working under him[1311]; the Land Allocation Committee[1312]; the Registrar of Titles;[1313] and the Village Council[1314] where the village land is involved, must always take prompt measures to react to land problems whenever and wherever they occur. The kind of efforts to be resorted to here include: avoiding making decisions affecting people's land rights without the people's participation in order to avoid the "*hatukushirikishwa*" (or we were not consulted) syndrome whose impact over the peace and security of the people in this country cannot be said to be insignificant;[1315] making and keeping proper records of holders of rights of occupancy to avoid the long-term problem of double allocation, ensuring proper procedures are followed whenever there is a need to move people out of their land, including proper notice of the government's intention to move them and prior payment of prompt and fair compensation; ensuring speedy attendance of processes such as granting and registration of documents of title; and avoiding to do what they are not legally empowered to do.

1308 See the Editor, "Kikwete's Stance on Land Soothing, the Guardian 26th March 2007.

1309 Ibid, section 8.

1310 Ibid, section 9.

1311 Ibid, section 11.

1312 Ibid, section 12.

1313 Section 4 of the Land Registration Act, [Cap. 334 R.E 2002].

1314 Section 8 of the Village Land Act, [Cap. 114 R.E 2002].

1315 Ibid, section 3 (1) (i).

In a word, they should avoid to be seen as agents of or instigators behind land problems. This recommendation does not stem from a vacuum. History has recoreded an event in which some residents in Kibamba, Dar es Salaam, were given a one month notice to vacate their lands in order to give room for a specified government pilot project in the area, and that they were required to do so when no prior compensation was paid by the government. The order brought these residents to loggerheads with the land administrators in the area. Thanks to Hon. Dr. John Pombe Magufuli, the Minister for Lands, Housing and Human Settlement Development (as he then was) who intervened to calm the situation as he addressed a public meeting involving the victims, by insisting that:

> *When the Government decides to evict residents from a certain area, it has to compensate them first before carrying out any exercise. The 30 day order is both uncalled for and bad taste. Be informed that the Government has extended the notice to four months pending an official communication from the ministry.*[1316]

Not only that but, again, the case of *Nizar Shell L'aadawy Muhanna v Registrar of Titles and Another*[1317] is critical to the Registrar of Titles who purported to do what the law did not authorise him to do, thereby causing a land problem which was latter resolved by the court. The background of the case is that: there was an advertisement in a general notice through Government Gazette advertising the loss of a Certificate of Title in respect of Plot No. 76, United Nations Road, Upanga which was initially issued in the name of the appellant. The advertisement indicated that the holder thereof was dead and that in the absence of any objection, a new Certificate would be issued in the name of the applicant who is also the second respondent, a widow of the late Muhanna. Essentially, the appellant objected to the notice very strongly on grounds that: he was not dead but alive; the Certificate was not lost but was in his possession; and he was the registered owner of the suit property. On the other hand, the second respondent maintained that the property was part of her late husband's properties and that the suit property was bequeathed to her through a will. The Registrar was confronted with these rival arguments, and he decided to make an investigation about the issue of ownership to establish who was entitled to the property, where he purported to act

1316 JOHN, Paul, "Magufuli calms down Kibamba" in The African Friday, January 18, 2008 at p. 4.

1317 [1995] TLR 217 (CA).

under section 105 of the then *Land Registration Ordinance*. He came to the conclusion that the property correctly belonged to the respondent's father and that she was bequeathed the same through a valid will. The appellant was aggrieved and he successfully found his way to the Court of Appeal.

> *However, we are satisfied that if the High Court judge on first appeal had not assumed that the Registrar had such powers of investigation and had specifically addressed his mind to the above provisions of s 105, he would most certainly have found that that section gives no such powers to the Registrar of Titles. That section as quoted above only empowers the Registrar of Titles to determine questions regarding whether his register should be corrected or an entry therein cancelled. Any other inquiry or investigation to be undertaken by him must be either expressly or impliedly authorised or required by the Ordinance or any rule made thereunder. The present proceedings did not involve a dispute over entries in the Land Register requiring the Registrar of Titles to determine whether any registration or entry should or should not be made in the Land Register or that what is in the register should be corrected or cancelled. It involved the question whether the land in dispute registered in the appellant's name was the appellant's property or his late father's. The dispute therefore involved the ownership of registered land. There is no provision both in the Land Registration Ordinance and in the rules which authorise or requires the Registrar of Titles to make investigations and determine such substantial issues as land ownership. The investigation and proceedings by the Registrar were therefore undertaken without jurisdiction they were thus null and void.*

To the general citizenry, knowledge about rights and obligations on land matters is extremely important. Citizens must be made to know that having rights or claims of rights to land goes together with reciprocal duties or obligations to respect the law as well as rights of others in the neighbourhood and in the remote. Everyone has the duty to respect the land rights of others, for example, by not daring to trespass into the land of another; the duty to seek to settle land disputes amicably or through the judicial process instead of resorting to the "self-help" rule; the duty to know the laws and rules of procedure governing claims over the right to land, and the incidental duty, finally, to respect court orders. Also some other moral duties, such as will writing to divide property and avoid chaos in families should always be taken on board.

To policy makers and legislators, the message is that legislation is always an open-ended process. Legislators should always strive to fill the gaps in land legislation by reconciling various pieces of legislation that seem to contradict or conflict with each other, and to enact new laws to meet the demands of the growing community of the Tanzanian citizenry. It was well seen in Chapter One above, that when cases of illegal evictions became rampant in South Africa and threatened social harmony the State adopted the *Prevention of Illegal Eviction from Unlawful Occupation Act, 1998* to combact the vice and restore the social order. It is this call to legislators which requires them to think of bringing in a similar legislation in Tanzania, as similar cases of illegal evictions tend to dominate the scene of land administration in Tanzania. We are quite aware of, and we praise the legislators for passing, the *Unit Titles Act*[1318] and the *Mortgage Financing (Special Provisions) Act.*[1319] The former was enacted for a fourfold purpose: to provide for the management of the division of building into units, clusters, blocks and sections owned individually; to provide for issuance of certificates of unit titles for individual ownership of units, clusters or sections of the building; to provide for management and resolution of disputes arising from the use of common property, and; to provide use of common property by occupiers other than owners.[1320] The latter, on the other hand, has been enacted for the purpose of amending certain laws with the view to providing further provisions for mortgage.[1321] Tanzanians, including the President and the Minister[1322] in the forefront, have great hope in the functioning of these two Acts. Let us wait and see!

To the would-be practitioners (land law students) and the practitioners (members of the bar), the knowledge on land law and practice is not an option. You need to be well-acquainted with the same in order to be able, not only to offer quality, reliable and reputable professional services (professional advice and appearance) to the needy clients, but also to assist the courts to reach just and fair decisions.

1318 Act No. 16 of 2008.

1319 Act No. 17 of 2008.

1320 See the long title to Act No. 16 of 2008.

1321 See the ling title to Act No. 17 of 2008.

1322 While delivering his monthly speech in January 31, 2009 President Kikwete did not hesitate to tell Tanzanians that these laws have been uniquely and especially enacted to emancipate Tanzanians from housing problems. His Excellency said in Kiswahili that "*Ni sheria za aina yake ambazo zitasaidia sana kuinua maisha ya watu...Ni Sheria za msingi zinazoleta mabadiliko muhimu katika maisha yetu.*"

To courts of law, their brand "Temples of Justice" must be guarded under all possible means at the courts' disposal. Courts should stand by the rules and principles of natural justice to ensure that public trust and confidence in courts is maintained. To this end, courts are duty bound not only to handle cases with great care and to ensure that cases are disposed of within the quickest possible time, but also to decide cases without fear or favour. In Khalifa Seleman Saddot v Yahya Jumbe & 4 Others,[1323] the Court of Appeal of Tanzania quashed the proceedings and the order of the High Court of Tanzania at Mwanza (Mrema, J.)[1324], which had nullified the disposition of a property by the 1st respondent to the applicant, without according the applicant the right of a hearing. The Court raised its voice very high and stated at p. 9 that:

> *We wish to emphasize the audi alteram partem rule of natural justice which requires a person to given a hearing before adverse action is taken against his or her property, interests or person. The learned Judge contravened this principle of natural justice when he nullified the disposition of the suit property without giving the applicant owner thereof, a hearing. As the Court decided in the cases cited above, such arbitrary nullification offends the right to be heard. In the premises, we quash and set aside the nullification of the sale of the property on Plot No. 23 Block 'T' Rwagasore Street, Mwanza. We hereby order that the matter be remitted to the High Court for hearing on the disposition, inter partes, so that the applicant purchaser can be heard on the same.*

In short, courts have a duty to ensure equality of rights to all who come to the courts to seek judicial remedies. In other words, no one may loose a right to land for reasons related to his social status, including the state of being poor and/or marginalized. The public comment from the two extracts below invites courts to make a reflection of their role in the administration of land law in this country:

> *Failure by the High Court to issue judgment on a court case filed three years ago by Mabwegere villagers in Kilosa district a over land dispute is the major factor behind the brutal killings of farmers that occurred at Kakenge hamlet on October 27 this year.*[1325]

1323 Court of Appeal of Tanzania at Mwanza, Civil Application No. 20 of 2003 (Unreported).

1324 Miscellaneous Application No. 16 of 2000.

1325 See LUHWANGO, Rodgers, "The Cost of Delayed Justice", in the *Guardian*, Sunday, November 9, 2008 at p. 3. The comment is taken in the instance of the recent land dispute between farmers and villagers in Kilosa District that claimed the lives of 7 people on 27 October 2008.

> *Ni vigumu mwananchi wa kawaida kumshinda kigogo mwenye pesa zake. Wawekezaji wa Misenyi ni vigogo na wengine ni waheshimiwa serikalini. Kuwashinda mahakamani ni ndoto.*[1326]

We recommend the above obligatory measures, while we are aware of the various constraints or potential constraints, including: corruption, which is turning into a virus in all areas of life not excluding the land administration sector; the illiteracy and poverty of the majority of our people; the understaffing of our public institutions, including the courts of law, which are the legal guardians of the people's rights to land; financial limitations on the part of the government; and the market forces which purport to dictate terms unfriendly to the poor and the marginalized who, in reality, form the majority of Tanzanians. Notwithstanding these constraints, we invite all stakeholders to utilise most profitably the modest available opportunities for the benefit of all citizens.

1326 KARUGENDO, Privatus, "Simama Imara Rais Kikwete, unao Umma", in Raia Mwema, January 23-29, 2008 at p. 17. The comment follows President Kikwete's move to intervene in the reported land dispute that erupted involving the natives of Misenyi District, Kagera, on one hand and the investors running the ranch project in the area where the villagers were ordered to vacate the area, but they maintained that they had been in the area for over four generations, and the occupied village was legally registered in 1970.

Appendixes

Appendix-1

SALE

THE LAND ACT, 1999, NO. 4 OF 1999
Contract For A Disposition of A Right Of Occupancy
(Under Section 64)

TITLE NO.	**00000**
LAND OFFICE NO:	**111111**
LAND:	**PLOT NO: 22**
BLOCK:	**T(HIGH DENSITY)**
KISIWANI AREA	
DAR ES SALAAM	

THIS AGREEMENT is made this ***1st*** day of ***January***, 2011

Between

NKAKA KYOMO KIBILA of P. O. Box 0001, Dar es Salaam (hereinafter called "the **Vendor**") of the one part.

And

KAFUMU MUGO NYOKOLA of P. O. Box 0002, Dar es Salaam (hereinafter called "the **Purchaser**") of the other part.

WHEREAS:

a. The Vendor is the owner of landed property over all that land known as Plot No. 22 (High Density), Kisiwani Area, Dar es Salaam (hereinafter to be referred to as "the property")

b. The Vendor is desirous of selling to the Purchaser and the Purchaser is desirous of buying from the Vendor the property at the consideration of Shillings Forty Million (40,000,000/=) free from any encumbrances whatsoever.

NOW THIS AGREEMENT WITNESSETH as follow:-

1. DESCRIPTION OF THE LAND

The land the subject of this **Contract** is all land known as **Plot No. 22 (High Density)** comprised under **Certificate of Title No. 00000 Land office No.11111** located at **Block "T" KISIWANI AREA, DAR ES SALAAM,** with all the buildings and other fixed improvements thereon.

2. CONSIDERATION

The consideration of this transaction is Shillings Forty Million only (Sh. 40, 000,000/=)

3. PAYMENT

The Purchaser has paid to the Vendor the sum of Tshs. 40,000,000/= (receipt of which is acknowledged by the Vendor on the date of execution of this agreement.

4. EXECUTION OF THE DEED OF TRANSFER

i. Simultaneously with the signing of this Contract there have also been signed such Deeds and all other transfer documents as are prescribed under the Land Act, 1999.

ii. The Vendor covenants to execute such further relevant documents and afford to the Purchaser such assistance as the Purchaser may require for the purpose of vesting in the Purchaser the full benefit of the property.

5. DELIVERY OF POSSESSION OF THE PROPERTY TO THE PURCHASER

The Vendor shall deliver the Property to the Purchaser promptly after receipt of the Purchase price as per clause 3. of this agreement.

6. CONSENT TO TRANSFER

The Parties hereto recognize that this Contract of Transfer of a Right of Occupancy and Deed of Transfer are subjected to the approval of the Commissioner for Lands. The Vendor assisted by the Purchaser shall take all necessary and reasonable steps to obtain the said Commissioner's Consent.

7. COSTS

The Purchaser shall be responsible for payment of Stamp Duty, Registration fees, Valuation fee, Approval and Notification fees as may be assessed in respect of this transfer.

IN WITNESS WHEREOF the parties hereto have duly executed these presents in the manner and on the day and year hereinafter appearing.

SIGNED and **DELIVERED** by the said]
NKAKA KYOMO KIBILA who is known to me]
personally/identified to me by........................] **......**
gned..................
..]
VENDOR
.... the latter being known to me,]
before me this ...... day of ...., 2011]
SIGNATURE: ....
(To be filled by an advocate/witness)
POSTAL ADDRESS: .... Oficial Stamp
....
QUALIFICATION: ....

SIGNED and **DELIVERED** by the said]
KAFUMU MUGO NYOKOLA who is known]
to me personally/identified to me by..............] ....
ned....................

.... the latter being known to me] **PURCHASER**
before me this ...... day of ...., 2011]
SIGNATURE: ....
(To be filled by an advocate/witness)
POSTAL ADDRESS: .... Official Stamp

....

QUALIFICATION: ....
DRAWN BY:-
....
Kigusha & Partners (Advocates),
Kwimbe Street,
P. O. Box 0000,
Dar Es Salaam

Appendix- 2

LEASE

THIS LEASE is made this ***1st*** day of ***January*** 2010 **BETWEEN**

NKAKA KYOMO KIBILA of P.O.Box 00000, Dar es Salaam (hereinafter referred to as "the Landlord" which expression shall where the context so admits include the persons deriving title under him) of the one part,

AND

KAFUMU MUGO NYOKOLA of P.o.Box 00002 Dar es Salaam (hereinafter called "the Tenant") of the second part, which expression shall where the context so admits include his successors and assignees in title.

WHEREAS the Landlord is the registered owner of the building erected on land comprised in Title No 0000 and located and/or situated on Plot No. 22 Kisiwani area, Dar es Salaam.

AND WHEREAS the Landlord desires to let the said building to the Tenant for residential purposes only on terms and conditions stated in this Lease.

AND WHEREAS the Tenant agrees to the same.

(1) The monthly rent is agreed at Two Hundred Thousand Shillings (Shs. 200,000/= per month).

(2) The rent shall be paid yearly in advance on 1st January each year.

(3) The tenancy shall commence from the 1st day of January and it is to expire on 31st December 2010.

(4) The Tenant HEREBY COVENANTS with the Landlord as follows, namely:

a. To pay the reserved rent yearly, and to use the demised premises for residential purposes only.

b. To keep the interior of the demised premises and all additions thereto and all the fittings, furniture and fixtures therein and all the sanitary and water apparatus thereof in good and tenantable repair and conditions (fair tear and wear and damage by fire or tempest excepted).

c. To keep the interior of the demised premises and the appurtenances thereof including doors, windows and other fixtures, fittings, fastening, electrical wires and fittings, water drains and other pipes and painting and decoration thereof in good and substantial repair and good condition.

d. Not to carry on or cause to be carried on in or upon the demised premises or any part thereof any trade or business whatsoever.

e. To permit the landlord and his agents with or without workmen and others at all reasonable times of the day to enter upon and view the condition of the demised premises and forthwith (so far as the Tenant is liable) to execute all repairs and works required to be done under a written notice given by the Landlord PROVIDED ALWAYS that if the Tenant shall not within fourteen days after service of such notice commence and proceed diligently with the execution of the repairs and works mentioned in such notice (so far as aforesaid) it shall be lawful for the Landlord to enter upon the demised premises with his workmen and execute such repairs and works and the cost thereof shall be a debt due from the Tenant to the Landlord and be forthwith recoverable by legal action.

f. Not to do or permit anything in or upon the demised premises or any part thereof which may be or become a nuisance or annoyance or damage to the Landlord or other occupiers of other properties in the neighbourhood.

g. Not to hold or permit to be held any sale by auction or otherwise of the demised premises.

h. Not to do anything whereby any insurance of the said building against fire may be rendered void or voidable or whereby the premium for any such insurance may be liable to be increased and to indemnify the Landlord against increased or additional premiums which by reason of any act or default of the Tenant or his guest may be required for effecting of keeping up any such insurance.

i. Not to assign, sub-let or part with the possession of the demised premises or any part thereof under any circumstances whatsoever.

j. To keep and maintain a dust-bin in accordance with the Municipal Health Regulations and to pay for its removal.

k. To pay and discharge all charges of electric power, water and land telephone used or consumed in the demised premises.

l. At the determination of the tenancy hereby created to yield up the demised premises and all fixtures and fittings thereof to the Landlord in such good and tenantable repairs as shall be in accordance with the covenants hereinbefore contained on the part of the Tenants.

m. Not without the previous consent in writing of the Landlord or his agent to make or permit to be made any alteration or addition to the demised premises or cut or injure or alter any of the walls or timbers thereof and to keep the demised premises to its present state.

n. At the expiration or soon after the determination of the term hereby granted to peacefully surrender and yield up to the Landlord the demised premises with any addition thereto in good and tenantable repair and condition in accordance with the foregoing covenants.

o. Not to install water tank in any part of the building except on the terrace of the building with the consent of the Landlord which shall not be unreasonably withheld.

(5) The Landlord HEREBY COVENANTS with the Tenant as follows:

a. That during the said term of the tenancy the Landlord will pay and discharge all existing rates, taxes, duties and outgoings payable in respect of the demised premises and of the said building.

b. That the Landlord will during the said term keep in good tenantable repair the exterior and main structure of the demised premises and on receipt of notice from the Tenant to remedy any structural faults or faults of construction affecting the covenant and proper use of the demised premises, both internally and externally provided that such faults are not attributable to neglect of the part of the Tenant or his agents or employees.

c. That the Landlord will keep the said building insured against loss or damage by fire.

(6) The Landlord and Tenant HEREBY EXPRESSLY AGREE AND DECLARE that:

a. If the rent hereby reserved or any part thereof shall be unpaid for ten days after becoming payable (whether formally demanded or not) or if any covenant on the Tenant's part herein before contained shall not be performed or observed then and in any of the said cases it shall be lawful for the Landlord at any time thereafter to terminate this agreement with the right of action for possession to the Landlord for any breach of the Tenant's covenants herein contained.

b. If at any time during the term hereby granted the demised premises or any part thereof shall be destroyed or damaged by fire (not occasioned by the willful act, neglect or default of the Tenant or his/ her visitors, servants or employees) or act of God or force *majeure* then and in any such case and so often as the same shall happen the rent hereinabove or a fair and just proportion thereof according to the nature and extent of the injury or damage sustained shall cease and be suspended so long as the premises hereby demised or the destroyed or damaged part thereof shall remain uninhabitable or unfit for use by reason of such destruction or damage and if any dispute shall arise between the Landlord and Tenant in regard to the amount of the abatement so to be made of the said rent or the period for which the said rent or any part thereof shall be suspended or otherwise in relation thereto the same shall be referred to the proper Court.

c. The Landlord shall not disturb the Tenant's peaceful occupation of the demised premises if there is no breach of the Tenant's covenants.

d. This lease is for a fixed term of One year only from the date of commencement.

e. The Landlord may in his absolute discretion renew (or decline to renew) the lease for a further period of one year.

IN WITNESS WHEREOF the Landlord and Tenant have respectively executed this DEED on the day, year and in the manner hereinafter appearing.

SIGNED and DELIVERED by the said]
NKAKA KYOMO KIBILA who is **known**]
to me personally/identified to me by........]
.....................................the latter being]......Signed.........
known to me personally this..........day of] **LANDLORD**
..................................2011.]
Signature:...
Name: ....
(To be filled by an advocate/witness)
Address:... Official Stamp
Occupation:...
SIGNED and DELIVERED by the said]
KAFUMU MUGO NYOKOLA]
who is known to me personally/ identified].......Signed..........
to me by.............................the latter] **TENANT**
being known to me personally, in my presence]
this .... day of...............2011.]
Signature:...
Name: ....
(To be filled by an advocate/witnes)
Address:... Official Stamp
Occupation:...

DRAWN BY:

....

Kigusha & Partners (Advocates),
Kwimbe Street,
P.o.Box 0000,
Dar es Salaam.

Appendix- 3

MORTGAGE OF A RIGHT OF OCCUPANCY

(Under section 113 of the Land Act)

C.T No. 00000
L.O No 11111
L. D No 22222

I, **NKAKA KYOMO KIBILA** of P.O. Box 00000, Dar es Salaam who is the Mortgagor HEREBY MORTGAGE the right of occupancy registered under the above reference and all buildings and developments thereon to **MUFUMO TANZANIA BANK LIMITED** of P.O. Box 33333, Dar es Salaam ("the Mortgagee") to secure the indebtedness as hereinafter appears upon the following terms and conditions.

DEFINITIONS.

1. In this deed the following terms shall have the following meanings:

"Borrower"	means **WAO LAW FIRM** of P.O. Box 5555, Dar es Salaam.
"Indebtedness"	means the facility, interest on it and all other money from time to time owing on the security of this deed and any document(s) supplemental to it.
"Fcility"	means Loan Facility of Tanzania Shilling Five Hundred Million (500,000,000/=) only.
"Mortgagor"	means a mortgagor as defined under the Land Act.
"Mortgagee"	means a mortgagee as defined under the Land Act.
"Parties"	means the parties to this deed.
"Property"	means the Right of Occupancy and all buildings and developments thereon known as Plot No. SK/999/3, Katumba Street, Dar es Salaam, comprised in Certificate of Title to a Right of Occupancy, Title No. 30303 (Land Office No. 11111).

"Property taxes" means the land rent and all taxes, rates, assessments, duties, charges and outgoings now or at any time payable in respect of the property.

FACILITY, COVENANT TO PAY AND CHARGE

2.1. The Mortgagee has agreed to grant the facility to the Borrower, upon the terms and conditions which are specifically spelt in the Loan Facility letter dated 1st January 2008 (hereinafter to be referred to as "the facility letter").

2.2 The Mortgagor hereby agrees to become jointly and severally liable with the Borrower to pay to the Mortgagee the amounts outstanding on the facility on the due dates of payment and discharge all obligations and liabilities whether actual or contingent now or hereinafter due to the Mortgagee.

2.3 The amount secured by this deed is Shillings Five Hundred Million (Tshs.500, 000,000/=) as described in the facility letter and for the payment of the Mortgagee's costs and expenses incurred (on a full indemnity basis) in connection with the enforcement of this mortgage.

2.4 All costs, charges and expenses incurred hereunder by the Mortgagee and all other moneys paid by the Mortgagee or its Receiver in perfecting or otherwise in connection with this security or in respect of the Property including all costs of the Mortgagee or its Receiver of all proceedings for enforcement of the security hereby constituted or for obtaining payment of the monies hereby secured or arising out of or in connection with the acts authorised by this deed shall be recoverable from the mortgagor as a debt and shall bear interest accordingly and shall be charged on the Property.

2.5 A demand for payment or any other demand or notice under this deed may be made or given by any Manager or Officer of the Mortgagee or any branch thereof by letter addressed to the Mortgagor and sent by post to or left at the last known place of business or abode of the Mortgagor.

1.6 A Certificate by an Officer of the Mortgagee as to the amount for the time being due from the Mortgagor to the Mortgagee and/ or as to the interest after demand from time to time payable hereunder and/or as to the amount of costs and expenses incurred by the Mortgagee from time to time (including internal costs and expenses) shall be conclusive evidence (and shall be admissible as such) for all purposes against the Mortgagor.

1.7 The Mortgagor as a beneficial owner hereby charges by way of legal mortgage all and every interest in and over the Property with the payment of the indebtedness to the Mortgagee.

INSURANCE

3. The Mortgagor shall keep the Property insured against fire and such other risks as the Mortgagee shall from time to time direct for its full reinstatement value for the time being with an insurance company approved by the Mortgagee in the joint names of the Mortgagor and the Mortgagee and shall duly and punctually pay all premiums and money necessary for effecting and keeping up that insurance and on demand produce to the Mortgagee the policy of insurance and the receipt for any premium payable in respect of it.

REPAIRS AND PROPERTY TAX

4.1 The Mortgagor shall keep the Property in good repair and condition and shall permit the Mortgagee or its agent at all reasonable times until the mortgage is discharged to enter and examine the state and condition of the property.

4.2 The Mortgagor shall punctually pay all property taxes, rates, charges and rent and comply with any covenants and other provisions affecting the property and produce to the Mortgagee on demand such evidence as the Mortgagee reasonably requires of the Mortgagor's compliance with this covenant.

RESTRICTION ON LEASES, TRANSFER OR ASSIGNMENT.

5.1 The Mortgagor shall not without the Mortgagee's written consent grant or agree to grant any lease or tenancy of the property or any part of it or accept or agree to accept a surrender of any lease or tenancy of it.

5.2 The Mortgagor shall not without written consent of the Mortgagee transfer or assign or agree to transfer or to assign the property or any part thereto.

BORROWER'S DEFAULT

1.1 If the Borrower fails to perform or observe any of its obligations hereof and under the facility letter the Mortgagee shall be entitled but not obliged to take such steps as it thinks fit in or towards making good the Borrower's default without becoming liable as Mortgagee in possession and for that purpose to enter the property.

1.2 All money paid by the Mortgagee in the exercise of its rights under this deed shall be money properly paid by it and the Mortgagor shall pay them to the Mortgagee on demand with interest at the rate of interest on the facility from the date of payment by the Mortgagee until the date of payment by the Mortgagor.

POWERS OF SALE AND APPOINTMENT OF RECEIVER

7.1 The Mortgagee's power of sale and other powers under this deed and of appointing a Receiver shall arise on the date of this deed and shall accordingly be exercisable by the Mortgagee immediately if:

- The Mortgagee demands payment of any money secured by this deed and repayable on demand and it is not paid immediately; or
- Any payment of any money payable by the Mortgagor under this deed or the facility letter as the case may be is in arrears whether legally demanded or not; or
- The Mortgagor or Borrower as the case may be fails to comply with the any of its obligations under the facility letter or this deed or any other document (s) supplemental to it or them and the failure (if capable of being remedied) remains unremedied after being called to the Mortgagor's attention by the Mortgagee; or
- Any steps are taken by any person to enforce any rights in respects of the Property.

1.2 The Mortgagee may appoint by writing any person or persons (whether an officer of the mortgagee or not) to be Receiver (s) and Manager (s) (herein after called "the Receiver") which expression where the context so admit include the plural and any substituted Receiver (s) and Managers of all or any part of the Property.

1.3 The Mortgagee may from time to time determine the remuneration of the Receiver and may remove the Receiver and appoint another in his place.

1.4 The Receiver shall (so far as the law permits) be the agent of the Mortgagor (who shall alone be personally liable for the Receiver's acts, defaults and remuneration) and shall have powers in the same name of the Mortgagor or otherwise to do the following things namely:

1.4.1 To take possession of, collect and get in all or any part of the Property and for that purpose to take any proceedings as he shall think fit;

1.4.2 To commence and/ or complete any building operations on the Property or any part thereof and to apply for and obtain building permission approvals and any other permissions, consents or licences in each case as he may in his absolute discretion think fit;

1.4.3 To raise money from the Mortgagee or others on the security of the Property or otherwise;

1.4.4 To provide such facilities and services for tenants and generally to manage the property in such manner as he shall think fit;

1.4.5 To sell, let or lease or concur in selling letting or leasing and to vary the terms of, terminate or accept surrenders of leases or tenancies of the Property or any part thereof in such manner and for such term with or without a premium with such rights relating to other parts thereof and containing such covenants on the part of the Mortgagor and generally on such terms and conditions (including the payment of money to a lessee or tenant on a surrender) as his absolute discretion he shall think fit;

1.4.6 To make arrangements or compromise with the Mortgagee as he shall think fit;

1.4.7 To make and effect all repairs, improvements and insurances;

1.4.8 To appoint Managers, Officers, Contractors and Agents for the aforesaid purposes upon such terms as to remuneration or otherwise as he may determine;

1.4.9 To do all such other acts and things as may be considered to be incidental or conducive to any of the matters or powers aforesaid and which he lawfully may or can do;

1.5 The Mortgagee is hereby authorised whether in its own name or in the name of the Mortgagor to grant a lease or leases of the whole or any part or parts of the Property with such rights relating to other parts thereof and containing such covenants on the part of the Mortgagor and generally on such terms and conditions (including the payment of money to a lessee or tenant on a surrender) and whether or not a premium as the Mortgagee in its absolute discretion shall think fit;

1.6 In no circumstances shall the Mortgagee be liable to account to the Mortggagor as a Mortgagee in possession or otherwise for any moneys not actually received by the Mortgagee;

1.7 All powers of the Receiver hereunder may be exercised by the Mortgagee whether as Attorney of the Mortgagor or otherwise;

ATTORMENT

1. The Mortgagor irrevocably appoints the Mortgagee as its Attorney to execute any document or do anything which is required for any of the purposes of this deed or the exercise or enforcement of any of the Mortgagee's rights and remedies under it.

FREEDOM FROM ACCOUNTABILITY

2. If the Mortgagee enters into possession of the Property or part of it, it may from time to time at pleasure go out of such possession and shall not be liable to account as lender in possession while in fact out of possession if notice of such fact is within seven days after its happening served on the Mortgagor.

INTERPRETATION

1.1 Reference to any part to this deed shall where the context permit include its successors in title;

1.2 The headings to clauses are inserted for convenience only and shall not affect the construction of this deed;

1.3 Reference in this deed to anything which any party is required to do or not to do shall include its acts, defaults and omissions whether

-direct or indirect

-on its own account, or

-for or through any other person, and

-those which it permits or suffers to be done or not done by any other person.

1.4 No failure, delay, forbearance or indulgence by the Mortgagee in exercising any right or remedy shall operate as a waiver thereof nor shall any single or partial exercise or waiver of any right or remedy preclude its further exercise or the exercise of any other right or remedy.

LAW AND JURISDICTION

1.5 This deed shall be governed by and construed in accordance with the Laws of the United Republic of Tanzania and the Mortgagor agrees (subject to its pecuniary jurisdiction) to submit to the High Court of Tanzania, Commercial Division, for the determination of any questions, differences, enforcement or disputes relating to or arising from this deed.

IN WITNESS WHEREOF the Mortgagor and the Mortgagee have executed this deed the day and year first above written.

Signed and delivered by the said]
NKAKA KYOMO KIBILA who is]
known to me personally/ who has]
been identified to me by…………] Signed ………………
………………………the latter being] **MORTGAGOR**
known to me personally in my]
presence this …… day of …….. 2011]
Signature:……………………………..
Name :……………………………..
(To be filled by an advocate/witness)
Address :…………………………….. Official Stamp
Occupation: …………………………..

Sealed with the Common Seal of]
MUFUMO TANZANIA BANK LIMITED]
and delivered in the presence of us this] Seal of the Company
.... day of .... 2011]

Signature:...
Name: ....
Address: ....
Qualification: Director/Company Secretary
Signature:...
Name: ....
Address: ....

Qualification: Director/Company Secretary

DRAWN BY:

Kigusha & Partners (Advocates),
Kwimbe Street,
P.o.Box 0000,
Dar es Salaam.

Appendix- 4

LAST WILL AND TESTAMENT

THIS IS THE LAST WILL and testament of me **NKAKA KYOMO KIBILA**, Resident of Dar es Salaam, Tanzania, of P.O.Box 00000, which I make this 1st day of January 2010.

1. I hereby revoke all former Wills and other testamentary dispositions heretofore made by me and DECLARE this to be my LAST WILL.

2. I appoint my wife **KABILIZI KYOMO KIBILA** and my son **KIJELA KYOMO KIBILA** to be jointly the Executors of this my Will.

3. I give devise to my said wife absolutely for her benefit and use unconditionally my house on Plot no 176, Block "D", Mao Estate in Dar es Salaam for her own absolute and benefit.

4. I bequeath the following specific legacies:

   a. To my son **KIJELA KYOMO KIBILA,** all my ordinary shares in the Company known as Kagaju Breweries Ltd.

   b. To my daughter **KALIGALIGO KYOMO KIBILA** my motor – car, TOYOTA Saloon with Registration No T 000 AAC.

5. I bequeath the following pecuniary legacies:

   a. To my son **KIJELA KYOMO KIBILA**, the sum of Tshs. Million Fifteen Thousands (15,000,000/=).

b. To my daughter **KALIGALIGO KYOMO KIBILA**, the sum of Tshs. Million Ten Thousands (10,000,000/=).

6. I devise and bequeath all the residual of my real and personal estate whatsoever and whosesoever not hereby or by any codicil hereto otherwise expressly disposed of as to my lands and as to my personal estate absolutely into my said wife, **KABILIZI KYOMO KIBILA** for her absolute use and benefit.

7. I further direct that should my wife die in my lifetime then and only then I give devise and bequeath all my real and personal property whatsoever and wheresoever situated to my said daughter and my said son in equal shares for their respective use and benefit absolutely PROVIDED THAT if any one of them shall die in my lifetime leaving issue who have not attained the age of 18 years then such issue shall take by substitution and if more than one equal share per stripes the share of my estate which such deceased daughter or son of mine would have taken if she or he had survived me but so that no issue shall take whose parent is alive and so capable of taking.

IN WITNESS WHEREOF I, the said **NKAKA KYOMO KIBILA** being the testator have to this my LAST WILL set my hand this 1st day of January 2010.

SIGNED AND AKNOWLEDGED by the above named]
NKAKA KYOMO KIBILA, the Testator as and for his]
LAST WILL in the presence of us both present at the]
same time who at his request in his presence and]… Signed
in the presence of each other have hereunto subscribed]**STATOR**
our names as witnesses.]

Signature:…………………………………………..
Name:…………………………………………...
(To be filled by a witness)
Address:……………………………………………
Occupation:………………………………………...
Signature:…………………………………………
Name:…………………………………………..
(To be filled by a witness)
Address:……………………………………………
Address:…………………………………………..
Occupation:………………………………………..

DRAWN BY:

……………………………………………………

Kigusha & Partners (Advocates),
Kwimbe Street,
P.o.Box 0000,
Dar es Salaam.

List of Cases

A

Abdallah Chapila v Mwinyigoha & Another, (1965) L.C.C.AD/30/65 (Unreported).

Abdallah Salanga & 63 Others, Court of Appeal of Tanzania at Dar es Salaam, Civil Application No. 4 of 2001 (Unreported).

Abdul Sadiki v Wilfred Rutakinikwa, [1988] TLR No. 167 (HC).

Abdulkadri Mohamed v Registrar of Titles, [1992] TLR No. 21 (CA).

Abdulrasul Ahmed Jaffer and 2 Others v Parin A. Jaffer and Another, Court of Appeal of Tanzania at Dar es Salaam, Civil Appeal No. 5 of 1994 (Unreported).

Abualy Alibhai Aziz v Bhatia Brothers Ltd [2000] TLR 288 (CA).

Adler v Blackman, (1953) 1 Q.B No. 146 (UK).

Aggrawal v Dhillon, [1969] HCD No. 167.

Agro Industries v Attorney General, [1994] TLR No. 43 (CA).

Aldin Latimer Clark Muirhead and Co, [1894] 2 Ch. No. 437.

Alexkor Limited and the Government of the Republic of South Africa v The Richtersveld Community and Others, Case No. CCT 19/03 (South Africa).

Alli Mangosongo v Chrispina Magenje, [1977] LRT No. 18 (HC).

Ameleck Ngajilo v Nuru Mohamed, District Land and Housing Tribunal for Temeke District at Temeke, Land Appeal No. 33 of 2006 (Unreported).

Ami v Safari and Others, [2001] 1E.A No. 3.

Amina Tratibu Mbonde v Selemani Ahmed Mtalika, [2000] T.L.R. 56 (HC).

Amodu Tijan v The Secretary Southern Nigeria, (1921) A.C 399.

Angelo Bisiki v Antonia Bisiki and Others, [1989] TLR No. 225 (HC).

Anna Benedict v Mrisho, East African Court of Appeal, Civil Appeal No. 41 of 1976 (Unreported).

Anna Benedict v Seif Mrisho and Anothher, [1977] LRT No. 36 (HC).

Asha Shemzigwa v Halima A. Shekigenda [1998] T.L.R. 245 (HC).

Assistant Registrar of Buildings v Fredrick Kibwana, [1987] TLR No. 84 (CA).

Attonery General v Lohay Akonay & Another [1995] TLR No. 80 (CA).

Attorney General v Motor Mart and Exchange Limited, (1960) E.A 689.

Attorney General v Sisi Enterprises Ltd, [2006] TLR 9 (CA).

Atuganile Mwaitege v Timoth Makalinga, High Court of Tanzania at Dar es Salaam, (PC) Civil Appeal No. 34 of 1999 (Unreported).

Aziz Daudi Aziz v Amin Ahmed Ally and Seleman Wagharibu, Court of Appeal of Tanzania, Civil Appeal No. 36 of 1990 (Unreported).

B

Balley v Barnes, (1894) 1 Ch No. 25 (UK).

Barend Petrus Barkhuizen v Ronald Stuart Napier, Constitutional Court of South Africa, Case No. CCT 72 of 2005 (South Africa).

Benjamine Kamau Murima and Others v Glady's Njeri, Kenya Court of Appeal Reports, Vol. 8, p. 64 (Kenya).

Beno Chelele t/a General Intergrated Firm v National Housing Corporation and 2 Others, High Court of Tanzania (Land Division) at Dar es Salaam, Land Case No. 96 of 2004 (Unreported).

Berabera Ujamaa Village v Abubakari Bura, [1983] TLR No. 219 (HC).

Bernado Ephrahim v Holaria Pastory & Another, High Court of Tanzania at Mwanza, Civil Appeal No. 70 of 1989 (Reported in [1990] L.RC. (Const.) 757.

Bi Amina Katume v Eustace Ndyakowa, [1968] HCD No. 13.

Bi Hawa Mohamed v Alli Seif [1983] TLR No. 33 (CA).

Bibi Makongoro v Issa, (1970) HCD No. 192.

Biggs v Hoddinnott, (1898) 2 Ch. No. 307 (UK).

Bilimbasa Zakaria v Jervas John, [1983] TLR No. 67 (HC).

Bp Bhatt and Another v Habib Versi Rajan, [1958] E.A 536.

Bridle v Ruby and Another, [1988] 3 WLR No. 191 (UK).

C

Celestina Paul v Mohamed Hussein, [1983] TLR No. 291 (HC).

Centre on Housing Rights and Eviction v Republic of Sudan, African Commission on Human and Peoples' Rights, Communication 295 of 2005 (Unreported).

Colonel Cashimir v Naginder Singh Matharu, [1988] TLR 163 (HC).

Congleton Corporation v Pattison, (1808), 10 East 130, 135 (UK).

CRDB Bank Ltd v Mazrui Commission Agent Co. Ltd and 4 Others, High Court of Tanzania (Commercial Division) at Dar es Salaam, Commercial Case No. 94 of 2002 (Unreported).

D

Deocres Rutabana v Deus Kashaga, [1981] TLR No. 122

Dero Investiment Ltd v Heykel Berete, Court of Appeal of Tanzania at Dar es Salaam, Civil Appeal No. 92 of 2004 (Unreported).

Diamond v Campbell Jones and Others, (1960) 1 ALL ER 583 (UK).

Didas Rwakalila & 3 Others v Thomas Matondane [1992] TLR No. 314 (CA).

Dillon v Public Trustee of New Zealand, [1941] A.C No. 294 (UK).

Director of Lands and Mines v Sohan Singh, [1952] 1 TLR 63.

E

Edward Msango v Aga Khan Sports Club, High Court of Tanzania at Dar es Salaam, Civil Application No. 15 of 2005 (Unreported).

Edwin Simon v Adam Mbale, [1983] TLR No. 410 (HC).

Elizabeth Mtawa v Hassan Mfaume Risasi, High Court of Tanzania at Dodoma, Civil Application No. 12 of 2001 (Unreported).

Elizeus Rutakubwa v Jason Angelo, [1983] TLR No. 365 (HC).

Emma Kichika Kea v Anna Musa Mbaga, High Court of Tanzania (Commercial Division) at Dar es Salaam, Commercial Case No. 84 of 2000 (Unreported).

F

Fans William Muze v Kalumela Mlula, High Court of Tanzania (Land Division) at Dar es Salaam, Misc. Land Appeal No. 3 of 2005 (Unreported).

Fatuma Ghachae v Mariam Ghachae and National Housing Corporation, High Court of Tanzania (Land Division) at Dar es Salaam, Land Case No. 261 of 2004 (Unreported).

Ferdinandi s/o Lumbogo v Ngeiyamu s/o Kajuna, [1982] TLR No. 142.

Frontier Dispute between Burkina Faso and the Republic of Mali, I.C.J Reports, 1986 p. 582.

Fumo Co. Limited and National Housing Corporation v Jujent Import-Export Co. Ltd, High Court of Tanzania at Dar es Salaam, Civil Appeal No. 135 of 1999 (Unreported).

Furaha Mohamed v Fatuma Abdallah, [1992] TLR No. 205 (HC).

G

George A. Mmari and Anande A. Mmari v Afra Fuime, [1995] TLR 146 (HC).

George Shambwe v National Printing Co. Ltd, [1995] TLR No. 262 (CA).

Ghina Abass v Peter Sylvester, High Court of Tanzania (Land Division) at Dar es Salaam, Misc. Land Appeal No. 5 of 2006 (Unreported).

Godwin Ndewesi and Another v Tanzania Audit Corporation, Court of Appeal of Tanzania at Dar es Salaam, Civil Application No. 57 of 1994 (Unreported).

Gregory Mtafya v Zainabu Lyimo, [1976] LRT No. 3.

H

Hamid Mbaye v The Brigade Commander, [1984] TLR 294 (HC-Z).

Hamis Sakaya v Beda Joseph & Others, Regional Housing Tribunal of Dar es Salaam, Application No. 134 of 2001 (Unreported).

Hamisi Sinahela v Assan Mbele, [1974] LRT No. 28 (HC).

Hamson D. Ghikas v Ludwina G. Ghikas, [1992] TLR No. 288 (CA).

Haruna Mpangoas & Others v Tanzania Portland Cement Company Ltd, Court of Appeal of Tanzania at Dar es Salaam, Civil Reference No. 3 of 2007 (Unreported).

Hawabai Franjee Petit v Secretary of State of India, [1915] 39 Bom. 279 (India).

Hemed S. Tamin v Renata Mashayo, [1994] TLR No. 197 (CA).

I

Ibrahim Korosso and 134 Others & Legal and Human Rights Centre v Thomas Ole Sabaya and District Commission for Serengeti District, Commission for Human Rights and Good Governance, Case No. HBUB/S/1032/2001/2002 MARA.

Ibrahim Kusaga v Emmanuel Mweta, [1986] TLR No. 78 (CA).

Idda Mwakalindile v NBC Holding Corporation, [2001] 1 E.A Na. 148.

International Drilling Fluids Ltd v Louisville Investment (Uxbridge) Ltd, (1986) 2 WLR No. 581.

Ismail Bushaija v Republic, [1991] TLR No. 100 (HC).

Issa Batenga v Kheri Batenga and Another, Court of Appeal of Tanzania at Dar ves Salaam, Civil Rereference No. 6 of 1995 (Unreported).

Issa Omary v Masood Issa, High Court of Tanzania at Dar es Salaam, Misc. Civil Cause No. 4 of 2001 (Unreported).

Issa Warsama v Salima Bhanji, [1984] TLR No. 122 (CA).

J

Jackosn Reuben Maro v Hubert Sebastinian, Court of Appeal of Tanzania at Arusha, Civil Appeal No. 84 of 2004 (Unreported).

Jayantilal P. Rajan v City Council of Dar es Salaam, [1983] TLR 385 (HC).

Jeremiah Venant v Clementina Alexander, [1983] TLR No. 137 (HC).

Jibu Sakilu v Petro Miumbi, [1993] TLR No. 75 (HC).

John Agricola v Rashid Juma, [1990] TLR No. 1 (HC).

John Ngomoi v Mohamed Ally Bofu, [1988] TLR No. 63 (HC).

Jones v Gardiner, [1902] 1 Ch. No. 191 (UK).

Joshua Maswi & 145 Others v BP Tanzania Limited & 2 Others, High Court of Tanzania at Dar es Salaam, Misc. Civil Cause No. 9 of 2003 (Unreported).

Juthalal Velji Ltd v The THB Estate Ltd, [1983] TLR No. 391 (HC).

Juma Goboka v Halima Mohamed, [1975] LRT No. 1.

Jumanne s/o Mazebele v Bukombe s/o Kihongwe, High Court of Tanzania at Dodoma, (PC) Civil Appeal No. 76 of 2002 (Unreported).

K

Kasubi v Kakubukubu, High Court of Tanzania at Mwanza, Civil Appeal No. 23 of 1987 (Unreported).

Khalifa Seleman Saddot v Yahya Jumbe & 4 Others, Court of Appeal of Tanzania at Mwanza, Civil Application No. 20 of 2003 (Unreported).

Kibwana Mohamed v Republic, [1980] TLR No. 321.

Kijakazi Mbegu and 5Others v Ramadhani Mbegu [1999] TLR 174 (HC).

*Kreglinger v New Patagonia Meat and Storage Co., (*1914) A.C No. 25 (UK).

L

Lalata Msongawale v Henry Mwamliama, [1979] LRT No. 3 (HC).

Land Officer v The Motor Mart and Exchange, (1953-1955) 2 TLR 295.

Lausa Alfan Salum & 106 Others v Ministry for Lands, Housing and Urban Development & National Housing Corporation, [1994] TLR No. 237 (CA).

Legal and Human Righs Centre v Ole Sabaya and 4 Others, High Court of Tanzania (Land Division) at Dar es Salaam, Misc. Land Application No. 22 of 2005 (Unreported).

Legal and Human Rights Centre v Ole Sabaya and 4 Others, Court of Appeal of Tanzania at Dar es Salaam, Civil Appeal No. 88 of 2006 (Unreported).

Leila Jelaludin Haji v Shaffin Jelaludin Haji Jamal, High Court of Tanzania at Dar es Salaam, Civil Case No. 372 of 2001 (Unreported).

Leonce Mtalindwa v Mariadina Edward, [1986] TLR No. 120 (HC).

Letisia Bugumba v Thadeo Magoma & Another, High Court of Tanzania at Mwanza, Civil Appeal No. 8 of 1989 (Unreported).

Leyla Nassoro Kiruka v Muakwe Mohamed Muakwe & Another, High Court of Tanzania (Land Division) at Dar es Salaam, Land Case No. 10 of 2003 (Unreported).

Likengele Faru Parutu Kamunyu & 52 Others v Ministry of Tourism, Ntural Resources and Environment [2000] T.L.R. 160 (CA).

Lucia Paulo v Lenna Ndege, High Court of Tanzania (Land Division) at Dar es Salaam, Misc. Land Appeal No. 48 of 2006 (Unreported).

Lukasi Masinori Kateti v Oloo Sebege, [1969] HCD No. 111.

Lutataza Biteye v Haji Seleman, [1975] LRT No. 43 (HC).

Lweshabula Mzinja v Juliet Jacobo, High Court of Tanzania (Land Division) at Dar es Salaam, Misc. Land Appeal No. 7 of 2005 (Unreported).

M

M/S Ilabila Industries Ltd & 2 Others v Tanzania Investment Bank and Another, Court of Appeal of Tanzania at Dar es Salaam, Civil Application No. 159 of 2004 (Unreported).

M/S Ilabila Industries Ltd and 2 Others v Tanzania Investiment Bank and Another, High Court of Tanzania (Commercial Division), Commercial Case No. 27 of 2002 (Unreported).

Maagwi Kimito v Gibeno Werema, [1985] TLR No. 132 (CA).

Mabo and Others v Queensland (No. 2) H.C.A 23 (Australia).

Mahlomi v Minister of Defence, 1999 (1) SA 124 (CC) (South Africa).

Manungwa Lutalamila and 2 Others v Martha Lutalamila, [1982] TLR No. 98.

Manyara Estate Ltd and Another v National Development Credit Agency, (1970) EA No. 177.

Mariam Ghahae v Fatuma Ghahae, Court of Appeal of Tanzania at Dar es Salaam, Civil Appeal No. 43 of 2009 (Unreported).

Maritime Boundary between Cameroon and Nigeria, I.C.J Reports, 2002 p. 303.

Martin Mbujilo v Elizabeth Lucas, High Court of Tanzania at Tabora, (PC) Civil Appeal No.6 of 2003 (Unreported).

Masanga Musoba v Mdee Lukuba, High Court of Tanzania at Mwanza, Civil Application No. 67 of 1984 (Unreported).

Mazaher Limited v Murray K. Chume, High Court of Tanzania (Commercial Division) at Dar es Salaam, Commercial Case No. 89 of 2002 (Unreported).

Mbaruku v Chomonyogoro, (HCD) No. 406.

Methusela Paul Nyagaswa v Christopher Mbote Nyirabu [1985] TLR 103 (CA).

MIC (T) v Tanzania Telecommunications Company Ltd (TTCL), High Court of Tanzania (Commercial Division) at Dar es Salaam, Commercial Case No. 146 of 2002 (Unreported).

Michael Leseni Kweka v John Eliafe, Court of Appeal of Tanzania, Civil Appeal No. 51 of 1997 (Unreported).

Mills and Another v Silver and Another, [1991] WLR No. 324 (UK).

Mkakofia Mariananga v Asha Ndisia, [1969] HCD No. 204.

Mkamangi Elifuraha v Mwinyishehe Mwinyishehe, [1991] TLR No. 191 (CA).

Mkubwa Said Omar v S.M.Z, [1992] TLR No. 365 (CA).

Mohamed Alladitta v El-Harthi, [1955] 22 E.A.C.A No. 84.

Mohamed Dossaji Frederick Lwezahula, High Court of Tanzania (Land Division) at Dar es Salaam, Land Case No. 25 of 2004 (Unreported).

Mohamed Hassan Hole v Keya Jumanne Ramadhani, Court of Appeal of Tanzania at Dodoma, Civil Appeal No. 19 of 1992 (Unreported).

Mohamed Hassan v Mayasa Mzee & Mwanahawa Mzee, [1994] TLR No. 224 (CA).

Mohamed Hasssan Hole v Keya Jumanne Ramadhan, Court of Appeal of Tanzania at Dodoma, Civil Appeal No. 19 of 1992 (Unreported).

Mohamed Iddi Mjasir v Mrs Jayalaxmi Jayantilal Joshi, [1993] TLR No. 274 (CA).

Mohamed Suleiman and 16 Others v Republic, High Court of Tazania at Dare es Salaam, Criminal Appeal No. 97 of 2003 (Unreported).

Mohamed Yusufu v Tunda Kassim, (1968) HCD No. 487.

Mrs Clara D'Souza v Charles Frank Kanyamala, [1974] LRT No. 27.

Mtoro Bin Mwamba v Attorney General [1953] 2TLR 327.

Mtumwa Ally Said and Another v Mwamtoro Ally Said, High Court of Tanmzania (Land Division) at Dar es Salaam, Land Appeal Case No. 48 of 2006 (Unreported).

Mtumwa Rashid v Abdallah Iddi and Salum Omari, Court of Appeal of Tanzania at Dar es Salaam, Civil Appeal No. 22 of 1993 (Unreported).

Mtumwa Shahame Baya Kondo & 111 Others v Principal Secretary, Ministry of Works & Attorney General, High Court of Tanzania (Land Division) at Dar es Salaam, Land Case No. 31 of 2004 (Unreported).

Muhena Bin Said v Registrar of Titles (1948) 16 E.A.C.A 71.

Mulbadaw Village Council & 67 Others v NAFCO [1984] TLR No. 15 (HC).

Musa Makono v Rehema Hassa, (1967) HCD No. 159.

Mutual Benefits Limited v Patel and Another, [1972] E.A 496.

Mwajuma Mohamed Njopeka v Juma Said Mkorogoro, High Court of Tanzania at Dar es Salaam, (PC) Civil Appeal No. 6 of 2001 (Unreported).

Mwalimu Omari & Ahmed Baguo v Omari A. Bilali [1999] TLR 432. (CA).

Mwanahawa Muya v Mwanaidi Maro, [1992] TLR No. 78 (CA).

N

National Agricultural and Food Corporation (NAFCO) v Mulbadaw Village Council and Others, (1985) TLR No. 88 (CA).

National Bank of Commerce Ltd v Manna Investment (Pty) Ltd and 2 Others, High Court of Tanzania (Commercial Division) at Dar es Salaam, Commercial Case No. 84 of 2002 9Unreported).

National Bank of Commerce v Dar es Salaam Education and Office Stationary, [1995] TLR No. 272 (CA).

National Bank of Commerce v Suleiman Nassoro Ally, [1989] TLR No. 67 (CA).

National Bank of Commerce v Walter, Court of Appeal of Tanzania at Dar es Salaam, Civil Appeal No. 31 of 1995 (Unreported).

NBC Holding Corporation v Shirika la Uchumi na Kilimo (SUKITA) and 63 Others, High Court of Tanzania (Commercial Division) at Dar es Salaam, Commercial Case No. 24 of 2001 (Unreported).

Nicolaus Komba v Kondrad Komba, [1988] TLR No. 172 (HC).

Nittin Coffee Estate Ltd and 4 Others v United Engineering Works Ltd and Another, [1988] T.R.L No. 203 (CA).

Nizar Shell Laadway Muhanna v Registrar of Titles and Another, [1995] TLR No. 217 (CA).

Noakes & Co. Ltd v Rice, (1902) A.C No. 24 (UK).

Ntiyahela Boneka v Kijiji cha Ujamaa Mutala, [1988] TLR No. 156 (HC).

Nuru Hussein v Abdul Ghani Ismail Hussein [2000] TLR 217 (CA).

O

***O**lam Tanzania Limited Property International v Baraka Mkondola*, High Court of Tanzania (Land Division) at Mtwala, Land Appeal No. 14 of 2007 (Unreported).

***O**lam Tanzania Limited and 3 Others v Seleman S. Selemani and 4 Others*, Court of Appeal of Tanzania at Mtwara, Consolidated Civi Revision No. 2, 3,4,5, &6 of 2010, ruling made on 11th October 2010 (Unreported).

***O**mari Mohamed v Awadhi Abdallah*, [1992] TLR 35 (HC).

***O**mari v Bilali*, High Court of Tanzania at Dar es Salaam, Civil Appeal No. 22 of 1987 (Unreported).

***O**noratha Della and Others v Peera*, (1970) HCD No. 22.

P

***P**artman Garments Industries Ltd v Tanzania Manufacturers Ltd*, [1981] TLR 303 (CA).

***P**atrick Kimilo v Shaweji Ulinda & Another*, Court of Appeal of Tanzania at Dar es Salaam, Civil Application No. 99 of 2001 (Unreported).

***P**aul Michael Simbaine v Asia Hassan Ramadhan*, High Court of Tanzania at Dar es Salaam, Civil Appeal No. 150 of 1999 (Unreported).

***P**eter Mbararia and Another v Peter Tabu Massawe*, High Court of Tanzania at Moshi, (PC) Civil Appeal No. 34 of 2003 (Unreported).

***P**ort Elizabeth Municipality v Various Occupiers*, Case CCT 53/03 (South Africa).

***P**ort v Griffith*, (1938) 1 ALL ER No. 295.

***P**residential Parastatal Sector Reform Commission v Data Machine Limited & 3 Others*, High Court of Tanzania (Land Division) at Dar es Salaam, Land Case No. 248 of 2004.

***P**rovinnchandra Mohanlal Mevada & 2 Others v Muhimbili Medical Centre and Another*, Court of Appeal of Tanzania at Dar es Salaam, Civil Appeal No. 106 of 2001 (Unreported).

***P**S Parmer and A. Adamjee v Paul E. Maro*, [1990] TLR No. 67 (CA).

R

Ramadhani Kambi Mkinga v Ramadhani Saidi, [1985] TLR No. 140 (HC).

Ramadhani Mussa v Francis Migilimo and Another, High Court of Tanzania at Tabora, (DC) Civil Appeal No. 13 of 2002 (Unreported).

Ramnik Vaghella v Mohamendra Vaghella [2000] T.L.R. 223 (CA).

Rashid Halfan v Pandael Singa and National Housing Corporation, High Court of Tanzania (Land Division) at Dar es Salaam, Land Case No. 173 of 2004 (Unreported).

Re Andrews, [1953] 1 WLR 1105 (UK).

Re Callagham, [1983] 3 WLR 1076 (UK).

Re Innocent Mbilinyi, (1969) HCD No. 283.

Re Kibiego (1972) E.A No. 179.

Re Leach [1985] 3 WLR 413 (UK).

Re the Estate of the Late Rabiuzima Matiro Mboro, High Court of Tanzania at Moshi, Probate and Administration Cause No. 2 of 1998 (Unreported).

Re the Estate of the Late Suleman Kasundwa, (1965) E.A No. 247.

Regina A. Kalukwa v Zubeil Katumwa, [1988] TLR No. 85 (HC).

Registered Trustees of the Masjid Al-Kadiria v Ali Muhidini and 6 Others, High Court of Tanzania (Land Division) at Dar es Salaam, Land Appeal No. 9 of 2006 (Unreported).

Republic v Abdulrahman s/o Sima, (1972) HCD No. 182.

Republic v Daudi Mdee, High Court of Tanzania at Dar es Salaam, Criminal Session Case No. 8 of 1999 (Unreported).

Republic v Mohamed Suleiman and 16 Others, Court of Resident Magistrate of Dar es Salaam, at Sokoine Drive, Criminal Case No. 2552 of 2002 (Unreported).

Riggs v Palmer, Court of Appeal of New York, Decision of October 8, 1889 (USA).

Riziki Habib v Fatuma Juma, High Court of Tanzania (Land Division) at Dar es Salaam, Land Case No. 102 of 2004 (Unreported).

Rye v Rye, (1962) AC No. 496 (UK).

S

Saffique A.S Dhiyebi v Presidential Parastatal Sector Reform Commission, High Court of Tanzania (Land Division) at Dar es Salaam, Land Case No. 46 of 2004 (Unreported).

Said Seleman Masuka v Anwar Z. Mohamed, Court of Appeal of Tanzania at Dar es Salaam, Civil Application No. 5 of 1997 (Unreported).

Salima Hussein v Hussein Ibrahim Sadiki & Sons, Court of Appeal of Tanzania at Dar es Salaam, Civil Appeal No. 55 of 2000 (Unreported).

Salmin Mohamed v Abdu Mohamed, [1986] TLR No. 251 (HC).

Salum Juma Mzeru v Omari Ubaya, [1984] TLR No. 31 (HC).

Salum Mateyo v Mohamed Mateyo, [1987] TLR No. 111 (HC).

Samson Kishosha v Charles Kingongo Gabba, [1990] TLR No. 133 (HC).

Samwel Olunga Igogo and 2 Others v The Social Action Trust Fund and 4 Others [2005] TLR 343 (HC).

Samwel v Jerrah Timber & Wood Paving Corporation, (1904) AC No. 323 (UK).

Sarjit Singh v Sebastian Christom, [1988] TLR No. 24 (HC).

Scolastica Benedict v Martin Benedict, [1993] TLR No. 1 (CA).

Shaban Nassoro v Shabani Simba, (1967) HCD No. 233.

Shah v Abdulla, [1964] E.A 742.

Shaidu Juma Kopwe v Seleman Musa, High Court of Tanzania (Land Division) at Dar es Salaam, Land Case No. 18 of 2006 (Unreported).

Shell and BP Tanzania Ltd v Wilbard Fulgence Rwenyagira, [1984] TLR No. 251 (CA).

Shinyanga Regional Trading Co. Ltd & Another v National Bank of Commerce, [1997] TLR No. 78 (CA).

Shomary Abdallah v Abdallah Hussein and Another, [1991] TLR No. 135 (HC).

Silvery Nkangaa v Raphael Albertho, [1992] TLR 110 (HC).

Simon Byanyuma v A.E Haliday, High Court of Tanzania (Land Division) at Dar es Salaam, Land Case No. 24 of 2004 (Unreported).

Simon Ngeleja v NBC, High Court of Tanzania at Dar es Salaam, Civil Case No. 154 of 1999 (Unreported).

Simon Osita v Adrianus Serere, (1967) HCD No. 21.

Sofia Njali v Mire Artan Ismail and Another, High Court of Tanzania at Dar es Salaam, Civil Revision No. 82 of 2002 (Unreported).

Sofia Said and Yusuf Mohamed Musa v Awadh Ahmed Abeid and 3 Others, [1992] TLR No. 29 (CA).

Standard Charted Bank Ltd v Walker & Another, (1983) 3 ALL ER No. 938.

T

Tanzania Tractors Manufacturing Co. Ltd/ PSRC v Gracious Mwanguya and Another, High Court of Tanzania at Dar es Salaam, Civil Appeal No. 203 of 2001 (Unreported).

Tatu Abdallah v Waziri Musa, [1975] LRT No. 7.

Territorial Dispute between Libyan Arab Jamahiriya and Chad, ICJ Reports, 1994 p. 6.

The Social and Economic Rights Action and Social Rights v Nigeria, African Commission on Human and Peoples Rights, Communication No. 155 of 1996 (Unreported).

Thomas Matondane v Didas Rwakalila and Others, [1989] TLR No. 210 (HC).

Tito Saturo & 7 Others v Matiya Seneya and Others, High Court of Tanzania at Arusha, Civil Case No. 27 of 1985 (Unreported).

V

Village Chairman KCU v Anthony Hyera, [1988] TLR No. 188 (HC).

Violate Kahangwa and Jovin Mutabuzi v The Administrator General and Mrs Eudokia Kahangwa, [1990] TLR No. 72 (CA).

W

Waziri Maneno Choka v Abas Choka, Court of Appeal of Tanzania at Dar es Salaam, Civil Appeal No. 51 of 1999 (Unreported).

William Rajabu Mallya & 2 Others v Republic, [1991] TLR No. 38 (CA).

Y

Yoke Gwaku & 5 Others v NAFCO and Another, High Court of Tanzania at Arusha, Civil Case No. 52 of 1988 (Unreported).

Young Wook v Yun Hun Hwa, High Court of Tanzania at Dar es Salaam, Probate and Aministration Cause No. 20 off 2001 (Unreported).

Yusufu Same and Hawa Dada v Hadija Yusufu, Court of Appeal of Tanzania at Dar es Salaam, Civil Appeal No. 1 of 2002 (Unreported).

Z

Zakaria Barie Bura v Theresia Maria John Mubiru, [1995] TLR 211 (CA).

Bibliography

AGARWAL, Bina, (1994): *A Field of Ones Own: Gender and Land Rights in South Asia*, Cambridge: Cambridge University Press.

AGARWAL, Bina, "Gender and Land Rights Revisited: Exploring New Prospective via the State, Family and Market" in RAZAVI, Shahra, (ed.), (2003): *Agrarian Change, Gender and Land Rights*, Blackwell Publishing, pp. 184-224.

AN-NA'IM, Abdulaah, Ahmed," Human Rights in the Muslim World" in HAYDEN, Patrick, (ed.), (2001): *The Philosophy of Human Rights*, First Edition, Paragon House, pp. 315-335.

ALFREDSSON, Gudmundur, "The Right to Property" in EIDE, Asbojorn, *et al.*, (1992): *The Universal Declaration on Human Rights: A Commentary*, Scandinavia University Press.

ARISTOTLE, (1962): *The Politics*, Penguin Books.

AVIRGAN, T., and HONEY, M., (1983): *War in Uganda: The Legacy of Idi Amini*, Dar es Salaam: Tanzania Publishing House

BARKER, David & PADFIELD, Colin, (1996): *Law*, 9th Edition, Madesimple Books.

BATUNGI, Nasani, "Land Tenure Reform in East Africa: Some Reflections on the Formalization of Customary Tenure," a Technical Paper Presented during the C.A.S.L.E Conference on Sustainable Land Management in Africa, held at Bagamoyo, Tanzania, 14th -17th March, 2006. See a compilation published by UCLAS Publishing Centre.

BIKAAKO, Winnie and SSENKUMBA, John, "Gender, Land and Rights: Contemporary Contestations in Law, Policy and Practices in Uganda" in WANYEKI, L. Muthoni (ed.), (2003): *Women and Land in Africa: Culture, Religion and Realizing Women's Rights*, London: and New York, Zed Books Ltd; Cape Town: David Philip Publishers.

BIKIE, Elise, H. & LOGO, Patrice, Bigombe, "Women and Land in Cameroon: Questioning Women's Land Status and Claims for Change" in WANYEKI, Muthoni (ed.), (2003): *Women and Land in Africa: Culture, Religion and Realizing Women's Rights*, London: and New York, Zed Books Ltd; Cape Town: David Philip Publishers.

BRIGGS, John, "Villagization and the 1974-6 Economic Crisis in Tanzania", *Journal of Modern African Studies*, Vol. 17, No. 4 (Dec., 1979), pp. 695-702.

BURKE, Barlow, *et al.*, (2004): *Fundamentals of Property Law*, Second Edition, LexisNexis.

CAPOTORTI, Francesco, (1991): *Study on the Rights of Persons belonging to Ethnic, Religious and Linguistic Minorities*, New York.

CHIPETA, B.D., (2002): *Civil Procedure in Tanzania: A Student's Manual*, Dar es Salaam: Dar es Salaam University Press Ltd.

CHUWA, Goodluck and MURUKE, Zainab, "Marriage and Spousal Relationships under Islamic Law" in *The Tanzania Lawyer*, Vol.1 No.3, (2007), pp. 27-42.

COLDHAM, Simon, "Land Tenure Reform in Tanzania: Legal Problems and Perspectives", *Journal of Modern African Studies*, Vol. 33, No. 2 (June, 1995), pp. 227-242.

CORY, H. and HARTNOLL, M.M., (1945): *Customary Law of the Haya Tribe*, Tanganyika Territory, London: Frank Cass.

COULSON, A., (1982): *Tanzania: A Political Economy*, Dar es Salaam: Oxford University Press.

COULSON, N.J., (1971): *Succession in the Mulsim Family*, Cambridge: Cambridge University Press.

DAHRE, Johansson, (2002): *The International Discourse on Indigenous People: A Compilation of Legal and Political Documents*, Sociologiska Institutionen, Lund.

DIGBY, Kenelm, Edward, (1892): *An Introduction to the History of the Law of Real Property*, Fourth Edition, Oxford: Clarendon Press.

DZODZI, Tsikata, "Securing Women's Interests within Land Tenure Reforms: Recent Debates in Tanzania," *Journal of Agrarian Change*, Vol. 3, Nos. 1 & 2, January 2003, pp. 149-183.

EAST AFRICA LAW SOCIETY, (2007): *Digest on Human Rights and Access to Justice*, LawAfrica Publishing Ltd.

ERGAS, Zaki, "Why Did the Ujamaa Village Policy Fail? Towards a Global Analysis", *Journal of Modern African Studies,* Vol.18, No.3, (Sep. 1980), pp. 387-410.

FIMBO, G.M., "Customary Tenure and the Court of Appeal of Tanzania" in BISIMBA, H.K & PETER, C.M (eds.), (2007): *Law and Justice in Tanzania: Quarter of A Century of the Court of Appeal*, Dar es Salaam: Mkuki na Nyota Publishers, pp.139-159.

FIMBO, G.M., (2004): *Land Law Reforms in Tanzania*, Dar es Salaam: Dar es Salaam University Press Ltd.

FIMBO, G. M., "Privatization, Private Investment and the Land Law", A Paper Presented during Training on Land Law Reforms in Tanzania, Centre for Continuing Education, University of Dar es Salaam, May 7th-9th 2003.

FIMBO, G. M., "Participation of Local Communities in Land Administration and Management", *Nyerere Law Journal,* Vol. 1 (2003), pp.1-12.

FIMBO, G. M., "Land Delivery Systems in the Land Acts: The Land Act, 1999 and the Village Land Act 1999." (Undated Paper).

FIMBO, G.M., (2010): *The Land Law of Tanzania: A Case Book*, Dar es Salaam (Unpublished).

FRANK, Thomas, M., "The Stealing of the Sahara", *American Journal of International Law,* Vol. 70, No. 4 (October, 1976), pp. 694-721.

GALATY, John G., "Losing Ground: Indigenous Rights and Recourse across Africa", *Cultural Survival Quarterly*, Issue 22.4, January 31, 1991.

GONDWE, Zabron Steven, (2001): *Manual for Transfers of Rights of Occupancy* (Revised Edition 2010), Dar es Salaam: Mkuki na Nyota Publishers Ltd.

HAYTON, David, J., (1982): *Megarry's Manual of The Law of Real Property,* Sixth Edition, London: Stevens & Sons Ltd.

HITCHCOCK, Robert and VINDING, Diana (eds.), (2004): *Indigenous People's Rights in Southern Africa*, IWGIA, Document No. 110, Copenhagen.

ILIFFE, J., (1969): *Tanganyika under German Rule 1905-1912*, Cambridge:

Cambridge University Press.

ILIFFE, J., (1979): *A Modern History of Tanganyika*, Cambridge: Cambridge University Press.

JACOBO, Abel, "Foreign Aid in Agriculture: Introducing Israel's Land Settlement Scheme in Tanzania", *African Affairs*, Vol. 71, No. 283 (April, 1972), pp. 186-194.

JAMES, R.W., (1971): *Land Tenure and Policy in Tanzania*, Toronto: University of Toronto Press.

JAMES, R.W. and FIMBO, G.M., (1973): *Customary Law of Tanzania: A Source Book*, East African Literature Bureau, Dar es Salaam.

JAPHETI, Kirilo and EARLE E. Seaton, (1967): *The Meru Land Case*, Nairobi: East African Publishing House.

JESSE, James E.C.M., (2002): "Rent Control Legislation in Tanzania: A Critical Review of Security of Tenure in Residential Rental Housing", LL.M Dissertation, UDSM.

JESSE, James E.C.M., "The End of Protection from Forced Eviction through the Repeal of the Rent Restriction Act in Tanzania," *The Tanzania Lawyer*, Vol.2, No. 2 (2008), pp. 63-75.

JOHNSSON, Christina, (2002): *National States and Minority Rights: A Constitutional Analysis*, Uppsala: Universitet.

JUMA, I., "Problems of the National Land Policy" in *Change*, Vol. 5, First Quarter, 1997, pp. 18-30.

KANIKI, Abdulrahman O.J., "Prevention of Corruption in Land Administration and Delivery in Tanzania: A Brief Glance at the 'New' Land Law Regime", *The Justice Review*, Vol. 7, No. 1, 2008, pp. 117-137.

KANJI, Nazneen, *et al.*, (2002): *Promoting Land Rights in Africa: How do NGOs make a difference?* London: International Institute for Environment and Development (IIED).

KANOGO, Tabitha, (1987): *Squatters and the Roots of Mau Mau 1905-63*, London: James Curiey; Kenya: Heinemann: Athens: Hoi University Press.

KAPINGA, Wilbert B.L., "Some Reflections on the Presidential Commission Report and the National Land Policy" in *Change*, Vol.5, First Quarter, 1997, pp. 9-17.

KENNY, Phillip H. & HEWITSON, Russell, (1994): *Property Law*, London, Dublin, England: Butterworths.

KILSON, Martin L., "Land and the Kikuyu: A Study of the Relationship between Land and Kikuyu Political Movements," *The Journal of Negro History*, Vol. 40, No. 2, 1955, pp.103-153.

KIRONDE, Lusuga J.M., " Rent Control Legislation and the National Housing Corporation in Tanzania 1985-1990", *Canadian Journal of African Studies*, Vol. 26, No. 2, 1992, pp. 306-327.

KIRONDE, Lusuga J.M., "Improving Land Sector Governance in Africa: The Case of Tanzania", Paper Prepared for the 'Workshop on "Land Governance in Support of the MDGs: Responding to New Challenges", Washington DC, March 9-10 2009.

KOROWICZ Marek St., "The Problem of International Personality of Individuals" *The American Journal of International Law*, Vol. 50, No. 3 (Jul., 1956), pp. 533-562.

LEGAL AND HUMAN RIGHTS CENTRE, *Tanzania Human Rights Report*, 2005.

LEGAL AND HUMAN RIGHTS CENTRE, *Tanzania Human Rights Report*, 2007.

LEGAL AND HUMAN RIGHTS CENTRE, *Tanzania Human Rights Report*, 2009.

LEVY, D.G., *et al.*, (eds.), (1980): *Women in Revolutionary Paris, 1789-1795*, Urban: University of Illinois Press.

LITTLE, Marilyn, "Colonial Policy and Subsistence in Tanganyika 1925-1945", *Geographical Review*, Vol. 81, No. 4. (Oct., 1991), pp. 375- 388.

LOBULU, Ben, "Dispossession and Land Tenure in Tanzania: What Hope from the Courts?" *Cultural Survival Quarterly*, Issue No. 22.4 of January 31, 1991.

LOCKE, John, (1978): *Two Treaties of Government*, (Trans. Cambridge Bibliographical Society 1952), J.M Deut & Sons Ltd.

LUGOE, F.N., "Policy derived challenges impact greatly on land administration" in *The Guardian*, Wednesday September 12, 2007.

LUOGA, F.D.A.M, "The Tanzanian Bill of Rights" in PETER, Chris Maina and JUMA Ibrahim, (eds.), (1998): *Fundamental Rights and Freedoms in Tanzania*, Dar es Salaam: Mkuki na Nyota Publishers, pp. 37-46.

MACKENZIE, Judith Anne, (1993): *A Practical Approach to Land Law*, Fourth Edition, Blackstone Press Ltd.

MAKARAMBA, Robert, "The Secular State and the State of Islamic Law in Tanzania" in JEPPIE, S. *et al*, (eds.), (2010): *Muslim Family Law in Sub-Saharan Africa: Colonial Legacies and Post- Colonial Challenges*,

Amsterdam: Amsterdam University Press.

MANJI, Ambreena, "Gender and the Politics of the Land Reform Process in Tanzania" *Journal of Modern African Studies*, Vol. 36, No. 1 (Dec., 1998), pp. 645-667.

MAPUNDA, O.B. and MPANGARA, G.P., (1969): *The Maji Maji War in Ungoni*, East African Publishing House.

MASHAMBA, Julius Clement, "Preempting Justice: The Repugnancy of Customary Law in Tanzania" *The Tanzania Lawyer*, Vol. 2, No. 1, 2008, pp. 59-79.

MCADAM, Doug, *et al.*, (2001): *Dynamics of Contention*, Cambridge: Cambridge University Press.

MELANDER, Goran, *et al.* (eds.), (2004): *The Roul Wellenberg Institute Compilation of Human Rights Instruments*, Second, revised edition, Leiden/Boston: Martinus Nijhoff Publishes.

MGULLU, Francis Peter, (1978): "Housing: A study of Tanzania's National Sites and Services Schemes," LL.M Dissertation, University of Dar es Salaam.

MHOJA, Monica E. Magoke, "Impact of Customary Inheritance on the Status of Widows and Daughters in Tanzania: A Challenge to Human Rights Activities" in BOND, Johanna (ed.), (2005): *Voices of African Women: Women's Rights in Ghana, Uganda and Tanzania*, Durham, North Carolina: Carolina Academic Press.

MIGIRO, Mtengeti Rose, "The Division of Matrimonial Property in Tanzania", *Journal of Modern African Studies*, Vol. 28 No.3 1990, pp. 521-526.

MINDE, Elizabeth Maro, "Law Reform and Land Rights in Tanzania", A Paper presented to the XVI International Aids Conference, Toronto, Canada 13th 18th August, 2006.

MKAPA, Benjamini William, "The Legal System Should be More Accessible and Affordable to More Tanzanians" in BISIMBA, H.K. & PETER, C.M. (eds.), (2007): *Law and Justice in Tanzania: Quarter of A Century of the Court of Appeal*, Dar es Salaam: Mkuki na Nyota Publishers, pp. 33-41.

MOYO, Sam, "The Political Economy of Land Acquisition and Redistribution in Zimbabwe 1990-1999", *Journal of Southern African Studies*, Vol. 26, No. 1 (Mar., 2000), pp. 5-28.

MONSON, Jamie, "Relocating Maji Maji: The Politics of Alliance and Authority in Southern Highlands of Tanzania, 1870-1918", *Journal of African History*,

Vol. 39, No. 1 (998), pp. 95-120.

MUNDEME, S., "Formalizing Informal Land Markets in Tanzania: The Role of the Private and Public Sectors", Paper Presented at the International Conference on the Interaction between Formal and Informal Urban Land Management in Africa, Dar es Salaam, 25-26 November 1999.

MWAIKUSA, J.T., "The Policy Paper and Its Implications on Pastoral Lands" in *Change*, Vol. 5, First Quarter, 1997, pp.31-36.

MWAIKUSA, J.T., "Tanzania's Constitutional History and Development" in BINCHY, William and FINNEGAN, Catherine, (eds.), (2006): *Human Rights, Constitutionalism and the Judiciary: Tanzanian and Irish Perspectives*, Dublin: Clarus Press, pp. 3-19.

MWAIPOPO, Rita Alice, "Gender and the Law in Tanzania: Aspects of the Position of Women on Land and Property" in BINCHY, William and FINNEGAN, Catherine, (eds.), (2006): *Human Rights, Constitutionalism and the Judiciary: Tanzanian and Irish Perspectives*, Clarus Press.

MWAKILEMA, I.T., "Right to Property: Study of the Law of Marriage Act 1971 and Widows Inheritance of Matrimonial Property Upon Their Spouses Deaths", Advanced LL.M Coursework Paper, University of Dar es Salaam, (Unpublished).

NATIONAL LAND FORUM, "Azimio La Uhai (Declaration of NGOs and Interested Persons on Land" in *Change*, Vol. 5, First Quarter, 1997, pp. 72-76.

NOWAK, Manfred, (2003): *Introduction to the International Human Rights Regime*, Martinus Nijhoff Publishers.

NYERERE, Julius Kambarage, (1966*): Freedom and Unity: A Selection from Writings and Speeches 1952-1965*, Dar es Salaam: Oxford University Press.

NYERERE, Julius Kambarage, (1968): *Ujamaa: Essays on Socialism*, Dar es Salaam: Oxford University Press.

OCHALA, James Obol (ed.), (1969): *Land Law Reforms in East Africa*, Milton Obote Foundation.

OGENDO, Okoth, "Legislative Approaches to Customary Tenure and Land Reform in East Africa" in TOULNINE, C and QUAN, J (2000): *The Evolving Land Rights, Policy and Tenure in Africa*, London: IIED.

PENTASSUGLIA, Gaetano, (2002): *Minorities in International Law: An Introductory Study*, Strasbourg: Council of Europe Publishing.

PETER, Butt, "Native Title Takes Off", *Australian Law Journal*, Vol. 69, No. 1

January 1995, pp 8-12.

PETER, Chris Maina, (1989): *Foreign Private Investiment in Tanzania*, Konstanz: Hartung-Gorre Verlag.

PETER, Chris Maina, (1997): *Human Rights in Tanzania: Selected Cases and Materials*, Rudiger Koppe Verlag. Koln.

PETER, Chris Maina, "Human Rights of the Indigenous Minorities in Tanzania and the Courts of Law", A Paper presented at the University of Bergen, Norway, February 2007.

PETER Chris Maina, "Blocking Fundamental Rights and Freedoms in Tanzania: The History of the Bill of Rights", *The Justice Review*, Vol. 7, No. 1, 2008, pp. 1-35.

PHILIP, Adam, (2006): "The Law on Consent of a Spouse in Securities: A Case Study of Commercial Banks in Dar es Salaam", LL.B Dissertation, UDSM.

PREECE, Alun A., "The Impact of the Law Inheritance on the Family", A Paper Presented at the 7th Australian Institute of Family Studies Conference, Sydney Convention and Exhibition Centre, Darling Harbour Sydney, 24-26 July 2000, at p.3.

RICHARD, Barlett, "The Mabo Decision", *Australian Property Law Journal*, Vol. 1 No. 3, December 1993, pp. 236-261.

RWEGASIRA, Abdon, (2006): "Human Rights, Law and HIV/AIDS Infection: A Focus on the Vulnerability of Women in Tanzania", Advanced LL.M Coursework Paper, University of Dar es Salaam. (Unpublished).

RWEYEMAMU, Anthony H., "Managing Planned Development: Tanzania's Experience", *Journal of Modern African Studies*, Vol.4, No. 1 (May, 1966), pp.1-16.

RWEZAHURA, Bart and WANITZEK, Ulrike: "The Constitutionalization of Family Law", *Open University Law Journal*, Vol. 1, No. 2, December 2007, pp. 110-131.

SAWYERR, Akilagpa, "Discriminatory Restrictions on Private Disposition of Land in Tanganyika: A Second Look," in OCHOLA, James Obol (ed.), (1969): *Land Law Reform in East Africa*, Militon Obote Foundation.

SHIVJI, Issa G., "Land: The Terrain of Democratic Struggle" in *Change*, Vol. 5, First Quarter, 1997.

SHIVJI, Issa G., "Grounding the Debate on Land: The National Land Policy and Its Implications" in *Change*, Vol. 5 First Quarter, 1997, pp. 37-47.

SHIVJI Issa G., "Reflections on the Women Question and Land: Some Debating Points" in Change, Vol.5, First Quarter, 1997, pp. 64-71.

SHIVJI, Issa G., and KAPINGA, Wilbert. B.L., "Implications of the Draft Bill for the Land Act" in *Change*, Vol.5 First Quarter, 1997, pp. 48-63.

SHIVJI, Issa G., (1998): *Not Yet Democracy: Reforming Land Tenure in Tanzania,* IIED/HAKIARDHI/ Faculty of Law, University of Dar es Salaam.

SHIVJI, Issa G., "Lawyers in Neoliberalism: Authority's Professional Supplicants or Society's Amateurish Conscience," Valedictory delivered on the occasion of formal retirement from the University of Dar es Salaam, delivered on 15th July, 2006.

SMITH, Rhona M.S., (2005): *Textbook on International Human Rights*, Second Edition, Oxford University Press.

STREN, Richard E., "Underdevelopment, Urban Squatting and the State Bureaucracy: A Case Study of Tanzania," *Canadian Journal of African Studies*, Vol. 10, No. 1, 1982, pp. 67-91.

TENGA, Ringo W. and KAKOTI, George, "The Barabaig Land Case: Mechanism of State Organised Land Grabbing in Tanzania" in HANNE, Veber *et al.*, (eds.), (1993): *Never Drink from the Same Cup: Proceedings of the Conference on Indigenous Peoples in Africa*, Tune. Denmark: IWGIA Doc. 74.

TENGA, Ringo W., "Minority Rights in Tanzania", in FINNEGAN, Catherine, and BINCHY, William, (eds.), (1995): *Human Rights, Constitutionalism and the Judiciary: Tanzanian and Irish Perspectives*, Clarus Press, pp. 71-91.

TENGA, Ringo W., "Legislating for Pastoral Land Tenure in Tanzania: The Draft Bill" in Horn F., (ed.) (1998) *Economic, Social, and Cultural Rights of the Maasai*, Rovaniemi: The Northern Institute for Environmental and Minority Law, University of Lapland.

TENGA, Ringo W., "Legitimizing Dispossession: The Tanzanian High Court's Decision on the Eviction of Maasai Pastoralists from Nkomazi Game Reserve", *Cultural Survival Quarterly*, Issue 22.4, January 31, 1999.

TENGA, Ringo W. and MRAMBA, S.J, (2008): *Manual on Land Law and Conveyancing in Tanzania*, Tumaini University, (Unpublished).

THORNBERRY, P., (1991): *International Law and the Rights on Minorities*, Oxford: Clarendon Press.

TULLY, J., "Aboriginal Property and West Theory Recovering Middle Ground" in Paul *et al.*, (1994): *Property Rights*, CUP, London, at p. 153.

TWAIB, Fauz, (1994): *The Legal Professional in Tanzania*, Dar es Salaam University Press.

TYABJI, F. B., (1919): *Principles of Mohamedan Law in Brotish India*, 2nd Edn, Buttherworths & Co.

UNITED REPUBLIC OF TANZANIA, (1992): *A Policy on Women in Development in Tanzania*, Ministry of Community Development, Women Affairs and Children.

UNITED REPUBLIC OF TANZANIA, (1997): *National Land Policy*, Second Edition, Dar es Salaam: Ministry of Lands and Human Settlement Development.

UNITED REPLIC OF TANZANIA, (2002): *National Human SettlementS Development Policy*, Dar es Salaam: Government Printers.

VERMA, S.K., (1998): *An Introduction to Public International Law*, New Delhi: Prentice-Hall of India.

WACHIRA, George Makundi, "The Role of Courts in Protecting Indigenous Peoples' Rights to Land and Resources in Kenya and South Africa" in the *East African Journal of Peace and Human Rights*, Vol. 13, No. 2, 2007, pp. 240-269.

WALKER Cherryl, "Piety in the Sky? Gender Policy and Land Reform in South Africa," in RAZAVI Shahra, (ed.), (2003): *Agrarian Change, Gender and Land Rights*, Blackwell Publishing.

WANYEKI, L. Muthoni, (ed.) (2003): *Women and Land in Africa: Culture, Religion and Realizing Women's Rights*, London and New York: Zed Books ; Ltd, Cape Town: David Philip Publishers

WOLLSTONECRAFT, Mary, (2004): *A Vindication of the Rights of Women*, Penguin Books.

WRIGHT, J., "The OSCE and the Protection of Minority Rights" in *Human Rights Quarterly* Vol. 18, 1996, pp. 190-205.

YAKUBU, M.G., (1985): *Nigerian Land Law*, London: Macmillan.